Sister Churches

# Sister Churches

*American Congregations and Their Partners Abroad*

JANEL KRAGT BAKKER

OXFORD
UNIVERSITY PRESS

# OXFORD

UNIVERSITY PRESS

Oxford University Press is a department of the University of Oxford.
It furthers the University's objective of excellence in research,
scholarship, and education by publishing worldwide.

Oxford   New York

Auckland   Cape Town   Dar es Salaam   Hong Kong   Karachi
Kuala Lumpur   Madrid   Melbourne   Mexico City   Nairobi
New Delhi   Shanghai   Taipei   Toronto

With offices in

Argentina   Austria   Brazil   Chile   Czech Republic   France   Greece
Guatemala   Hungary   Italy   Japan   Poland   Portugal   Singapore
South Korea   Switzerland   Thailand   Turkey   Ukraine   Vietnam

Oxford is a registered trademark of Oxford University Press
in the UK and certain other countries.

Published in the United States of America by
Oxford University Press
198 Madison Avenue, New York, NY 10016

Library of Congress Cataloging-in-Publication Data
Bakker, Janel Kragt.
Sister churches : American congregations and their partners abroad / Janel Kragt Bakker.
pages   cm
Includes bibliographical references and index.
ISBN 978-0-19-932821-5 (pbk: alk. paper)—ISBN 978-0-19-932820-8 (cloth: alk. paper)
1. Christianity-Developing countries. 2. Missions, American-Developing countries.
3. Christian Union. 4. Missions and Christian union. I. Title.
BR500.A1B35   2013
270.09172′4—dc23      2013012866

1 3 5 7 9 8 6 4 2

Printed in the United States of America
on acid-free paper

# CONTENTS

## ACKNOWLEDGMENTS

I am indebted to many individuals and institutions for their support of this project. When it began as a doctoral dissertation, this project was skillfully shepherded by my director, William Dinges. The other members of my dissertation committee—the late Dean Hoge, Anthony Pogorelc, and John Ford—lent valuable insight as well. Charles Jones, Associate Dean for Graduate Studies in the School of Theology and Religious Studies at The Catholic University of America, and fellow graduate students Christine Brickman Bhutta, Chris Born, and Todd Scribner also offered helpful feedback. Funding was generously provided by Catholic University's Johannes Quasten Scholarship and Hubbard Dissertation Fellowship. I am also grateful to the Louisville Institute, especially staff members Jim Lewis and Sheldon Sorge, for generous underwriting of my dissertation research and writing as part of the Louisville Institute's 2008–2009 dissertation fellowship program.

This project was also advanced through a postdoctoral fellowship in Religious Practices and Practical Theology at Emory University's Candler School of Theology during the 2010–2011 academic year. The Institute for the Study of American Evangelicals, the Seminars in Christian Scholarship at Calvin College, and the Collegeville Institute for Ecumenical and Cultural Research were other entities that helped this book come to fruition. The editorial team at Oxford University Press, and Theo Calderara in particular, patiently walked the manuscript through various revisions and skillfully saw to its continued improvement.

Various colleagues in the academic study of religion deserve mention for their constructive criticism of the manuscript as well as their professional cheerleading. I am especially grateful to Leticia Campbell, Arun

Jones, David King, Tom Long, Gerardo Marti, Jenny McBride, Mark Noll, Kevin Offner, Paul Olson, Don Ottenhoff, Paul Otto, Amy Reynolds, Bob Priest, Martin Vander Meulen, Miroslav Volf, and Steve Warner.

Without the generosity of time and spirit of the nearly one hundred respondents who granted sometimes lengthy interviews without the prospect of personal gain, this project would not have been possible. Erika Bakker, Kim Darling, and Sara VanBronkhorst skillfully and efficiently transcribed most of these interviews. The late Kit Collins and the other members of the staff at the Center for Educational Design and Communication kindly provided office space and camaraderie while I worked. Too numerous to mention, many friends and family members supported the project by caring for my children, expressing interest in my research, asking important questions, and helping me live a balanced life. Susan Bayer-Larson, Nancy Brenneman, Margot Eyring, Miriam Gerber, Del Glick, Sarah Krueger, Kristin Kobes DuMez, Elisabeth Kvernen, Danica Lefever, Trisha Posey, Matt and Carolyn Tapie, and Heather Tomlinson deserve particular mention. I am also especially grateful to my parents, Roger and Glenda Kragt, and my husband, Laryn Kragt Bakker, for their consistent encouragement and many sacrifices on my behalf. My living children, Alleia and Reuben, have added immeasurable joy to my life and helped focus my work. My deceased daughter, Caritas, whose brief life was intertwined with this book, still breathes into its pages.

Sister Churches

# Introduction

*Side by Side, Shoulder to Shoulder*

IN 1999, REVEREND LAMONT KOERNER, Lutheran campus pastor at the University of Minnesota, spent several months teaching Old Testament courses at Tumaini University in Tanzania—an institution that had been founded three years earlier by the joint efforts of the Saint Paul Area Synod of the Evangelical Lutheran Church in America and the Iringa Diocese of the Lutheran Church in Tanzania. Moved by his cross-cultural encounter and wanting to pass along the same opportunity to his students, Koerner formed a partnership and exchange program between Lutheran students at the University of Minnesota and students at Tumaini University. The program was designed to encourage both American and Tanzanian students to develop a global perspective, to apply students' professional interests to needs in Tanzania, to foster Tanzanian self-sufficiency, and to work side by side across cultural barriers in the name of the Christian gospel—promoting what Lutherans call the "accompaniment" model of mission.

Several years later, Koerner became the associate coordinator of the companion relationship between the Saint Paul Area Synod and the Iringa Diocese of Tanzania. Seeing this position as an extension of his work with students, Koerner's role was to help Lutheran congregations in the Saint Paul area build long-term, faith-based partnerships—otherwise known as "companion congregation," "twinning," "sister church/parish," or "congregation-to-congregation" relationships—with Lutheran congregations from the Iringa Diocese.[1] As he traced the origin of such partnerships, Koerner explained that after the fall of colonialism in the middle of the twentieth century, Christian churches in the global South, especially those with ties to the West, were seen as being complicit in oppression. A crisis in mission ensued as many southern Christians spoke out about indignities they had suffered and many northern Christians retreated from involvement in the global South. Koerner noted that as many American Lutheran leaders wrestled with their role in international mission efforts, they began looking for opportunities for a fresh start. "What was happening in mission was that God was calling us over there to change what we were doing."[2] In consultation with global southern Christian leaders, American Lutherans dreamed of a path ahead that was neither isolationist nor domineering. They began looking for models of engagement that would allow them to serve and learn with their southern counterparts, "shoulder to shoulder." Out of this dream and similar dreams among other Christian groups, the sister church model of mission was born.

Based on the ideal of partnership in mission, congregation-to-congregation relationships are designed to foster mutuality between northern and southern partners. The model eschews unidirectional sending of resources and human capital from so-called mother to daughter churches by blurring the lines between sender and receiver, donor and dependent. Proponents of sister church relationships place a high premium on solidarity, the sharing of power between Christians from North and South, sustainable development, and interpersonal cross-cultural relationships at the grassroots level.

While congregation-to-congregation relationships vary significantly in the ways they are envisioned and carried out in particular contexts, they generally represent the approach to mission voiced by Lamont Koerner. Beginning in the 1980s and becoming increasingly popular among Christians from a variety of traditions, sister church relationships reflect changes to the map of world Christianity in the twentieth century and a growing commitment to eschew patterns of colonialism in mission. Recognizing that Christianity is numerically and, in many ways, spiritually stronger in the global South than it is in the global North—while the imbalance in material resources runs in the opposite direction—proponents of sister church relationships maintain that, in different ways, both northern and southern Christians stand to gain by entering into relationships with each other.

## Rationale

The contemporary landscape of global Christianity differs radically from previous eras, and new patterns of transnational engagement have emerged. The following study taps into the revolution in mission and refashioning of global Christianity by examining select North/South congregation-to-congregation partnerships. Among the various angles from which to approach the evolving relationships among Christians around the globe, the sister church phenomenon is worthy of study because, despite its growing influence, its dynamics and outcomes are largely uncharted by scholars. Indeed, while much attention has been given to the growth and vitality of Christianity in the global South, less has been given to the links between churches in the two hemispheres.[3] Adding nuance to the accounts of encounters between northern and southern Christians in which segregation, friction, or exploitation are dominant motifs, this study depicts border-crossing relationships within the global church that are also marked by interconnectivity and collaboration. This book also challenges prominent notions about the relationship between religion and globalization, which tend to instrumentalize religion as a political weapon, ignore important religious differences, or strip religion of its potency. As this book illustrates, globalization encourages religious pluralization over secularization, allowing religious groups to expand their influence around the world and to foster greater bonds among adherents.

## Scope and Method

This book combines ethnographic case study with historical research to explore the sister church model of mission as it is embedded in specific contexts. It focuses specifically on the North American side of the relationships, analyzing the attitudes and experiences of a group of parishioners in the Washington, DC, area whose congregations are involved in sister church relationships. This study explores the extent to which these North American Christians at the grassroots level are cognizant of the changes in global Christianity and the degree to which their words and behavior reflect new currents in missiology such as the ones Koerner described.

In his multicongregational study of the relationship between church and community in a black urban neighborhood, Omar McRoberts describes his work as an attempt to balance the sweeping "landscape" style of qualitative research with the more intimate "portraiture" style of single-church ethnographies. The result of McRoberts's research, in his words, is "part analysis and anatomy of a local urban system, part religious and cultural interpretation, part structure, part meaning."[4] Similarly, my research method was designed to promote both breadth and depth of understanding. I aimed to paint a meaningful portrait of each case while not losing sight of the big picture. I cannot claim that my research is representative of North American sister church initiatives at large, nor can I claim that every meaningful aspect of each case is thoroughly examined and illuminated. But, like McRoberts,

I trust that the cases I explore emerge as fully developed, historicized, and unique entities that are nonetheless signs of broader processes at work.

Especially in the social sciences, scholars of religion increasingly insist that religion is best understood not as the abstract theological systems of religious institutions and the elites that control them but as a constellation of symbols, devotion, and practices—rituals chief among them—of those who sit in the pews. While this study is concerned with both attitudes and behavior, text and performance, leaders and followers, its main focus is experience at the grassroots level. "A cardinal goal of any religious ethnography," says Brenda Brasher, ". . . is to advance our understanding of lived religion, that is, religion as it is commonly practiced."[5] The large number of congregational cases and individual respondents in my study precluded me from conducting the sort of subterranean probing of individuals that is a strength of phenomenological analysis. Though individual idiosyncrasies were of interest to me, I was most concerned with the shared construction of meaning. I aimed to understand the distinctiveness of the sister parish model of mission and the dialectic relationship between North American Christians' participation in congregation-to-congregation partnerships and their posture toward their counterparts in the global South. It was with these goals in mind that I developed my diversified method.

## Selection and Access

In order to examine the dynamics of the international congregation-to-congregation phenomenon at the grassroots level among American Christians, I selected twelve congregations located within two hundred miles of Washington, DC, as cases for my study.[6] As a way of comparing congregation-to-congregation relationships among Christian traditions with different theological frameworks and types of ecclesiastical polity, I chose three Roman Catholic, three Presbyterian (Presbyterian Church in the United States of America), three Anglican (Anglican Mission in America or Convocation of Anglicans in North America), and three Baptist (Progressive National Baptist Convention) congregations. Respectively, the four traditions represent the general categories of North American Christians delineated by historians and social scientists: Catholic, mainline/conciliar, evangelical, and Black.[7] Among Christian bodies with a significant presence in the Washington, DC, area, the four chosen traditions/denominations emerged as most workable and available for study within each category.

Any congregation within my geographic and denominational proscriptions involved in an international relationship was eligible for my study as long as: (a) the partner was another congregation in Africa, Latin America, or Asia, (b) leadership in both congregations formally recognized the relationship, (c) the duration of the relationship was two years or more at the time the study began, (d) the relationship involved some form of personal interaction beyond sending and receiving money, and (e) at least some members of the North American congregation, beside the clergy, were involved in the relationship in some fashion.

Beyond the dynamics of their international partnerships, I selected congregations for my sample on the basis of size, physical and cultural environment, ideological orientation, and demographic trends among their memberships. I attempted to generate a diverse sample of American congregations, keeping in mind that the Washington, DC, metropolitan area, just like every geographic region, is idiosyncratic on several scores and that congregations that participate in sister church relationships represent a particular subset of congregations.[8]

In-depth, semi-structured interviews with ninety individuals served as the primary means of data collection. Between October of 2007 and November of 2008, I interviewed seventy-two people at the congregational level. Using an interview template as a springboard for my conversations with respondents, I interviewed an average of six individuals in each of the twelve congregations. Through purposive and snowball sampling, I generated a list of respondents in each congregation, striving for diversity in point of view, position of power, demographic characteristics, length of attendance, and level of involvement in the sister church relationship. The appendix contains information on each respondent pertaining to these variables. In each congregation, I sought to interview one member of the pastoral staff, one or two key project leaders (such as the chair of the partnership committee or the delegation leader), two or three project participants, and one or two nonparticipating parishioners.

In addition to interviews, I gathered data at the congregational level through other qualitative and ethnographic techniques such as direct observation and examination of written documents and other social artifacts. I attended worship services, sat in on sister church presentations and events, and combed congregational literature such as bulletins, newsletters, brochures, websites, and blogs. Several respondents also gave me access to travel journals, reflections, or articles they wrote in connection to their participation in their congregation's partnership.

To triangulate my observations and analyses at the congregational level as well as to provide historical and cultural context to the specific cases in my study, I interviewed eighteen representatives of sister church initiatives or programs in denominations or parachurch organizations at the national level. While I could not interview representatives from all agencies involved in the phenomenon, I selected a broad swath of organizations, giving special attention to the traditions from which my sample derived. Many of the respondents also provided me with unpublished literature pertinent to the sister church phenomenon, which I also consulted to enrich my interview material. Within the study, the names and all identifying information for each congregation and respondent at the congregational level were changed in order to comply with federal guidelines for the protection of human subjects. Since the interviews with representatives from denominational and parachurch agencies solicited oral histories from public figures, these interviews were exempt from such requirements.

## Respondent Bias and Validity

An inescapable reality of social scientific research is that both researchers and respondents are necessarily biased. As far as respondents' testimonies are concerned, it is important to remember that each person's experiences are in many ways singular, and each person's account of a given phenomenon is biased by his or her station and perspective. Religious people are not necessarily more biased than anyone else, but relying on firsthand information from people within the religious communities under scrutiny has its own set of perils. Congregational leaders, for example, are prone to describe events and processes through the lens of an idealized sense of what their congregation should be in addition to, or instead of, what is actually happening. Parishioners, while perhaps less invested in the good name of their congregations, are nonetheless also susceptible to selective, enhanced memory and to glossing over or distorting information that does not neatly cohere with their theological commitments or views of themselves and their communities.[9]

To guard against the undue influence of such possible biases, I chose respondents to reflect the diversity within a congregation.[10] I solicited interviews with both highly involved insiders and marginal participants, with long-time members and relative newcomers. I also sought balance of perspective by finding respondents who were not referred to me by gatekeepers and key informants. Aware that the biases of a key contact often leads to biased sampling, I tried to diversify my sources of contacts for potential respondents. I was also cognizant of the strengths and limitations of my primary method of gathering data. Interviewing is a powerful medium for hearing individual stories, diverse perspectives, and minority voices that might otherwise go unnoticed. Another strength of interviewing is that it allows access to unobservable phenomena like attitudes, personal feelings, and individual interpretations. Yet, no interview should be understood as a completely accurate account of objective reality. With this in mind, I also gathered data from other sources. Direct observation and use of congregational literature helped make up for the weaknesses of the interview medium.

Data Analysis

The central goal of my research was to shed light on the sister church phenomenon by close examination and comparison of the details of particular iterations of this phenomenon. Ethnographic case study was the overarching research paradigm I employed for this study.[11] While many case studies focus on a single example of a phenomenon, my selection of twelve sister church relationships enabled me to conduct cross-case analyses for comparison purposes.[12] Relying on John and Lyn Lofland's approach for deciphering patterns within a given research topic, I looked for frequencies, magnitudes, structures, processes, causes, and consequences within my data.[13] This book is structured according to the Loflands' schema. Chapters 1 and 2 concentrate on magnitudes and frequencies. Chapter 3 focuses on processes while chapter 4 addresses structures, chapter 5 examines causes, and chapter 6 concentrates on consequences. The concluding chapters synthesize these categories to create a fuller picture of the whole.

Within the larger paradigm of case study, I also approached the material I collected in the field phenomenologically. I sought to illuminate the lived experiences of my respondents by analyzing the stories they told and the reflections they offered. Narrative analysis was particularly useful. Part of my research goal was to understand the attitudes of North American Christians with regard to the church in the global South and the meaning these North Americans associated with their cross-oceanic religious encounters. Respondents' stories and reflections on their experiences proved to be the most illuminating window into their attitudes and senses of meaning. Moreover, phenomenological analysis enabled me to better enter into the experiences and perspectives of my respondents.

While phenomenological analysis is most useful for interpreting individuals' understanding of their experiences, I also found narrative analysis helpful for shedding light on the collective experience of congregations. Narratives play an essential role in congregations' self-understanding and empowerment.[14] Moreover, the atmosphere and dynamics of an event are best expressed through narratives, and narratives are an excellent method for describing a congregation's culture, processes, and theology.[15] Thus, not only did I analyze the narratives of my respondents, I also used narrative to describe the sister church relationships in my study. Chapter 3 tells the story of each congregation-to-congregation relationship, as much as possible in the collective voice of respondents themselves.

It can be argued that any work of sociology demands a historical footnote. A given phenomenon is always and everywhere part of a larger historical context. Chapters 1, 2, and 6 acknowledge this reality by attempting to situate the cases within a larger picture of mission history, both globally and in the North American context. Oral histories provided by representatives of denominational and parachurch bodies, primary sources specific to these organizations, and scholarly secondary literature were combined to present an account of the historical context of international congregation-to-congregation partnerships. Because my study relies so heavily on historical analysis to complement field research, it could be described as an ethnohistorical study.

## Point of View

Every account is told from a particular vantage point. This book focuses on the testimony of North American Christians, most of whom were members of Washington, DC–area congregations involved in international congregational partnerships. Since North Americans arguably represent the largest force in Christian mission, dominate western Christianity, and are widely perceived to lag behind the rest of the world in international collaboration and global understanding,[16] their attitudes and behaviors with regard to international religious engagement are of critical interest. The distinctiveness of the sister church model of mission and the role of congregation-to-congregation relationships in the lives of participating North American congregations and individuals are thus important subjects for investigation.

In addition to facilitating a careful probe of North Americans' participation in the sister church phenomenon, limiting field research to the northern side of sister church relationships enabled a manageable scope for this project. Unfortunately, however, this decision also highlights the bias of northern respondents and leaves at least half of the story of each of the profiled relationships largely untold. The perspectives of southern participants and outcomes of sister church relationships in their congregations in the Southern Hemisphere are intimated throughout the book, but only through the perspective of scholars (both northern and southern) and northern respondents. This book tells the story of twelve American congregations involved in international partnerships, both highlighting idiosyncrasies and making comparisons across cases. While it points to themes and trends that are broader than the lives of these congregations, this study leaves much to be told by others voices.

Over the last generation, postcolonial criticism has drawn attention to modern scholars' propensity to tell a Eurocentric story in the guise of objectivity.[17] My aim, rather than to enshrine western assumptions or meta-narratives, is to recognize that American Christians speak with particular voices and represent particular cultural assumptions and values. While this book focuses on the attitudes and behaviors of American Christians, I try not to confuse the perspective of my subjects or my own vantage point as a scholar with a "view from nowhere." Nor do I suggest that American Christians speak for their counterparts in other parts of the world, especially those in subaltern positions.

## Outline of the Book

Chapter 1 sets the stage for this study by charting the demographic changes in world Christianity over the twentieth century as well as the evolving structures of global religious engagement. It chronicles the crisis in Christian mission in the context of the fall of colonialism and describes the trajectory of mission theory and practice that has taken shape over the last several decades. Placing the sister church phenomenon within this broader context, it highlights how the border-crossing dynamic of globalization as well as structural and philosophical shifts in global Christianity propel new forms of international faith-based engagement.

Chapter 2 chronicles the history and development of the congregation-to-congregation model of mission in North America, exploring how this model reflects the religious landscape of North America as well as trends in mission among North American Christian bodies. Chapter 3 shifts to the grassroots arena, homing in on the experience of twelve congregations involved in sister church relationships. As a way of comparing these relationships among Christian traditions with different theologies, cultures, and types of ecclesiastical polity, three Roman Catholic, three mainline Presbyterian, three evangelical Anglican, and three African American Baptist congregations—twelve congregations in all—are studied qualitatively. Chapter 3 tells the story of each of these twelve relationships from the perspective of respondents from the Washington, DC–area congregations.

Comparing and contrasting the twelve relationships with one another, the book proceeds topically. Comparison is intended to illuminate both ideological and organizational dimensions of sister parish relationships as well as to draw out a typology of these relationships. Chapter 4 considers the structures and dynamics of the studied relationships, presenting profiles of congregations and participants. This chapter highlights the role of immigrants and other transnational figures in sister church relationships as well as the leadership structures under which the profiled relationships operated. Chapter 4 addresses questions regarding the balance of local autonomy and hierarchical oversight. It also explores common themes in participating congregations' cultures of spirituality.

Chapter 5 examines the purpose of sister church relationships from the perspective of respondents, analyzing the collective action frames that propel participation in sister church relationships. Featuring a typology of sister church relationships, it draws attention to the tension between projects and relationships and the tension between "this worldly" and "other-worldly" concerns evidenced in the sister church relationships. This chapter also highlights shared notions among participating congregations regarding the purpose of sister church relationships. It explores how the Washington, DC–area churches distanced themselves from other models of mission, particularly those associated with colonialism.

Chapter 6 concentrates on the outcomes of sister church relationships, especially with regard to the lives of participants. This chapter explores respondents' claims that congregation-to-congregation relationships represent an effective model of mission and bring about a significant amount of good in the lives of northern and southern participants alike. While the effects of sister church relationships on southern participants and communities are only suggested through second-hand testimony, northern respondents' accounts of the changes in their own lives and communities are much more telling. In addition to presenting respondents' assessments of the effects of sister church relationships, this chapter also addresses questions regarding the reliability of such accounts.

As chapter 7 explains, formidable challenges stand in the way of sister church relationships achieving their goals. Raising issues of material inequalities, cultural barriers, racism, pitfalls of development theory, logistical difficulties, troublesome personalities, interpersonal conflict, and weaknesses in the frames that undergird sister church relationships, this chapter explores the factors that threatened to derail the profiled sister church relationships and compromise their positive outcomes.

Conversely, chapter 8 describes how respondents still esteemed the sister church model as an attractive, viable, and effective means of cross-cultural Christian engagement, despite the weight of these challenges.

This chapter addresses how sister church relationships take advantage of cultural trends and contemporary circumstances, both in North America and around the globe. It considers the sister church phenomenon as a product of the processes of globalization wherein borders are collapsed and time and space are compressed through technological developments. Focusing on the American context, chapter 8 explores questions regarding the relationship between the sister church phenomenon and contemporary religiocultural trends such as the growing interest in practice-oriented spirituality and the surge of grassroots mobilization efforts. It also discusses how sister church relationships take advantage of the interpenetrating relationship between the global and the local in the contemporary milieu.

## Terminology

The term *encounter* has been widely used to describe how people meet and interact with the "other," especially in colonial settings.[18] *Encounter* is a word that connotes both synchronicity and confrontation. This study examines sister church relationships as a venue in which Christians from around the world encounter one another in the contemporary period. For the American Christians profiled in this study, encountering coreligionists from the global South through congregation-to-congregation partnerships was often an experience of friendship and abrasion simultaneously. Participants sought to relate to their cohorts as partners and equals, but entrenched hierarchies and vast disparities in access to resources constantly threatened to undermine their relationships with Christians from other parts of the world.

Since 1978 when Edward Said's publication of *Orientalism* first lent currency to the term *postcolonial* in the western academy, postcolonialism has burgeoned into a robust, multilayered and theoretically diverse field of inquiry and critique.[19] Set in the wake of the demise of modern colonial empires, at least in a formal sense, this study employs the term *postcolonial* sparingly and mostly as a denotation of a historical era in which most locales that were colonized in the modern era have gained political independence. *Colonial*, correspondingly, describes the project of European political domination from the sixteenth to the twentieth centuries until the national liberation movements of the 1960s. The field of postcolonial studies has unearthed important debates and made valuable contributions to scholarship and cultural reflection, but venturing into the theoretical territory of postcolonialism was largely outside the scope of this study.

While the partnership or accompaniment approach to mission is tangentially related to various strands of postcolonial thought in its attention to the dignity and agency of colonized peoples, this missiological discourse more precisely addresses cross-cultural religious engagement and was more accessible to respondents than the discourse of postcolonial theory.

*Globalization* is another sticky term relevant to this study. *Globalization* is often used indiscriminately, thus making the definition contested territory and the very use of the term problematic. But, as James Mittelman has argued, globalization is a helpful concept inasmuch as it highlights the growing consciousness of the world as a single place and the compression of time and space witnessed by the contemporary era.[20] The integration of economic, political, and cultural systems across the globe— which has come to be known as globalization—is not unique to the current time period. However, these processes are powerful and dominant in the contemporary milieu. *Globalization* is used throughout this study as a shorthand for an expanding sense of interconnectedness and borderlessness that is prominent in today's world.

In addition to serving as a description for processes of integration, globalization is also invoked as a theory of historical development. The predominant theory of contemporary globalization holds that the world is becoming more homogenous and that the processes of globalization in today's world perpetuate structures of western—and principally American—hegemony. Critics of this cultural-homogenization approach to globalization, on the other hand, draw attention to resistance to westernization among various groups of people living outside of North America and Europe. They note increasing fragmentation in the global cultural landscape. Endorsing neither the universal-culture theory of globalization nor the famed "clash of civilizations,"[21] this book envisions globalization as the potential engine not just of homogenization or conflict but also of cross-cultural exchange.

## Contributions

This study demonstrates that sister church relationships represent both philosophical shifts in the understanding of Christian mission and changing structures of global religious engagement. The twelve profiled partnerships intimate that at least some relationships between Christians from North and South challenge both the prevailing patterns of colonialism and the expectations of leading contemporary globalization theorists. As sister church relationships show, emerging trajectories of religious globalization are marked not only by cross-cultural conflict but also by cross-cultural connectivity. While disparities in access to power and resources posed formidable barriers to mutuality, participants in sister church relationships sought to relate to their counterparts as equals and partners in ministry. As respondents' accounts show, some paired congregations restricted the flow of physical resources from North to South in order to avoid situations of patronage and exploitation. Other respondents distinguished between spiritual and material capital, contending that paired congregations achieve solidarity not through equivalence but through enriching each other in different ways. Respondents did not just seek to reach out to southern Christians and their communities. They also esteemed southern Christians as saints and teachers.

While international congregation-to-congregation relationships run the risk of reproducing inequalities rather than overcoming them, they also bear significant potential for pushing against the currents of systemic injustice, ideological stalemate, cultural division, and religious privatization. According to Lamont Koerner, in many ways sister church relationships are nothing short of subversive. Especially because they encourage northern Christians to release a sense of entitlement and willingly give up power, sister church relationships face many uphill challenges.

> [Western] Christianity will change kicking and screaming every inch of the way, because we have become a religion of the empire. And we don't like to give up power. We have had influence and we have had authority . . . and by golly we are not about to give this up. When we start feeling the pull and change of being this much more organic faith that really questions all other authority and power, that scares the liver out of us. We are scared to death that we are going to lose our standing. And we don't know what that means.[22]

Despite the difficulties in realizing the goals of the sister church model of mission, however, Koerner was filled with hope. He testified that American Christians' sense of what is important starts to change on a one-to-one level, as they encounter coreligionists in their sister congregations.

> People experience fear about losing power and anxiety about the future because they don't have personal experience and they don't understand. But when they sit with someone, face to face and faith to faith, that encounter, far from making them more afraid, takes away the fear. It helps them to see the face of this other person who has this deep and abiding faith that they

are in awe of. And that is the kind of way that the change will happen in a non-threatening way. It is this type of interface that will be the change agent within the church.[23]

Side by side, shoulder to shoulder, explained Koerner, northern and southern Christians are partnering together to join the mission of God to the church and the world.

CHAPTER 1 | Christendom Turned Upside Down

*The Global Context of Sister Church*
*Partnerships*

FOR MUCH OF ITS history, Christianity has been perceived as a western religion. Despite its rootedness in the Near East, its flourishing in North
Africa and Southwest Asia for the first millennium of the Common Era,
and its long history as a minority religion in various regions around the
globe, since the Constantian period, Christianity has been securely linked
to the culture and peoples of the North Atlantic. And until recently, the
majority of those who identified themselves as Christians were Europeans
or of European descent. If it ever was fitting to speak of Christianity as a
western religion, however, it is no longer appropriate. Over the course of
the twentieth century, the number of Christians in Asia, Latin America,
and Africa combined grew by 1,130 percent, compared to a 79 percent
growth rate in North America and Europe combined.[1] There are now more
Christians in either Africa or Asia or Latin America than there are in North
America, and the total number of affiliated Christians in the global South
eclipses the number in the West by more than five hundred million by conservative estimates.[2] Sixty percent of professed Christians live in the
southern continents of Asia, Latin America, Africa, and the Pacific, a proportion that grows annually.[3] Numerically speaking, the map of "Christendom" is radically different in the twenty-first century from those of
previous centuries.

For a western audience, Andrew Walls, Philip Jenkins, and Lamin
Sanneh have been the most prominent heralds of the news that the demog-
raphy of the world's population of Christians has shifted so dramatically.
In his influential account of the "southernization" of Christianity, Philip
Jenkins predicts that by 2050, only one in every five Christians will be a

non-Hispanic white and a typical Christian will be "a woman living in a village in Nigeria or in a Brazilian *favela*."[4] Jenkins argues that this transformation of Christianity is the most significant change in the contemporary world. Lamin Sanneh likens the magnitude of worldwide Christian resurgence to a tidal wave,[5] and Andrew Walls describes the current situation as a post-Christian West and a post-western Christianity.[6] "Perhaps the most striking single feature of Christianity today," writes Walls, "is the fact that the church now looks more like that great multitude whom none can number, drawn from all tribes and kindreds, people and tongues, than ever before in history."[7]

These scholars and others have also argued that aside from changes in the demographics of world Christianity, systems of governance, mission, and culture have also evolved. "The dissolution of Christendom," writes Walls, "made possible a cultural diffusion of Christianity that is now in the process of transforming it."[8] Jenkins envisions a new Christendom based in the Southern Hemisphere, launching a "revolutionary new era in world religion."[9] Global southern Christians, distinct both in worldview and praxis from Christians in North America and Europe, are becoming progressively influential on the global religious stage.

The sister church phenomenon is an outgrowth of this refashioning of global Christianity, representing shifting patterns of global religious engagement and a new paradigm in the theology and practice of mission. Attempting to break free from the outmoded and patronizing metaphor of a mother/daughter relationship, northern and southern Christians who participate in these relationships seek to encounter one another in a relationship of equals—both churches contributing to a common mission of serving each other and the world.

## The Ascent of Global Southern Christianity in the Twentieth Century

Christian communities in the global South are increasingly steered by indigenous leaders, theology, and practice.[10] While many locales in the global South were initially introduced to Christianity through the efforts of Westerners in the 1800s—"the great missionary century"[11]—Christianity has been embraced by global southerners on their own terms. After World War II and in the context of decolonization, western missionaries were often forced out of their posts, many internalizing the "Go home!" message they had received from the communities they served, and some—particularly those from mainline denominations—questioning the missionary endeavor altogether. Meanwhile Christianity grew exponentially in the global South through local efforts. In Africa, African Initiated Churches (AICs) multiplied by leaps and bounds. In Latin America, Pentecostalism as well as base ecclesial communities proliferated. In China, despite the persecution of Christians accompanying the Cultural Revolution, Protestants grew to thirty-six million. During the same period that the North Atlantic mission effort seemed to collapse in failure, ordinary people in Africa, Latin America, and Africa were receiving and transmitting the gospel at a grassroots level, and the gospel was retranslated into the cultural modes that cohered with the worldview and ethos of local situations.[12] Dana Robert and Lamin Sanneh both point to the power of reading the Bible in the vernacular in this indigenization process. In their translation of the Bible into local languages and their promotion of literacy, western missionaries had paved the way for nationals to receive the gospel. Once nationals had access to the scriptures in their own idiom, they were empowered to make the faith their own. Similarly, the emphasis on "freedom in the Spirit" within the Pentecostal movement allowed for flexibility in different social and cultural contexts.[13] Rather than functioning as an import, Christianity was incarnated in local cultures.[14]

Because of its thorough integration into local contexts in the global South, the character of the Christian faith in the Southern Hemisphere has departed from versions of the faith represented by western missionaries and, indeed, dominant forms of the religion in the North Atlantic at large. Although Christianity is specifically and uniquely embodied in each culture, some general patterns can be discerned. Writing about the spread of evangelicalism in the global South, historian David Martin draws attention to the strength of spiritism outside the West. Regardless of their stripe, Christians in the global South take spiritual warfare seriously and often literally. Pentecostals and evangelicals in particular, whose ranks have swelled most dramatically in the global South, have been largely cut loose from western structures of professionalization and legitimation and are generally indifferent to the liberal western intelligentsia. Christians in the global South tend to fuse ancient and postmodern, see reality in binary terms, and believe that God blesses the faithful in material ways.[15] Jenkins describes the dominant culture in emerging world Christianity as "traditionalist, orthodox, and supernatural," having more in common with the culture of medieval or early modern Europe than with contemporary western culture.[16] In *The New Faces of Christianity*, Jenkins points to a biblical literalism and traditionalism in the global South which differs markedly from the prevailing liberal interpretation of the Bible in the North.[17]

Despite the clashes of worldview that are readily apparent within global Christianity, global southern clerics are assuming new ascendancy in the church in the West and the church at large. With the 2013 election of Argentine cardinal Jorge Bergoglio to the papacy, the Roman Catholic Church made history by selecting its first southern pope. In the face of a shortage of native-born priests in Europe and North America, an increasing number of African, Latin American, and Asian priests are now serving in the global North. The Anglican Communion has also seen a shift in power and leadership structures. Africa is the numeric heart of Anglicanism and has unofficially replaced Canterbury as the leadership hub as well. More Christians worship in Anglican churches in Nigeria each week than in all the Episcopal and Anglican churches of Britain, Europe, and North America combined.[18] The African bishops represent a powerful voice among the Anglican primates, pressuring the Anglican Communion to censure the US Episcopal Church for its ordination of a gay bishop in 2003. Moreover, since then a number of American parishes have broken ties with the US Episcopal Church and placed themselves under the leadership of southern clerics such as Nigerian Archbishop Peter Akinola and Rwandan Archbishop Emmanuel Kolini. Approximately one thousand congregations have joined the Anglican Church in North America, founded in 2009 as a rival body to the Episcopal Church. The Anglican Church in North America maintains close ties to Latin American and African Anglican leadership and is seeking recognition as a province in the Anglican Communion.[19]

Another example of the growing influence of southern Christians on global Christianity is the "reverse mission" phenomenon.[20] While international missionary enterprises continue, an increasing number of missionaries hail not from Europe or North America but rather from Asia, Africa, or Latin America.[21] Seventh-Day Adventists, for example, send international missionaries from nearly all of the 204 countries in which the church has a presence. Among Adventists, there are as many non-North Americans serving in North America as there are North Americans serving around the world.[22] Arguably, the leading missionary nation is now South Korea, which sends out a remarkably large number of missionaries in proportion to its population.[23] In every continent there are now hundreds of Korean missionaries. The Korean Research Institute for Missions reported that in 2008 there were 18,035 Korean missionaries (up from only ninety-three in 1979) serving in 177 countries around the globe. The mission field of these missionaries is overwhelmingly local people in the countries served rather than Korean immigrants in these countries.[24] Brazil and Nigeria also send scores of missionaries around the globe, and Europe now receives more missionaries than Africa.[25] According to Claudia Währisch-Oblau, Europe is home to

> hundreds or even thousands of African, Asian, and Latin American Pente-
> costal and Charismatic migrant churches which do not see themselves so
> much as 'diaspora churches', as a 'home away from home' for their mem-
> bers; but rather as part of the outreach movement of the *missio Dei*.[26]

While Africa, Latin America, Asia, and Oceania still receive more missionaries than they commission, these four continents send out and support
more than one hundred thousand foreign missionaries. And although the
United States continues to send out the most missionaries around the globe,
it is also the country that receives the most missionaries from other lands.[27]
While many of the missionaries that the United States receives minister to
immigrants or expatriate communities, others specifically target native-
born populations. Considering American culture to be post-Christian, these
missionaries aim to re-evangelize unchurched Anglo-Americans.[28] Of
course, in addition to North-South and South-North mission, there is also
South-South mission (e.g., Brazilians in Mozambique) and North-North
mission (e.g. Americans in France), making mission today truly from everywhere to everywhere.

## European and North American Responses
## to the Rise of Southern Christianity

While global southerners are embracing a changing reality, inhabitants of
the North Atlantic are often surprised to discover the shifting centers of
gravity for the Christian religion. "Few developments in our day have
been more striking and less anticipated than the emergence of Christianity
as a world religion," writes Lamin Sanneh. World Christianity's thrust at
the very moment of colonialism's demise combined with its record of
prosperity apart from European denominational structures especially lend
a dramatic appearance to the phenomenon.[29] In the century that has elapsed
since the heralded World Missionary Conference in Edinburgh in 1910,
Christian history has unfolded in a way that the conference participants
never would have predicted. While the Edinburgh delegates had identified
cooperation between the missionary-sending nations as key to world
evangelization, missionary-receiving nations ended up taking on the torch
of evangelization while missionary-sending nations went to war with one

another. Edinburgh delegates predicted that young volunteers from Europe and North America would continue to flood the mission field, unaware that war, economic hardship, and changing sentiments would pull such volunteers elsewhere. These delegates also assumed that western empires around the globe would provide stable conditions under which missionaries could work effectively; little did they know that colonial empires would soon crumble into the dust. And perhaps most fundamentally, the delegates took for granted the perseverance of Christendom as a base for world evangelization, unaware of the wave of secularization soon to take over European institutions. In short, nearly every one of Edinburgh's conclusions proved to be false.[30] The mushrooming growth of Christianity in the global South, primarily due to national efforts no less, comes as a surprise to many in the West.

Some Europeans and North Americans are not only perplexed but also unnerved by the radical change in world Christianity. Using statements voiced by the liberal leadership of the American Episcopal Church as a chief example, Sanneh argues that southern Christianity is considered distasteful, reactionary, and threatening by many in the church in the West. "Christianity has continued to blossom against nationalist intolerance at home and Western objections abroad, provoking a skeptical West to add the cultural gap to the poverty gap to distance itself from the new Christianity. The West limits its role in the new Christianity to taking precautions against too close an encounter with it, except where the West can tame it," writes Sanneh.[31] Philip Jenkins dramatically argues that the world is on the eve of a historical turning point, a "Second Reformation" as significant for the Christian world as the original Reformation. "There is increasing tension between what one might call a liberal Northern Reformation and the surging Southern religious revolution, which one might equate with the Counter-Reformation," inevitably producing an "enormous rift" in global Christianity.[32]

However, in light of multiple trends in transcontinental engagement, Jenkins's and Sanneh's depictions of a global culture clash among Christians is overstated. Some Christians in the West have responded to the crisis in mission and demise of colonialism by withdrawing from missionary activity and distancing themselves from the southern church altogether. Ashamed of colonialism, yet equally put off by the theological and cultural posture of southern Christianity, these folks tend to engage southern Christians only on the level of conflict or charity—and in the best case, social advocacy. Conversely, others have ignored the crisis in mission by carrying on "business as usual." In so doing, they tend to perpetuate paternalistic, outmoded, and often dehumanizing approaches to cross-cultural engagement. Yet, these bifurcated patterns of response do not tell the whole story.

Beside the examples of avoidance and dominance, there is growing evidence of connectivity. Western Christians, and North American Christians in particular, have become more—not less—engaged with the global church in recent decades.[33] In their engagements around the world, some western Christians are espousing relationships based on partnership and mutuality. Eschewing one-directional sending of resources and human capital from so-called old to new churches, Christians from around the world are attempting to fashion a new breed of contemporary transnational relationships that blur the lines between sender and receiver, donor and dependent. These nascent patterns of engagement, accompanied by fresh missiological insight, have emerged as a corrective to the dominant mode of mission in the modern era. Such partnerships between Christians across cultural and economic divides are not without historical precedents; nor are these contemporary partnerships immune to the same paternalistic tendencies that their architects recognized in the colonial mission enterprise and sought to rectify. Even so, colonial mission efforts serve as a foil to proponents of sister church relationships and other such partnerships as they seek to encounter Christians in other parts of the world as brothers and sisters.

## The Crisis in Colonial Mission

There is no shortage of criticism leveled against the western missionary effort around the globe in the modern colonial period. The modern western missionary effort was indelibly linked to the concept of Christendom, wherein "Christian nations" stood in contrast to "heathen lands," and Christianity constituted not only religious forms but also territories, cultural forms, political structures, and legal systems.[34] "Christianity, Commerce, and Civilization" was the marching cry of the endeavor, and western missionaries often took for granted the legitimacy of European empire-building and worked under a rubric of conquest and control. Often closely linked to colonial enterprises and self-consciously exporting western culture alongside the Christian gospel, missionary efforts in the eighteenth and nineteenth centuries especially have been indicted for paternalism, Orientalism, cultural elitism, and territorialism.[35] Modern mission was based on a precritical understanding of culture, in which people take their own culture to be self-evidently normative. These missionary efforts also have long been criticized for fostering dependence on western powers among nationals. Though many missionaries themselves were well-intentioned, they functioned within systems and cultural assumptions that sometimes did more harm than good and left many nationals with a bitter taste in their mouths.

Recent scholarship has offset this line of argument by pointing out that great numbers of nationals experienced the message of western missionaries as empowering rather than disabling, especially when it was translated into their native language. There are numerous examples of western missionaries in the modern period who criticized colonialism, celebrated indigenous cultures, or sought to build genuine cross-cultural friendships with the people they encountered in the field.[36] Moreover, missionaries helped develop important infrastructure such as schools and hospitals that eventually aided the move toward political independence from colonial power.[37]

A second censure has come from historians of mission who point out that, in the grand scheme of things, the western missionary enterprise in the colonial era is only a brief period in the history of the transmission of the Christian faith. Rather than being a western export to other regions of the world, over the course of Christian history, the gospel has migrated across numerous cultural divides. Moreover, in various instances of the transmission of the Christian faith into a new territory or culture, the conquest metaphor is just one facet of one stage in a long process of cultural encounter.[38] Thus, the western colonial missionary endeavor should not be seen as normative for mission efforts in general.

Nonetheless, the European and North American missionary movement in the colonial period—particularly in the nineteenth century—was a massive and influential phenomenon. Jump-started in Britain by William Carey's 1772 tract entitled *An Enquiry into the Obligation of Christians to Use Means for the Conversion of the Heathen*, the modern European missionary endeavor grew to include some thirty Protestant missionary societies and an accompanying surge of missionary passion among Catholics by 1825.[39] By the end of the nineteenth century, the number of Protestant missionary societies soared into the hundreds. Western missionaries found a footing in every part of the globe, and every nominally Christian country in Europe and the North Atlantic and almost every denomination took part in the international missionary cause.[40] Stephen Neill estimates that by 1900 there were ten thousand Protestant missionaries from the West serving around the world.[41] Although they represent a staggering growth from previous eras, these numbers appear quite modest when compared to the hundreds of thousands of Christian workers from the West serving around the globe today. The significance of the modern missionary movement lies more in its reach and symbolism than in its numeric value. Kenneth Scott Latourette's depiction of the nineteenth century as the "great century" in church history offers a window into the enthusiasm and confidence of the modern missionary endeavor:

> Never before had Christianity, or any religion, been introduced to so many different peoples and cultures. Never before in a period of equal length had Christianity or any other religion penetrated for the first time as large an area as it had in the nineteenth century. Never before had so many hundreds of thousands contributed voluntarily of their means to assist the spread of Christianity or any other religion.[42]

Due to the scope of the modern missionary movement, the nineteenth century was widely perceived by westerners of the time to be the greatest period of Christian impact in history.

Thus, when crisis struck, it struck hard. From the 1880s onward, but especially after World War II, the peoples of the nonwestern world increasingly resisted the political, cultural, and religious control of Europeans operating under the concept of Christendom. Global southerners grew impatient with the coerciveness inherent to expansionist Christendom.[43] Indigenous political and religious movements began to surge around the global South, often in reaction to western mission efforts. By 1970, African churches in particular were calling for a moratorium on western missions because of the perception that these missions stunted the growth of local initiatives.[44] Particularly through the Latin American Episcopal Conference (CELAM) of the Catholic Church, Latin Americans also registered strong critique of European and North American mission efforts in the 1960s and 1970s, drawing attention to their deficiency in cultural understanding and propensity to create dependency.[45] Meanwhile, many northerners themselves grew weary of the constraints of the old order. It became increasingly clear that western-inspired Christendom was a past rather than a present reality. Based on experiences in the field, the development of human sciences, and the general post-war intellectual milieu, many scholars and missionaries in the Catholic and mainline Protestant traditions began to develop a critical view of culture, to question the "universal rationality" of the Enlightenment, and to see the importance of the integrity of each local context.[46] According to South African missiologist David Bosch, with regard to Christian mission, the

Enlightenment paradigm of universal reason and universal good sowed the seeds of its own undoing once it became clear that these "universals" were in fact western and modern contingencies.[47] On the other side of the spectrum, conservative Christians vehemently emphasized the "orthodoxy" that liberals had allegedly abandoned. On top of the denominational divisions that already impeded the missionary effort, ideological battle lines were drawn in the church to the discredit of the Christian faith in the eyes of many outsiders.

The factors coalesced to spell crisis for the modern missionary endeavor, including the mass exodus—both forced and voluntary—of western missionaries from their posts in the 1960s and 1970s. Increasingly aware of nationals' resentment of their way of doing ministry, and decreasingly confident about the efficacy of their work, many European and American missions agencies scaled back their mission efforts, some turning instead to secularized relief and development efforts while others focused on social programs at home. Among Catholics, many missionary priests serving in Latin America left the mission field and returned to Europe or North America. Others left the priesthood altogether. Many progressive western Christians lost confidence in both the method and message of modern mission—and perhaps even the Christian gospel itself—and thus all but abandoned the modern missionary movement. Conservative Christian bodies filled the vacuum by aggressively proclaiming a parochial gospel preoccupied with individual sin and salvation. By and large, mission in the global South became an increasingly local affair.

The mid-century crisis called into question the entire apparatus of modern mission and the very legitimacy of western involvement in the global South. Yet, crisis often gives birth to change. Out of the ashes of modern mission, new theories, techniques, and approaches to mission have arisen among Catholics and Protestants alike—often as a result of dialogue between and among global northerners and southerners. While vestiges of the modern western missionary endeavor still abound around the globe, new patterns of mission have emerged alongside the modern approach to mission. The partnership model of mission that is becoming increasingly popular has been bolstered by a tidal wave of missiological reflection over the last half century. In the wake of the overthrow of colonial regimes, the collapse of the modern western missionary endeavor in the global South, and the coming of age of the southern church, a significant cadre of both Catholic and Protestant missiologists have called for a new approach to mission.

## The Missiological Revolution: *Missio Dei*, the Local Church, and the Call to Partnership, Contextualization, and Holism

On the Catholic front, a new missiology was built on the theological reflection of missionaries, the ecumenical movement, liberation theology, and the Second Vatican Council.[48] Vatican II revolutionized the way the Catholic Church perceived itself and its mission. Instead of seeing the church solely as institutional hierarchy, the ecclesiology of Vatican II also emphasized the church as the people of God. It also called ordinary Catholics to assume the mission of being a sacrament to the world and to an all-embracing human solidarity.[49] *Ad Gentes* insisted that missionary activity is essential to the very nature of the Church and underlined the importance of both witness and dialogue. Vatican II called Christians to be missionaries wherever they find themselves and highlighted the unique identity of the local, national, and regional churches—while reminding the faithful that no single unit is sufficient unto itself.[50] While these themes have precedents in the Catholic theological tradition, Vatican II helped resurrect them in order to revive and reform mission.

In the spirit of the Second Vatican Council, Catholic missionary theology over the last several decades has highlighted the importance of incarnation, accompaniment, and solidarity. Since the middle of the twentieth century, and especially over the last thirty years, an incarnational vision of mission has begun to replace the colonial missiology that valorized the lone missionary risking his or her life to "convert the heathen," and "bring light into darkness." Catholic missiologist Robert Schreiter notes that the colonial approach to mission often borrowed from military metaphors of engaging in combat, winning territory, and planting European Christianity on foreign soil.[51] Whereas the colonial model emphasized the distance between church and world, religious and lay, Europe and its colonies, the theology of incarnation promoted by the documents of the Second Vatican Council focuses instead on the "Word entering the world."[52] Postconciliar missiology also encourages missionaries to see themselves as fellow sojourners with the people they serve, to walk alongside of them rather than ahead of them. Solidarity, which can be seen as the consequence of accompaniment, is another emphasis of contemporary Catholic missiology. Solidarity, says Schreiter, means "inserting oneself into another's reality and struggling with others for the sake of liberation."[53]

Subsequent reflection in the wake of Vatican II continued to emphasize solidarity and liberation as crucial components of mission, especially with regard to the poor. At the historic Latin American Bishops' Conference at

Medellín in 1968, the bishops called on the whole Church to transform situations of sin into a just social order and brought into focus the Church's "preferential option for the poor."[54] Medellín stressed that the well-being of the poor is integral to evangelization. An important premise of the liberation theology that was popularized by Medellín and by theologians such as Gustavo Gutiérrez and Leonardo Boff was that the poor are dignified when they participate in their own liberation—hence the importance of the formation of base ecclesial communities. Although both liberation theology and base communities have been met with mixed reviews within the Catholic Church and have waned in influence over the last twenty years, their contributions to contemporary Catholic missiology and practice remain significant. The call to partnership among rich and poor, North and South, as well as the value of the voices of marginalized people are themes that continue to resonate today.

Other significant points of reference for late twentieth-century Catholic missiology include *Evangelii Nuntiandi* (1975) and *Redemptoris Missio* (1990). Pope Paul VI's apostolic exhortation, *Evangelii Nuntiandi*, affirmed that mission is not defined by geography; instead every local church is missionary by its very nature. *Evangelii Nuntiandi* also placed the reign of God as the central theological focus of mission, teaching that mission is the Church participating in the kingdom of God. Pope John Paul II's encyclical, *Redemptoris Missio*, emphasized the reciprocity and universality of mission: "Cooperating in missionary activity means not just giving but also receiving. All the particular churches, both young and old, are called to give and to receive in the context of the universal mission, and none should be closed to the needs of others."[55]

On American soil, the United States National Council of Catholic Bishops also sketched out the principle of universality in *To the Ends of the Earth* (1996) and *Called to Global Solidarity: International Challenges for U.S. Parishes* (1997). *To the Ends of the Earth* deems every local church as both mission-sending and mission-receiving,[56] while *Called to Global Solidarity* offers a similar message: "We are members of a universal Church that transcends national boundaries and calls us to live in solidarity and justice with the peoples of the world. . . . [P]arishes need to be more Catholic and less parochial."[57] These influential documents, among others, drove home the notion that mutuality is essential for mission.

Contemporary missiological reflection among Catholics, while varied, builds on the postconciliar emphases of incarnation, accompaniment, and solidarity. It often employs the principle of *missio Dei* to insist that there is but one mission, the mission of God that is shared by the Church. This mission has two directions: to the church itself and to the world.[58] Stephen Bevans and Roger Schroeder describe the trajectory of Catholic missiology today as "prophetic dialogue" in which people are respected for who they are but also called into continual conversion.[59] Similarly, Robert Schreiter notes that guideposts of incarnation, accompaniment, and solidarity draw the Church in a mission of reconciliation—participating with God in healing and restoring broken relationships and societies. Prevailing contemporary Catholic missiology insists that mission be accomplished through partnership. This missiology balances the local and the universal, stressing the role of each local parish—whether northern or southern—in the call to universal evangelization.

Protestant missiology has followed along a similar vein—often using different terminology to express ideas similar to incarnation, accompaniment, solidarity, liberation, and reconciliation. This overlap is not accidental. Indeed, Protestants and Catholics are collaborating in the theology and practice of mission as never before. The ecumenical movement, which rose to prominence during the early twentieth century among mainline Protestants as a propellant for mission, has in turn significantly affected contemporary concepts of mission. While the ecumenical movement had largely been a Protestant phenomenon prior to Vatican II, it has subsequently proceeded in conversation with Catholic theologians. Both Protestants and Catholics call for cooperation in mission. Instead of viewing mission as competition for souls, Christians of all stripes are increasingly seeing mission in the broader context of participation in God's kingdom, wherever it may be found. Even evangelicals, who have frequently stood in opposition to the ecumenical movement, are progressively embracing collaboration with other Christian traditions. Between 1977 and 1984 evangelicals and Roman Catholics came together for a series of meetings called *The Evangelical-Roman Catholic Dialogue on Mission* in which they agreed on the goals of common witness, worship, evangelism, and social action.[60] Pentecostals also joined with Catholics in 1997 to produce a joint document on common witness. "Why do apart what we can do together?" their report asked rhetorically.[61] Though evangelicals have been leery of what they perceive to be politicalization and secularization of the gospel among conciliar Protestants, they are embodying an increasingly conciliatory posture toward churches affiliated with the World Council of Churches (WCC) as well, often at the urging of global southerners sensitive to the negative impact of divisiveness on mission.[62] This collaboration has resulted in both a shared vision for mission and a shared practice of mission.

Both mainline and evangelical Protestant missiologies have witnessed incredible ferment over the last generation, leading to new emphases on partnership, contextualization, holistic ministry, and the primacy of local congregations. In fact, prominent missiologists such as David Bosch and Charles Van Engen identify nothing short of a paradigm shift in missiology over the last generation.[63] In his description and endorsement of an "emerging ecumenical missionary paradigm" in his heralded 1991 magnum opus, *Transforming Mission: Paradigm Shifts in Theology of Mission*, South African Reformed missiologist David Bosch writes that in this new paradigm, the heart of mission is connection. Mission is the church-with-others.[64] "Everywhere the church is in the diaspora, in a situation of mission."[65] The new missiology also premises mission on unity in the church, abandoning the distinction between "sending" and "receiving" churches and favoring mutuality over hierarchy. In the new paradigm, mission is conceived as a two-way process in which people offer mutual spiritual encouragement to one another. Protestant missiology that embraces the new paradigm, like its Catholic counterpart, appropriates the concept of *missio Dei*, commissioning Christians to participate in God's mission to the world by living both in solidarity with the world and fidelity to Jesus and the church.

Within the new paradigm, partnership in ministry is a key motif. Among conciliar Protestants, the language of partnership first came to the fore after the 1947 meeting of the International Missionary Council (IMC), an organization that resulted from the Edinburgh conference. In an effort to overcome the patterns of dependency between "younger" and "older" churches, the IMC recognized that all churches around the world were "worthy partners in the task of evangelism"—thus rendering the distinction between "older" and "younger" churches obsolete.[66] The IMC's 1952 meeting reflected the emergence of the concept of *missio Dei* in missiological discourse. The classical doctrine of *missio Dei* as God the Father sending the Son, and God the Father and Son sending the Spirit was expanded at this meeting to include the Trinitarian God sending the church into the world. *Missio Dei* places God at the heart of missionary activity and reconstructs mission as an activity of the Trinity in the world, with churches from around the globe participating together in God's mission as partners.[67] According to David Bosch, the 1952 IMC meeting was a watershed for thinking about mission. Afterward, Christians of virtually all persuasions embraced the concept of *missio Dei*.[68] The IMC, which merged with the WCC in 1961, continued to challenge the unidirectional "sending" of mission from West/North to South in subsequent decades and to advocate for partnership in mission.[69] Reciprocity, mutuality, and interdependence were to be the hallmarks of partnership in mission—learning to share together in m*issio Dei*.[70]

Among evangelicals, who are often criticized for carrying on mission efforts as if still in the height of colonialism, the *missio Dei* concept and the partnership approach to mission have gained traction as well. At mid-century, evangelicals strongly reacted against the ecumenical movement that was prominent among conciliar Protestants. Forming several mission agencies in the 1960s as counterpoints to the more liberal WCC and IMC, evangelicals sought "to offer a biblically based alternative to ecumenism."[71] In contrast to conciliar Protestants' more horizontal approach to mission in which social justice and liberation are paramount, evangelical mission bodies typically endorse a more vertical view of mission that emphasizes individual reconciliation with God and sees proclamation of salvation as the paramount task of mission. Despite this friction over the message and goal of mission, evangelicals increasingly also embrace a more egalitarian method of mission. Clause 8 of the monumental 1974 Lausanne Covenant, for example, states:

> God is raising up from the younger churches a great new resource for world evangelisation, and is thus demonstrating that the responsibility to evangelise belongs to the whole body of Christ. . . . Thus a growing partnership of churches will develop and the universal character of Christ's church will be more clearly exhibited.[72]

According to Bruce Camp, while the "supporting church" and "sending church" models are still dominant in evangelical mission, a new "synergistic church" model is emerging that is based on "joint action by agents that, when taken together, increases the effectiveness of both."[73] In this model, interdependence between western and nonwestern churches is prized, and each local church is called to be proactive in mission.

Among Catholics, mainline Protestants, and evangelicals riding the currents of the new missiological paradigm, the central role of the church in mission, particularly at the local level, has received increased attention. While *missio Dei* was initially conceived as a correction to a church-centered view of mission in its insistence that the church does not mandate mission or acquire territory but rather participates in God's outreach to the world, *missio Dei* was later appropriated to reinvigorate church-based mission. At the Willingen meeting of 1952, WCC delegates confessed: "We are convinced that mission work should be done through the Church. We should cease to speak of missions and churches and avoid the dichotomy."[74] More recently, as part of The Gospel and Our Culture Network, mainline missiologists Darrell Guder, Craig van Gelder, and their colleagues have launched the *Missional Church* project. In the sense of *missio Dei*, they point out, mission is the charter not of individuals or of agencies but of the church as God's instrument in the world.[75] While evangelical mission has largely fallen under the purview of parachurch ministries and unaffiliated individuals, it has also seen a renewed emphasis on ecclesiology in the last generation. James Scherer argues that in the Lausanne movement from 1966 to 1986, evangelicals increasingly moved toward church-centered mission with the local church being viewed as the principal agent of evangelism.[76] The Lausanne Covenant states that "The church is at the very center of God's cosmic purpose and is his appointed means of spreading the Gospel."[77] At the second Lausanne conference in 1989, parachurch ministries were called to play a supporting role in mission, letting churches themselves take the lead.

Accompanying this focus on the centrality of the church is a recognition of the importance of the local parish. Lesslie Newbigin, another influential missiologist of the "new paradigm," speaks of the local Christian congregation as a "hermeneutic of the gospel." In the local body of believers, says Newbigin, the gospel is truly encountered and lived.[78] As early as 1949, conciliar Protestants encouraged western missionaries to integrate into local churches, becoming "in every respect" members of the churches they served.[79] Evangelicals, too, have reiterated the importance of the local church, referring to it as the primary instrument for world evangelization in Lausanne II.[80] Among Catholics, the power of the witness of the local parish, which was highlighted in *Sacrosanctum Concilium* and *Evangelii Nuntiandi*, has remained a central focus.[81] Fortified by liturgy, prayer, and sacrament offered in the context of the local parish, the faithful are equipped to go into the world to preach Christ.[82] Pentecostal theologians also echo this sentiment. Simon Chan writes that "Eucharistic worship does not end in cosy fellowship, but in costly mission to the world."[83] Mission, according to the new paradigm, flows out of the life and witness of the local church.

Contextualization, the Protestant counterpart of the predominantly Catholic notion of inculturation, is another prominent marker of "new paradigm" missiology.[84] Discourse about contextualization maintains that the gospel, while always culturally situated, is captive to no one culture. Instead, the gospel is to be uniquely embodied in each local culture. Advocates of contextualization also recognize the problematic link between western culture and the Christian faith in modern mission efforts.[85] While some evangelicals have been leery of the concept of contextualization out of a fear of syncretism and pluralism, many have come to embrace it—thanks largely to the voices of global southerners critical of the western trappings of the gospel preached in their lands by missionaries from Europe and North America. At the first Lausanne conference, Indian doctor B. V. Subamma argued persuasively that the church needed to better adapt to local cultural climates so that "each ethnic unit in each land" could "follow its own culture" instead of having to embrace a foreign culture along with the Christian faith.[86] Latin American theologian René Padilla was also a major voice for the contextualization of the gospel at Lausanne and beyond. Based on the incarnation event in which God becomes present as a human among humans, Padilla lifted up a truly indigenous church.[87] Though their notion of contextualization is more muted and cautious than the conciliar definition, many evangelicals have come to recognize that rather than being a jewel of western culture, the Christian faith is at once universal and particular to each local culture.[88] Billy Graham, a premier evangelist who was once an anthropology student at Wheaton College, also recognized the problematic linkage of Christianity to western culture. In an introductory address at Lausanne, he quipped, "When I go to preach the gospel I go as an ambassador for the kingdom of God, not America."[89]

Largely because of increased attention given to local contexts, missiological reflection in the postcolonial milieu has also highlighted the social dimensions of the gospel.[90] In the 1960s, in fact, the documents produced by the World Council of Churches perceived mission almost exclusively in terms of working for justice in the world. More recently, missiologists in conciliar Protestant circles have sought out a more "holistic" approach to mission, one that includes both proclamation and activism, personal conversion and social transformation. Many evangelicals, who tend to stress proclamation above all else in mission, have been reintroduced to the social side of the gospel over the last generation—though prominent evangelical organizations such as Bread for the World and World Vision have long stressed ministry to physical needs as an important priority in mission. Latin American evangelicals René Padilla, Orlando Costas, and Samuel Escobar brought social justice issues into the fore for evangelical missiology. Padilla, while eschewing liberation theology for its Marxist undertones, declared at Lausanne that "Jesus' work had a social and political dimension . . . the kingdom of God." The church, then, is not an "otherworldly religious club" but a "sign of the kingdom of God . . . given a mission oriented toward the building of a new humanity."[91] Escobar, a Peruvian Baptist, reflects on the multidimensional nature of the missionary task, advocating a missiology of "radical discipleship," which sees action for justice as an integral and constitutive part of evangelism.[92] Although contemporary evangelicals are sometimes criticized for creating an artificial dichotomy between social justice and personal transformation—with personal transformation being perceived as paramount—signs of an integrative gospel that ministers to the full range of human needs are also apparent among evangelicals.[93]

The new missiology—based on the notion of *missio Dei*, the centrality of the local church, and the call to partnership, contextualization, and holistic ministry—is certainly not embraced by all Christians involved in mission today. In fact, especially in North America, a significant number of churches and mission agencies function according to what Escobar calls "managerial missiology." They are concerned more with statistics, techniques, inventiveness, entrepreneurialism, leadership strategy, pragmatism, and numerical growth than with theological or anthropological reflection.[94] Embodied in the church-growth movement pioneered by David McGavran and the Fuller Seminary School of Intercultural Studies, the managerial model has fostered numerous mission efforts among evangelicals (who now overwhelmingly dominate international mission endeavors among North Americans) that are "organized, focused, well-managed, and even scientific" in their approach to ministry.[95] While the managerial model is arguably still dominant in North American mission, it has been increasingly challenged as evangelicals apply a critical eye to past assumptions and embrace a new missiological paradigm. At the turn of the twenty-first century, members of the World Evangelical Fellowship recognized the modern roots of the managerial approach, thereby joining Escobar in repudiating its overconfidence, reductionism, lack of cultural awareness, and ethnocentrism.[96] In the spirit of Lausanne, in dialogue with conciliar Protestants and Catholics, and in deference to Christians in the majority world, many evangelicals have rediscovered a holistic, service-oriented model of mission, says Escobar.[97]

Across Christian traditions and around the globe, new currents in missiology continue to swell. Rather than being the exclusive domain of western academics, "new paradigm" missiology includes the voices of majority-world Christians. These voices may, in fact, be the most salient in the mix—the dominant force in turning Christendom and its mission upside down.

## Grassroots Developments: Trends in the Practice of Mission

The revolution in mission has not been purely, or even principally, a cerebral affair. At the grassroots level as well, several trends suggest that the colonial mode of mission has given way to very different patterns of religious engagement between North and South. The practice of mission, like the theology of mission, is quite different in the postmodern world than in the modern era. While traditional relationships and patterns still exist, a new paradigm in the practice of mission has also emerged.

Changing economic and political structures around the world have dramatically altered patterns of North-South religious engagement. Economically and politically, first the colonial enterprise of European empire-building and then the Cold War system of bipolar blocs have been replaced by a polycentric milieu featuring the resurgence of ethnic groups, the emergence of regional spheres of influence, and the reinforcement of the nation-state. The integration of economic, political, and cultural systems across the globe—otherwise known as globalization—is a powerful and dominant force in our time. Although it can be argued that globalization is still a colonizing force in the American dominance of multinational corporate capitalism and the exportation of cultural modes, our world is increasingly polycentric. Flows of resources, power, and information are multidirectional and multidimensional. Through travel, the press, and technology, North Americans in particular are in contact with Africans, Latin Americans, and Asians more than ever before.[98]

Made possible by globalization, transnational religious connections—consisting of flows of people, information, goods, services, and other resources across national boundaries—have become increasingly pronounced and of greater interest in recent decades.[99] Whereas the arena of "foreign mission" used to be limited primarily to religious professionals, ease of travel and communication has enabled more and more lay people to become personally involved in international relationships and ventures of a religious nature. Robert Wuthnow and Stephen Offutt report that an estimated 1.6 million US churchgoers participate in short-term mission trips to other countries each year.[100] Increased migration and "reverse mission" efforts have also enabled greater contact between majority-world and minority-world groups and individuals. The face of the "other" is no longer out of reach. Based on this heightened level of contact, members of disparate cultures and locales have the opportunity to better their knowledge of one another's situations, build respect, and work toward meeting needs more effectively. Moreover, even though the distribution of power and resources is still grossly uneven in the contemporary world, the political, economic, and cultural milieu of globalization at least affords the opportunity for new voices to be heard and new loci of influence to emerge.

In addition to the propelling force of the contemporary global political and economic climate, new patterns of cross-cultural religious engagement have also emerged on the ground in light of the grassroots situation of the churches in the global South. As "younger" southern churches have matured, their expressed needs have changed. A new generation of leadership has emerged in southern churches. Generally, what they seek from North American Christians is not control, management, or programming but rather solidarity and equipment for ministry. The situation could be described as post-postcolonial.[101] Whether they affiliate with European or North American denominations or function independently of such apparatuses—Asian, Latin American, and African churches have developed well-articulated agenda and increasingly sturdy structures of leadership, especially in the last generation. Westerners are simply not in a position to control and dominate majority world Christianity. The swelling membership and influence of African Initiated Churches and other independent Christian bodies in the global South is also a sign that northern missionaries are no longer in a position to exercise unilateral control. To the extent that northern mission agencies and congregations have altered their approach to mission in the global South, the impetus for reform has come as much from the changing grassroots situation and the voices of global southerners as it has any sort of ideological reformation on the part of western Christians.

Whereas the political opportunities and mobilizing structures mentioned above have doubtlessly contributed to fresh patterns in the practice of mission, so too has framing, which can be defined as the "conscious strategic efforts by groups of people to fashion shared understandings of the world and of themselves that legitimate and motivate collective action."[102]

The widespread condemnation of the norms under which colonial mission is often perceived to have operated, combined with the broad-scale currency of the new missiology, have been influential in the contemporary practice of mission. Moreover, whatever the direct influence of the new missiology at the grassroots level, many contemporary Christians—especially in the West—have internalized the norms of equality and self-determination inherent to the philosophy of political liberalism. In the United States in particular, the traction of the discourse on multiculturalism and the civil rights movement have signaled a cultural shift in shared beliefs and understandings regarding acceptable patterns of engagement between persons of European and non-European descent, between power brokers and those lacking access to power. Various organizations and initiatives within the field of Christian mission have adopted these secular and religious ideologies, developing frames of thought to mobilize their constituents. Georg Wilhelm Friedrich Hegel's famous notion that ideas have legs takes on particular weight in the emergence of social movements like the sister church phenomenon and other iterations of the new paradigm in mission.

Due to fresh missiological reflection, the evolution of cultural sentiment regarding equality and self-determination, seismic shifts in the global cultural-political landscape, the coming of age of the church in the Majority World, and various other latent factors, new patterns in the practice of mission have become dominant in the last thirty years. Some of these changes simply refashion western imperialism in new garb. But many coalesce with the new paradigm missiology as they concretize—albeit imperfectly—the rhetoric of partnership, contextualization, and holistic mission.

One marked change is the restructuring of the global missionary apparatus, especially on an institutional level. Christian missionary efforts in our time are increasingly decentralized, independent, locally targeted, and internationally sourced. Since the middle of the twentieth century, most mainline mission agencies based in the West have integrated their mission projects in the global South into local churches. Mission institutions such as schools and hospitals were also gradually turned over to local churches. Many mainline mission agencies eventually dissolved or restructured their boards of foreign missions, scaling back the number of missionaries they sent to the global South and working to build partnerships with national churches.[103] Shifting their model of service from *mission station-to-people group* to *church-to-church relationships*, it is not uncommon for mission agencies based in the West to "send" personnel to the global South only in response to a request from national or local churches. Moreover, these mission agencies are less likely to play the role of captain or even the role of intermediary. Instead, they function as trainers, technical assistance providers, and resource suppliers.[104]

In the contemporary postcolonial milieu, one path of missionary institutions birthed in the modern world has been to scale back and refocus their efforts. Another has been to globalize. For example, World Evangelical Fellowship, a network that represents 420 million evangelicals,

100 international organizations, and churches in 128 nations, shifted its international headquarters from the United Kingdom to Singapore in 1987 and elected its first nonwestern international director in 1992.[105] Many other formerly western agencies have followed suit. And a host of new sending agencies have popped up outside of the West. South Korea has become a center of international mission-sending agencies, with the latest count at 190.[106] Unlike the missionary societies formed in the nineteenth century, today's international agencies and alliances for mission are decentralized. They eschew top-down leadership in favor of networks and collaborative efforts, and they encourage church-based initiatives, especially at the local level.

As an even greater affront to organizational bureaucracy, a significant amount of missionary activity is taking place independent of mission agencies and denominations. Congregation-based international initiatives are increasingly common. "Unreached peoples are adopted, teams are sent to visit and pray, and, in many cases, long-term personnel are deployed, often without reference to mission agencies," Todd Johnson writes with regard to the role of local congregations in mission today.[107] It has become common for the institutional backing of the congregation to be circumvented, as independent evangelists raise their own support to travel across the world on a mission, unaffiliated groups of college students engineer their own international service projects, and internet surfers send money to distant cyber friends.

The composition of missionary personnel has also evolved considerably. Mission efforts around the globe are predominantly driven by laypeople and short-term workers rather than clergy and "career" missionaries.[108] The colonial model of mission, wherein a relatively small and isolated group of western career missionaries lived—often in their own enclaves—for extended periods in the global South, has been replaced by much more voluminous, decentralized, and fluid flows of transnational engagement. David Barrett and his colleagues report that out of the world's 443,000 foreign mission workers serving around the globe in 2005, 218,000 were laypersons and 410,000 were short-term missionaries who served abroad from two weeks to under one year.[109] While institutional decentralization and a lay-dominated, short-term missionary force do not necessarily facilitate the actualization of "new paradigm" missiology, they at least create conditions in which the redistribution of power is possible and local cultures are more likely to be celebrated.

International mission is indeed from everywhere to everywhere in our time. Yet Americans still dominate the arena both numerically and financially.[110] Arguably, Americans are also the most aggressive exporters of culture among international missionaries, and they are often recognized as the founders of the managerial model of mission decried by missiologists of the new paradigm.[111] On top of all this, the principal vehicles of mission among Americans since the nineteenth century have been voluntary societies and parachurch organizations, many with few ties to the institutional church. Coupled with the xenophobic clamor of a small but high-ranking cadre of liberal American Christians, it is easy to see why American Christians are often judged as hostile to dominant forms of majority-world Christianity and imperialistic in their missionary efforts.

Even on the North American scene, however, harbingers of a fresh prototype in the practice of mission abound.[112] A significant number of North American Christians involved in mission are challenging the modern approach to mission and self-consciously trying to do things differently. And many of their attitudes and practices are gaining traction in mainstream mission efforts as well. In their rhetoric, if not in their behavior, North American Christians who journey to Africa, Latin America, or Asia are less likely than their predecessors in the colonial era to take for granted paternalistic attitudes toward the "other" in the global South. They are also more likely to form relationships that are based—at least ostensibly— on partnership and mutuality. Relief and development efforts have come to outweigh direct evangelization efforts in the Majority World, especially among mainline Christians, and both evangelicals and mainline Christians have increasingly focused on a holistic gospel joining word and deed. Many missionary agencies have shifted their attention from sending northern career missionaries into regions of the global South to supporting and training nationals. In fact, Protestant international mission agencies based in the United States employ three nationals working in their own countries for every two Americans they deploy abroad.[113] Additionally, North American Christians have become increasingly doubtful about the desirability and effectiveness of exporting American culture with evangelism. Eschewing a precritical approach to culture, international ministry bodies frequently offer training in cross-cultural exchange and attempt to foster respect for host cultures among North Americans traveling to the global South. While Catholics and mainline Protestants have led the call to increased cultural sensitivity, evangelicals have also followed suit. Whether Catholic, mainline Protestant, or evangelical, many sending agencies have shifted their rhetoric away from charges to "convert the heathen" toward calls to "build relationships" and "learn while serving."

As Dana Robert has observed, establishing intercultural relationships has become both a means of mission and an end in itself in today's context of globalization. Tracing the history of relationality in mission over the course of the last century, Robert notes that the high value placed on cross-cultural personal friendships by many missionaries in the first half of the twentieth century gave way to more modest "partnership" ideal at mid-century—lest western missionaries be perceived as communists, colonialists, or attempted spokespersons for Africans and Asians. During the 1960s and 1970s, argues Robert, colonial guilt and pressure for reparations turned ideals of partnership into development projects that often eclipsed the personal and faith commitments of the friendship ideal, even though personal friendships were still important behind the scenes.[114] In today's mission milieu, however, relationality has regained currency as the longing for cross-cultural friendship has become a powerful motivation—often stronger than evangelism or social service—for mission.[115] While projects of various types are still central to most contemporary mission efforts, relationality has been elevated to new levels.

## The Sister Church Phenomenon: An Illustration of "New Paradigm" Mission

One example of the changing approach of North American Christians to their counterparts in the global South, and a forerunner in the implementation of "new paradigm" missiology, is the sister church phenomenon.[116] Since the early 1980s, and especially in the last decade, a significant number of North American congregations representing diverse Christian traditions have forged long-term relationships with partnering congregations in the global South. These congregation-to-congregation partnerships are typically driven by grassroots efforts, centered around the local church as the operative unit in mission, lay led, and democratically or representatively governed. Although sister church relationships are envisioned and carried out in various ways, generally speaking, from the North American vantage point, they represent a vote of confidence for indigenous churches in the global South, an acknowledgment of the demographic changes in the map of Christendom, and an attempt to promote the contextualization of Christianity. Within the congregation-to-congregation partnership model, a high premium is placed on mutuality and collaboration, both ecumenically and geographically. Power sharing, North/South solidarity, and personal relationships are also highly valued—often in contrast to efficiency or tangible "results." At least in intent, the sister parish model is all but "managerial."

In the ideal, North/South congregation-to-congregation relationships embody a missiology based on partnership, contextualization, and solidarity among Christians from vastly different worlds. The degree to which sister church partnerships could be considered anticolonial or collaborative varies with each relationship. At times, power is shared unequally, contextualization is incomplete, and lines between "sending" and "receiving" communities are more fixed than not. In some respects, in some cases, sister church relationships are just another iteration of western imperialism, little more than veiled attempts to tame or co-opt Christianity in the global South. But in other respects, in many cases, sister parish relationships illustrate a missionary approach that Central Africans might refer to as *bega kwa bega* or *maboko na maboko*, mission "shoulder to shoulder" or "hand in hand."[117] Taken as a whole, this model represents an attempt to embody "new paradigm" missiology and embrace an upside-down Christendom. Indeed, for many North Americans who have awakened to shifts in global Christianity and the accompanying need for a new approach to mission, the sister parish model has come as a breath of fresh air. It is to this story that this study will now turn.

CHAPTER 2 | Beginnings

*The History and Development of the Sister Church Model Among North American Christians*

MIKE VALLEZ NEVER PLANNED to become an activist. And at first glance, Vallez—a civil engineer and father in his mid-fifties who resides in Utah—did not appear to be much of a prophet or revolutionary. In his spare time, however, Vallez was deeply immersed in dreams and initiatives that he believed had the capacity to change the world drastically. As Vallez saw it, international partnerships between grassroots faith-based communities are the key to eradicating global poverty: "The vision of millions of people, working within faith-based groups connected between the developed world of the 'haves' with the developing world of the 'have-nots' is the emerging vision I see for creating a world without poverty or economic insecurity."[1] As founder of Global Faith Partners, an organization that facilitated sister church relationships, Vallez was a dedicated evangelist of this vision.

Vallez first became acquainted with the sister church phenomenon when his suburban Minneapolis Catholic parish partnered with a parish in Chimbote, Peru, in 1996. At first only a curious onlooker in the relationship, Vallez grew to be personally involved when he joined a ten-day well-drilling delegation from his parish to Chimbote in 2002.[2] While participating in this delegation, Vallez was emotionally touched by relationships he formed and impressed by the mutuality that he witnessed and experienced. After traveling to Peru a second time, Vallez became all the more convinced of the efficacy of the sister parish model:

Unless one has experienced the transcendental/spiritual aspects of being involved in this special kind of giver-receiver relationship at a group and individual level, it is difficult to describe on paper. However, the experience is one of personal transformation for everyone involved. The structural framework for affecting human solidarity on a profound level is in place.[3]

When he returned home, Vallez felt compelled to facilitate similar experiences for others.

In 2004, in the interest of forming a mechanism to match congregations to one another, Vallez began assembling a list of contacts who were influential in the sister church movement, the names gathered through word of mouth. One by one, he contacted these leaders of other initiatives from around the country to hear their stories and glean from their experiences. Soon, he had formed a steering committee to construct a vision and mission for what would become Global Faith Partners. In the process, he met Lutherans from the Saint Paul Area Synod who had been partnering in Tanzania for the last fifteen years. These Lutherans introduced Vallez to a visiting Tanzanian Catholic priest, who soon invited Vallez to Tanzania. In late 2005, Vallez traveled around Tanzania, enrolling parishes in Global Faith Partners. Over the course of a month, Vallez had enrolled one hundred parishes whose leaders were interested in linking with US Catholic parishes. The next spring, Vallez arranged for five Tanzanian priests to visit the United States. He funded their tickets, found host families to provide lodging, planned meetings for them with scores of church officials, and showed them around the Mall of America and the Minnesota countryside. Vallez also helped the Tanzanian priests make personal calls to dozens of Catholic parishes in the Minneapolis area, resulting in sister parish relationships between Minnesota parishes and each of the parishes the priests pastored back home in Tanzania. While Vallez's relocation to Utah and the demands of two other projects stemming from his trip to Tanzania eventually rendered Global Faith Partners' parish-matching program inactive, Vallez continued to tout the partnership model of mission and encourage the formation of sister church relationships informally.[4]

According to Vallez, on-the-ground, cross-cultural encounters between people of faith, like the ones he experienced in Peru and Tanzania, are potent agents of social change, "helping to fill the 'missing link' in global human development."[5] In Vallez's eyes, sister church relationships not only change conditions in the global South but also profoundly transform those involved on both sides.

I believe that when we experience solidarity with our fellow brothers and sisters in the way of mutual giving and receiving, our souls join with others in filling up a river of abundance that promises to irrigate all souls with the holy waters of love and generosity.[6]

Compelled by the power of his own experiences and the testimonies of those who have also participated in sister church relationships, Vallez became an unlikely evangelist for the sister church movement among North American Christians.

## Overview of the Sister Church Phenomenon Involving North American Christians

Mike Vallez's story is unique, but Vallez is certainly not alone in his zeal for international congregational relationships. International partnerships between northern and southern communities—and particularly congregation-to-congregation relationships—have become widely popular among denominational representatives, staff members of mission agencies, and leaders of parachurch organizations in the United States over the past thirty years. This enthusiasm for sister church relationships is mirrored at the grassroots level. "'Partnership' has become something of a buzzword in mission right now," said Dan Shoemaker, president of Reciprocal Ministries International (RMI), a nondenominational evangelical organization that facilitates congregational partnerships, "and sister church relationships are an ideal way to live out partnership."[7]

While formalized sister church relationships are most common among Catholics and mainline Protestants with centralized denominational structures, they span virtually all Christian traditions and denominations. Participants in sister church relationships can be found among traditionalists and progressives, liberals and conservatives. Congregations composed of recent immigrants as well as established congregations—be they predominantly Anglo, Black, Latino, Asian American, or multiethnic—are involved in international linkages. Since its birth in the early 1980s and especially over the last fifteen years, the sister church movement has mushroomed among American Christians. "As a growing phenomenon," wrote Vallez, "it appears that the human propensity to connect in these types of relationships has become a 'meme'."[8] Like a vine, the movement has spread throughout American Christianity as communities of faith enter intentional relationships with other Christians around the globe.[9]

Northern and southern Christians who participate in sister church relationships seek to encounter one another as equals—both churches contributing to a common mission of serving each other and the world. Proponents of such partnerships place a high premium on solidarity, the sharing of power between Christians from North and South, and interpersonal cross-cultural connections at the grassroots level—often in contrast to efficient programs or measurable results.

Generally, the northern partner in the relationship is significantly wealthier than the southern partner, and financial and material support are usually a component of the relationship. In addition to donations of money, food, clothing, and educational or religious supplies, many northern congregations involved in sister parish relationships organize delegations to their partner congregations annually or biannually. The expressed purpose of these trips is often service, but sometimes the mission is solidarity or friendship-building instead of, or in addition to, working. Stated goals and purposes of sister church relationships in general also vary greatly, often based on members' theology and social ideology, but sometimes based on polity or practical considerations. Yet, the mode in which these relationships are intended to function—whether it be called accompaniment, partnership, or mutuality—is almost universal.

Notwithstanding the disparities between partners, most participants in sister parish relationships aspire to at least some level of mutuality and equality. "Ideally," says a 2003 report published by the Center for Applied Research in the Apostolate (CARA), "these relationships are, or become, partnerships of mutual support, so that both parishes benefit from the relationship as they become partners in solidarity."[10] In the interest of mutuality, many congregation-to-congregation partnerships feature letter-writing campaigns among parishioners, intercessory prayer for the other congregation, or return visits from members of the southern parish. Moreover, northern participants commonly acknowledge that while they give to their southern partners in physical ways, they receive countless nontangible gifts from their southern partners. While sister parish relationships do not erase global inequality or paternalism, they pay tribute to the refashioning of the world map of Christianity in the twentieth century and represent shifting patterns of global religious engagement.

Despite the growing scope of the sister church movement, its dynamics and outcomes are largely uncharted by scholars. Because of the dearth of literature published on sister church relationships in general and American participation in particular, this chapter relies largely on oral history to tell the story of this burgeoning movement from the vantage point of American participants. Based on semistructured interviews with eighteen representatives of denominational agencies or parachurch organizations, as well as a variety of literature published by these groups, this chapter traces the historical development of the sister church model of mission among American Christians.

## Grassroots Cross-Cultural Encounters: The Engine of the Sister Church Movement

Mike Vallez's story is a particular illustration of a common theme in the history of international church partnering programs in which American Christians participate. Both the partnership approach to mission and concrete expressions of partnership like the sister church phenomenon arose organically out of grassroots experiences. Among scores of congregations from across the continent, representing virtually all Christian traditions, international congregation-to-congregation partnerships have been formed on the backbone of transformative, personal, cross-cultural encounters of both organizers of programs and parishioners themselves.

In the context of decolonization, rapid globalization, innovations in transportation and communication technology, the rise of global political and humanitarian movements, the creation of the Peace Corps, and the burgeoning of new mission societies, the number of North American Christians traveling to the global South for religious or humanitarian purposes increased markedly in the 1960s and 1970s from previous decades.[11] Since then, the number of North American sojourners to Africa, Latin America, and Asia has multiplied exponentially. Of course, North American Christians have also come into closer contact with Christians from other parts of the world through increased migration of southerners to North America. The firsthand encounters between North American Christians and fellow believers they have met around the world inspired sister church programs and relationships among various Christian traditions. Of the eighteen representatives of denominational or parachurch agencies who were interviewed for this project, nearly all referenced the personal encounters of their founders, key program personnel, or constituents as the impetus for the sister church programs they administer. While missiology, interdenominational and interorganizational collaboration, and programmatic innovations have made relevant contributions to partnership programs, these programs are rooted in personal cross-cultural encounters.

Among American Catholics, the encounters that gave birth to sister parish programs and relationships largely took place in the 1960s and 1970s in Latin America. In response to the calls of Popes John XXIII and Paul VI for North Americans to join in solidarity with Latin Americans, more and more US bishops began sending their priests to Latin America to occupy posts as missioners. Lay missioners from those same dioceses also became active in Latin America, thus transforming the North American Catholic presence in Latin America from members of religious communities to diocesan priests and laypersons—people directly connected to local parishes back home. Though these missionaries worked within a traditional sending model of mission, they saw firsthand what was happening on the ground in Latin America and told stories of what they witnessed to Catholics in US parishes.[12] Further impetus for grassroots connections between North and Latin Americans came in the late 1970s with Salvadoran Archbishop Oscar Romero's plea to the universal church, and especially the Catholic Church in North America, to stand with the people of El Salvador and bear witness to the abuses they suffered.[13] Parachurch agencies involved in faith-based North/South partnerships—such as Christians for Peace in El Salvador (CRISPAZ), Sister Parish, and the SHARE Foundation—along with numerous diocesan or independently initiated partnerships were formed in response to the call for witnesses, solidarity, and aid by Romero and other members of the Latin American Bishops' Conference.

Catherine Nerney, president of Small Christian Community Connection, which links individuals to small Christian communities (otherwise known as base ecclesial communities) and communities to each other, marveled at the origins of faith-based, cross-cultural partnerships among Catholics, whether between parishes or other groups:

> People don't even know they're doing something that later someone will study as a specific movement or project of some kind. They just begin to reach out. And then they find themselves so enriched by the faith, life, and love of [the people they reach out to], that they are the ones who are changed.[14]

Many projects and relationships between North American and Latin American Catholic communities arose organically, said Nerney, and later evolved into more sustained and intentional programmatic efforts.

Mary Campbell, coordinator for Companion Synod Relationships in Latin America and the Caribbean with the Evangelical Lutheran Church in America, told a similar story about the impetus for companion congregation relationships among Lutherans and other Protestants. The accompaniment approach to mission, said Campbell, arose out of encounters between US Christians—mostly Catholics and Lutherans, but also other mainline and evangelical Protestants—and their Latin American counterparts in the

1980s on Latin American soil. According to Campbell, the large number of US Christians who visited Latin America in the 1980s did so because they wanted to help. Conscious of the ravages of war, corruption of governments, and poverty plaguing communities in El Salvador, Guatemala, Colombia, Honduras, and Nicaragua—and disturbed by the role played by the US government in Latin America's political conflicts—these Christians wanted to give voice to a different perspective from their government and show their solidarity and support to Latin Americans.

While many North Americans initially saw themselves as benefactors, said Campbell, they soon "discovered that they were learning so much about faith from their Latin American brothers and sisters that this wasn't just a giver/receiver relationship. It really was a relationship of mutuality."[15] Concerted, faith-based, solidarity initiatives emerged as North Americans simply began to "walk alongside" impoverished and oppressed people, explained Campbell. As North American Christians got to know Christians in Latin America, they discovered that their Latin American brothers and sisters had as much to give and teach as they did to receive and learn. These North Americans also realized that what their brothers and sister wanted from them was not solutions or programs but friendship and advocacy. Often "falling in love" with the communities they encountered, North American missioners felt compelled to continue the relationships they had started. And because of the success of these early linkages, organizations such as Campbell's began to create sister church matching and facilitation programs on a broader scale.[16]

While their purposes often diverged from Catholics and mainline Protestants, evangelical Protestants from the North also visited the global South in record numbers in the last quarter of the twentieth century thanks to the burgeoning of the short-term mission (STM) movement. In 1965, student researcher Thomas Chandler noted only 540 individuals from North America involved in short-term mission around the globe. By 1989, an estimate from the Fuller School of World Mission put the number at 120,000, while three years later it had more than doubled to 250,000, and by 2000 the number neared a million.[17] The STM movement and the sister church movement are two trends in mission with common origins. While there is significant overlap in the two phenomena, the models differ philosophically and practically. Yet, among evangelicals, the smaller church partnership phenomenon functions as a branch growing out of the trunk of short-term mission efforts.

Dan Shoemaker of Reciprocal Ministries International described how RMI's congregational partnership program arose in the context of short-term mission trips. As evangelical missionaries to Haiti in the 1970s, Shoemaker's parents, Herb and Shirley Shoemaker, were asked to host short-term youth and adult church teams from the United States. Whereas the Shoemakers celebrated enhanced personal ministry, encouragement of the national church, and renewal of faith among North American visitors as results of short-term mission encounters, they also recognized that short-term mission trips' effectiveness was limited by a lack of accountability, shared history, ongoing commitment, cultural understanding, and depth of relationships. The Shoemakers perceived that short-term volunteers from the United States were often profoundly moved by their encounters with the Haitians they met, but these Christians lacked the organizational support to follow through with the relationships they had started. In an attempt to enable North American Christians to continue to engage in cross-cultural mission while adjusting the parameters of their ministry to facilitate more effective, manageable, personal, mutual, and long-term mission activity, the Shoemakers began to match US and Haitian congregations in a sister church program.[18] "Our sister church program came out of the personal experience of my parents and myself as missionaries," said Dan Shoemaker.

> We saw sister church relationships as an effective way to do ministry. [North Americans] like the idea of having a cross-cultural experience and serving in the Third World. They don't want to just give money or support a missionary. They want to get their hands dirty. So, sister church relationships are a very effective way to do that. People get to get their hands dirty, and the work they do is more effective than short-term trips.[19]

Among North American Catholics, mainline Protestants, and evangelicals, what have become formal sister parish relationships arose informally and often spontaneously out of grassroots, cross-cultural encounters with inhabitants of the global South. The same can be said for immigrant and ethnic-minority congregations—which may or may not fit into the categories delineated above—involved in international partnerships. For these congregations, in fact, the personal connections to the congregations with which they partner are often much more visceral. For immigrant congregations in North America, partner congregations might be composed of friends or relatives. Linkages between African American and African or Caribbean congregations are often formed around the bonds of a common heritage or background. Whatever the case, the vast majority of broadscale sister church programs as well as scores of individual partnerships began because northern and southern Christians met, established bonds, and sought to develop the relationships they had formed.

## The Institutional History of the Sister Church Phenomenon

Due to space constraints, the following account is only an overview of the sister church phenomenon among American Christian institutions. By examining the movement in its Catholic, mainline, evangelical, and Black Church contexts, this chapter attempts to represent the spectrum of North American Christianity in which sister church relationships are situated. Although this account is far from comprehensive, it incorporates sample stories from all sides of the movement in addition to featuring the most prominent denominations and agencies. This account also takes into consideration the diversity in polity and demography of North American congregations that participate in the sister church movement as well as the varied role that institutions perform in congregation-to-congregation relationships.

### Denominational Bodies

#### Catholics

While rooted in the North/South exchanges of the 1960s, 1970s, and 1980s, the institutionalized sister parish phenomenon among Catholics burgeoned in the 1990s. Since then, it has been increasingly popular. Bill Nordenbrock, mission director for the Mission Society of the Precious Blood, maintained that "parishes that embark on these relationships are testing new waters. . . . For a United States parish to enter into an ongoing relationship with a faith community in the missions is to choose to embrace a new way of being a parish."[20] While international sister church relationships involving US Catholic parishes date back at least to the 1980s, the vast majority of parishes that have become involved in sister parish relationships have done so since 1990. The 2001 National Parish Inventory found that almost half of the twinning relationships among respondents were less than five years old, and 90 percent were the first twinning relationship in which the US partner had been involved.[21] Almost all Catholic sister parish relationships are less than twenty years old, with the largest surge of interest coming since 1995.[22] Although no comprehensive numerical data on sister parish relationships has been generated since the 2001 report, it appears that the number of parishes involved in parish-to-parish relationships continues to grow.[23]

The response to the 1995 National Council of Catholic Bishops (NCCB) parish survey (with 1,717 parishes responding) indicated that 12 percent of US parishes were involved in sister parish relationships.[24] More recently, the Center for Applied Research in the Apostolate (CARA) found that 18 percent of parishes surveyed through the 2001 National Parish Inventory (with 4,670 parishes responding) were engaged in a "relationship of support" with another parish outside the United States, with 83 percent of international partners being in Latin America.[25] In their survey of eleven US dioceses, the United States Catholic Mission Association (USCMA) found that the percentage of parishes partnering within the various dioceses ranged from 3 percent to 15 percent.[26] It is difficult to determine exactly how many of the nineteen thousand US parishes are involved in sister church relationships. The CARA study reports that nearly fourteen hundred parishes have a faith-based partnership abroad or with a poorer US parish, while the US Bishops' 1997 statement, *Called to Global Solidarity*, lists seventeen hundred relationships in Latin America alone.[27] The Archdioceses of Cincinnati and St. Paul-Minneapolis, along with the Dioceses of Richmond and Nashville, are leaders in the American Catholic Church's sister parish effort. Cincinnati has more than fifty parishes involved in the endeavor, nearly one quarter of the parishes in the archdiocese.[28] Haitian parishes are especially popular partners for US Catholic parishes. In her study of parish partnerships, anthropologist Tara Hefferan identified more than three hundred thirty US parishes partnering in Haiti.[29]

Among Catholics, the great majority of parish-to-parish partnerships are initiated by someone in the parish, whether a parish priest, parish council, or layminister.[30] Although the CARA survey found that two-thirds of parish respondents said that their diocese promotes sister church partnerships,[31] the dioceses or other levels of the Church hierarchy are peripheral forces in the sister parish movement at best. Less than 10 percent of sister parish relationships are initiated by bishops, and the level of diocesan support for parish twinning varies greatly by diocese.[32] Some US bishops embrace more radical notions of solidarity, liberation, and justice in Latin America. Others, leery of liberation theology, prefer to focus on religious formation and/or less controversial areas of social concern such as education and health care in Latin America. Still other bishops have directed missional attention away from Latin America altogether in favor of concentrating on local concerns.

This ambivalence is reflected at the grassroots level as well, as many US Catholics involved in mission in Latin America have shifted focus from advocacy and systemic restructuring to catechesis and pastoral concerns.

For instance, a 2005 USCMA survey found that nearly one third of US missioners serving internationally were engaged in pastoral ministry as their primary work activity. Education, health care, administration, and priestly/religious formation were successively the next highest ranked activities. Less than 3 percent of missioners serving abroad, by contrast, worked primarily in social justice, social transformation, or social work.[33] Data collected on sister parish relationships also reveal that solidarity and justice are not always prioritized in practice. The CARA study found that intercessory prayer and providing material support were the central priorities of US parishes involved in sister church relationships.[34] The USCMA study conceded that although building "mutual relationships of solidarity" is often the expressed goal of sister church relationships, these relationships may reflect very different priorities as they are carried out.[35] Yet, while the emphasis of sister parish relationships vary among Catholics, these relationships continue to be popular at the grassroots level.

Mainline Protestants

Among mainline Protestants in the United States, Lutherans boast of the most far-reaching and developed congregation-to-congregation partnership program. "Companion congregation" relationships, as they are called among Lutherans, date back to 1988 when the Evangelical Lutheran Church in America (ELCA), which was formed that same year through the merger of three American Lutheran bodies, launched its "companion synod" program.[36] A year before, the Saint Paul Area Synod (SPAS) entered into a relationship with the Iringa Diocese of the Lutheran Church in Tanzania through the efforts of Owdenburg Mdegalla, bishop of the Iringa Diocese, and Arnold Blomquist, national councilperson for the ELCA, who had met each other through the work of Lutheran Global Volunteers in Tanzania. This relationship soon became the pilot companion synod relationship for the ELCA as Mdegalla and Blomquist together drafted formal guidelines for the Iringa partnerships in 1989.[37]

In the beginning, the Iringa partnership was little more than a formal meeting between bishops, but it soon blossomed into a sprawling grassroots movement. The first companion congregation relationship was formed out of the Iringa partnership in 1990.[38] Since then, sixty congregations have entered into a relationship with companion congregations through the Iringa partnership. Additionally, more than one thousand people have traveled back and forth between Saint Paul and Iringa. As a result of the partnership, Tanzania's first private university has been founded, more than nine hundred students in Iringa have received scholarships, numerous construction and well-digging projects have been completed, a pastoral exchange program has flourished, visiting scholars have enjoyed stays in both countries, and health care facilities in Tanzania have been significantly expanded.[39]

While the Saint Paul Area Synod's partnership with the Iringa Diocese is the most developed example of the ELCA's companion synod program, all sixty-five ELCA synods have entered into companion relationships.[40] As Mary Campbell explained, the ELCA chartered its companion synod program in the early 1990s as an effort to enliven the denomination's international relationships and participation in the Lutheran World Federation.[41]

Especially since the mid-nineties, the ELCA has bolstered the companion synod program, seeing it as a key means of implementing the accompaniment approach to mission. In 1995, the ELCA's Division for Global Mission (DGM) called for a re-evaluation of the ELCA's activity in Latin America. Based on experience learned through bilateral international relationships as well as conversations with other members of the Lutheran World Federation, the ELCA revamped is vision for mission around the concept of accompaniment, which it defines as "walking together in a solidarity that practices interdependence and mutuality."[42] Said Campbell:

> One thing that came out really clearly in our consultations in the 1990s with other members of the Lutheran World Federation, was that they saw themselves as independent church bodies and weren't looking for a giver-receiver relationship. They were looking to be accompanied and for relationships of mutuality.[43]

Accordingly, the ELCA's strategic plan for mission in the twenty-first century became to implement the vision of accompaniment throughout its international mission programs and relationships. To that end, in 1998, Herbert Chistrom, Presiding Bishop of the ELCA, issued a directive to all ELCA synods to seek out and develop a companion church relationship with a diocese somewhere else in the world.[44]

As a national body, the ELCA only facilitates the companion synod program, leaving companion congregation relationships to be organized at the synodical level.[45] Because the ELCA is affiliated with Sister Parish, an ecumenical parachurch organization, ELCA congregations also have the denomination's blessing to link with Latin American congregations under Sister Parish's oversight. Some ELCA congregations circumvent both the companion synod program and Sister Parish and form relationships with other congregations based on their own contacts and resources. Because of the varied avenues through which Lutheran companion congregation relationships are facilitated, said Campbell, it is difficult to gauge the number of congregations involved. Of the eleven thousand congregations in the ELCA, Campbell claimed that a "significant minority" are involved in congregation-to-congregation relationships.[46]

As a denomination, the ELCA has the most developed vision and the most extensive implementation of the sister church model among Protestants. But other denominational mission agencies are also charting this territory. Sister church relationships are popular among many Baptists, especially in mainline denominations. While the Southern Baptist Convention, the largest American Baptist body, does not facilitate sister church relationships, several other Baptist denominations sponsor thriving programs. The 1.5 million-member American Baptist Church (ABC) has been sponsoring sister church relationships between ABC congregations and other congregations around the globe for the last twenty-five years, and especially in the last ten years.[47] According to Charles Jones, Area Director for Europe, the Middle East, and North Africa for the International Ministries division of ABC, partnership is the cornerstone of International Ministries' approach to mission.[48] "The story of International Ministries," says the division's website, is "a story of surprise about God's power to bring people together in partnership with God—and with one another."[49] International Ministries currently supports thirty-five to forty ABC congregations engaged in partnerships, matches made through the five regional areas of the ABC.[50]

Many of the initial congregation-to-congregation relationships among ABC congregations were aided by Baptist Peace Fellowship of North America (BPFNA), which encouraged sister church relationships over the last quarter of the twentieth century in an effort to build international trust and peace. More recently, this role has been ceded to International Ministries, other intermediaries, and congregations themselves. Given the congregational polity of Baptists, many individual congregations affiliate with more than one Baptist convention or association. Others are completely independent. Thus, in addition to the congregations matched through International Ministries, it is likely that numerous other ABC congregations have also forged congregational partnerships. Sister church relationships among Baptists are organizationally decentralized. International Ministries recognizes and embraces this fact, seeing its role in the movement as offering education and encouragement to congregations who choose to partner in almost limitless ways.

While the ABC's church partnership program arose out of a long history of relationships, for another mainline Baptist group, the Alliance of Baptists, a linking program grew out of a more recent history of common dissent. The Alliance, a small, nongeographical association of roughly one hundred twenty progressive Baptist congregations, forged a close relationship with the Fraternity of Baptist Churches of Cuba. Both the Alliance and the Fraternity are comprised of churches that were formerly connected to the Southern Baptist Convention and either left the denomination or were expelled because of their progressive theological commitments. In 1988, after both groups had recently formed, friendship blossomed between leaders of the two associations as they learned of their common trajectory.[51]

Stan Hastey, minister for mission and ecumenism with the Alliance, has been a key liaison in the formation of most of the congregational partnerships among members of the two bodies. In 1993, while attending the Fellowship of Baptist Churches of Cuba's annual gathering, Hastey was "absolutely captivated" by this "new group of Baptists." Hastey recalled:

> That visit transformed my viewpoint and led me back to deal with a foundational issue, I think, for all Christians. And that is, are we not all missionaries in some sense? Are we not all called to the same mission?[52]

Since that visit, which he described as a "conversion experience," Hastey has returned to Cuba twenty-six times. He has introduced most of the twenty Alliance congregations that participate in sister church relationships to their Cuban partner congregations. Because of the testimonies of the initial partnering congregations, other congregations have been eager to forge partnerships as well. Based on what the Alliance calls "a shared commitment to an enlightened understanding of mission," Alliance and Fraternity congregations aspire to missionary work that flows "in two directions," embarking on relationships between "co-equal partners with no masters."[53]

For Methodists, the concept of two-directional mission is related to the polity of connectionalism.[54] Under the rubric "In Mission Together," and on the basis of connectional missiology, more than one thousand United Methodist congregations in the United States partner with other congregations around the world.[55] Patrick Friday, director of the In Mission Together partnership program of the United Methodist Church's General Board of Global Ministries, reported that this program is "designed to assist churches to engage in shared mission and ministry with a developing congregation or in the development of a relationship that could lead to a new congregation."[56] While social justice and holistic ministry are part of the DNA of United Methodist mission, said Friday, In Mission Together's direct purpose is to strengthen existing congregations and plant new ones in Eastern Europe and Southeast Asia. In Mission Together began in the 1990s, in response to a growing sentiment among United Methodists at the grassroots level that the work of church planting was unfinished. According to Friday, until the 1960s, international church planting was a key part of United Methodist mission efforts. In the 1960s and 1970s, the United Methodist Church halted church-planting efforts internationally in the name of ecumenism and decolonization. But in the eighties, said Friday, two things happened: key denominational leaders began reconsidering this retrenchment, and large numbers of Methodists at the grassroots level began traveling to other regions of the world on their own initiative. In Mission Together eventually formalized some of these efforts by connecting US congregations, districts, and conferences to emerging missions or congregations around the world, while many other missional partnerships and efforts continue among United Methodists outside the auspices of Global Ministries.

Friday stressed that international congregational partnerships are very much grassroots initiatives among United Methodists. In fact, roughly half of the international partnerships involving United Methodist congregations in the United States are initiated by the congregations themselves. The General Board of Global Ministries celebrates local grassroots efforts, seeing its own role as facilitating rather than directing or controlling relationships. Encouraging and affirming the role of local congregations in mission in a global setting, the General Board of Global Ministries seeks to come alongside partnering congregations, providing a trained third-party facilitator to assist them in developing linkages. Because congregations are often relatively ignorant of colonial history and common pitfalls in international mission, Global Ministries help American congregations develop cultural sensitivity and a commitment to shared ministry. "What we are asking congregations to do," explained Friday, "is move away from 'parachute drops'" and toward long-term, hand-in-hand partnerships. "We are very contextual in our approach," continued Friday, "and every relationship is different. . . . But the partnership piece is key—what we Methodists call 'connectionalism' is crucial to our ministry."[57]

Like the United Methodist Church and many other denominations, the Presbyterian Church of the United States of America (PC[USA]) also embraces the partnership approach to mission. In 2003, the PC(USA) formally adopted this approach on a national level when the General Assembly published "Presbyterians Do Mission in Partnership," a document which embraces the principles of (1) shared grace and thanksgiving, (2) mutuality and interdependence, (3) recognition and respect, (4) open dialogue and transparency, and (5) sharing of resources in all mission in which Presbyterians participate.[58]

Within the PC(USA), congregational partnerships grew out of presbytery-to-presbytery relationships, which commenced in the late 1970s. Given that presbyteries are made up of congregations, congregational partnerships are a natural part of presbytery pairing, said Doug Welch, Africa area coordinator for the PC(USA)'s World Mission program.[59] Welch reported that of the 173 PC(USA) presbyteries, between 110 and 115 have paired with another presbytery outside of the United States. And out of 11,000 to 11,500 PC(USA) congregations, Welch estimated that roughly eleven hundred are involved in international relationships with other congregations. While some congregation-to-congregation relationships emerged through presbytery linkages, others originated out of the travels or personal connections of parishioners. The relationships that arise informally at the congregational level tend to be thinly connected to presbytery and denominational leadership. Thus, Welch said, it is difficult for World Mission to gauge the scope and generalize the dynamics of sister church relationships among PC(USA) congregations. But as an agency, World Mission does not balk at this lack of control. Like the United Methodist General Board of Global Ministries and many other denominational mission agencies, World Mission increasingly sees its role as offering resources and guidance to congregations, and then standing back and letting them do their work.

Embracing the model of partnership while playing a limited role in the operations of sister church relationships is a common theme among mainline denominational mission agencies. The Episcopal Church, the United Church of Christ, the Disciples of Christ, and almost all other predominantly white mainline Christian denominations in the United States sponsor or support international congregation-to-congregation relationships in some way. Most do not directly facilitate partnerships at the congregational level. Instead, they loosely oversee relationships between synods, diocese, presbyteries, and districts, encouraging these smaller bodies to promote partnerships on the congregational level while offering resources and support for such endeavors. However, many representatives of mainline denominations and mission agencies argue that though their role in congregation-to-congregation partnerships may be minimal, their support for them is unequivocal. Since the birth of the ecumenical movement and especially over the last quarter century, mainline denominations see partnership as the marrow of mission. And increasingly, they recognize the local church as the engine for mission all over the world. Nearly all mainline mission agencies have authored and widely circulated statements lauding the merits of the accompaniment or partnership approach to mission, and most have developed some sort of initiative to carry out the ideals such documents promote. While these initiatives do not set the parameters for the sister church phenomenon in a firm way, they do give it buoyancy and form.

### Evangelicals

Evangelical congregation-to-congregation initiatives are usually undertaken on an ad-hoc basis. Few evangelical denominations directly orchestrate partnership programs. Umbrella evangelical organizations such as the National Association of Evangelicals and the Willow Creek Association do not track mission efforts among their constituents, and there are fewer research institutes among evangelicals than there are among mainline Protestants and Catholics. Thus, it is difficult to determine the magnitude of the sister church phenomenon among evangelicals.

Formal sister church programs are less common among evangelical denominational agencies than they are among mainline Protestants and Catholics, and they are especially rare among fundamentalist and Pentecostal organizations. Compared to Catholics and mainline Protestants, American evangelicals are latecomers to the partnership model of mission. While support for this missiological approach isn't as far-reaching as it is in mainline and Catholic circles, the idea of partnership is increasingly embraced by many evangelicals.[60] Evangelicals represent one-third of the American populace and more than 40 percent of affiliated Christians in the United States,[61] and their participation in international mission is proportionally higher than their counterparts in Catholicism, mainline Protestantism, or the Black Church. Evangelical mission efforts around the globe are not only prevalent, they are also diverse. Within the variety of mission efforts among evangelicals, expressions of partnership—such as congregation-to-congregation relationships—are gaining traction.

Among American megachurches, the vast majority of which are evangelical in orientation, sister church relationships are especially popular. In a recent survey of 405 US megachurches conducted by Robert Priest and his colleagues, fully 85 percent reported that their congregation has one or more church-to-church partnerships with congregations abroad. Commenting on the survey, Priest surmised:

> There appears to be a widespread pattern of church-to-church partnerships, supervised or monitored by highly mobile megachurch mission pastors, enabled by field missionaries and national church leaders, funded from the U.S. congregational base, linked through short-term mission trips, and carried out as an extension of the U.S. megachurch and its vision for ministry.[62]

Members of megachurches, along with many other evangelicals, belong to churches whose polity is congregational rather than connectional or hierarchical. Loose evangelical networks such as Bible church associations tend to be even less directive than historic denominational mission agencies, leaving the facilitation of mission efforts to parachurch organizations, congregations themselves, and individuals.

Evangelical denominational mission agencies face some of the same challenges as their mainline counterparts, such as diminished resources, weakening influence over constituent congregations, and increased competition with other actors in the field. Moreover, given the popularity of individualistic piety in evangelical circles, evangelicals often undertake mission efforts as individuals or ad-hoc groups rather than congregations. That said, several evangelical denominational mission agencies do take an active role in international congregation-to-congregation relationships. And some that do not directly facilitate congregational partnerships encourage their constituent congregations to form linkages through other channels.

One example of an evangelical denominational agency that facilitates congregation-to-congregation partnerships is Covenant Merge Ministries, a ministry of the Department of World Mission of the Evangelical Covenant Church. Under the rubric of "enabling multi-cultural relationships and committed partnerships for the kingdom of God," Merge Ministries facilitates mission trips involving teams from Covenant congregations—initial contacts they hope will develop into long-term relationships with international host ministries.[63] According to Dale Lusk, executive director of Merge Ministries, the program began in 1992 in the wake of consultations between Lusk and representatives of the Evangelical Covenant Church in Mexico. Seeking to redress the perceived lack of connectedness between the Covenant Church in the United States and in Mexico, the program was founded to send members of Covenant congregations from the United States to Mexico on short-term mission trips. While it started as an STM program, Merge Ministries has evolved to embody the long-term partnership ideal, said Lusk. Currently, approximately sixty Covenant churches from the United States send groups to various locations around the global South through Merge Ministries each year, about one-third of which form long-term partnerships with their host congregations.[64]

Another example of a denominational mission agency in the evangelical tradition that is involved in the sister church phenomenon is the International Ministries division of Converge Worldwide, formerly the Baptist General Conference (BGC). Converge Worldwide has just begun to embrace the sister church model of mission. In 2006, Converge Worldwide and the Baptist Conference of the Philippines initiated Decade of Change, a "new mission partnership platform to establish a movement of reproducing disciples, leaders and congregations." One of the projected outcomes is establishing ten sister church partnerships with a shared vision of planting middle-class community churches.[65] A focus on church planting has been a historical commitment of the Baptist General Conference. Carrying out this mission in the context of partnership, on the other hand, is a newer commitment, reflected in the BGC's recent name change. "'Converge Worldwide' is the Baptist General Conference's new missional name," explains the denomination's website about the 2008 decision. "Our focus is to Connect, Ignite and Transform: connecting churches and leaders to spiritually ignite movements of transformational churches."[66] Initiatives such as the pilot sister church program reflect this new focus on partnership and connection.

Among evangelical denominations, the most developed and wide-reaching partnership programs are found among affiliates of the newly constituted Anglican Church in North America (ACNA), which formed in 2009 among "orthodox" Anglican groups that broke fellowship with the Episcopal Church.[67] Compared to the modest scope of Merge Ministries' program, the embryonic nature of Converge Worldwide's congregational partnership efforts, and the absence of sister church programs among most evangelical denominations, these realigned Anglicans have enthusiastically embraced the sister church model of ministry. With strong links to Anglican provinces in the global South and a keen attachment to the worldwide nature of the Anglican Communion, it is no wonder that evangelical Anglican bodies are leading the way in the sister church movement among conservative American Protestants. Members of the Anglican Communion have long prided themselves in a sense of the church's global connectedness, and since 1963 Anglicans have formally embraced the accompaniment approach to mission under the banner of "Mutual Responsibility and

Interdependence in the Body of Christ."[68] As a consequence of this commitment to partnership in mission, in 1982, the Episcopal Church called on every diocese to establish a companion diocese relationship and encouraged the formation of sister parish relationships as well.[69] In 1998, the Lambeth Conference reiterated this call for the whole Anglican Communion, declaring that "the time has come for significant new initiatives in encouraging all dioceses to develop companion relationships across provincial boundaries, as part of the process of developing the cross-cultural nature of the Anglican Communion."[70]

Although the constituent congregations of the Anglican Church in North America no longer affiliate with the Episcopal Church, they share in the legacy of its commitment to cross-cultural relationships within the church. Moreover, many ACNA affiliates still fall under the leadership of Anglican churches in Africa or Latin America.[71] Since these North American Anglican churches are themselves members of the Anglican Church of Uganda, Nigeria, Rwanda, or another southern province, it seems only natural for them to partner with southern congregations that share the same spiritual authority. The Anglican Global Mission Partners, the mission arm of the Anglican Communion Network, has recently begun to link American Anglican parishes to parishes overseas, with a particular focus in Southeast Asia.[72] Sharing of Ministries Abroad (SOMA) is another linking organization. SOMA facilitates short-term mission trips that evolve into long-term parish-to-parish partnerships in some instances.[73]

For the Anglican Mission in the Americas (AMiAs), which was formed in 2000 as a missionary outreach of the Anglican Province of Rwanda and identifies as a "ministry partner" of the ACNA, sister church relationships enjoy prominence as a direct outgrowth of the organization's identity.[74] Representing roughly one hundred forty congregations throughout North America, AMiAs has celebrated the vibrancy of Anglicanism in Africa by joining its ranks; AMiAs operates under the authority of the Province of Rwanda and its archbishop, Emmanuel Kolini. In 2004, to "provide a unique opportunity for individual AMiA[s] churches to build relationships with local parishes in Rwanda in order for each to benefit relationally and spiritually,"[75] AMiAs launched a sister parish pilot project featuring partnerships between nine congregations in North America and nine in Rwanda.[76] According to Tim Smith—canon and former chief executive officer of AMiAs—the pilot project grew out of conversations between Smith, Archbishop Kolini, and Bishop Chuck Murphy, chairman of AMiAs, that took place soon after AMiAs was founded. These leaders wanted to enable local Rwandan and AMiAs parishes to be on mission together, as mutual partners in a common calling to ministry. From the beginning, "Sister-to-Sister" relationships were envisioned as distinct from short-term missions or other project-based endeavors, and the "overriding and primary" relational goal of the Sister-to-Sister program was clearly articulated to all participants. Because of the positive reception of the pilot project and the transition of AMiAs from a missionary outreach to an integral member of the Province of Rwanda, the Sister-to-Sister program has expanded to include thirty-five AMiAs congregations.[77] To express its commitment to this program, AMiAs is developing infrastructure to support participating congregations, complete with a Sister-to-Sister "desk" at the denominational level, parish training programs, and literature to articulate the goals and dynamics of Sister-to-Sister relationships.[78] While most evangelical denominations have little to do with the sister church phenomenon and a few are modestly or tangentially involved, AMiAs embraces international sister church relationships as core to its identity.

### African American Protestants

Of the seven major historical black denominations that, together, are often labeled the "Black Church,"[79] none formally sponsor international congregational partnership programs. The absence of sister church programs is generally not due to a lack of support for the partnership strategy. A document adopted by the 2007 annual session of the National Baptist Convention, entitled "A Global Vision for Unity, Mission, and Evangelism," speaks for many in the Black Church tradition when it lauds missional relationships of "genuine partnership between churches of the North and those of the South" and calls on the Black Church to provide a "unique role of leadership . . . so that a special space can be provided and strengthened . . . where relationships, built on mutual trust, are strengthened between all parts of the Christian family."[80]

Many leaders in African American mission are especially sensitive to the potential for paternalism in international mission efforts given the place of African Americans in the history of colonialism.[81] Yet, international missionary activity has historically been an ambiguous arena for African Americans, as "the interests of white Americans (both paternalistic and overtly racist) intertwined in complicated ways with the missionary zeal of black Americans."[82] At the grassroots level, international mission efforts among African American groups have at times unwittingly perpetuated colonial frames of paternalism and dependency fostering.[83] And as

David Emmanuel Goatley, executive secretary of Lott Carey Foreign Mission Convention, argued, compared to predominantly Anglo Christian institutions in the United States, institutions that are part of the Black Church tend to be younger, less well funded, and more locally focused.[84] Because of these factors, international sister church programs are uncommon in the Black Church, and the relationships that do exist are usually formed on an informal basis.[85]

Parachurch Organizations

Denominational agencies play a significant part in the formation and sustenance of some international congregation-to-congregation partnerships. But in many cases involving an intermediary, it is a parachurch agency rather than a denominational board that fills this role. In *The Restructuring of American Religion*, sociologist Robert Wuthnow documents the declining significance of denominationalism in American religion since World War II, complete with the clouding of individual denominational identities and the weakening of denominational organizations.[86] Wuthnow also points to the dramatic growth of religious special purpose groups in the United States in the 1970s and 1980s. These parachurch organizations' orientation is toward a specific objective rather than a theological tradition, and most of them are either interdenominational or nondenominational.[87] The waning of denominations and waxing of parachurch organizations in American religious life are trends that are mirrored in the history of the sister parish phenomenon. Among Catholics, for example, the CARA report found that 49 percent of responding parishes involved in sister parish relationships had worked with parachurch groups that foster partnerships with Latin American churches.[88] Many mainline and evangelical congregations also rely on parachurch organizations or other intermediaries instead of or in addition to church hierarchies or denominational agencies for assistance with parish partnerships. Especially in the early years of the sister parish movement, parachurch organizations served as important catalysts.

Intermediaries in the sister church phenomenon include the following faith- or community-based nonprofit organizations:

Aid to Special Saints in Strategic Times (ASSIST Ministries)
Catholic Relief Services (CRS)
Christians in Action
Church Twinning International (CTI)

Comunidad Oscar Arnulfo Romero (COAR)
Council of Protestant Churches in Latin America (CEPAD)
Food for the Hungry
Global Faith Partners
International Partners in Mission (IPM)
Light for Life
Parish Twinning Program of the Americas (PTPA)
Parish Without Borders
Partners International
Reciprocal Ministries International (RMI)
Small Christian Community Connection
Sister Parish, Incorporated
SHARE Foundation

Most of these agencies are based in the United States, while a few are
Latin American or multinational. Many of these groups, such as CRS,
COAR, Parish Without Borders, and PTPA are Catholic in identity, although they do not fall under the jurisdiction of the Church hierarchy.
Others, like Sister Parish, IPM, and Global Faith Partners are ecumenical,
catering to both Catholic and mainline Protestant congregations. Several
parachurch organizations, such as ASSIST Ministries, Christians in Action, Food for the Hungry, Reciprocal Ministries International, and Light
for Life, are evangelical in orientation, while Church Twinning International is unique as an African American Protestant organization. In addition to these faith-based organizations, a few secular organizations, such
as the SHARE Foundation, facilitate grassroots partnerships among various types of groups including churches.

The scope and function of parachurch intermediaries in congregation-to-
congregation relationships varies greatly. Some organizations serve exclusively as technical-assistance and training providers. Others not only provide
resources for participants but also match congregations to each other, facilitate visits between congregations, provide opportunities for advocacy, require accountability and reporting from participating congregations, help
participants formulate partnership agreements, and arbitrate conflicts and
misunderstandings in the relationships they sponsor. In addition to
functional variety, intermediaries also differ in scope. Some intermediaries
work with various types of groups wishing to partner with global southern
communities—youth groups, schools, civic associations, clubs, even
towns—in addition to congregations, dioceses, or other ecclesiastical bodies.
Most of the intermediaries work with only a few dozen congregations, and

some advocate for congregational partnerships as a model of mission rather than providing practical services.

Since an exhaustive account of parachurch congregational linking efforts would be inordinately lengthy and tedious, the following is a snapshot of how intermediaries fit into the story of the sister church movement—focusing on the most prominent organizations but also recognizing the diversity of programs.

Parish Twinning Program of the Americas, a Catholic intermediary that facilitates more parish partnerships involving US congregations than any other organization, boasts the oldest and most developed program on the national scale. PTPA started informally in 1978 and officially became incorporated as a nonprofit in 1992.[89] The seeds of PTPA were planted by a small-town Tennessee businessman, Harry Hosey, who had visited Haiti yearly for a decade and was increasingly steered toward advocacy by the poverty and degradation he witnessed during his trips. Back in Nashville, Hosey told his story to the people of St. Henry's Catholic parish, who soon made a commitment to provide ongoing financial aid to Haiti. At St. Henry's, Hosey also met Theresa Patterson, who became a long-term ally and the eventual director of PTPA. Patterson accompanied Hosey on a trip to Haiti, and the two soon decided to invite other parishes into twinning relationships.[90] According to PTPA's website, Hosey dreamed that "if every parish in North America would adopt a parish in the Third World, then we could really begin to change the world."[91]

By 1995, when PTPA was featured in the United States Conference of Catholic Bishops' report on the relationship between the Church in the United States and the Church in Latin America, 292 parishes spanning the continental United States were twinned with Haitian parishes through PTPA.[92] In 1999, PTPA expanded its twinning program to include Mexico and other countries in the Caribbean and Central and South America. Currently, PTPA facilitates more than three hundred forty linkages between Catholic parishes in the United States and parishes in Latin America, making it the largest citizen-to-citizen network joining the two regions.[93] Since 1978, PTPA parishes have sent more than $22 million in aid to their Latin American partners. Three-quarters of Haitian parishes are twinned to a US group through PTPA.[94]

Sister Parish, Incorporated, an ecumenical organization that has facilitated international congregational partnerships since 1988, joins PTPA as an anchor in the sister parish movement in the United States. In the only monograph written on the sister parish phenomenon prior to 2000, Richard Fenske, founder of Sister Parish, tells the story of the organization's genesis. After a second "conversion experience" in 1968 in which he awakened to the plight of the majority of the world's population and the call to social justice, Fenske, a Lutheran pastor, became highly involved in a refugee resettlement program. Perplexed by the US government's willingness to grant political asylum to refugees fleeing communism but not economic asylum to refugees from impoverished Latin American countries, Fenske took a sabbatical in Nicaragua in search for answers.[95] There, he became convinced that most North Americans either misunderstood or were ignorant of the plight of Latin Americans. He also began to entertain the idea that personal contact at the grassroots level could be a key component in changing these misguided perceptions among North American Christians.

In 1987, Richard Fenske met Vicki Schmidt, a Lutheran laywoman from Minnesota who was also interested in introducing North American Christians to the lives of the Latin American masses. The two came together to create a pilot sister parish program, the key component of which was yearly North-South and South-North delegations—complete with home stays and other opportunities to build close relationships. Sister Parish was incorporated in 1988 and sent its first northern delegation to Central America in 1989 and its first southern delegation to the United States in 1993. By 1998, it had organized fifty delegations and facilitated more than thirty partnerships of three years or more among Catholics, Lutherans, Methodists, and Episcopalians in the United States, El Salvador, and Guatemala. Seventeen partnerships are active today, and the organization is now codirected by one US citizen and one Central American, with central offices in Guatemala City.[96]

Parish Twinning Program of the Americas and Sister Parish are the most prominent organizations in the modern history of congregational partnerships. While not as well-known, the evangelical Reciprocal Ministries International dates back as far as PTPA and Sister Parish. Facilitating sister church partnerships informally since 1980 and officially since 1987, RMI "has been in the business of sister church partnerships before it was 'the thing to do,'" quipped its president, Dan Shoemaker. RMI facilitates relationships between twenty congregations in North America and their partners in Haiti or Guatemala in order for these congregations to "minister to one another and together to the world."[97] While RMI used to be the only evangelical organization of its kind, over the last fifteen years more and more evangelical mission or relief and development agencies have latched onto the congregation-to-congregation model of mission.

Several evangelical parachurch agencies have recently launched sister church programs or other initiatives based on the partnership ideal. While parish partnerships are the cornerstone of PTPA, Sister Parish, and RMI, for other organizations it is one program among many—a recent initiative begun in an effort to improve or expand upon existing programs. For example, Food for the Hungry, a large evangelical international relief and development organization, which was formed in 1971 as a "compassionate response to a hurting world," launched a church partnership program called "Community to Community" (C2C) in 1997. Food for the Hungry's mission is to "walk with churches, leaders and families in overcoming all forms of human poverty by living in healthy relationship with God and His creation."[98] To that end, according to Alisa Schmitz, Food for the Hungry's senior director of advocate and short-term team ministry, the Community to Community program was birthed as a way to further engage congregations in Food for the Hungry's ministry.

> We found that if we only stayed at arms' length and asked for money from people, then we wouldn't be getting the full transformation that we could. So we have really been trying to offer opportunities for engagement, where people and churches can come alongside of us and minister along with us rather than staying at a distance.[99]

Approximately forty congregations in the United States partner with a community in the developing world through C2C. "By getting personally involved with the poor, churches are able to see and experience the transformation that comes from a strong relationship," says Food for the Hungry's literature about the C2C program.[100]

The SHARE Foundation is another nonprofit that facilitates a partnership program in addition to other initiatives—though as a community-based foundation, SHARE's mission and vision is distinct from that of Food for the Hungry. SHARE calls North Americans into "deeper communion within the service of justice" in order to "build a new El Salvador today."[101] The Foundation began in 1981 as a direct response to Salvadoran martyr Archbishop Romero's plea for the people of the world to join hands in solidarity with Salvadorans in response to the brutal fourteen-year war and accompanying civil rights abuses in El Salvador. SHARE helps coordinate close to fifty relationships among Lutherans, Presbyterians, and Roman Catholics in North America and El Salvador.[102] Although SHARE is not a religious organization, it embraces ideas of solidarity and partnership that are similar to those of many Christian mission agencies involved in sister church initiatives.

Another illustration of the breadth of the sister church phenomenon is the work of Church Twinning International. A large majority of North American participants in international congregational partnerships are of European descent. Church Twinning International, on the other hand, exclusively links African American congregations to African congregations—seeking to "affect a peculiar link between the two," a "physical and spiritual bond of mutual acceptance" designed to produce a "common concern for their united people."[103]

This concept was first introduced to Sidney Holston, founder of CTI, in 1981, when Andrew Denteh, then vice president of the Methodist Church of Ghana, visited Holston's home in Georgia and shared his idea to pair African American congregations in the American south with Ghanaian congregations. Since 1984 when CTI was incorporated, ten US congregations have signed "Deeds of Twinning" with African and Caribbean congregations. Through these efforts, nearly five thousand African American Christians have participated in a congregation-to-congregation relationship.[104] CTI is unique not only in the demographic composition of participating churches but also in the purpose of the relationships it facilitates. CTI's vision is decidedly Afrocentric. While many organizations laud the cross-cultural education and enrichment of North American participants as one of the byproducts of sister church relationships, for CTI, exposing African Americans to the cultural legacy of Africa is one of the chief goals. "I may need a bone marrow [transplant] from Africa," said Sidney Holston pointedly, illustrating CTI's belief that African Americans benefit from congregation-to-congregation relationships just as much as their African counterparts.[105]

In scope and purpose, parachurch agencies play widely varying roles in the phenomenon of international partnerships between congregations. What virtually all of these parachurch organizations have in common with one another and with denominational agencies that are also involved in such efforts is that their role in sister church relationships is to offer support and resources rather than to control these relationships. "We have changed from being an agency that is doing *for* the churches to being an agency that is facilitating their participation," stated Charles Jones of the American Baptist Convention, speaking of the about-face in the role played by denominational and parachurch ministries over the last generation. "We are more like consultants now," continued Jones, "bringing all the advantages of our long history before congregations so they will be educated in their going and in their doing."[106] While denominational and parachurch agencies play a key role in the phenomenon by linking many congregations and helping them navigate their sister church relationships, the lifeblood of the model comes from local congregations rather than overarching denominational agencies or parachurch organizations. Although the sister church model leans on umbrella institutions for resources and longevity of partnership, it is fueled by grassroots efforts and functions bottom up rather than top down through institutional channels.

## Congregations

The most influential institutions in the movement are neither denominational agencies nor parachurch intermediaries. Congregations themselves are the driving agents behind the sister church phenomenon. While either denominational or parachurch organizations commonly match congregations to their sister parishes, in the majority of cases these intermediaries exercise very little control over congregation-to-congregation relationships once they begin. Often, the intermediaries are enlisted at the behest of congregations and not the other way around. And while many relationships involve an intermediary in some way, perhaps as many or more function independently—birthed and maintained not through the efforts of denominational bureaucracies or even the promptings of visionaries but through person-to-person encounters at the grassroots level.

The circumvention of intermediaries is especially pervasive among US megachurches involved in the sister church movement. Robert Priest and his colleagues found that nearly half of all megachurches act as their own sending agency for missionaries and mission ventures.[107] Though small and moderately sized congregations lack the resources of megachurches, they too have shifted their relationship with denominational boards and other intermediaries.

Over the last two decades, numerous scholars have called attention to an institutional crisis in American religion. Although their affinity for "spirituality" has not waned, Americans do not evidence the same denominational loyalty, deference to church authority, and willingness to support religious bureaucracies as did previous generations.[108] The decline of denominationalism has only intensified since 1988 when Wuthnow first called attention to the trend. Though parachurch agencies flourished in the 1970s and 1980s, they too have fallen on rough times in the last twenty years.[109] In the contemporary setting, both denominational agencies and parachurch organizations commonly confront significant budget deficits, necessary cutbacks in staff and programming, and dwindling numbers of constituents. In the face of shrinking financial and moral support and the increasing demands of organizational maintenance, mission agencies in particular—whether at the denominational or parachurch level—have been forced to reduce their programming and scope.[110] Some Christian agencies have survived the institution crisis in American religion by reinventing themselves—often shifting into a supporting role rather than a leading role in their constituent relations. The sister church phenomenon is an illustration of this restructuring. Those intermediaries who remain relevant have shifted their strategy to empowering local congregations and supporting grassroots initiatives.

The sister church movement has weathered this storm—even managing to thrive and grow in the midst of America's religious institutional crisis—because it is rooted in local communities rather than in vast bureaucracies. While congregations have not been immune to the sickness plaguing larger religious institutions,[111] they continue to form the backbone of religious life in North America. In fact, over the last fifteen years an entire body of literature has emerged in the sociology of American religion to draw attention to the vitality and import of local congregations.[112] Moreover, the sister church movement draws on the bonds of even more tightly knit communities than local congregations—since sister church committees and delegations often serve as intimate *petites églises* within their larger congregations.

## Conclusion

Among North American Christians, the sister church model of international mission has become widely and increasingly popular since its birth in the 1980s. Drawing on the missiology of accompaniment/partnership and solidarity, denominational agencies and parachurch organizations representing most Christian traditions in North America have implemented programs to facilitate international congregation-to-congregation partnerships. But missiology and intermediaries are not the most salient agents in the sister church movement. Whether facilitated by denominational agencies, parachurch organizations, pastoral leadership, or parishioners themselves, congregation-to-congregation relationships are overwzhelmingly driven by local Christian communities and the power of their cross-cultural experiences.

The sister church phenomenon is at once decidedly local and global. No longer content to engage other regions of the world through media, giving, or other people's stories alone, scores of American Christians seek to personally interact with their counterparts in Latin America, Asia, Africa, and beyond. Through congregation-to-congregation relationships, they do so in the context of their own local communities. Typically circumventing religious bureaucracies and organizational hierarchies, their sister church relationships allow them to develop interpersonal cross-cultural relationships at the grassroots level. Sister church relationships afford the global Christian community with a unique opportunity for connectedness and kinship. The structures of congregational partnerships create new possibilities for American mission efforts and open doors for global engagement among coreligionists in the contemporary setting.

Mike Vallez's visit to Peru on a delegation with his parish, which set in motion a series of sister church relationships and programs, is just one example of the significance of grassroots North/South encounters to the phenomenon. In fact, such encounters are the most important element in the story of the sister church movement. Since grassroots movements proceed from the bottom up rather than the top down, they are difficult to chronicle. This chapter's treatment of the history of the sister church movement is incomplete because it does not give full attention to the unique local contexts in which the sister church model of mission is embodied. The following chapter tells the stories of twelve congregations in the mid-Atlantic religion involved in international partnerships with other congregations. While these accounts do not represent the experiences of all northern congregations involved in the movement, much less southern partners, they offer a window into how the sister church model is embodied on the ground. And in so doing, they add texture to the story of international partnerships among American congregations.

CHAPTER 3 | Tales of Twelve Sister Church
Relationships

GIVEN ITS GRASSROOTS ORIENTATION, the best way to study the sister church phenomenon is by focusing on the accounts, artifacts, and activities that collectively build the culture of mission in participating congregations and parishes.[1] Since congregational partnerships are overwhelmingly powered by entities and efforts at the local level, it is data gathered in local congregations that can best illuminate the dynamics of the movement. This chapter hones in on the stories as well as the material and ritual cultures of twelve congregations in the Washington, DC, area that have twinned with other congregations in Latin America or Africa. In order to facilitate comparison of congregation-to-congregation relationships among Christian traditions with different theologies, cultures, and types of ecclesiastical polity, the stories of three Roman Catholic, three mainline Presbyterian, three evangelical Anglican, and three African American Baptist congregations are told below.

The stories are told largely from the perspective of leaders and congregants representing the North American partners in these relationships, leaving the accounts of global southerners for another study directed by different purposes. The most prominent voices behind these narratives are pastors, who articulate perspectives that are biased by their experiences and commitments, yet who often serve as the chief decision-makers and liaisons in the relationships in which their congregations participate. When available, congregations' official accounts of their partnerships—published in newsletters, websites, brochures, and bulletins—are also woven into the following narratives. The voices of other actors, both at the center and the margins of the highlighted relationships, can be heard as well, drawn out more fully in subsequent chapters.

## Saint Clement Catholic Church and Paroisse Catholique du Sacré-Coeur, Pignon, Haiti

For Saint Clement Catholic Church, a multiethnic suburban parish of five thousand members that came into being in 1960 in the "spirit of the Second Vatican Council," compassion, justice, and the universality of the Catholic Church were values held dear to the parish community.[2] From 1994 onward, Saint Clement attempted to live out those values in a sister church relationship with Sacré-Coeur parish in Pignon, Haiti. While Saint Clement's parish was composed largely of middle- and upper-class well-educated professionals, Sacré-Coeur was composed mostly of subsistence farmers and sharecroppers who earned an average of two hundred dollars in yearly income and who were lucky to have even an elementary education. Saint Clement's annual budget for its church and school was 3.5 million dollars, while Sacré-Coeur ran a church, three remote chapels, fourteen elementary schools, and a secondary school on a budget significantly less than one hundred thousand dollars. Despite their vast differences, Saint Clement and Sacré-Coeur were united by a common faith and a commitment to help the people of Pignon "build a better future for themselves, their families, and their community."[3]

The sister parish relationship between Sacré-Coeur and Saint Clement was birthed in the mind of Bernadette Bellemy, a Haitian American who immigrated to the Washington, DC, area in the late 1960s. A social worker, Bellemy strongly desired to do something to help her native country ever since immigrating. Bellemy explained that growing up in a privileged family in Haiti in the 1940s had sheltered her from the poverty around her. "Haiti is divided into two parts: you have the 'haves' and the 'have-nots,' and no middle class. But since my family put me in a shell to 'protect' me, I didn't really understand what was going on in the country until I came to the U.S. and started studying the situation," said Bellemy.

The more she studied, the more Bellemy felt called to "do something." And by 1985, when Bellemy heard about Theresa Patterson and her work with Parish Twinning Program of Americas, Bellemy was settled into a career, her children were out of the house, and she was ready to put her dream into action.

After corresponding at length with Theresa Patterson and receiving multiple profiles of Haitian parishes eligible for "being adopted," Bellemy approached Saint Clement's pastor in 1986 about forming a relationship. First told that Saint Clement "didn't have the money" to enter into a sister parish relationship, Bellemy was persistent and continued appealing to

Saint Clement's leadership about the prospect. By 1992, Monsignor Arnold Monroe had begun his tenure at the parish, and he and the parish council agreed to pursue a sister church relationship. Not wanting to bias the outcome, Bellemy stayed out of the decision about which sister parish to choose. Saint Clement finally selected Sacré-Coeur two years later because of their sense that Sacré-Coeur was the most remote and faced the greatest need of all the options. Bellemy recalled that she was quite uncomfortable with the choice at first. "My friends in Haiti were telling me, 'No one goes to Pignon. What are you talking about? You might have to take a little boat!'" Despite her reservations, in 1996, Bellemy was a member of the first delegation from Saint Clement to visit Sacré-Coeur, accompanied by Theresa Patterson, Monsignor Monroe, and one other Saint Clement parishioner. Although the delegation did not have to travel by boat as Bellemy had feared, it did take them eight hours to drive the one hundred miles between Port-au-Prince and Pignon. Whereas Bellemy would have been forbidden to visit Pignon as a child living in Port-au-Prince, she ventured there five times as an adult living in suburban Washington, DC, through the sister parish relationship.

Starting in 1996, Saint Clement sent a delegation of six to eight parishioners to Pignon every January. Delegations from Saint Clement to Sacré-Coeur typically conducted medical and dental clinics, participated in construction and sanitation projects, and provided educational enrichment programs. Delegation members were often doctors, nurses, dentists, engineers, and teachers from the parish. They usually reported about their trip to the rest of the congregation each year in a lengthy program following a "Lenten Supper" in February. Saint Clement also sponsored a visit from Sacré-Coeur's pastor each year, who reported on the progress of projects that Saint Clement sponsored in Pignon. Saint Clement sent about fifty thousand dollars in aid to Sacré-Coeur annually, whether in special collections or school sponsorship pledges. The parish also periodically sent shipments of educational and medical supplies. Through the sister parish project, a high-achieving secondary school educating two hundred fifty students was introduced to the Pignon community, eighteen hundred elementary-aged children were educated and fed in parish schools each year, dozens of people received necessary surgeries, several cisterns and other sanitation projects were completed, and extensive medical and nutritional training efforts were undertaken.

In the late 1990s, Saint Clement hired a director of social concerns to facilitate the already burgeoning sister church relationship. While Saint Clement's director of social concerns oversaw a long list of ministries, the sister parish relationship took up most of her time and energy. Other members of Saint Clement's sister parish committee also dedicated generous portions of their resources to the relationship on a volunteer basis. For example, one long-time member, Jack Napoli, spent the majority of his free time helping his friends from Pignon launch a microenterprise coffee-marketing venture, a project that spun out of the sister church relationship. According to Monsignor Monroe, over the years Saint Clement's relationship with Sacré-Coeur became a core part of Saint Clement's identity. "It has caught the conscience and imagination of the parish," he declared.

## Our Lady of Sorrows Catholic Church and Iglesia Católica María Reina de la Paz, San Salvador, El Salvador

The Church of Our Lady of Sorrows, a seven-thousand-member, predominantly white, wealthy, Jesuit parish located in a prestigious urban neighborhood, also participated in a long and productive relationship with a parish abroad. For Our Lady of Sorrows, however, the sister parish relationship suffered decreasing prominence in parish life in the years just prior to the study. Our Lady's sister parish relationship with María Reina de la Paz, located in an impoverished neighborhood on the outskirts of San Salvador, began in 1989 in the midst of El Salvador's brutal civil war. The seeds of the relationship were sown three years earlier when John Mountford, then pastor of Our Lady of Sorrows, spent several weeks in Reina de la Paz, listening to the testimonies of parishioners. Most of Reina de la Paz's early members were war refugees who fled their homes in the countryside in the early 1980s and settled along the railroad tracks in a former garbage dump in San Salvador, founding Reina de la Paz in their new community in 1984.

Several parishioners of Our Lady of Sorrows were inspired by their pastor's stories from the Reina de la Paz community as well as the calls of Oscar Romero and other Catholic leaders for solidarity with the Church in El Salvador. They approached Our Lady's parish council about formalizing a relationship of solidarity and aid with Reina de la Paz. After receiving approval, the relationship commenced with the formation of a sister parish committee, a visit from Reina de la Paz's pastor to Our Lady, and a delegation to Reina de la Paz that same year.

From the time the sister parish relationship began onward, Our Lady of Sorrows parishioners took countless trips to Reina de la Paz and received visitors from Reina de la Paz in return on two occasions. Projects supported by the sister parish relationship included a preschool program for small children in the Reina de la Paz parish; a microcredit organization to support small businesses; health, dental, and eyeglass clinics; a sewing cooperative; a bakery; the construction of a new church building; and a cooperative farm on the outskirts of the city. More recent projects included a foster-care program, an elder day-care center, legal assistance, and an evangelization effort in the poorest margins of the parish. Our Lady's parish-to-parish committee served as the primary liaison with the parishioners of Reina de la Paz, leaning on the SHARE Foundation for technical assistance and support. In addition to facilitating delegations to Reina de la Paz, the committee sponsored a Christmas craft sale to raise funds for Reina de la Paz. The majority of Our Lady of Sorrows' financial gifts to Reina de la Paz came from a portion of the church's tithe to nonprofit organizations. With a 3.5 million-dollar budget, Our Lady of Sorrows gave 350,000 dollars in grants to a collection of nonprofits each year, and twelve thousand dollars of that sum was allocated for Reina de la Paz.

The twinning committee at Our Lady of Sorrows also worked with the liturgical staff to remember Reina de la Paz in Our Lady Sorrows' liturgies, especially on special occasions for Reina de la Paz's parishioners, such as the celebration of the birthday of Oscar Romero. Because several Our Lady parishioners involved in the sister parish relationship worked professionally in international business or development in Latin America, individual visits from Our Lady parishioners to Reina de la Paz were not uncommon. Over the years, deep friendships formed among several members of the two communities. Because of these bonds as well as the Jesuit legacy of social justice espoused by their parish, several members of Our Lady of Sorrows advocated for their friends at Reina de la Paz with the US and Salvadoran governments—political territory that is usually avoided in sister church relationships.

Despite the long history of the relationship between Our Lady of Sorrows and Reina de la Paz, several members of the parish-to-parish committee expressed disappointment, frustration, and weariness in light of the state of the relationship at the time when the interviews were conducted. Janice Thompson, who joined the committee several years prior when she noticed a decline in the prominence of the sister church relationship at Our Lady of Sorrows, lamented that the committee had dwindled as most of the people who were passionate about the relationship in years passed moved on from Our Lady of Sorrows. In the minds of many of those who stayed involved, in recent years the pastoral staff had not prioritized the twinning relationship among the parish's many projects and ministries. Moreover, differing appraisals of US foreign policy in El Salvador caused tension within the twinning committee, and the pastoral staff discouraged advocacy efforts in order to avoid offense. Despite these challenges, Thompson, for one, was optimistic about the future of the sister church relationship: "I'm really hopeful that we can start something big. The situation has never been worse for our sister parish in El Salvador, but there has never been a better opportunity for Our Lady of Sorrows."

Encouraged by the arrival of a new pastor at Our Lady of Sorrows— whom she described as "young, educated, bold, passionate about social justice"—as well as a corresponding hike in the number of people becoming involved in the Reina de la Paz partnership, Thompson looked forward to rebuilding the floundering relationship.

## Saint Mariana of Jesus Catholic Church and Iglesia Católica Nuestra Señora de los Ángeles, San José, Costa Rica

Saint Mariana of Jesus Catholic Church was similar to Saint Clement in its demography and similar to Our Lady of Sorrows in the struggling state of its sister church relationship. A multiethnic suburban parish located in a research and technology thoroughfare, Saint Mariana was composed of roughly thirteen hundred families and had a budget in excess of a million dollars. Saint Mariana was a parish constituted by cultural groups with distinct masses and ministries. Mass was conducted in Filipino, Spanish, Taiwanese, and English each week, and parishioners hailed from all over the world. Beginning in 2005, Saint Mariana participated in a sister parish relationship with Nuestra Señora de los Ángeles in a slum of San José, Costa Rica. Nuestra Señora was a poor but vibrant parish, composed largely of young people. Since the neighborhood was plagued by high rates of crime and substance abuse, most parish outreach activities were centered around nutrition, religious education, enrichment, and intervention for children and youth. Saint Mariana aspired to support these activities both physically and financially, but the main thrust of the relationship—at least in the minds of the twinning committee members—was building a mutual partnership of solidarity and cross-border evangelization.

In the fall of 2002, in the midst of Saint Mariana's campaign in which parishioners were asked to prayerfully consider how they could use their gifts to serve God and the church, Ricardo Flores, a fifth-generation Mexican American who was an administrator at a Catholic international relief-and-development organization, began to consider using his expertise to help Saint Mariana get involved in a parish twinning relationship. Familiar with the concept through his occupation and passionate about getting Saint Mariana parishioners to awaken to the needs and the faith of others around the globe, Flores soon started floating the idea of forming a parish twinning relationship among the clergy and other parishioners at Saint Mariana. Together with Hortense Tshombe, a Congolese immigrant, Flores got permission from Saint Mariana's pastor to form an International Twinning Committee (ITC) in 2003 to explore the field of potential partners and determine a vision for the project. That summer, the ITC conducted a parish-wide survey and discovered that more than half of the parish wanted to twin with a parish in Latin America. Soliciting help from Parish Twinning Program of the Americas, the committee eventually settled on Nuestra Señora. According to Flores, this parish was chosen because of the committee's perception that Nuestra Señora was an accessible partner for Saint Mariana—Costa Rica being close enough to facilitate uncomplicated travel and considered safer than most areas of Central America. Nuestra Señora was also perceived as being in need without being utterly impoverished. The committee hoped that relative parity would promote friendship and also feared that Saint Mariana's parishioners would be unwilling to travel to settings more dissimilar to their own.

After spending months laying out plans for the relationship, the ITC invited "Pa Jairo" Baca, pastor of Nuestra Señora, to visit Saint Mariana in the summer of 2004. The following summer, the relationship officially got underway when a fact-finding delegation from Saint Mariana—accompanied by a PTPA representative—returned the visit to build communication and shared commitment. Saint Mariana sent several delegations to Nuestra Señora in the following years. But unlike the initial fact-finding delegation, the later trips also included work on projects laid out by Baca, such as building a cafeteria and painting several homes in the community. According to Ricardo Flores, delegations were the life blood of the twinning relationship. Saint Mariana hosted a visit from Baca every year and hoped to sponsor visits from other members of Nuestra Señora in the future. The two communities also prayed for each other regularly, and Saint Mariana gave around twelve thousand dollars in tithes and offerings to Nuestra Señora each year.

While Saint Mariana's ITC first envisioned the relationship with the instruction of its native-born population in mind, the committee also sought to involve Latinos at Saint Mariana in the sister church relationship—hoping to provide an opportunity for immigrants who attended the Spanish mass to better integrate into Saint Mariana's parish life. In fact, for the first few years of its existence, the ITC conducted its meetings in

Spanish. However, whether because of their perceptions that Costa Ricans did not face as many challenges as the residents of their home countries, their disconnectedness from the administration of the relationship, their own financial challenges, or other reasons, Saint Mariana's parishioners who attended the Spanish mass did not become involved in the sister parish relationship. Nor did the relationship gain prominence in Saint Mariana's general parish life as the initial members of the ITC had hoped. Flores used the analogy of a departing airplane to describe the state of the relationship: "Our sister church relationship is off the ground, but it hasn't reached a high altitude yet where it can cruise." Saint Mariana faced several difficulties throughout the tenure of the relationship: the ITC suffered high turnover, only a small minority of Saint Mariana's parishioners were active in the relationship, a recent youth delegation to Nuestro Señora was plagued by infighting, and Saint Mariana's new pastor had not supported the partnership as unequivocally as the former pastor. Despite these setbacks, Flores and other members of the ITC remained hopeful that their sister church relationship would stabilize and even flourish.

## Kensington Woods Presbyterian Church (PC[USA]) and Narok Presbyterian Church, Limuru, Kenya

Beginning in 1987, Narok Presbyterian Church in the Limuru Mission Area of Kenya functioned as the "second home of ministry" for the parishioners of Kensington Woods Presbyterian Church in an exurb of Washington, DC[4] The Limuru Mission Area, the site where Scottish Presbyterian missionaries first arrived in Kenya in 1898, had been all but abandoned by the Presbyterian Church by the late 1980s. With the support of Kensington Woods Presbyterian, twenty years later the Limuru Mission Area was home to twelve congregations, a vocational training center, a primary school, an orphan-care program, and several preschools administered by the Presbyterian Church of East Africa. Narok Presbyterian Church also experienced a renaissance after the partnership began. Its members, most of whom were subsistence farmers, had come to worship in an attractive cinderblock sanctuary and send their children to Limuru Mission schools.

The northern partner in the relationship, Kensington Woods Presbyterian, was founded in 1980 in the newly constructed "planned community" of Kensington Woods. The Kensington Woods congregation was composed of six hundred fifty members when the study took place, many of whom were civil servants, social workers, educators, or health-care professionals.

Although the congregation was mostly white and middle to upper class, a dozen nationalities, various ideological and political perspectives, and an array of life paths were represented. With a budget of nearly a million dollars, the congregation supported a staff of ten and numerous local, national, and international ministries—the Limuru partnership prominent among them.

The particularities of Kensington Woods's sister church relationship were tied to the personal history of the congregation's senior pastor, the Reverend Doctor Ruth Eaton, who had served the congregation since 1984. As a college student in the 1960s, Eaton spent a summer in Kenya as a volunteer with Operation Crossroads Africa, John F. Kennedy's inspiration for the Peace Corps. Following her time of service, Eaton maintained contact with one of her counterparts from the program, a Kenyan woman from the Limuru area who spent several years studying in the United States. Early in her tenure at Kensington Woods, Eaton received a letter from her friend, explaining the difficulties faced by the friend's home village in Kenya. It just so happened that the Kensington Woods congregation was looking for an opportunity to get involved in international mission when Eaton received the letter. Stirred by her friend's letter and seeing an opportunity for collaboration, Eaton contacted the Presbyterian Church of East Africa to see if there were any projects in Kenya that Kensington Woods could join as a long-term partner. As Eaton drafted her letter, she was guided by the philosophy of Operation Crossroads Africa, which was founded by African American Presbyterians in the context of African decolonization. Designed to combat the patriarchal systems of colonialism and "build bridges of friendship and understanding" between Africans and Americans, Operation Crossroads Africa sends young Americans to work with young Africans at the grassroots level.[5] Similarly, Eaton's letter specified that Kensington Woods was not seeking a one-way mission but rather a "partnership based on mutual trust, faith, and respect."[6] At the time, the Presbyterian Church of East Africa was in the process of making plans to redevelop the Limuru Mission Area, so Eaton's correspondents quickly suggested that Kensington Woods partner with Narok Presbyterian in service to the Limuru community.

While Kensington Woods occasionally received grants from it presbytery for its work in Limuru during the tenure of the relationship, the congregation's sister church relationship functioned independently of the mission efforts of the General Assembly of the denomination as well as the Mid-Atlantic Presbyterywide partnership in another region of Kenya. Despite lack of outside direction for the partnership, Kensington Woods developed an extensive network of opportunities for its congregation to get involved in ministry in Limuru. Every three years, Kensington Woods sponsored a month-long trip to Kenya for a dozen of its members to "experience first hand worship and working together with the Kenyans" in Limuru.[7] To facilitate these work camps, Kensington Woods developed a "global ministry intern" position, filled on several occasions by a college student or retiree from the congregation who spent several months in Limuru before the rest of the delegation arrived, preparing for the trip and serving as a liaison between the two communities. Through the summer work camps, the members of the two congregations built classrooms, dormitories, a water storage tank and a staff house in the Mission Area. Kensington Woods's delegation members were also afforded daily opportunities to worship with their Kenyan hosts. Shared Bible studies, discussion groups, celebrations, and meals were prominent features of the time together as well. Kensington Woods's parishioners typically offered professional training, technical assistance, and religious education while in Kenya, but they also received from their Kenyan friends as they learned how to prepare food over an open fire and step traditional dances. Eaton baptized dozens of children, served communion on numerous occasions, preached in most of the twelve congregations, and administered pastoral care to countless members of the Limuru community over the years. Spiritual encouragement also traveled both ways, as Kensington Woods's parishioners who spent time in Kenya overwhelmingly reported being enriched by the faith of those they encountered in Limuru. "Our primary purpose is building relationships as one body in Christ, and seeing the power of the Holy Spirit at work, which is not bound by nation's boundaries or by cultural differences," said Eaton about the work trips.[8]

In addition to the work trips, the Kensington Woods congregation found numerous ways to connect to their Kenyan partners. A vibrant pen-pal program and mutual liturgical recognition helped keep the bonds between the Kensington Woods and Narok congregations strong. Financially, Kensington Woods supported the Limuru area in various ways. The congregation provided salary support, scholarships, meal supplements, educational materials, and construction supplies for new classrooms in Limuru's schools. Kensington Woods also helped provide Bibles, hymnals, and pews for the village churches of Limuru. In the late 1990s, it supplied the funds to build a new church building for Narok Presbyterian. Narok showed appreciation to their partners at Kensington Woods by designing their sanctuary in the same style as the Kensington Woods sanctuary. Kensington Woods also hosted a large silent auction each year to increase the partnership's visibility and raise money for the orphan-care program.

Pastor Eaton and the Limuru partnership committee took seriously the task of keeping the relationship strong and active: "[Our partnership] is a bond of the Holy Spirit that is part mystery and part plain hard work."[9] Because they believed that their work together with the Limuru community was a "small cooperative effort toward the building of the Kingdom of God,"[10] the leaders of the Limuru partnership from Kensington Woods were duly motivated.

## Mount Shannon Presbyterian Church (PC[USA]) and Bensonville Presbyterian Church, Carysburg, Liberia

Though Mount Shannon Presbyterian Church was remarkably similar to Kensington Woods in its size, theological and social leanings, demographic composition, and setting, its sister church relationship was remarkably dissimilar. In contrast to Kensington Woods's long-standing, stable, clearly designed, and intentionally mutual relationship, Mount Shannon's relationship was young, floundering, conflicted, and lopsided. Mount Shannon's troubled relationship with Bensonville Presbyterian Church and the Carysburg Mission in greater Monrovia, Liberia, highlights the complexities of mission in a postcolonial context.

The catalysts for Mount Shannon's sister church relationship were Priscilla and Charles Spencer, members of a prominent Liberian family who fled to suburban Washington, DC, in 1989 in the midst of Liberia's bloody civil war. While exiled from their home country, the Spencers attended Mount Shannon and were active in the congregation for fifteen years. In 2006, when relative peace was restored to Liberia, the Spencers decided to return home, feeling called to rebuild Carysburg Presbyterian Mission, a once-thriving medical clinic and school that was virtually destroyed in the civil war. Reaching out to the networks they had formed while living in the United States, the Spencers contacted the Reverend Doctor Henry Hunt, newly appointed pastor at Mount Shannon, to solicit Mount Shannon's help in their efforts in Carysburg and to invite Hunt to join the Carysburg Mission board.

Hunt had recently received correspondence from Ellen Turbot, the wife of Mount Shannon's previous pastor, encouraging Mount Shannon to support the Spencers. Given Mount Shannon's long-standing commitment of financial support for international mission, the close connection between the Spencers and the congregation, the timing of Torbot's letter, and Hunt's own feeling that the congregation needed a more hands-on approach to mission in Africa, Hunt said partnering with the Spencers was a "no brainer" for Mount Shannon. Hunt began brainstorming with Mount Shannon's session regarding the role the congregation would play in the ministry. Meanwhile, the Carysburg Mission board proposed that Mount Shannon form a sister church relationship with the Presbyterian congregation in Bensonville, the town adjacent to Carysburg Mission, hoping to expand the impact of Carysburg Mission into the broader community.

By the end of 2006, Hunt had joined the Carysburg Mission board, Mount Shannon's session had added a line item in its budget for Carysburg Mission, a sister church relationship was formalized between the Bensonville and Mount Shannon congregations, and Mount Shannon had begun plans to send both a container of supplies and a volunteer delegation to Carysburg Mission. In the following years, Mount Shannon started a pen-pal program between students who attend Mount Shannon's day school and students in the Carysburg primary school, directly raised more than eighty thousand dollars for the Carysburg Mission, and secured grants for the Carysburg Mission from secular and religious foundations.

In March of 2008, the congregation sponsored a "scouting delegation" of five volunteers who traveled to Liberia to explore ideas for the congregation's future involvement. Only two member of the delegation were actually members of the congregation: Henry Hunt and Don Lingard, a retiree serving on Mount Shannon's Interpretation and Stewardship Committee. The other three members were chosen for their professional expertise, upon which Mount Shannon's leadership hoped to rely as they assessed programmatic needs in Carysburg. Following the trip, delegation members reported their findings to the Mount Shannon congregation and suggested new ministry opportunities, but the congregation's leadership had difficulty determining their next steps in the relationship.

If the scope of projects supported and amount of money raised were the measure of success of sister church relationships, then Mount Shannon would be doing quite well. According to Don Lingard, who was very proud of Mount Shannon's work in Carysburg, supporting the Carysburg Mission gave Mount Shannon the opportunity to make the world a better place. "The way I see our projects is that rather than talking, we're walking," said Lingard. Lingard reported that the congregation had been very generous in their support of Carysburg and that parishioners were happy to help out as they were able. But according to Hunt, who envisioned Mount Shannon's involvement in Carysburg as an opportunity for (a) spiritual solidarity between the two communities and (b) the discipleship and education of his own congregation, Lingard and most of the rest of the congregation "just don't get it." Wary of the potential for building empires and fostering dependency in western philanthropic efforts in Africa, Hunt wanted his congregation to view the Carysburg relationship as a partnership in faith rather than a charitable project. To Hunt's chagrin, the sister church relationship between Bensonville and Mount Shannon remained underdeveloped, and Mount Shannon's Interpretation and Stewardship Committee generally took a project-centered approach to their involvement in the Carysburg Mission.

Tension in the relationship could be found not only between Hunt and some of the parishioners at Mount Shannon but also between Hunt and other members of the Carysburg Mission board—most notably Priscilla Spencer. Believing Spencer to be perpetuating classist norms in Liberia by favoring descendants of repatriated African American slaves over other Liberians, Hunt publicly questioned Spencer's leadership in the Carysburg Mission. Spencer, in response, criticized Hunt for interfering in a culture he did not understand. The two had yet to reconcile when the interviews were conducted, and the relationship between Mount Shannon and Carysburg limped along—handicapped by the disunity among the leadership.

## Third Presbyterian Church (PC[USA]) and Iglesia del Centro Presbiteriana-Reformada de la Habana, Cuba

Third Presbyterian Church, a historic, liberal congregation located in downtown Washington, DC, was involved in a sister church partnership with a similar congregation in downtown Havana that, unlike the Mount Shannon/Carysburg relationship, was decidedly not project-centered. Third Presbyterian and Iglesia del Centro intentionally structured their relationships around two-way friendship and sharing, but government restrictions also steered the partnership away from North/South philanthropy. Moreover, in the words of Gloria Feinburg, chair of the partnership committee, Third Presbyterian "just doesn't have much money to give." Although it had around six hundred fifty members and a budget near one million dollars, the majority of Third's parishioners were "very young or very old."[11] Many were employed by the government or humanitarian non-government organizations and had little discretionary income. Others were homeless and/or impoverished and made their way to Third out of their own need. Thus, rather than focusing on projects and financial giving, said Feinburg, the relationship between Third Presbyterian and Iglesia del Centro was centered around connecting people to people. Rather than writing checks or constructing classrooms, Third Presbyterian exchanged music, art, prayer, and friendship with its sister congregation in Cuba.

The relationship between the two congregations was prefaced by the Mutual Mission Agreement adopted by the Presbyterian Church of the United States and the Iglesia Presbiteriana-Reformada en Cuba in 1985, which attempted to rebuild historic links between the two churches and specified that presbytery and congregational partnerships would be a prominent way in which the two churches would work together in mission. Cuba Partners was formed under the auspices of PC(USA) World Mission to help facilitate such partnerships, and more than seventy-five relationships evolved among groups from the two churches to "forge mutually supportive relationships as brothers and sisters in Christ."[12] Iglesia del Centro had already formed sister church relationships with two other US congregations when Daniel Díaz, pastor of Iglesia del Centro, came to preach and teach a class at Third Presbyterian during a trip to the United States in the fall of 1998. But given the exuberant welcome that Díaz experienced at Third Presbyterian, he was glad to add Third to the list of partners. The relationship started informally as Third sponsored an adult Sunday school class on Cuba following Díaz's visit and sent a delegation to Havana in January of 1999. In the fall of 1999, the congregations again exchanged visitors as Iglesia del Centro hosted a visit from Third Presbyterian's pastor and Third Presbyterian welcomed parishioners from Iglesia del Centro to speak to their congregation. In December of 1999, the sessions of the two congregations formally adopted a five-year resolution establishing a sister relationship "to affirm and build on the unity of the Presbyterian Church under Jesus Christ through a mutual exchange of people, communication, spiritual understanding, Christian education and Bible study, theology, cultural understanding (art, music, theater), financial support, and political understanding."[13]

Despite the initial energy surrounding Third's sister church relationship in Cuba, by the early 2000s, both the senior pastor and the associate pastor at Third had moved on to other congregations, and the relationship fell into inactivity due to a lack of leadership and direction at Third. This changed in early 2004, when Gloria Feinburg, an elder at Third Presbyterian, visited Daniel Díaz and Iglesia del Centro while in Cuba for other reasons. A former Peace Corps volunteer who had recently retired from a career in international affairs, Feinburg decided that if there was interest between the two congregations, she would use some of her newly gained free time to revive the relationship. Unbeknownst to Feinburg, Díaz and the Reverend Doctor Robert Hamilton, Third's new senior pastor, had recently begun talking about renewing the relationship as well. That year, under Feinburg's leadership, Third Presbyterian sponsored two series of Sunday school classes to raise awareness and generate interest in Cuba and the Presbyterian Church there, and both congregations sent representatives to the Cuba Partners meeting. In May of 2005, the sessions of the two congregations signed an "Understanding of Partnership," committing to strengthen the relationship through shared gifts and activities.

After that, the two congregations carried out this commitment in several creative ways. Teams from Third Presbyterian visited Iglesia del Centro five times between 2005 and 2008, traveling to Cuba to make music, mark the one hundredth anniversary of the founding of Iglesia del Centro, and celebrate Advent with their Cuban brothers and sisters. During the music-making trip in early 2006, Third's choir director along with half a dozen choir members spent a week with Iglesia del Centro's chorus. Each choir introduced the other to their favorite music—Third learned the beat of *son*, a traditional Cuban rhythm, while Iglesia del Centro's choir learned American gospel pieces for the first time. During the Sunday morning worship service, the two choirs sang together in celebration of Iglesia del Centro's one hundredth anniversary. Learning of Centro's choir's desire to make an album of music they had composed, members of Third's choir raised a modest sum of money toward the effort. When a group from Third returned to Iglesia del Centro to celebrate Advent later that year, they were surprised to discover that Centro's choir had waited until Third's delegation arrived to launch their album.

According to Feinburg, this is just one of the many touching examples of how the two congregations honored and enjoyed each other. Third hired a liturgical artist to make matching stoles for Pastors Díaz and Hamilton and banners for each church to hang in their sanctuaries. Feinburg reminisced that the stole-giving ceremony moved both men to tears, and the liturgical artist, who wasn't even Presbyterian, found her work so meaningful that she decided to travel with Third to Centro on her own expense to help the two congregations make a quilt together during Third's next visit. Third Presbyterian celebrated Centro by planting a tree in Centro's honor, hosting Cuban-themed events, bringing Centro's prayer concerns to the congregation's attention through an elaborate bulletin board, and recognizing births, deaths, and special events at Iglesia del Centro as if they took place in their own congregation. Third also sponsored multiple visits from both leaders and parishioners from Centro, arranging for them to attend conferences and meet with other Presbyterian groups while in the United States. Financial contributions were modest and almost always directed to specific ends; for example, Third's library committee donated two hundred dollars to Iglesia del Centro's library committee to improve their collection, and Third's annual "Alternative Christmas Store" allowed parishioners to contribute to the endowment fund of a seminary related to Iglesia del Centro.

Several of Third's parishioners were quick to mention that money played only a small part in the relationship. The biggest gift that Third parishioners have given to their counterparts at Iglesia del Centro is the knowledge that Cubans have not been abandoned or forgotten, said Feinburg. Conversely, Iglesia del Centro's parishioners ministered to Third through their remarkable hospitality, testimonies, prayers, music, time, and willingness to challenge members of Third to advocate for the marginalized. Third's sanctuary and foyer were donned with several reminders of Iglesia del Centro's support for them—tapestries, letters, and photographs sent with love from one sibling to the other.

## Trinity Anglican Church (CANA) and the Cathedral Church of Saint James (Anglican Province of Uganda), Soroti, Uganda

Trinity Anglican Church was perhaps an unlikely candidate for an international sister church relationship. The 140-member all-white congregation was located in a rural area more than one hundred miles outside a major metropolitan area and was composed mostly of retirees from the military and federal government. In contrast to the Episcopal parishes in the area, Trinity was solidly conservative and evangelical. In 2006, in the wake of controversy surrounding the appointment of an openly gay bishop in the Episcopal Church, Trinity left the denomination to affiliate with the conservative Convocation of Anglicans in North America (which fell under the leadership of the Anglican province of Nigeria) and the Anglican District of Virginia. In the midst of this realignment, and partially because of it, Trinity built a close and vibrant partnership with the Cathedral Church of Saint James and its provost, the Very Reverend Doctor Paul Wamboga, in Soroti, Uganda.

The relationship between the two parishes hinged on evangelism, with each congregation equipping and assisting the other's efforts to preach the gospel in the community. Indeed, Trinity long prided itself on prioritizing mission. Parishioners were quick to quote Jesus' commission to take the gospel to Jerusalem (interpreted as the local community), Judea (the region), Samaria (distant lands in which other Christians live), and the ends of the earth (distant lands inhabited by "unreached" people groups). Trinity had sent out forty short-term mission teams in the fourteen years in which Craig Mora had been rector. For Trinity, the sister church partnership fell under the "Samaria" category. Trinity parishioners were eager to support Saint James in its ministry to Ugandans' physical, and more important, spiritual needs. According to respondents, parishioners from the Cathedral Church of Saint James were also eager to see the Christian faith grow and strengthen in Virginia. Though most of Saint James's parishioners struggled to meet their own basic needs of survival, the congregation rarely appealed to Trinity for aid.[14] The Cathedral Church of Saint James was a congregation of more than fifteen hundred people; it was perceived as a pillar of the Anglican Church in Uganda and a hub of community life. Its leaders in particular supported so-called reverse-mission efforts in the United States—a country reputed to have lost its footing in faith and morality—and the partnership with Trinity allowed them a chance to participate in reverse mission.

The partnership between Trinity and Saint James can be traced back to a telephone call Craig Mora received from Edwina Thomas, director of Sharing Mission of Ministries Abroad USA (SOMA), an Anglican short-term mission agency specializing in cross-cultural evangelism, in late 2002. Mora had previously participated in several short-term mission trips sponsored by SOMA, and Thomas had become a friend of the Mora family. In this particular call, Thomas asked Mora to play the reverse role in a short-term mission trip; she wondered if Mora and his congregation would consider hosting three Ugandans—a priest, an evangelist, and a layperson—for an evangelistic mission trip to rural Virginia. Piqued by the idea of reverse mission and excited to draw his congregation into his passion for international evangelism, Mora quickly consented. Mora recalled that his past interactions with African Christians had also prepared him for the relationship that would develop. While in seminary in the early 1990s, Mora came to know a small group of African students who, like him, were preparing for the priesthood. He remembers being "blown away" by the depths of their faith. Later, during a mission trip to Kenya, Mora was again captivated by the zeal, peace, and joy he witnessed among the African Christians he met. Thus, when the three Ugandan men made the trip to Virginia in June of 2003, preaching at Trinity Anglican and leading an evangelistic crusade in the community, Mora was not surprised by the deep level of respect and friendship that emerged between his guests and his congregation. Mora and Wamboga particularly befriended each other. After the trip, the two men exchanged frequent letters to maintain the friendship and explore possibilities for joint mission in the future.

In the course of conversations between Mora and Wamboga, it was Wamboga who suggested that Trinity form a sister church relationship with the Cathedral Church of Saint James. As the two priests discussed the potential relationship, Wamboga laid out his vision for the partnership: first, prayer and encouragement were to be central features. Second, the two congregations would share in each other's ministry. Wamboga wrote: "We can exchange ideas on how to do ministry and mission. We can visit each other. The people of Uganda are so hospitable. They are ready to receive and share the love of Christ with you. Come and share the message with our people." And third, Trinity could support Saint James's Soroti House Project, an income-producing commercial venture used to fund Saint James's orphan care, mission work, and pastoral salaries.

The two congregations made good on each of these commitments after the partnership began. While Wamboga completed a doctoral program in the United States in the years following his initial trip to Trinity, he visited the congregation each spring to develop relationships, preach, and minister at Trinity and the surrounding community. Between his first visit in 2003 and the time the interviews were conducted in 2008, Wamboga returned to Trinity five times, on one occasion joined by his wife and another by five of his sons who were touring in the United States as the "Living Hope Salvation Choir." Evangelist Samuel Nangai also returned to Trinity on two occasions to preach to the congregation and the community. In 2005, Mora led a ten-day trip to Saint James with five parishioners from Trinity. During their stay, the team visited schools, participated in worship, evangelized in the community, distributed eyeglasses, gathered in hosts' homes for meals each evening, and spoke to the Mothers' Union and intercessory prayer team at Saint James. Prayers for the brothers and sisters of Saint James were voiced regularly at Trinity, in the formal settings of liturgy and prayer ministry gatherings and informally among parishioners. Several parishioners who had hosted Ugandan visitors or traveled to Saint James exchanged regular correspondence with their friends in Uganda. According to Mora, most people in the congregation thought of Wamboga as a personal friend. Trinity gave around twenty thousand dollars to Saint James since the beginning of the partnership, mostly through special collections gathered for specific purposes, such as school fees for the twenty-six children—some biological but most adopted—in the Wamboga household or chairs and a tent for gatherings of the Mothers' Union.

Respondents from Trinity unanimously argued that Saint James had made the greater contribution to the relationship, even though money flowed in the opposite direction. Saint James's intercessory prayer team—fifty persons strong—prayed for Trinity daily since the partnership began. Several interviewees reported that this prayer support was an invaluable asset to Trinity, particularly as the congregation made the decision to leave the Episcopal Church. "Our relationship with Saint James has made us more resolved than ever that we are on the correct path of having left the Episcopal Church and aligned under the archbishop of Nigeria," said Remy Duke, Trinity's delegate to the Anglican District of Virginia. Inspired by the strength of their brothers' and sisters' prayerfulness, conviction, and faith, Trinity parishioners were emboldened in their confrontation with the Episcopal Church because of Saint James's encouragement. The controversy also strengthened the sister church relationship, since both parties were assured that the other was on the same side. In fact, according to Edward and Jean Francis, both participants in the 2005 delegation to Uganda, members of the two congregations joked that they were both rebel colonies of England and its liberal church—bonded together in common dissent.

## Living Faith Anglican Church (AMiA) and Murambi Parish (Anglican Province of Rwanda), Gatsibo, Rwanda

Living Faith Anglican Church, an evangelical church plant birthed in 2003 in the living room of its founder and rector, Dave Rice, grew to more than three hundred members and planted two additional congregations in the first five years of its history. Living Faith rented space from another congregation in a trendy urban neighborhood. The vast majority of its members were white, under forty, single, middle-class professionals—many of whom worked for the federal government or nonprofit organizations. Living Faith was closely linked with the Anglican Church in Africa from the beginning. With a Reformed background and seminary training at an interdenominational evangelical seminary, Rice was drawn into the Rwandan Anglican Mission in America because of personal relationships he had made with Thad Barnum, who went on to become an American bishop in the AMiA, and Barnum's Rwandan mentor, Bishop John Rucyahana. "I realized that there was something really extraordinary about these relationships, that there was depth of discipleship and depth of Christian friendship that I hadn't experienced before," said Rice about his decision to seek affiliation with AMiA, which had started in 2000 by the Province of Rwanda to provide "asylum" to conservative Episcopal churches marginalized or closed by the US Episcopal hierarchy.

Living Faith's connection to the church in Rwanda was consistently nurtured and prioritized by Rice and the vestry members. According to

Rice, the parish's relationship with Rwandan Christians and submission to global southern leadership was a compelling reason many chose to affiliate with the congregation. In the interest of building on its African connections, in early 2005 Living Faith's leadership sought inclusion in a pilot sister church project recently approved by the House of Bishops in Rwanda. To facilitate cooperation and communication between churches situated on two continents yet part of the same church, the project paired one congregation in each diocese in Rwanda with an AMiA congregation. Archbishop Emmanuel Kolini himself specifically chose the parish of Murambi in the diocese of Gatsibo to partner with Living Faith. Murambi was situated in a rural area in the northeast corner of Rwanda. Like Living Faith, Murambi was a vibrant and active parish, and its pastor, Archdeacon Fabi Gataraiha, was also well loved by the congregation. Because of Gataraiha's dynamism, the Murambi congregation's warm reception of Living Faith, and the two congregations' complementary strengths, many of those involved in Living Faith's sister church relationships saw their partnership as an ideal match: Murambi provided "Rwandan parents to American children." Murambi was a "church full of mommas in Rwanda," and Living Faith a "church full of young singles in America."[15]

Living Faith was mostly comprised of unmarried and/or childless young adults and Murambi of people in all ages belonging to large families; this fact was not lost on either party. Several Living Faith congregants were eager to speak of Murambi's role in mentoring and discipling parishioners at Living Faith, especially in matters of marriage and family. Visits from Fabi Gataraiha, his wife Shiyra, and other representatives from Murambi to Living Faith featured seminars on marriage and family. Murambi women laid hands on single women who participated in Living Faith's delegations to Rwanda, asking for God to select a spouse for each woman. Pastor Rice related that prayer and counsel were a critical part of Murambi's ministry to Living Faith. When members of the sister church had come to the United States, they had spent the lion's share of their time meeting with groups and individuals from Living Faith to offer prayer support and encouragement. In fact, during their last visit, said Rice, the Gataraihas canceled all of the sight-seeing excursions that Living Faith's partnership committee had planned for them, preferring instead to eat and pray with Living Faith parishioners. The same dedication to the spiritual development of Living Faith's members could be seen during visits to Rwanda as well. Pastor Rice recounted:

> Of the thirteen people who were part of our first delegation to Rwanda, eleven were singles in their twenties or thirties. Our friends at Murambi

were profoundly troubled by this. They saw healthy, mature, Christian believers well on in years, from their perspective, who were unmarried and
without prospects for marriage. I think they read it through the lens of a
western culture that has blown sexuality out of control. So they began to
pray. They prayed for us then, and they have prayed for us all the time since
then. And when we took that first delegation in 2005, I think we had one
wedding in our church that year, and this past year we had twenty-five engagements! It's been a real joke, I think, among many people here, that
we've written to Murambi and asked them to stop praying. We can't handle
any more weddings; we don't have any free weekends!

Rice's humorous story illustrating how seriously the Murambi parish
took their role in praying for their partner church is just one example of the
people of Living Faith's great pride in perceiving themselves to be in a
relationship of equality—even submission—with an African church.
Living Faith members involved in the sister church relationship were conscientious about treating their counterparts in Murambi with deference
and respect. They laughed politely at Fabi Gataraiha's jokes, carefully edited their correspondence to Murambi, read widely about the Rwandan
genocide, and spoke of Murambi's parishioners as saints of great faith.
Living Faith patterned their women's ministry after Murambi's women's
ministry, hosted public events in Washington, DC, featuring speakers from
the Gatsibo diocese, and produced a documentary on the stories of their
friends in Murambi.

Because of this desire for equality and awareness of the potential pitfalls
of international mission, Living Faith's Cross-Continental Partnership Council (CCPC) was leery of giving monetary gifts or sponsoring projects in
Murambi. For the first two years of the partnership, in fact, the two congregations focused exclusively on building their relationship. In August of
2005, Living Faith sent a team to Rwanda for ten days to get acquainted with
the Murambi parish and the Anglican Province of Rwanda. While in Rwanda,
Living Faith's delegation spent time worshiping, eating, and recreating with
the Gataraihas and Murambi parishioners. They did not engage in any work
projects or make recommendations for development during the trip. Although they brought several thousand dollars along to distribute while in
Rwanda, the team decided to give just five hundred dollars to the Murambi
parish. The rest of the funds, they determined, would be distributed only after additional prayer, reflection, and consultation with the Murambi leaders.

After another year and a half of dialogue and relationship building with
Murambi, which included a month-long visit from the Gataraihas in the

summer of 2006, Living Faith's CCPC "felt that it was ready to explore ways of assisting Murambi with meeting material needs."[16] Living Faith received a letter from Murambi with a request for assistance in several areas. Most notably, Murambi asked for funds to purchase a tipper lorry for community use. While the CCPC was at first skeptical about whether buying a dump truck should be a top spending priority for Murambi, they were eventually convinced. After months of deliberations and correspondence between the two parishes, Living Faith decided to wire funds for the tipper lorry, school supplies, and medical implements. Feeling cautiously comfortable about offering material support in the midst of a relationship of mutuality, Living Faith's CCPC continued to give modest sums of money to the Murambi parish while stressing spiritual connection as the cornerstone of the partnership. In the summer of 2007, another large team from Living Faith traveled to Murambi, and several Living Faith parishioners who traveled to Africa professionally also paid visits to Murambi parish. Fabi Gataraiha returned to Washington, DC, twice to visit Living Faith after his first trip, accompanied by other leaders in the Murambi parish. Through open dialogue and consistent prayer, the CCPC hoped to avoid the damage that they know resource-sharing can cause. As the two parishes continued to walk together down the road of partnership, said Aaron Thomas, president of Living Faith's CCPC, they held fast to the "three principles of partnership" articulated by Archdeacon Gataraiha on the night in which Living Faith's first delegation to Rwanda was introduced to the Murambi parishioners: unity, charity, humility.[17] While Living Faith's partnership with Murambi may look similar to a donor/recipient relationship, stated Thomas, it was the posture of mutual respect, deference, and celebration of common bonds that made all the difference.

## Christ the King Anglican Church (AMiA) and Iglesia Nueva Jerusalén (Independent), San Fernando, Nicaragua

Christ the King Anglican Church was a congregation of two hundred, with an annual budget of six hundred thousand dollars, located on a wooded campus in a wealthy outer suburb. The rector and most of the parishioners at Christ the King were highly conservative in both their theology and their politics. The liturgy at Christ the King was classical and formal. The all-male clergy and liturgical assistants wore vestments, while several women in the pews wore head coverings and dark dress suits. Most of Christ the King's members were white, middle to upper class, and middle aged or older. Few young adults worshiped at Christ the King, but families with children did dot the sea of baby boomers and elderly. Like Living Faith, Christ the King was also a member of the Rwandan Anglican Mission in America. In 2001, more than 90 percent of Christ the King Episcopal Church's members voted to leave the denomination, leaving the building the church owned and the name "Episcopal" with a handful of parishioners loyal to the denomination. The next year, the new Christ the King Anglican Church affiliated with the AMiA out of a sense that the Rwanda Anglican Church would "be a safe home, theologically speaking."[18]

Christ the King forged several connections with other Anglicans in Africa. Given Christ the King's close proximity to a Reformed seminary, two Anglican priests from Tanzania were part of the congregation while studying in seminary in the late 1990s. Later, both of these men became bishops in Tanzania, and Christ the King supported their work through financial contributions at the diocesan level in Tanzania. More recently, Christ the King began making contributions to a Rwandan diocese through the AMiA affiliation as well. The church's congregation-to-congregation relationship, however, was with a church that was neither African nor Anglican but rather Latino and nondenominational charismatic.

Beginning in the summer of 2005, Christ the King parishioners embarked on an annual trip to San Fernando, Nicaragua, to lead vacation Bible school for children, facilitate adult Bible studies, make improvements to church property, help repair buildings damaged by recent hurricanes, and fellowship with the people at Iglesia Nueva Jerusalén. In addition to the summer mission trip to Nueva Jerusalén, which was the hallmark of the relationship, Christ the King sponsored a medical fund for community members of Nueva Jerusalén as well as a fund for offsetting educational costs for children in San Fernando. Individuals at Christ the King used the relationship for a springboard for other activities: a group of women sold hand-crafted items from the Nueva Jerusalén community, one man started a microfinance program in San Fernando, and another man telephoned a friend from Nueva Jerusalén every Sunday.

Nueva Jerusalén and Christ the King first became acquainted through Food for the Hungry, an evangelical relief and development organization. Marla Hines, an employee of Food for the Hungry who attended Christ the King in the early 2000s, knew of the devastation of war, hurricanes, and poverty in Nicaragua and suggested to Christ the King's mission committee that they explore getting involved in Food for the Hungry's work there. The wife of Christ the King's rector at the time was Nicaraguan, and her family had endured much suffering during the Nicaraguan civil war.

"So, with those kind of relationships, needs became known. And it was 'something to do' for missions," said Canon Peter Russell, rector.

The congregation's first trip to San Fernando in 2005 was facilitated and led by Food for the Hungry. While Christ the King's delegation quickly fell in love with the San Fernando community, said Cory Kimsey, who served as Christ's the King's delegation leader every subsequent year, they were dissatisfied with the work of Food for the Hungry. According to Kimsey, since the team had already educated themselves on Nicaragua before the trip began, Food for the Hungry "wasted the team's time" by requiring them to spend several days in Managua learning about the history and culture of Nicaragua before proceeding to San Fernando. Kimsey reported that Food for the Hungry also charged exorbitant rates and was unwilling to provide Christ the King with an expense report. In addition, the team was uncomfortable with the "leftist undertones" of Food for the Hungry's training program.

Yet, while in San Fernando the Christ the King delegation forged bonds with Pastor Juan Mendoza and other members of Iglesia Nueva Jerusalén, and the relationship soon took on its own steam. In March of 2006, Kimsey and four other Christ the King parishioners returned to San Fernando to see if they could continue to visit and support the community without the help of Food for the Hungry. Christ the King visited Nueva Jerusalén each summer after that. Christ the King decided to focus their relationship on Iglesia Nueva Jerusalén rather than the San Fernando community at large. Kimsey observed:

> When we worked in the San Fernando community at large with Food for the Hungry, there were a lot of bystanders who were just watching the North Americans do the work. And a lot of people were looking for handouts. But with Nueva Jerusalén it is more of a partnership. We do the work together, Pastor Juan is accountable, and we've built a relationship of trust with him.

Kimsey joked that while Food for the Hungry refused to share their financial records, Pastor Juan Mendoza often sent him receipts unprompted.

According to Peter Russell, the somewhat unlikely bonds between Christ the King and Iglesia Nueva Jerusalén persisted and strengthened over the course of the relationship. Maintaining those bonds of Christian fellowship—rather than advancing projects—became the focal point of Christ the King's involvement.

> At first, I think we saw this venture as a mission project. But now, relationships are so active and ongoing, so the purpose is really maintaining Christian

relationships with people we have gotten to know. In other words, it's not a theological commonality—well, we both love Jesus, but they are not Anglicans, you understand. They are Baptists, we are Pedobaptists, they're Pentecostal, we're Reformed. You get it. But these relationships are incredibly strong. Let me put it this way, if I said, "We aren't interested in Nicaragua anymore," it would cost me incredibly politically. And people would still go down, if I said "no." That's how strong it is. Not that I am of the mind to say "no," but that's just to convey how powerful those relationships are that have been built up over the years.

The San Fernando community at large was well-connected to North Americans; in fact, in the mid-2000s a guest house was built just to host the steady stream of North Americans who volunteered on a short-term basis in San Fernando. But Corey Kimsey argued that the partnership between Christ the King and Nueva Jerusalén stood out among San Fernando's encounters with North Americans. "People from Nicaragua tell me that our church is different. People in our congregation just know that Nicaraguans are equals and they treat them accordingly. I don't know what it is other than a biblical sense of humility." Moreover, he maintained that both congregations firmly believed that hope for the community comes from spiritual transformation and not any sort of program. Thus, despite their differences, Christ the King and Nueva Jerusalén undertook a common quest to "provide hope that only comes from Jesus—especially to people who have so little."

## Victory Baptist Church (PNBC) and Ebenezer Baptist Church, Frankfield, Jamaica

Victory Baptist Church, an 800-member exclusively African American congregation located in an economically depressed area of Washington, DC, enjoyed a reputation for being a pillar in the community. The church ran a day care, after-school program, food pantry, clothes closet, and credit union in addition to sponsoring an evangelism team, a thriving music program, a visitation ministry to the sick and homebound, an annual revival, and an active Christian education program—all this on a one-and-a-half million dollar budget. While Victory Baptist focused most of its ministry efforts on the local community, said Lola Evans, Victory's associate minister of evangelism and outreach, the church did its best to meet people's needs wherever it found them. To that end, for the ten years prior to the study, Victory had been in a "relationship of support" with Ebenezer Baptist Church in Frankfield, Jamaica. Unlike many international congregation-to-congregation relationships, Victory's arrangement with Ebenezer was decidedly project-centered and one-directional. Victory's pastor, mission board, and parishioners tended to be unaware of the legacy of paternalism in international mission efforts. All the same, they saw the folks at Ebenezer Baptist as brothers and sisters. And since "these brothers and sisters needed a church, we built them a church," said Evans.

In 1995, Ebenezer Baptist, one of three congregations in Pastor Exley Fraser's circuit in a rural area of western Jamaica, decided to begin constructing a new church building to replace the small, dilapidated facility that housed worship services. "They were trying so hard to build that church, and it was so badly needed—but somehow or another they couldn't even get it off the ground," recalled Anita Wallace, former chairperson of Victory Baptist's board of mission. Things began to change a few years later when Exley Fraser and his wife, Vivian, met Reverend Milton Barclay, pastor of Victory Baptist and Jamaican by birth. Barclay was traveling in Jamaica with two representatives of the Foreign Bureau of the Progressive National Baptist Convention who had asked him to accompany them on their relationship-building trip because of his Jamaican background. Fraser showed Barclay and the PNBC representatives Ebenezer's steadily declining facilities as well as the building site, explaining that the congregation simply didn't have the funds to proceed and pleading with Barclay for help. Barclay quickly pledged one thousand dollars to the project from Victory Baptist.

Several months later Fraser sent a letter and photograph to Victory detailing the progress of the building project. "In this photo, they were taking sand and water and trying to build this church by hand, even the women and children. So, after seeing this first picture, Pastor Barclay decided that we would take on this project and make sure that the church got built. And we did," Wallace reported proudly. Over a period of several years, at Barclay's discretion, Victory sent sixteen thousand dollars out of their mission budget to the Ebenezer congregation. Along the way, Fraser continued to send photographs and letters as the structure went up, which Victory's board of mission assembled onto a bulletin board. Cynthia Adams, Victory's chairperson of the board of mission, remembered that at one point, Victory received a photograph with the edifice of the new sanctuary completed all the way up to the roof and a note that funds had dried up to continue building. Together with several other US churches whose pastors the Frasers met while attending an annual PNBC convention, Victory raised the money to put the roof on the sanctuary. In 2005, the new sanctuary finally complete, Adams, Wallace, Barclay, and his wife, Francine, and a deacon from Victory Baptist traveled to Jamaica for the dedication of the new building they had funded. "That was an 'oh happy day' for me and the others from Victory," said Wallace. "We got to see the fruits of the giving and labor." Adams added: "The folks at Ebenezer were high in the spirit. They were truly grateful. And indeed, it was one of the greatest celebrations I have ever seen in terms of building a church and seeing people come together to worship God."

While the relationship between Victory and Ebenezer centered mostly on the construction of Ebenezer's sanctuary, other exchanges have also taken place. In between the time they first met Milton Barclay and Exley Fraser's death in 2004, the Frasers twice traveled to Washington, DC, to visit Victory Baptist, and both Exley and Vivian preached to the Victory congregation. After her husband's death, Vivian Fraser became the pastor at Ebenezer and maintained correspondence with Milton Barclay. After the dedication of Ebenezer's sanctuary, Victory's board of mission sent hymnals, educational materials, second-hand clothes and shoes, and small financial gifts to the Ebenezer congregation. Collecting one thousand pairs of shoes in the wake of Hurricane Dean and figuring out how to ship them to Jamaica was no small task, remembered Wallace. Victory Baptist tried to help Ebenezer meet some of the physical needs of its members, but the focus of their support for Ebenezer was always "to fulfill Matthew 28:18–20, to go into all the world and preach the gospel," said Barclay. Victory Baptist was surrounded by plenty of need in its own congregation and community. But in the minds of Barclay and the members of the board of mission at Victory, having a place to worship God is a paramount human need. Even though the sixteen thousand dollars Victory gave to Ebenezer for sanctuary construction could have been used in countless other ways in Victory's own neighborhood, seeing the Ebenezer congregation "joyfully coming to praise God" was well worth the sacrifice.

## Thirteenth Street Baptist Church (PNBC) and Sharon Circuit of Baptist Churches, Black River, Jamaica / Umzito Baptist Church, Umzito, South Africa

The Reverend Doctor Lionel Morris, senior pastor at Thirteenth Street Baptist Church, considered himself a mission-minded pastor in the business of creating a mission-minded congregation. When Morris first came to Thirteenth Street Baptist in 2000, he initiated a major strategic planning process aimed to galvanize the congregation around a shared sense of mission and vision. The results of this process were a vision statement and a mission statement that undergirded all of Thirteenth Street's ministries. Thirteenth Street's mission was "to lead souls to Christ, to demonstrate the standard of Christian living, and to spread the Gospel of Jesus Christ." The church's vision was "to glorify God by being fruitful disciple makers of Jesus Christ."[19] This commitment to evangelism was taken very seriously; Morris explained that every ministry at Thirteenth Street Baptist was required to demonstrate to him how they were living out the church's mission and vision.

Morris appointed the church's evangelism, hospitality, deacons', and deaconess' ministries to manage Thirteenth Street's local outreach efforts in its struggling urban neighborhood as well as inreach efforts to the five hundred households that are part of the congregation. Internationally, however, all of Thirteenth Street's efforts were orchestrated directly by Morris. "We support international mission in two ways," said Lawrence Jones, assistant to Morris, "through our financial giving and through the work of Pastor Morris." Morris established several long-standing interchurch relationships in Africa and the Caribbean on a pastor-to-pastor basis. Beyond listening to Morris's reports, packing boxes of supplies, and writing checks, no one at Thirteenth Street besides Morris was directly involved in these relationships. Morris mentioned that he would like to see members of his congregation form delegations to Jamaica and South Africa to get to know their international ministry partners, but for the time being he represented them vicariously as he traveled.

Shortly before coming to Thirteenth Street Baptist, Lionel Morris co-founded African Impact Ministries—an organization established to build churches and train church leaders in Nigeria—with a Nigerian colleague named Isaac Eze from Morris's seminary days. In 1998 Morris traveled to Nigeria with Eze to preach in remote churches and teach a class for Nigerian pastors. When Morris transferred to Thirteenth Street Baptist, he pulled the congregation into African Impact's ministry. After Eze moved to the United States, he preached at Thirteenth Street on several occasions, and the congregation supported African Impact financially. However, Morris directed most of the church's international mission efforts to the work of the Lott Carey Baptist Foreign Mission Convention.

In 2005, Morris began participating in Lott Carey's pastoral excellence program, which was designed "to transform the ministry visions and magnify the pastoral impacts of African American pastors through executing multiple ministry immersions in African and African Diaspora contexts with consistent peer groups for mentoring and networking."[20] The relationships that Lionel Morris formed with Wesley Lewis, pastor of the Sharon Baptist circuit in Black River, Jamaica, and Oliver Zange, pastor of Umzito Baptist Church in Umzito, South Africa, stemmed directly from Morris's participation in the Lott Carey program and became the cornerstones of Thirteenth Street's international mission activity.

Thirteenth Street Baptist had a long history of support for the Lott Carey Convention. Through Morris's participation in the pastoral excellence program, he strengthened these ties and drew Thirteenth Street Baptist into Lott Carey's newly refashioned approach to international ministry. In the Lott Carey pastoral excellence initiative, African American pastors commit to a three-year program, which includes a mission trip each year, initially to Guyana, then Jamaica, and finally southern Africa. On each trip, the pastors spend two weeks living and working with local church pastors in those countries, fully sharing in ministry. Morris explained that while Lott Carey continued to embrace its founding mission, to spread the gospel to the outermost ends of the earth, in recent years the Convention became more committed to working alongside nationals in Africa and the Caribbean as partners and equals. The Lott Carey Convention also increasingly deferred to local Baptist conventions in the areas in which it worked around the globe.

For his part, Morris poured himself into the pastoral excellence program and formed relationships with partnering pastors that extended well beyond the bounds of the program. Morris's acquaintance with Wesley Lewis, pastor of the five rural congregations that made up the Sharon Circuit in Black River, Jamaica, began with written correspondence in 2005 as part of the Lott Carey program. In the spring of 2007, Morris traveled to Black Water, where he preached at a revival service and a youth service in the Sharon Circuit and stayed in Lewis's home. Morris quickly learned that Jamaican circuit pastors like Lewis are heavily taxed by a grueling travel schedule, a mountain of responsibility, and an inadequate income. While in Jamaica, Morris did all he could to encourage Lewis and lighten his load, and when Morris returned home, he quickly adjusted Thirteenth Street's mission budget to include supplementary funds for Lewis's salary.

In early 2008, Morris traveled to Umzito, South Africa, where he was paired with Oliver Zange, pastor of Umzito Baptist Church. Morris recalled that when the two first met, Zange, in his late sixties, was expecting a much older man than Morris, in his early forties, for the peer mentoring relationship. The two men hit it off quickly despite their age difference, and at one point Zange's wife, Florence, remarked, "I have three daughters and no sons; you are now my son."[21] Both before the trip and after, Thirteenth Street, at Morris's direction, responded to Zange's request for leadership and Sunday school materials. "What's unique about our relationship with Pastor Zange and Umzito Baptist is that it doesn't center around money. They told us that money was not important. What they really need, Pastor Zange said, is material to help them train their leaders and establish a church school."

Morris recruited the Christian education ministry at Thirteenth Street to gather leftover materials from the Sunday school closets, pack up unneeded books "that were just collecting dust" in Morris's study, and buy discounted material from Christian education suppliers—all to be shipped to Umzito.

Morris said that he would like to see his congregation's connectedness to Umzito Baptist, the Sharon circuit, and African Impact in Nigeria strengthened over the years to come. In particular, he dreamed of organizing a delegation to Africa so members of his congregation could bear witness to their faith, minister to people's needs, and be encouraged by their brothers and sisters in the faith in Nigeria or South Africa. But in the meantime, he was proud that 12 percent of Thirteenth Street's half-a-million-dollar budget was dedicated to mission and outreach. And he was thankful for the congregation's receptiveness to hearing about his travels and supporting his relationships around the globe.

## Mount Calvary Baptist Church (PNBC) and Jangalia Baptist Church, Hezamara, India / Resurrection Temple Missionary Baptist Church, Georgetown, Guyana

Mount Calvary Baptist Church was a historic African American congregation of six hundred members, located in a gentrifying urban neighborhood. More than 10 percent of the church's 800,000 dollar budget was dedicated to mission, and the congregation long supported numerous missionary ventures overseas. In fact, delineating the boundaries of Mount Calvary's sister church relationships was difficult given that Mount Calvary "adopted" half a dozen congregations, schools, or orphanages around the world. Jangalia Baptist Church in Hezamara, India, and Temple Missionary Baptist Church in Georgetown, Guyana, stood out as the most prominent of these, which Mount Calvary's church administrator, Jocelyn Parker described as "churches we support" rather than "sister churches" or another corresponding term.

Mount Calvary first became linked to Jangalia Baptist Church in 2004 when Clancey Brown, Mount Calvary's long-time senior pastor, met Chandra Rupini at the local Missionary Baptist Ministers' Conference, over which Brown presided. Rupini, a prominent Baptist pastor and church planter in India, requested Mount Calvary's prayers and financial support for Jangalia Baptist, the congregation he served, as well as a new congregation being planted nearby under Jangalia's auspices. After that, Mount Calvary sent money each year to Rupini to support the two congregations, and Rupini returned every year to preach at Mount Calvary and bring greetings from Jangalia Baptist. Jocelyn Parker explained that in addition to the regular offerings, Mount Calvary's thirty-person-strong missions ministry organized special projects to support Jangalia Baptist and other ministries. For example, one year Mount Calvary's annual angel tree was dedicated to Pastor Rupini's tailoring ministry in India. Each angel on the tree represented a sewing machine donated to the ministry. Jangalia Baptist and the other ministries Mount Calvary supported were embedded in the church's material culture not just at Christmas but also through flags prominently displayed in the front of the sanctuary along with a large map marked with the location of each ministry.

Mount Calvary's support for Resurrection Temple began more recently following Clancey Brown's visit to Georgetown, Guyana, with the Lott Carey Foreign Mission Convention's pastoral excellence program in 2006. Brown was matched with Carolyn Luckhoo, pastor of Resurrection Temple, in a peer-to-peer mentoring relationship. While in Guyana, Brown led a five-day revival at Resurrection Temple. On the last day of the revival, Brown recalled, Resurrection Temple's diaconate "got up and voted me as the father of their church." Even though Luckhoo was an older woman, explained Brown, she and the congregation recognized that the church needed male "covering" and Luckhoo needed a spiritual mentor. The rest of the congregation was introduced to Reverend Luckhoo the following year when she traveled to Mount Calvary while in the United States visiting family. Luckhoo participated in Mount Calvary's community day and worship service and also attended the Washington, DC, Baptist Convention ministers' meeting while in the area. Before Luckhoo returned home, Olivia West, president of Mount Calvary's missions ministry, gathered her team together to pack a barrel of school supplies, Sunday school curriculum, and hymnals for Luckhoo to bring back to her congregation. Mount Calvary also sent eyeglasses, clothing, and refurbished computers to Resurrection Temple. Although most of the communication between Mount Calvary and Resurrection Temple, as well as Mount Calvary and

Jangalia, went from pastor to pastor, several members of the mission ministry formed personal relationships with both Luckhoo and Rupini and corresponded with them through e-mail and letters.

According to Clancey Brown, Mount Calvary's support for Jangalia, Resurrection Temple, and other overseas ministries was rooted in the church's very identity. "Like many Baptist churches, we have been missionary from our birth. And so, to be true to the name and to the mandate, we have to be missionary-minded. . . . You could say that a church that is not involved in missions is not a church at all. . . . When God blesses us, he blessed us to bless others, whether they are local or whether they are foreign or far away."

Given the strength of Christianity in Africa and Latin America, Brown explained that Mount Calvary's missionary ventures there were centered around discipleship, skills training, and economic empowerment. In India, however, evangelism was the central focus. Each year, Mount Calvary gave approximately twenty thousand dollars to support international ministries, most of which was dedicated to Chandra Rupini and Jangalia Baptist Church. Echoing Brown's description of Mount Calvary as missionary in its very nature, Olivia West explained that locally, "we just jump up and do, whereas internationally we tend to send money," hoping that the money sent would be used to advance the gospel in one way or another.

## Conclusion

Beyond the common quest for kinship with another community of faith in a distant locale, the stories of these twelve churches involved in sister church relationships vary greatly. Yet, each narrative raises questions about the measure of effectiveness, the role of individuals, the possibility of parity, the influence of time, and the structure of power in sister church relationships—questions that lie at the heart of the movement. While twelve case studies derived from specific ecclesiastical contexts and a particular geographical region cannot hope to represent the sister church movement as a whole, they shed light on the path of North American churches that embark on a shared journey with a partner in another area of the globe. The stories told above provide data for analysis in subsequent chapters, which will draw out common themes in these accounts as well as highlighting differences. The following chapter will examine the organizational, identity, and logistical dynamics at work in the twelve case studies.

| Profiles

*Congregations and Individual Participants*
*in Sister Church Relationships*

WHEN RUTH EATON, SENIOR pastor of Kensington Woods Presbyterian Church, began to set in motion her dreams for a missional partnership with an East Africa community in 1986, contacting the denomination to which her congregation belonged seemed like a natural first step in the process. At that point in time, the PC(USA) was just beginning to encourage the formation of international presbytery-to-presbytery relationships and to articulate an accompaniment approach to mission. Eaton recalled that the General Assembly seemed rather bewildered by her idea of a long-term partnership between Kensington Woods and another faith community abroad. The General Assembly put her in touch directly with the Presbyterian Church of East Africa, and the relationship between Kensington Woods and the Limuru Mission Area evolved from there. Eaton recalled sending annual reports to the General Assembly in the early years of the partnership. Never receiving correspondence in return, she eventually stopped sending the reports.

In 1996, partly because of excitement among presbytery leaders generated by the Kensington Woods-Limuru relationship, the National Capital Presbytery entered a relationship with a presbytery in another area of Kenya. A decade later, the formal relationship crumbled because of conflicts over homosexuality, though projects were sustained under the auspices of several congregations within the National Capital Presbytery. The Kensington Woods-Limuru relationship, which was not subject to either denominational or presbytery oversight, steadily progressed and even flourished in the midst of this controversy—untouched by the politics of religious bureaucracies.

## Local by Nature

Kensington Woods's near circumvention of denominational or regional bodies as it formed and carried out its sister church relationship was typical for the twelve profiled congregations. Of the twelve congregations, only Third Presbyterian and Living Faith Anglican entered into sister church relationships as part of a denominational initiative. These congregations received occasional technical assistance from denominational bodies. However, the congregations themselves, in concert with their partners abroad, were solely responsible for designing and managing their relationships. Living Faith's international partnership committee even took on the would-be role of a denominational mission agency by educating other congregations on best practices in sister church relationships.[1] Of the other ten congregations, five relied on the help of parachurch organizations to birth their sister church relationships but maintained increasingly less contact with intermediaries over time. The remaining five congregations conducted their sister church relationships with little to no assistance from intermediary organizations.

Regardless of polity, theological tradition, or whether or not an intermediary was involved, the sister church relationships in the profiled Washington, DC–area congregations were steered by local congregational leadership. While most of the congregations paired with congregations within their tradition, these partnerships were formed primarily on the basis of grassroots networking rather than denominational oversight. Denominational or parachurch bureaucracies were unnecessary in effectively administering congregation-to-congregation relationships. The relationships functioned bottom up rather than top down through the chain of religious organization.

## Profiles of Congregations in Sister Church Partnerships

Given the fact that denominations and other intermediaries played only a small role in the profiled sister church relationships, it was the characteristics of the participating congregations and their members that set the course of the relationship, particularly on a structural level. The northern partners tended to be congregations with a vibrant community life, a missional outlook, and a willingness to alter or expand the roles allocated to congregations in their representative traditions. Beyond these commonalities, however, the congregations came in numerous varieties.

## Size and Budget

Most of the congregations were much larger than the national mean of 185 persons.[2] Each of the Catholic parishes had more than twenty-five hundred members on its roster. The large size of these parishes mirrored the national trend discovered by the CARA study, which found that US Catholic parishes involved in parish-to-parish relationships are typically on the larger end of the spectrum with an average of fourteen hundred households.[3] The Presbyterian and Baptist congregations were also large by comparison to other congregations in their traditions. Only the Anglican congregations were more modest in size, though two of the three were still larger than the national average: Living Faith had three hundred members; Christ the King, two hundred; and Trinity, one hundred forty. Based on the consensus of informants from denominational and parachurch linking programs as well as my own mapping of congregations across the Washington, DC, area involved in international partnerships, these numbers mirror national trends among congregations that participate in international sister church relationships. In order to sustain programs like sister church relationships, which require large amounts of time, money, and human capital, congregations often need to be bolstered by large numbers of members.

The more salient factor than size in the ability of congregations to support programs like sister church relationships, however, is monetary resources. Nancy Ammerman and her team found that congregations with budgets under fifty thousand dollars were much less likely than congregations with larger budgets to support international mission efforts sponsored by denominations or parachurch agencies.[4] Directly pertaining to sister church relationships, CARA found that those US Catholic parishes involved in sister parish relationships drew in an average of three hundred eighty thousand dollars in annual Mass collections.[5] The congregations in my study each managed annual budgets much larger than the national average of roughly eighty-six thousand dollars.[6] With the exception of Trinity Anglican, each of the congregations maintained annual budgets in excess of five hundred thousand dollars. At least two-thirds of the congregations maintained annual budgets of eight hundred thousand dollars or more, and two parishes had multimillion-dollar annual budgets.

For the larger and wealthier congregations, the sister church relationship tended to be one program among many—rivaling other initiatives for time, attention, and resources and often relegated to a subculture or special-interest group within the congregation. In these congregations, most parishioners were only tangentially involved in the relationship. At best, their participation was limited to giving money, receiving updates from the pulpit or other venues, and participating in liturgies in which the sister church relationship was recognized in some way. The partnership committee or other similar body, usually in conjunction with the pastor, was responsible for almost all aspects of the relationship. In the smaller Anglican churches, by contrast, the sister church relationships were a central part of congregational life. Other factors such as the tight ecclesiastical links to overseas church bodies also intervened in these situations, but the intimacy of these congregations seemed to promote widespread participation. At Trinity Anglican, for example, very few other programs competed for parishioners' attention and thus a large proportion of the congregation was involved in the sister church relationship. Trinity's relationship with Paul Wamboga and the Cathedral Church of Saint James was central to the identity of the congregation. Although Trinity was an anomaly among North American partnering churches because of its size, it made up for lack of resources in enthusiasm and focus.

## Demography

International sister church relationships can be found among predominantly white, predominantly black, multiethnic, and predominantly Latino congregations—immigrant or native-born—in North America. Of the twelve Washington, DC–area congregations, three were predominantly black, two were multiethnic, and seven were predominantly white.[7] Of the predominantly white congregations, only one was completely homogenous; all of the others featured at least some ethnic or racial diversity. Among Catholic parishes, CARA found that ethnic composition was not strongly related to support of a sister parish.[8] But because ethnicity functions differently in Catholic parishes from Protestant congregations—with Catholics being more likely to worship in parishes in which multiple ethnic groups are represented—this finding is not necessarily true for Protestant congregations as well.[9] Most Christian congregations in the United States that participate in international congregation-to-congregation relationships are predominantly white, largely because these congregations are the majority and because they tend to have greater access to material resources than other types of congregations.

International congregational pairing is uncommon among African American churches. And among efforts that do exist, relationships tend to be rather elemental. It was difficult to locate African American Baptist congregations involved in international relationships with other congregations, despite the large number of African American Baptist congregations in the Washington, DC, area. The three profiled congregations in this tradition each dealt only minimally with their partners beyond giving money. Moreover, in none of these congregations was the relationship perceived as a significant deviation from the sending model of mission. Historically, African American congregations in the United States, while often strongly committed to mission and evangelism, have focused most of their outreach efforts on the needs of the local community.[10] Combined with their lack of access to power and resources when compared to predominantly white churches as well as the relative youth of African American institutions, this local priority often renders would-be international mission efforts nonexistent or programmatically thin. Additionally, given the expectations placed on black churches to have well-developed social program, some black congregations may feel pressure to embellish their outreach efforts no matter how functional these efforts are in point of fact.

Immigrants from the global South represent an increasingly influential swath of North American Christianity and often perform crucial roles in congregation-to-congregation linkages. Out of the hundreds of thousands of people—mostly from the global South—who stream into the United States every year as immigrants, the great majority are Christian. "The new immigrants represent," as R. Stephen Warner aptly puts it, "not the de-Christianization of American society but the de-Europeanization of American Christianity."[11] Most worship, at least at first, in distinctly immigrant congregations. These immigrant congregations generally foster religious and cultural ties between immigrants and their homelands as well as connections between immigrants and their new lands.[12] The congregation-to-congregation partnerships that are formed between immigrant congregations in the United States and congregations in the global South are generally designed to link immigrants to their countries of origin as well as to provide aid to former compatriots facing more dire circumstances than immigrants who found their way to the United States. Because of the distinct nature of congregation-to-congregation relationships between immigrants in the United States and coethnics in their native countries, combined with the practical inability to cover sister church relationships among all possible groups, immigrant congregations are not featured in this study.[13] However, most of the predominantly white profiled congregations included at least a few nonwhite immigrants, students, or other sojourners from the global South. These transnational individuals were often key players in their congregations' sister church relationships.

As far as other demographic factors are concerned, the participating congregations were generally urban or suburban and composed of predominantly middle- to upper-class well-educated professionals. Many of the congregations contained large numbers of civil servants, educators, and other nonprofit sector workers. Most congregations' dispersions of age and family status were typical of American congregations, although Living Faith Anglican contained a disproportionately high percentage of singles in their twenties and thirties, and Trinity Anglican a high percentage of retirees. Since the sample was limited to a particular geographic area in which rates of population density, educational attainment, and income are higher than in many areas of the nation—not to mention the fact that the Washington, DC, area is a hub for both the federal government and nonprofit organizations—these characteristics are not necessarily representative of North American congregations that participate in sister church relationships.[14] However, given the fact that congregations with larger budgets are more likely to support sister church relationships, levels of income and educational attainment among participating congregations are also likely to be high in comparison to the mean.

## Polity

When the parish partnership model began to be implemented in the late 1980s, it was primarily among Catholics and mainline Protestants with centralized denominational structures and hierarchical or connectional polity.[15] In addition to the theological impetus for partnerships among these communities, institutional religious groups were perhaps more likely to participate in sister church relationships than nascent groups because of greater access to resources and more developed networks around the world.

However, the last fifteen years have made it especially clear that sister church relationships can thrive in the absence of the oversight of institutional bureaucracies. During that time period, nondenominational congregations with autonomous polity have increasingly established long-term bonds with other congregations, schools, or social service providers in the global South—usually through the efforts of clergy, missionaries, immigrants, or students with ties to both communities. While they are not as likely to be counted as part of a formal sister church program, such congregations are perhaps just as likely to imbibe the partnership approach to mission and to form sustained faith-based relationships at the grassroots level.[16] The growing ranks of Christian communities that reject a civic/bureaucratic model of organization have managed to find other ways to form meaningful and enduring international connections.[17] And even congregations that are denominationally affiliated often circumvent these channels in their missional connections in favor of informal networking.

While umbrella institutions sometimes lend stability to congregation-to-congregation relationships, informal networks and ad-hoc arrangements are perhaps just as effective in generating and maintaining these relationships. Of the twelve Washington, DC–area congregations, three were congregational in polity (Baptist), three were connectional (Presbyterian), and six were hierarchical (Roman Catholic and Anglican). The Anglican parishes, however, imbibed a congregational ethos rather than a hierarchical ethos in their collective identity; two of the three Anglican pastors reported that evangelical identity was more salient in their congregations than Anglican identity, and all three identified a fluid and nonauthoritarian leadership structure within the Anglican bodies to which their parishes belonged. As far as sister church relationships in particular were concerned, almost all of the partnerships operated nearly independently from denominational hierarchies. All but one congregation partnered with congregations in the same ecclesiastical tradition, and denominational networks usually helped bring the sister congregations together. For most, the reverse was also true: partnerships were conceived as tools to build a sense of shared identity among dispersed members of a particular tradition. Church traditions played a networking and sometimes theological role in the relationships, but they did not play a governing role. Beyond the structures of leadership within each congregation, church polity factored little in the administration of sister church relationships.

What sociologists of American religion have termed "institutional isomorphism" and "de facto congregationalism" are relevant trends in this regard. Institutional isomorphism refers to a general process of modeling that leads to convergence over time. Because institutions that copy the dominant organizational model in a given field have a competitive advantage and enhanced organizational legitimacy, over time organizations that perform similar functions will come to progressively resemble each other.[18] Based on this idea, Stephen Warner contends that in the United States, where the dominant model of religious organization is Protestant denominationalism, we see an "institutional bias of religion toward affectively significant associations under lay and local control."[19] De facto congregationalism implies that the local religious community is made up of those who choose to assemble together rather than by geographic units assigned by authorities, on which the parish concept is based. According to Warner, religious groups across the spectrum have been swept up by this centrifugal force in American religion, especially since World War II.[20] As a result, there is increasingly less variance in functional polity among religious bodies in the United States, a trend to which the sister church relationships in this study testified.[21]

Ideological Orientation

De facto congregationalism also implies that congregations in the United States are increasingly based on shared affinities or niches rather than geography or denominational identity. Although race, class, life cycle, and other demographic factors can be the source of these shared affinities, niche congregations can also be based on a common purpose or outlook.[22] How a congregation interacts with its outside environment can be constitutive of congregational identity. Indeed, de facto congregationalism implies that niche congregations can be formed out of a common commitment to mission. A commitment to mission is not necessarily a conservative or evangelical value. Mainline Protestant groups, for example, are just as likely to send out short-term volunteer teams as are conservative Protestants.[23] While they may define *mission* differently, congregations from across the spectrum could be considered missional.

Based on their study of congregations' involvement in their community through the Church and Community Project, Carl Dudley and Sally Johnson identified five types of congregational self-images vis-á-vis the rest of the world. The pillar church is guided by a sense of civic responsibility, and members see themselves as pillars in the geographic community and responsible for its well-being. The pilgrim church sustains members—who often represent a particular cultural group—as a community in their collective journey. The survivor church is also internally focused, reacting to crises in an overwhelming world and telling stories of the storms the church has weathered. The prophet church and the servant church, by contrast, are outwardly focused—the prophet church seeking to challenge the evils of the world in a bold and often entrepreneurial way and the servant church helping others quietly in modest, nonpolitical ways.[24]

Although the profiled congregations did not conform neatly to these ideal types, they tended to be outwardly focused with affinities to the servant church—and, to a lesser extent, the prophet church. With the exceptions of Third Presbyterian and Our Lady of Sorrows, the congregations shied away from political activism and controversial social issues in general, preferring to focus on felt needs in their congregations, local communities, and sister churches. Yet, each of the congregations imbibed a strong sense of responsibility to the world outside its walls. In many of the congregations, members described their churches as being "mission minded" or having an "international outlook." This characteristic was central to the collective identity of several congregations and a source of pride to many members. At Living Faith Anglican, for example, informants reported that the congregation's special connection to Rwanda was a focal point of congregational life.[25] In a description of her congregation, Victory Baptist's board of missions chair, Anita Wallace, boasted that "we are very focused on the spiritual and physical needs of others here." Trinity Anglican parishioner Gini Axelrod described Trinity's approach to mission as "enthusiastic and wide-reaching."

Beyond this missional outlook, congregations varied widely in their theological and social/political proclivities. Trinity and Christ the King Anglican were highly conservative congregations both theologically and socially. Members of Third Presbyterian, on the other hand, tended to be highly liberal in both arenas. The other congregations gravitated more to the middle of the spectrum. The pastors at Mount Shannon and Kensington Woods Presbyterian described their congregations as "moderate" within the mainline Protestant family. Members tended to espouse progressive theology while maintaining a permissive and philanthropic, yet precritical approach to social issues and action. Parishioners from the African American Baptist congregations generally maintained an evangelical theology alongside a progressive social agenda, a posture typical in the Black Church. Saint Mariana of Jesus and Saint Clement were "Vatican II" parishes, reformist-minded yet well within the mainstream of American Catholicism. As a Jesuit parish, Our Lady of Sorrows was a bit more progressive on the whole, prioritizing social justice to a greater degree than Saint Mariana and Saint Clement within its parish life. Finally, the majority of the members of Living Faith Anglican might be described as "new evangelicals." While continuing to embrace the biblicist, crucicentrist, conversionist, and evangelistic tenor of mainstream American evangelicalism, Living Faith parishioners were also passionate about social justice.[26]

A second typology, articulated by David Roozen, William McKinney, and Jackson Carroll in *Varieties of Religious Presence*, helps explain the ideological diversity among congregations that embrace a similar model of mission. Roozen, McKinney, and Carroll identify four ways in which congregations—Protestant, Catholic, and Jewish—relate to their context and live out their sense of how the faithful are called to live in the world.[27] The typology cuts across two dimensions: whether a congregation is "this worldly" or otherworldly and whether it is "member centered" or "publicly proactive." All of the congregations profiled in this study were more publicly proactive than they were member centered. Yet, along the "this worldly" versus otherworldly continuum, congregations could be found at widely different points. As the next chapter will explore in greater detail, the sister church model of mission is flexible enough to suit various purposes. For different reasons, it appeals to traditionalists and progressives, liberals and conservatives alike.

Perhaps differences between "this worldly" and otherworldly, otherwise known as liberal versus evangelical, are to some degree bridged or transcended by phenomena like sister church relationships. In most of the profiled relationships, both spiritual solidarity and social action on behalf of the oppressed were prominent aspects of the partnerships. Whether they viewed Christianity as the one true religion with exclusive claims to salvation or simply a useful metaphor for connecting to the sacred, members of participating churches prayed for and worshiped with members of their sister churches abroad. Whether they believed that this world is all there is or that this world is weigh station for the next, participants worked to meet the physical needs of their friends across the ocean. Whether they belonged to the Catholic, mainline, evangelical, or Black Church traditions, participants attempted to treat members of their sister churches as partners and equals.

The popular two-party thesis used to explain the American religious landscape of recent decades maintains that regardless of ecclesiastical affiliation, Americans are polarized into two camps: the conservatives, or orthodox, who stress individual responsibility and right belief and the liberals, or progressive, who stress social responsibility and the relativity of belief.[28] According to this bipolar schema, the two groups are bitterly and increasingly divided, the differences between them eclipsing all other types of ideological divisions. However, a growing body of literature suggests that the so-called culture wars have been overblown and perhaps even outmoded. In the pews, people tend not to identify with camps or parties but instead hold blended views on a variety of issues. According to the National Congregations Study, nearly 30 percent of congregations and 40 percent of members describe themselves as "right in the middle" between liberal and conservative.[29] The epistemology of modernity forces a choice between text and experience, revelation and science, propositionalism and expressivism. As the philosophy of the modern period breaks down in the contemporary milieu, a plane beyond these dichotomies of the liberal/fundamentalist schema has begun to appear.[30] Religious identity is ever more fluid and rationalism ever de-emphasized in favor of embodied knowing.[31] In this context, communities of Christians in various traditions are emphasizing a "holistic gospel," which marries social justice and personal piety. The sister church movement caters to these sentiments. While sister church relationships can be found among congregations that could be described as either conservative or liberal, their preferred habitat is congregations that don't fit neatly into either category.

## Leadership

While all of the profiled sister church programs were governed intracongregationally, within this structure were various leadership models. In each of the African American congregations, the pastor was almost single-handedly responsible for initiating, maintaining, and steering the international partnership(s). Laypeople were commissioned to assist at his discretion. By contrast, most of the other sister church programs were administered in committee by decentralized leadership, with or without the active participation of the congregation's lead pastor.

In cases such as Kensington Woods Presbyterian, the pastor played an active role in the relationship, but did so alongside the sister parish committee. Pastor Ruth Eaton, the chief architect of Kensington Woods's sister church relationship, had participated in each of Kensington Woods's delegations to Kenya. However, Kensington Woods's partnership committee and global intern were responsible for most of the details of the relationship. Likewise, Living Faith Anglican's rector, Dave Rice, was cooperatively involved in the administration of Living Faith's relationship with Murambi Parish in Rwanda. Rice enjoyed a close friendship with Pastor Fabi Gataraiha from Murambi and several other Rwandans. Still, he reported, Living Faith's Cross-Continental Partnership Council "are the ones who really drive this relationship." For example, it was not until the day of Living Faith's annual church retreat that Rice found out Pastor Fabi was coming to the event.

In still other cases, the head pastor was only tangentially involved with the sister church relationship. Third Presbyterian's senior pastor, Robert Hamilton, explained, "I have only really been involved in the Cuban relationship to the extent that I am asked to get involved." Similarly, at Christ the King Anglican, rector Peter Russell remarked that his congregation's relationship with Nueva Jerusalén has little to do with him and would likely continue even without his blessing.

At all three of the Catholic parishes, the pastor played only a minimal role in the sister parish relationship. At Saint Clement, sister parish leadership was helmed by Saint Clement's director of social concerns, whereas for the other Catholic parishes, volunteers were chiefly responsible for maintaining the partnerships. Our Lady of Sorrows and Saint Mariana of Jesus both had a staff person appointed to help oversee the sister parish relationships. At Our Lady of Sorrows, John DiGiovanni, serving a two-year term as the parish's social justice minister through Ignatian Volunteers, was the staff liaison to the Parish to Parish Committee. At Saint Mariana of Jesus, Diego Rodríguez, interim associate pastor and a Central American native, was appointed to a similar role. In each of these cases, however, it was the volunteer-led sister parish committee that was chiefly responsible for the relationship.

Leadership plays a crucial role for organizational success. Most thriving sister church relationships in the study, from the vantage point of the North American partners, were administered communally and empowered by lay leadership. When leadership *within* each congregation mirrored the broader designs of the relationship *between* the partner congregations—to promote mutuality—administration tended to function more smoothly and participation was stronger than if a more centralized and authoritarian structure were in place.[32]

Pastoral involvement, when collaborative and advisory rather than controlling, lent stability and prominence to the relationship within congregational life. Kensington Woods and Living Faith, congregations that enjoyed thriving and far-reaching sister church relationships, governed their sister church relationships by committee but enjoyed encouragement and input from the head pastors. Trinity Anglican rector Craig Mora played a more central role in Trinity's sister church relationship, largely because the small size of the congregation limited the development of elaborate organizational structures. Mora's deferential leadership style, combined with his strong popularity within the congregation and the vestry's active role in congregational affairs, muted the centralized leadership structure at Trinity Anglican, resulting in a sister church relationship marked by high levels of enthusiasm and lay involvement.

Congregations in which pastoral involvement in the sister church relationship deviated significantly from this collaborative role tended to have more handicaps. Pastoral leadership was strong in each of the African American Baptist congregations. Conflict or dissent was not pronounced in any of these congregations, but international partnerships were programmatically thin, largely uncritical in approach, and lacking in lay participation. Likewise, at Mount Shannon Presbyterian, where Pastor Henry Hunt was the central leader in the sister church relationship, congregational participation was also minimal. Partly because pastoral leadership is generally expected to be strong in African American congregations, Pastors Morris, Barclay, and Brown did not face opposition to their agenda with regard to the congregations they supported internationally. At Mount Shannon, on the other hand, where more democratic governance was expected, some informants expressed dissatisfaction with Hunt's strong leadership style and agenda.

Too little pastoral involvement also presented a barrier to smooth and generative sister parish relationship administration in some cases. At Our Lady of Sorrows, twinning committee members expressed frustration that the sister church relationship enjoyed little attention or promotion by the pastoral staff. Several pointed hopefully to the recent appointment of a new pastor with a reputation as a crusader for social justice, anticipating that his leadership might breathe new life into Our Lady's sister church relationship. At Saint Mariana of Jesus, the sister church relationship floundered because of ineffective, transitory, and conflicted leadership. In the eyes of several members of the sister parish committee, Saint Mariana's pastor saw the relationship as little more than an outlet for monetary giving, and its associate pastor who was appointed to help steer the relationship had very little enthusiasm for the initiative. One member described Pastor Peter Krakishaw's involvement in the relationship as both too little and too much—too little support and encouragement and too much input without knowing the dynamics of the relationship.

In cases in which minimal pastoral involvement did not appear to dampen the successful functioning of the sister church partnership, strong advocates for the relationship were still important. Whether they were other staff members or laypersons in the congregation, leaders were crucial in generating enthusiasm, developing a common agenda, and stabilizing congregations' participation in sister church relationships. Whatever their station, these leaders in functioning sister church relationships embodied what students of organizational leadership call the "transformational" style of leadership. Marked by charisma, inspirational motivation, intellectual stimulation, and individual consideration, their leadership style empowered parishioners and helped generate a shared sense of purpose.[33] Within the Washington-area churches, functional sister church leadership was generally decentralized in structure and transformational in style.

## Profiles of Individuals: Catalysts, Champions and General Participants

### Leaders

Within both centralized and decentralized organizational structures, individual leaders perform important roles. If organizations are too decentralized, it is difficult to develop a common purpose, to communicate effectively, and to garner sustained attention for a particular initiative. In their description of decentralized organizations, Ori Brafman and Rod Beckstrom identify "catalyst leaders" who transfer ownership, responsibility, and a shared sense of vision to others, and "champion leaders" who emerge to promote and carry out new ideas within the organization.[34] Catalyst and champion leaders were identifiable in each of the profiled sister church relationships, no matter the organizational structure. These roles were sometimes filled by pastors, while in other cases they were filled by other staff persons, members of partnership committees, charismatic parishioners, or even relative outsiders.

#### Catalyst Leaders

Catalyst leaders were often people who were connected to the congregation without being insiders—immigrants, international students, missionaries from the global South, or other transnational figures chief among them. They bridged oceans and cultures by personally connecting global southerners and North Americans—both logistically and symbolically. Turning the "other" into "one of us" by their presence in their congregations, they helped pave the way for partnership by transferring ownership and creating a sense of shared identity.

Many of the catalyst leaders in the profiled partnerships were immigrants from the global South. More than twenty-five million global southerners, most of whom are Christians, have immigrated to the United States since legislation changed dramatically under the Immigration and Nationality Act in 1965.[35] Immigrants have altered the social composition of American congregations, especially in recent years. In their survey of American congregations, for example, the National Congregations Study investigators found that predominantly white and non-Hispanic congregations were measurably more ethnically diverse in the late 2000s than in the late 1990s. The number of people in congregations with no immigrants decreased from 61 percent in 1998 to 49 percent in 2006–2008. And the number of people in completely white and non-Hispanic congregations decreased from 20 percent to 14 percent in the same time period.[36] While many new immigrants worship in immigrant congregations, enough worship in predominantly white, native-born congregations to significantly diversify such congregations.

Most of the profiled congregations included post-1965 immigrants. And in several cases these immigrants played key roles in the congregation's sister church relationship. At Saint Clement, the very idea of exploring a sister parish relationship started with a Haitian immigrant within the congregation, Bernadette Bellemy. Bellemy's persistence was largely responsible for the formation of Saint Clement's relationship with Sacré-Coeur, and her passion inspired the participation of many of her fellow parishioners. At Saint Mariana of Jesus, a Congolese immigrant teamed up with a fifth-generation Mexican American to initiate the sister church relationship. At Mount Shannon Presbyterian, it was political exiles Priscilla and Charles Spencer who initiated the sister church relationship. Natives of Liberia but members of Mount Shannon Presbyterian for fifteen years while receiving asylum in the United States, the Spencers encouraged Mount Shannon to link with Bensonville Presbyterian and the Carysburg Mission. When Christ the King Anglican's relationship with Nueva Jerusalén began, the rector's wife—who was a Nicaraguan refugee—heightened the congregation's attraction to Nicaragua and desire to forge a sister church relationship. Victory Baptist's partnership with Ebenezer Baptist in Jamaica also resulted from an immigrant connection. Since Victory's pastor, Milton Barclay, was a Jamaican immigrant, he was approached by the Foreign Bureau of the Progressive National Baptist Convention to assist with mission efforts in Jamaica. Once the initial connection was forged, Barclay was keen to draw his congregation into a more sustained relationship with Ebenezer Baptist in part because of his own ties to Jamaica.

At Trinity, Living Faith, and Christ the King Anglican, other types of what Peggy Levitt calls "transnational villagers" served as catalysts of sister church relationships.[37] Living Faith Anglican was drawn into the Anglican Mission in America and, by extension, their sister church relationship with Murambi Parish, because of rector Dave Rice's "deep respect" for leaders of the Anglican Church of Rwanda like Bishop John Rucyahana and Archbishop Emmanuel Kolini, both of whom traveled extensively in the United States and met face-to-face with Rice on several occasions. Christ the King Anglican became the worshiping community of two Tanzanian priests during their time in the United States as seminarians in the mid-1990s. Both of these men later became bishops in the Anglican Church of Tanzania, and Christ the King supported their work financially. According to Christ the King's rector, Peter Russell, the congregation's friendship with these Tanzanian priests warmed their hearts to the idea of becoming a "missionary outpost" of an African church through the Anglican Mission in America. The friendships also evolved into long-term financial support for both dioceses that the Tanzanian bishops oversee. And while the Tanzanian priests provided no direct linkage to Christ the King's sister church relationship with Nueva Jerusalén in Nicaragua, respondents from Christ the King speculated that the congregation's positive interaction with the Africans in their midst generated enthusiasm for international connections in general. Similarly, Trinity Anglican parishioners were drawn into a relationship with the Cathedral Church of Saint James in Uganda by becoming acquainted with its provost, Paul Wamboga, who visited Trinity on numerous occasions while a doctoral student in the United States. A conservative, all-white, rural Virginian congregation composed mostly of retirees, Trinity Anglican's partnership grew out of a relationship with Wamboga rather than any sort of postcolonial ethos within the congregation. Senior warden Earl Henderson explained that Trinity's exposure to Wamboga helped Trinity members see Africans in a new light and piqued their interest in cross-cultural relationships.

All of the immigrants, international students, exiles, or other transnational figures that were influential in these sister church relationships were rich in social capital and cross-cultural fluency. Immigrants such as Bernadette Bellemy, Milton Barclay, and Felix Mapanje, a leader at Kensington Woods Presbyterian, had been in the United States for decades. All three were well educated and well connected, both in their native countries and in the United States. Similarly, asylum-seekers Priscilla and Charles Spencer were well-endowed members of a prominent Liberian family with a dense web of international relationships and experiences. The African Anglicans who forged connections with American congregations during their studies or missionary ventures in the United States also enjoyed high levels of social capital and cultural proficiency in both the United States and their home countries. Trinity parishioner Edward Francis explained: "Paul Wamboga has lived within the American culture. He is not isolated from it; he does understand. That makes it easier for us to express our thoughts and ideas."

Like the immigrants, all of the sojourners from the global South who were in the United States temporarily spoke English fluently, had established powerful international connections, had become familiar with American culture, and were themselves persons of influence.

Not just global southerners traveling in North America but also North Americans traveling in the global South helped catalyze sister church relationships. Father John Mountford's summer sabbatical in El Salvador in the mid-1980s served as the impetus for Our Lady of Sorrows' relationship with María Reina de la Paz in San Salvador. Mountford's stories inspired the Our Lady of Sorrows parish to take action in war-torn El Salvador. The relationships he formed with individuals from María Reina de la Paz blossomed into a sister church relationship between his parish and theirs. At Trinity Anglican, Reverend Craig Mora had previously traveled to several locations in the global South with a parachurch mission agency. Returning to his congregation, he passed on his excitement for mission and passion for forming relationships with Anglicans in other parts of the world. While these native-born North American catalyst leaders did not bring the global South into their congregations in the same way as immigrant leaders, they did help their congregations identify with Christians in other regions of the world.

### Champion Leaders

In addition to serving as catalyst leaders, immigrants also functioned as champion leaders and long-term intermediaries in several instances. At Kensington Woods Presbyterian, Malawian immigrant Felix Mapanje chaired the orphan care program that Kensington Woods facilitated to help the Limuru Mission Area in its ministry to vulnerable children. Mapanje served three summers as a global mission intern for Kensington Woods, each term spending several months in Kenya as an intermediary between Kensington Woods and Limuru and organizing Kensington Woods's month-long delegation to Kenya. Mapanje explained that much of his role was "to bring some of the thinking of the Kensington Woods congregation to our friends and brothers and sisters in Limuru." Conversely, Mapanje believed that his African background helped him better understand Kensington Woods's Kenyan partners. While he maintained that there was a strong level of trust between the two communities, he conceded that miscommunication was always a risk because of cultural differences. Mapanje saw himself as mitigating this risk as an interpreter and translator. "I can relate very well to the people there, and they feel that I can be in the position to tell our friends here exactly how they feel. I can help everyone understand each other."

Like Mapanje, Bernadette Bellemy and Milton Barclay were also champion leaders, promoting the sister church relationship within their

American congregations and helping sustain the relationship through their ability to communicate cross-culturally and build trust between the communities.

Many other champion leaders, although they were not migrants with multinational identities, had significant cross-cultural experience. Committee chairpersons or other de facto project leaders usually had extensive international travel experience, and many had a professional background in international development. Ricardo Flores, chairperson of Saint Mariana of Jesus' sister parish committee, was a senior-level officer at a Catholic relief and development organization. Both Kevin Marino and Janice Thompson, the chair and the co-chair of Our Lady of Sorrows' Parish to Parish Committee, had doctoral degrees in international development and worked in that field for the US government. Living Faith's sister church committee president, Aaron Thomas, as well as several other members of the committee, were also federal employees working in international development. Third Presbyterian's committee head, Gloria Feinburg was a former Peace Corps worker with thirty years' experience in international business as a congressional aid. At Kensington Woods, Pastor Ruth Eaton had formerly served as a long-term volunteer in Africa, and Felix Mapanje worked for the International Monetary Fund. Pastor Henry Hunt at Mount Shannon had previously served as an agriculturalist in Africa, and social concerns director Kimberly Cook had a graduate degree in Catholic social teaching and extensive experience in international mission. Besides the African American congregations, only Christ the King Anglican was steered by leadership with no direct experience in international relief, development, or mission.

Participants

In the profiled congregations, most of the participants were relatively well endowed in social capital, discretionary resources, and cross-cultural exposure.[38] All of the interviewees from the African American congregations were black. Of the forty-six participants interviewed who attended the other congregations, three were black, two were Hispanic, one was Asian American, and forty were white. Four of these six people of color belonged to ethnically heterogeneous Catholic parishes, and all were highly assimilated into North American culture.[39] A disproportionate number of participants were older than fifty, while there was also a sizable number who were younger than thirty-five.[40] Many participants were single and/or childless, and several were empty-nesters; very few had dependents living at home. Of the handful of delegation members who were parents of minor children, in two cases their children were teenagers who were also part of the delegation. Men and women were represented in approximately equal numbers, although in the African American congregations most of the volunteers were women. While most participants were well-educated professionals, many were in flexible employment situations—students and retirees chief among them, along with teachers and self-employed contractors. These characteristics suggest that discretionary time was an important factor in participation, specifically for project leaders but also for anyone who traveled overseas. Discretionary income also seemed to be relevant to delegation participation, especially since most delegation members paid much, if not all, of their expenses. Just as congregations on the wealthy end of the spectrum are more likely to be involved in sister church relationships, so too, perhaps, are wealthier individuals.[41]

Besides discretionary time and money, experience was an important factor in participation. Most delegation members had previously traveled outside of North America, if not to the global South. A large number were employed in the fields of international development, medicine, social work, or other helping professions. In some churches, especially those with a project-centered approach to their sister church endeavors, delegation members were recruited specifically for their skills or expertise. Participants also self-selected on the basis of experience. Saint Clement's annual sister church delegation generally centered around medical missions. Health-care professionals—sometimes joined by educators, engineers, or construction managers—spearheaded the delegation's service trips. At Mount Shannon Presbyterian, Pastor Henry Hunt hand-selected members of the fact-finding delegation based on their professional expertise.

Within most of the congregations, sister church initiatives, once started, were driven by the efforts of a small group of people within the congregation. "For better or for worse," said Pastor Robert Hamilton of Third Presbyterian, "that is just how congregations work." Especially in larger congregations, many informants described those involved in the sister church relationship as a subculture within the congregation. Oftentimes members of these groups shared similar interests and demographic characteristics. When participation expanded beyond a cadre of experts or a clique of friends, however, sister church programs were generally more resilient and robust. Certainly, many congregations found it helpful for people with professional competencies in international development and/ or medicine, education, and other social services to be involved in their sister church relationships. These people helped their congregations think critically about goals and practices, and they lent insights as well as skills to projects. But, as many of these same experts were quick to assert, sister church relationships are qualitatively different from secular relief and development projects. And in many cases, furthering development projects and achieving measurable results were not the chief concerns of partnership initiatives. As the next chapter will detail, sister church relationships are generally designed to bring about relationships of solidarity between people of faith at the grassroots level. In this schema, homemakers, retirees, pastry chefs, college students, and physicists can be just as critical to effective sister church relationships as doctors, pastors, and humanitarian aid workers.

## Participants' Motivation

As the next chapter will explore, congregations involved in church partnerships embrace collective action frames to inspire and propel their sister church relationships.

The ideologies for collective action frames often help motivate individuals to participate. But this is not always the case. As Gary Marx and Douglas McAdam explain, ideology offers only a partial explanation for behavior. Individuals can be involved in a group phenomenon without a strong commitment to the ideology that undergirds that phenomenon. And for many people, ideology functions retrospectively; it flows out of participation rather than leading to participation, and it justifies action that has already taken place.[42] Moreover, individuals may not be fully aware of their motives, or their rhetoric surrounding their motives may not be completely honest. Volunteer motivation is a complex phenomenon in which ideology, altruism, perceived personal benefits, and social-structural factors all play a role.[43]

To shed light on the complexities of the volunteer impulse, Marx and McAdam identify two types of individual motivators for participants in social movements: individual characteristics and social-structural conditions.[44] Individual characteristics are psychological factors such as personality type, personal history, level of life satisfaction, interests, values, and outlook on life. Social-structural conditions, on the other hand, are the ways in which the social organization of a person's life may encourage or discourage participation. Social-structural factors include life-cycle stages and other demographic factors, as well as access to social capital and other resources.

Individual Factors

The previous sketches of leaders and participants in the profiled sister church relationships illuminate many common individual characteristics that inspired participation. Most participants had prior international travel experience and enjoyed interacting with and learning about people from other cultures. Many had previously participated in mission projects and been enriched by such experiences, and a good number worked professionally in international development. When asked why they became involved in their congregation's sister parish relationship, respondents frequently mentioned a love of travel, a personal interest in mission, a desire to "reach out" or "serve," or an aspiration to use professional skills or background in a volunteer context.

Religious or cultural tourism factored prominently in respondents' attributions for their involvement. Teenagers and young adults who participated, especially those who visited their sister church, often referenced a curiosity about the setting of their sister church. "I had never been to Africa," said Justin Hahn, a twenty-five-year-old member of Living Faith Anglican. "I always wanted to go any place on the continent. But Rwanda was my top choice. I was specifically drawn to the narrative of that country. With that being in the back of my mind, it was very appealing to join Living Faith's delegation to Rwanda."

Older participants often referenced a sense of curiosity as well, though their curiosity tended to be more targeted. Eleanor Banks, a seventy-four-year-old college Spanish instructor, explained that part of her inspiration to join one of Third Presbyterian's delegations to Cuba was that "Cuba was one of the countries that I had never been to, and obviously there are some unique reasons for wanting to travel there." Similar sentiments were voiced by numerous respondents, some of whom added that they were interested to see how their cohorts in other parts of the world practiced the Christian faith. In the words of Aaron Thomas from Living Faith,

I liked the idea of being a mission church of Rwanda. The shift from the First World sending missionaries to the Two Thirds World sending people to us is exciting. But on a day-to-day basis, it didn't mean anything to me or the rest of the congregation because it was happening on such a macro level. So part of the desire was just to get to know these people. Who are these people who stood up to the Archbishop of Canterbury and said, "We don't care if you don't give us money. We aren't threatened by poverty; we have that already."

Especially but not exclusively for realigned Anglicans like Thomas, there was something captivating and exotic about the faith of Christians in another part of the world that drew them into relationship.

A second theme that was commonly expressed by respondents was a general pull toward philanthropy. "Outreach to others is where I've always felt called," explained Milton Estelle, chair of Kensington Woods's sister church relationship, who has dedicated countless hours of service to Kensington Woods's local and international mission efforts over the years. Similarly, Olivia West of Mount Calvary Baptist related: "I got involved in the missions ministry because I like helping people. It is my gift, or so I found out later when I took a test on spiritual gifts."

Like Milton Estelle and Olivia West, many participants expressed a desire to give of themselves for the sake of others.

Third, a good number of people became involved in sister church relationships at least partially because they wanted to apply professional skills in a religious or volunteer context. Several participants who worked for large governmental or nonprofit agencies expressed a desire to work on a micro level—wherein they could interact with partners personally and perhaps even see tangible change—rather than administer colossal and depersonalized programs. At the micro level, several respondents explained, results are more visible and rewards are more tangible than at the macro level. Aaron Thomas from Living Faith Anglican put it this way:

> My job is in international development, but it is mostly emailing spreadsheets and the like. Like most people in this city who work on development issues, there is a real distance from the people. So, the stuff I do with the Rwandans is much more gratifying, and I feel like I have a chance of making a much greater impact at a much higher level than in what I do during the week.

Correspondingly, other professionals who applied their vocational skills in sister church settings commonly mentioned that it was gratifying to use their skills in situations in which they were so badly needed.

Participation in congregation-to-congregation relationships, for many individuals, was also a product of identity negotiation. As William Gamson notes, "Participation in social movements frequently involves enlargement of personal identity . . . and offers fulfillment and realization of the self."[45] The quest for personal fulfillment and self-realization goes hand-in-hand with the American therapeutic ethos in which participants were steeped. Several respondents reported that they were looking for an opportunity for spiritual or personal growth. Whether they were students with a thirst for adventure and a budding social conscience, middle-aged adults longing for an escape from tedium or personal tragedy, or retired folks looking for a newfound sense of purpose, participants often recognized that their participation was motivated by a desire for self-fulfillment as much as it was pleasing God or serving others.

## Social-Structural Factors

The profiles of leaders and participants also point to some of the social-structural factors that motivated participation. Like volunteers in general, the participants in congregation-to-congregation relationships were overwhelmingly well educated and endowed with discretionary time and money.[46] However, in any given congregation, social capital was a more salient factor in participation than physical capital. Social networks propelled participation in various ways, such as exposure and social pressure. There is substantial evidence to indicate that those who come into contact with volunteers are more likely to volunteer themselves.[47] In this vein, several respondents first became involved in a sister church relationship because of a friend or family member's participation. For example, Jolene McIntyre noted that she invested in Kensington Woods's relationship because of the transformation she noticed in her daughter, who had previously participated.

> As a teenager, my daughter went on our church's delegation to Kenya twice, and I saw the effects it had on her. It really directed her personal choices and her vocation. She went from being a typical teenager, spending her time shopping, to being a minimalist. Fifteen years later, she still owns only what can be moved in a car—though she no longer owns a car! She also has dedicated her professional life to AIDS prevention in Africa. I saw the changes in her, and I wanted to go too.

Another function of social networks was to encourage or pressure participation. People are much more likely to volunteer if they are recruited and more likely to give if they are directly asked, especially if they share an affective bond with the recruiter. Janice Thompson, a long-time member of Our Lady of Sorrows, explained that, for years, family friends who participated in the sister parish relationship encouraged her to get involved. Because of her professional expertise in international development, Thompson was an attractive recruit. Likewise, participants in various congregations were recruited for their language or professional skills. At Trinity Anglican, Reverend Craig Mora handpicked his congregations' delegation to Uganda.

Because Mora was highly esteemed in the congregation, his suggestion was flattering and persuasive in many cases.

Interpersonal ties or direct appeals from the sister church community also propelled participation. Immigrants from Latin America or Africa often played crucial roles in their sister church relationships, in many cases motivated by a desire to "give back" to their countries or continents of origin. Interpersonal ties forged between pastors or other congregational leaders and corresponding leaders from the global South also propelled participation. Similarly, in their 1995 survey of parish priests, the US National Conference of Catholic Bishops found that according to pastors, personal requests for help were the single strongest motivating factor encouraging people to contribute time, effort, and money to Latin America.[48] Moreover, the third most significant factor undergirding contributions to Latin America, according to parish priests, was interpersonal ties to Latin America.[49]

A third motivation related to social capital was the opportunity for interpersonal bonding. In his groundbreaking study of social capital, *Bowling Alone*, Robert Putnam shows how Americans have become increasingly disconnected from family, friends, neighbors, and democratic structures—a process that has left people feeling isolated and hungry for connection.[50] Part of Putnam's antidote to the decline of social capital is the fortification of religious congregations as civic institutions. As Putnam argues and many participants in my study seemed to intuit, bonding within a group and bridging between groups often go hand in hand. Participants got involved because they wanted to forge stronger personal relationships. More important, relationships were what sustained their participation. Several participants formed strong friendships with cohorts in their sister parishes—friendships that propelled regular correspondence and return trips to their sister parishes. But even for those participants who did not form deep or long-lasting relationships with cohorts in their sister parishes, many did form tight bonds with their fellow parishioners. Participation in a sister church relationship offered the opportunity for congregants to form or nurture various types of interpersonal relationships.

## Conclusion

While the congregations and individual participants were in many ways as diverse as they were numerous, several patterns in participation can be discerned. The profiled congregation-to-congregation programs were decidedly local; denominational or parachurch bureaucracies were unnecessary in their effective administration. Such intermediaries often performed the useful function of resourcing congregation-to-congregation relationships. They served congregations by helping them connect with their partners, determine the mission and vision for their relationships, ascertain best practices, and/or measure effectiveness. Their role was supportive and consultative rather than directive. The sister church programs relied on local congregations and their administrative structures more than on umbrella organizations.

At the congregational level, demography, leadership, and ideological orientation each played a role in how sister church relationships functioned. The congregations with active sister church programs tended to be much larger and wealthier than the national average. Discretionary wealth and an abundance of human capital enabled congregations to invest in their sister church programs. While formal church polity did not have a significant effect on the governance of sister church relationships, leadership structures within congregations, as well as expectations and cultures surrounding authority, were salient matters. Leadership in effectively functioning sister church programs was generally decentralized in structure and transformational in style. In these cases, pastors were usually active or at least supportive of the relationships without being managerial. Catalyst and champion leaders within the congregations, in many cases immigrants or other transnational figures, inspired parishioners to participate and helped sustain sister church relationships through good times and bad. While the presence of "experts" was often helpful, pairing efforts often fared better when the rank and file also became involved.

The congregations fell at various points along the liberal/conservative, progressive/traditional continuum, both sociopolitically and theologically. Beyond having a missional outlook and being "publicly proactive," congregations that participated in functioning sister church relationships did not necessarily share common ideological commitments. However, as the next chapter will explore, their ideological postures did help determine the goals parishioners envisioned for their sister church relationships as well as the way they went about trying to achieve these goals.

The next chapter will consider how congregations defined *effectiveness* with regard to their sister church relationships. The following chapter will discuss whether the twelve congregations approximated success as they defined it. Regardless of how sister church relationships were conceptualized or carried out, however, the organizational structures in which congregational partnership programs operated factored critically in their relationships. From the vantage point of the Washington, DC–area congregations, effective administration was a critical factor in the success of international partnerships.

CHAPTER 5 | Frames

*The Sentiments that Propel Sister*
*Church Relationships*

JUST BEFORE SHE STARTED attending Living Faith Anglican Church, Hailey Beckett, a thirty-year-old journalist and an active participant in Living Faith's relationship with Murambi Parish in Rwanda, had gone on a short-term mission trip to Barbados through her former church.

> During that trip, it became especially clear to me that there is something about traditional mission trips that doesn't jibe with me. I just don't "get" them. I'm always a bit suspicious when you just go somewhere for a couple of weeks and do a few "service projects" or pass out some tracts. You start wondering, *who is this actually for?*

Beckett had previously spent a year serving with AmeriCorps, during which she had come to understand that "you are doing these good things, but really it is mainly for your own character building. Were you really helping people in a significant way? No." Beckett explained that her team's AmeriCorps service was structured in one- or two-month increments in each location before moving on to another site. "Showing love and 'being Christ in the world' is great, but the relationships weren't getting established in a way that was actually building anything. We'd go and meet people and build up a flooded area or something, and then leave. It just felt kind of empty."

Beckett's disillusionment with the predominant patterns and assumptions of both contemporary evangelical mission practices and secular charitable programs propelled her toward Living Faith and its sister church relationship in Rwanda. Beckett could be characterized as idealistic, ambitious, and kindhearted. Her Christian faith inspired her to act for good in the world. But she was also sensitive to many of the pitfalls that have historically accompanied philanthropy. While she wanted to share her faith, she didn't want her witness to be received as coercive or disrespectful. While she wanted to make a positive impact, she sensed that it is long-term, locally initiated projects rather than short-term efforts by outsiders that make a real difference to communities. While she wanted to interact with the poor and marginalized, she was leery of patronizing, objectifying, or doing violence to those she served. And while she wanted to give of herself, she also sensed that human relationships are meant to be reciprocal.

For these reasons, Beckett strongly resonated with the way the Living Faith congregation framed its mission and its sister church relationship. Beckett used the analogy of courtship to describe this sense of resonance. "From the very beginning," she said, "it was like going from dating people here and there in college, to finally investing in a long-term relationship and saying, 'I could marry this person, so I'm going to have to deal with all their quirks and foibles and take the time to actually get to know them.'" Beckett explained that Living Faith's involvement in Rwanda centered around mutual relationships. She believed this focus on long-term, kinlike, reciprocal, loving relationships set Living Faith's model of mission apart from her previous negative experiences.

Hailey Beckett's expressed set of beliefs about the purpose and meaning of mission is an articulation of what social movement theorists call "collective action frames." Beckett's ideas, experiences, and reactions were in many ways her own, but they also tap into a broader trend. The partnership model of mission in general and the sister church phenomenon in particular harness and reinforce the sentiments of Beckett and her like-minded peers, transforming dissatisfaction with popular modes of mission and philanthropy and into a platform for a new course of action.

## Collective Action Frames

Social movement theory provides a helpful lens for understanding why congregations and individuals participate in congregation-to-congregation relationships and what they dream these partnerships will accomplish. In their synthesis of the various strains of social movement theory, Doug McAdam, John McCarthy, and Mayer N. Zald argue that three factors arise out of the literature as most salient to the emergence of social movements: political opportunities, mobilizing structures, and framing processes.[1] This chapter focuses on the third member of the triad: framing processes, or what sociologist Stuart Hall calls "the politics of signification."[2] To study framing processes is to delve into the collective "meaning work," or the production and maintenance of mobilizing ideas and meanings, for movement actors.[3] More specifically, social movement theorists Robert Benford and David Snow define collective action frames as "action-oriented sets of beliefs and meanings that inspire and legitimate the activities and campaigns of a social movement organization."[4] While closely related to ideology, frames are more functional and targeted. If ideology is a fairly pervasive and entrenched set of beliefs and values; frames extend, renegotiate, and direct ideologies to application in particular situations.[5]

Collective action frames are largely constituted by "core framing tasks." As Benford and Snow put it, frames are constructed as "movement adherents negotiate a shared understanding of some problematic condition or situation they define as in need of change, make attributions regarding who or what is to blame, articulate an alternative set of arrangements, and urge others to act in concert to affect change."[6] In other words, movement actors assemble frames by diagnosing a problem, proposing a solution, and inspiring action. In addition to these tasks, actors generate, develop, and advance collective action frames by attending to three processes that can be labeled as discursive, strategic, and contested. Frames are articulated and amplified in the context of wide-ranging and collaborative group discussion, goal-directed action, and conflict negotiation both among members of the movement and between movement actors and its detractors.[7] Perhaps the most salient element of framing processes in general is that they are strategic. Groups of people fashion shared understandings of the world and of themselves that legitimate and motivate collective action through the conscious and strategic efforts of collective action frames.[8]

## Framing Congregational Partnerships at the Macro Level

With regard to the sister church movement, the strategic element of collective action framing is readily apparent in the rhetoric of denominational and parachurch organizations that facilitate or encourage congregation-to-congregation relationships. Literature and interview responses from spokespersons of the sister church movement across the spectrum of American Christianity help illuminate the ideological milieu in which many of the profiled congregations found themselves.

## Solidarity over Charity

One of the most important concepts that frames the discourse on the purpose of sister church relationships at the macro level is solidarity. The general consensus among intermediaries that promote sister church relationships is that these relationships are designed to facilitate friendship and understanding across borders and to minister to human needs in the context of mutuality and respect. Architects of rhetoric at the macro level often reference a shift in mission from a charity-based model, or one-way flow of spiritual and material resources, to a solidarity-based model that relies on mutuality between the partners.

As part of their core framing task, many spokespersons diagnose the problem that the sister church model seeks to rectify as global inequality, caused at least partially by the foibles of colonial mission efforts. If colonial modes of mission fostered paternalistic relationships, undignified treatment of southerners by northerners, and southern dependency on northern handouts, then the sister church model attempts to correct these problems by promoting mutuality and justice in the spirit of solidarity.

From official church teaching—such as the Vatican II documents for Catholics, the Lausanne Covenant for evangelicals, and World Council of Churches proceedings for mainline Christians—to pamphlets published by denominational mission agencies to nonsectarian missiological texts such as David Bosch's *Transforming Mission*, the literature that is used to frame the purpose of sister church relationships highlights the importance of solidarity, or similar concepts, in mission. Under the rubric of communion, accompaniment, partnership, or solidarity, sister-church movement framers at the macro level stress that the model collapses the roles of giver and receiver in mission for the purpose of joint ministry to human needs.

The US bishops' statement, *Called to Global Solidarity*, which the US Catholic Mission Association found was the main document cited as theological motivation for twinning programs in the dioceses they surveyed, specifically lauds sister parish relationships as an example of effective action of behalf of global solidarity.[9] "We welcome 'twinning' relationships and encourage the development of these relationships in ways that avoid dependency and paternalism. These bridges of faith offer as much to U.S. parishes as their partners. We are evangelized and changed as we help other communities of faith."[10]

Defining solidarity as "action on behalf of the one human family, calling us to help overcome the divisions in our world," this bishops' statement makes use of familial metaphors to describe the parity to which sister church relationships aspire. Likewise, many northern proponents of sister church relationships speak of their coreligionists in the global South as "brothers and sisters" in an effort to encourage solidarity, seeking what anthropologists label "fictive kinship," wherein nonrelated persons are given kinship titles and treated as if they were family members.[11]

Yet, as the variety in the literature and interview responses suggests, solidarity is a rather amorphous concept that is sometimes interpreted in competing ways. Specifically, spokespersons and organizations struggle with how to frame the role of material support in congregation-to-congregation relationships. When one party in a relationship is clearly endowed with more capital than the other, how is the value of mutuality actualized?

Parish Twinning Program of the Americas, a Catholic intermediary with the oldest and widest-reaching partnership program on the national scale, answers this question by asserting that the flow of financial and material resources from the northern partner to the southern partner is a secondary goal of sister church relationships. PTPA primarily frames sister parish relationships as fostering the integration of mission and the universality of the Church into the daily experience and expression of faith of Catholics in both parishes. As the organization's literature explains, PTPA specifically chose the word *twinning* to describe their program because it implies mutual entrance into a close relationship. PTPA asserts that it supports both parishes in "developing a mutual and enriching relationship of sharing, solidarity and understanding."[12]

In the midst of this focus on mutuality, a central part of the mission of PTPA is "to serve those in need" in Latin America. The organization is clearly bent on alleviating social problems in Haiti and other Latin American countries. "Through this coming together the twin parishes are joined in their search for an ever-deepening faith and in their struggle to free themselves from the chains of poverty," states PTPA's literature. Trying to delicately balance the sometimes conflicting aims of charity and mutual solidarity, PTPA encourages North American parishes to provide material support for their sister parishes while also aiming to educate North Americans on social justice issues, provide resources for Latin American communities to empower themselves, and respect the complexity and beauty of other cultures.

Denominational agencies that facilitate sister church relationships also wrestle with how to promote mutuality in the context of material inequality. "We focus on relationships more than programs or giving money," said Charles Jones of the International Ministries division of the American Baptist Church. In a brochure on sister church relationships, International Ministries expounds upon this idea:

The desire of North Americans to share from their abundance with those in need is appropriate, even a mandate of Christian obedience. But there are complicating factors. We have become addicted to "checkbook discipleship." In North America we have absolutely no idea what Peter meant when he and John confronted the lame man sitting at the temple gate, saying "I have no silver and gold, but I give you what I have." (Acts 3:6) Our Christian brothers and sisters outside North America have significant gifts—unrelated to silver or gold—to impart to us. Thus, if we view our relation with them primarily as a vehicle for "aid" we may miss the point entirely.[13]

Lamont Koerner from the Saint Paul Area Synod of the ELCA reiterated this notion of mutual giving. While North American participants give of themselves through evangelism, material support, educational efforts, and program development in the context of their sister church relationships, he said, "We really try to discourage the sense of 'we are in this for charity.' We really try to be clear that this isn't about donors and recipients. We are all in the same boat here."[14]

Sister Parish, Incorporated, another leading organization in the field, eschews "charity" altogether out of a sense that it compromises mutuality. North-South financial support is not a constitutive part of the relationships Sister Parish facilitates. In fact, Sister Parish's policy is that no gifts besides photos, audio recordings, and of course friendship be exchanged during delegation visits. The mission of Sister Parish is to foster mutual understanding and commitment to peace and justice among people in the United States and Central America.[15] As founder Richard Fenske explained, Sister Parish aims to create a "personal spiritual crisis" in the lives of North American participants. "Transformation in the person and in the life of the congregation from which they come is the goal."[16] In addition to raising consciousness, Sister Parish embraces a vision of solidarity, reconciliation, and ecumenism. It seeks to help North and Central American Christians confront the "dominant culture of greed and materialism" together and build friendships across cultures.[17] In that spirit, Fenske insists that Sister Parish's northern delegations to Central America are not designed to "fix things" or change Central Americans. Central American partners are just as involved in decision-making as are North American partners, claims Sister Parish. Richard Fenske argues further that North Americans, in effect, get the "better deal" in sister church relationships, since they learn more from Central Americans than vice versa.

## A Distinct Model of Mission

In addition to framing congregational partnerships in the context of solidarity rather than philanthropy, another part of the framing task at the macro level is distinguishing the sister church model from other models of mission, with the "colonial" approach to mission and stand-alone short-term mission trips most pronounced among them. Framers not only point out the foibles of "traditional" modes of mission but also are tasked with articulating an alternative set of norms and arrangements. "General Guidelines for International Partnerships," a document published in 2004 by the Worldwide Ministries Division of the Presbyterian Church (USA), presents a clear example of this framing task at work. Doing mission in partnership, explains the document, entails seeking:

- To answer God's call in mission, *not to serve our own needs by "doing good"*;
- Opportunities for initiatives in mission by any partner, *not one-sided efforts*;
- Mutual respect, *not paternalism*;
- To be independent (self-propagating, self-supporting, self-governing) church partners with a missional vision, *not dependent churches focused on survival*;
- Interdependent partnerships that are of benefit to all partners, *not one-sided dependent relationships*;
- Mutuality, *not one-way mission*;
- Opportunities and recognition for "the least of these," *not exploitation to the benefit of the more powerful*;
- A growing web of partnerships, *not exclusive or private relationships*;
- To meet the holistic needs of churches and people(s), *not serve narrow agendas*;
- Open dialogue, prophetic challenges and mediation of differences, *not coercive or manipulative imposition of solutions*;
- To honor the integrity of the church context, structures and social dynamics, *not to subsidize another's central church life nor exert undue pressure to change or conform*[18]

By pitting the virtues of the partnership model of mission against the foibles of other models, these guidelines help distinguish the model in the missional field.

Spokespersons for congregational partnerships often attempt to further the cause by distancing themselves from colonial mission norms of yesteryear and their residual presence in the contemporary era. Referring to the ELCA's legacy of colonial mission, Mary Campbell explained that the ELCA now acknowledges with sadness that racism and arrogance were built into much of previous mission activity. Yet, thanks to new modes of mission such as companion programs, "what's great is being able to say, 'We're not going to apologize because many good things came out of that, but that's not where we are now.'" Another contrast between colonial mission practices and the sister church model, said Lamont Koerner, is that companion congregation scenarios are focused more on relationships than projects. "There are many unused dams in Africa left over from the colonial era," stated Koerner, referencing spokespersons' desire to avoid making the same mistakes. "Instead of initiating projects that we think people in Tanzania need, we walk alongside them as they initiate their own projects." But more than a shift in how projects are envisioned, Koerner pointed to a shift in the very goals of engagement—from project completion to personal transformation through relationships, both on the part of North Americans and global southerners.

In concert with Campbell and Koerner, Doug Welch from the PC(USA)'s World Mission division noted that Presbyterians are also "trying to rectify some of the mistakes made in the colonial era." Welch continued:

> Life is about learning from our mistakes and moving on. We have moved a long way since the colonial era in a variety of things. And one of the things we do as a denominational agency is work with our congregations and presbyteries to help them gain those learnings from the past, since they don't always have the same opportunity to experience the learning we have at the denominational level.[19]

Patrick Friday of the United Methodist Church agreed:

> The colonial piece looms large and brings concern and fear, which it should. In most places we try to explain to our teams, who haven't been trained in church history, that there is a backdrop to all of this, and some of it is negative. So we have to be very sensitive to these boundaries, these cross-cultural things.[20]

In addition to their critique of colonial norms, spokespersons for the sister church model of mission often distance themselves from the short-term mission movement—even though it is largely through short-term mission trips that sister church partnerships are sustained. Many spokespersons criticize stand-alone short-term mission efforts for lacking appropriate respect for nationals and local culture, for applying quick fixes rather than long-term solutions, for squandering resources, and for promoting paternalistic patterns of cross-cultural interaction. Dan Shoemaker, president of Reciprocal Ministries International, an evangelical parachurch organization in the congregational partnership crusade, traced the birth of RMI to the founders' sense that "short-term mission trips weren't working." Without a long-term mission commitment and a shared history, Shoemaker continued, short-term trips weren't effective in achieving lasting change in Haiti and bringing the US church into meaningful involvement.

Many advocates of congregation-to-congregation partnership claim that, in contrast to the short-term mission model, sister church scenarios foster long-lasting and mutually respectful cross-cultural relationships; promote contextualized and culturally sensitive ministry; tackle social problems with a collaborative, long-range view; and respect the integrity of local Christian communities. Yet, few of these advocates condemn short-term mission trips altogether. Rather, they hope that these trips will become embedded in long-term partnerships. As Doug Welch said, "We recognize that short-term mission trips are often how relationships are built, so we encourage congregations to think of their short-term trips in terms of long-term relationships. And we hope that congregations will begin to invest in a particular community."[21]

## Holistic Christian Mission over Proselytism

Though not all stand-alone short-term mission efforts are designed exclusively as evangelistic crusades, short-term mission efforts are also sometimes critiqued for compartmentalizing the human person by focusing on spiritual needs over against physical needs, and for their perceived coercive proselytizing techniques. Framers of the sister church movement, even those representing more conservative evangelical constituents, tend to eschew short-term evangelistic crusades in favor of holistic and contextualized Christian witness. Charles Jones said he is proud to be involved in partnership efforts on behalf of the American Baptist Convention because of the understanding of mission that informs his agency's work. "We don't see our role as going into developing countries to 'convert the heathens.' We recognize that God is already working in those countries, and we try to participate in what God is doing."[22]

Similarly, Patrick Friday boasted that United Methodists "endorse a holistic approach to mission—word and deed together." International sister church relationships coordinated through the United Methodist Church are often directly evangelistic, and partner congregations are usually located in areas of the world with very small Christian populations. But Friday said the program discourages both "the mentality that you are going abroad and converting people" and "parachute drops" wherein a congregation "sponsors" a pastor with a salary and a building and tells him to fill the church.[23] Instead, the program encourages ministry to the whole person, as well as ecumenism, cultural sensitivity, long-term relationships, and mutual giving and receiving between the congregations in partnerships.

While North American spokespersons for the sister church model tend to be leery of proselytism, most still frame congregational partnerships in directly religious ways. At the macro level, congregation-to-congregation partnerships are generally couched as spiritual, indeed "missional," relationships. Prayer, worship, mission, witness, and fellowship are advanced as key components of sister church relationships by many macrolevel actors. For example, ELCA literature states that the goals for participants in companion congregation relationships are to "be renewed and regenerated by the faith witnesses of Christians of another land and culture; deepen their experiences of being both givers and receivers of encouragement, witness and prayer support; be strengthened and challenged in their mission callings; and be informed of the life and mission of the church outside their own country."[24]

Proponents of sister church relationships also drive home the fundamentally religious nature of sister church relationships by referencing a scene from the biblical book of Revelation, which depicts Christians from all nations and language groups joining together in worship. Just as the Apostle John's vision in Revelation celebrates Christian fellowship across boundaries, so too sister church relationships embrace the unity of the church around the world.

Sister church relationships are designed not only to strengthen Christian bonds within the church but also to answer the call to participate in what ELCA literature describes as "God's mission to redeem the world." "The basis for this *accompaniment*, or what the New Testament calls *koinonia*, is found in the God-human relationship in which God accompanies us in Jesus Christ through the Holy Spirit."[25]

The operative question for sister church framers in this regard is not whether Christians should be engaged in mission but rather how they should be engaged. David Cline, a Lutheran pastor who has become a spokesperson for companion congregation relationships through his doctoral dissertation writes that "increasingly we no longer understand ourselves as the keepers of the Great Commission for the sake of the world but as companions in a shared journey with a shared commission."[26] In like manner, the American Baptist Church endorses sister church relationships as opportunities to "share life and mission with brothers and sisters in another part of God's world" and promises that sister church relationships make "mission come alive in the local church."[27]

The Alliance of Baptists also frames sister church relationships in the context of mission. According to the Alliance's manual for congregational relationships, the basis of partnership for Alliance congregations and their partners in Cuba is "a shared commitment to an enlightened understanding of mission."

> Together we recognize the importance of celebrating trans-cultural experiences that provide the framework for mutual enrichment of our respective journey of faith. We are learning how to share our testimonies of faith with one another and plumb the depths of mutual understanding. We see our missionary work as flowing in two directions. In short, our relationship is one of co-equal partners with no masters.[28]

The "enlightened understanding of mission" touted by the Alliance of Baptists doesn't reject the idea of evangelism altogether. Rather, the Alliance and other advocates of congregational partnerships encourage "doing evangelism in a more holistic sense." These are the words of Stan Hastey, minister of mission and ecumenism with the Alliance of Baptists. Hastey said that Alliance partners in Cuba have helped North Americans understand what evangelistic zeal, "in a good sense, not fire and damnation," looks like. "They bear witness to the living Christ in the most unlikely settings, often at great cost, inspiring us to do the same."[29]

## Friendly Toward Secular Culture, but not Co-opted

Most aspects of the collective action frames that inspire and shape sister church relationships are theologically oriented. However, sister church framers also tap into the wider cultural stock of images and values that inform secular cross-cultural interaction for North Americans. In fact, like many religious movements, sister church advocates often locate detractors within the ranks of the church rather than outside of it. Framers of the sister church movement tend to accept many of the socially liberal values articulated in the public discourse on human/civil rights, multiculturalism, and postcolonialism, even if they do not directly champion these values. Additionally, contemporary secular relief and development efforts, as well as secular cross-cultural exchange programs, are generally positively esteemed by framers of the sister church movement.

Even the term "sister church" makes overtures to Dwight Eisenhower's people-to-people/sister city program established in 1956 to foster human connections and cultural links between inhabitants of paired locales. Sister City International's mission to "promote peace through mutual respect, understanding, and cooperation—one individual, one community at a time" is remarkably similar to the concept of solidarity that serves as the foundation for most congregational partnership programs.[30] The Peace Corps, The Rotary Youth Exchange program, and various other secular citizen networking utilities help supply the sister church movement not only with ideological fodder but also with organizational templates around which to structure sister church relationships. Some congregations' partnerships are even facilitated by secular organizations, such as the SHARE Foundation, whose mission is to support the empowerment of poor and historically marginalized Salvadoran communities.[31] Congregational partnerships facilitated through SHARE illustrate that, although most framers consider the model to be fundamentally religious, values that are not directly religious also inform the movement.

Though sister church framers borrow from the cultural stock of the citizen-networking and international-development agendas, many also distinguish the sister church movement from these efforts. The history of European and North American secular development efforts in the global South in the postcolonial period, they claim, is one of mixed results. Much of the money has been wasted or poured into projects that were not embraced by the local population and thus not well used. And many efforts have had only short-term positive effects. Several framers maintain that grassroots, faith-based, partnership-oriented development efforts like sister church relationships are a more effective means of building a just global society than are secular efforts. According to Mike Vallez, founder of Global Faith Partners, spirituality is crucial to the effectiveness of sister church relationships. "If the failures of global development efforts in the past are to be changed to successes in the future, we must look at ways to tap the better aspects of human nature and spirituality to achieve the positive results we are looking for."[32]

The sister parish model of mission is conceptualized in different ways at the macro level. Some framers see evangelism as the primary goal of sister church relationships; others envision its chief purpose as spiritual friendship; others see it as social change in the global South; and still others view it as a change in consciousness on the part of North Americans. Despite these different emphases, there are strong common themes that run through the literature on the sister church model of mission and are articulated by spokespersons. Congregation-to-congregation relationships, according to framers, are spiritual partnerships, built around the concept of solidarity, designed to bring about personal and communal transformation. As a model, the phenomenon is distinct from secular relief and development initiatives, charity projects, stand-alone short-term mission efforts, and "colonial" modes of mission. It is this distinctiveness that is at the heart of framers' core framing tasks. Framers attempt to inspire congregations to participate in sister church relationships by convincing them that the sister church model is a more effective approach to mission than others in the field.

## Framing Among Participating Congregations

The core framing tasks of spokespersons of the sister church model of mission were reiterated at the congregational level, whether or not congregations officially participated in broader partnership programs. Respondents from the profiled congregations often articulated norms and objectives similar to those articulated by representatives from denominational and parachurch organizations. In general, the more intentional the congregation was about their sister church relationship, the more participants mirrored the frames of movement spokespersons. Leaders and participants at the congregation level championed the value of mutuality, embraced the goal of solidarity, and pitted the sister church model against other approaches to mission and development.

For several congregations, such as Christ the King Anglican, Mount Shannon Presbyterian, and Victory Baptist, sister church relationships were undertaken because of circumstance rather than because of a commitment to a particular model of mission. In most of the congregations, however, project leaders and often participants as well viewed their sister church relationship as the embodiment of a fresh and distinct approach to mission. Like movement spokespersons, they contrasted sister-church relationships with stand-alone short-term mission trips, colonial mission projects, and secular development efforts. Almost all respondents, at least in their rhetoric, embraced the idea of mission as mutual and two-directional, balking at any suggestion that their efforts be marked by paternalism or patterns of dependency. "We aren't going down there to fix their problems," quipped one respondent in a common refrain, "but rather to walk alongside them and offer our hands, hearts, and resources." Almost all respondents reported that their relationship was mutual and reciprocal, even when their description of the dynamics of the relationship betrayed this notion of equality.

## A Typology of Sister Church Relationships by Purpose

Even though almost all respondents at the congregational level maintained that mission is most effectively conducted in the context of relationships and that relationships are most effectively conducted in the context of mutuality, the twelve congregations varied significantly in terms of how their sister church relationships were designed. Typology is a useful analytical frame for understanding the way congregations envisioned their partnerships. As Max Weber noted, ideal types, although incapable of perfectly reflecting the characteristics of any given case, shed light on a larger phenomenon by facilitating comparison and disentangling complex structures and processes.[33] Two continua especially illuminate the framing process among congregations: the trajectory from "this world" to the "other world" and the trajectory from projects to relationships.

### This World Versus the Other World

As the previous chapter explained, the profiled congregations tended to be outwardly focused and mission minded, if loathe to act in controversial or political ways. By Roozen, McKinney, and Carroll's classification scheme, these churches were "publicly proactive" rather than "member centered." Another part of Roozen, McKinney, and Carroll's typology is whether congregations are "this worldly" or "otherworldly" in terms of how they relate to their context; on this score, the profiled congregations differed considerably.[34] Another way to describe this distinction is "evangelical" and "liberal." As R. Stephen Warner differentiates between the two poles, "The core of contemporary liberalism is an attitude toward the world; of evangelicalism, doctrines about God."[35]

Congregations could be found at various points along the "this worldly" versus "otherworldly" continuum, and sister church relationships usually reflected congregational posture on this score. In two of the three evangelical Anglican congregations, most respondents listed evangelism and/or spiritual encouragement as the chief purpose of their congregation's participation in their sister church relationship. "The goal is to provide hope," said Corey Kimsey, delegation leader for Christ the King Anglican, "especially to people who have so little. These people don't have any hope outside of Jesus, so they really need Jesus." At Trinity Anglican, Reverend Craig Mora reported that the central purpose of the relationship was for each community to support each other spiritually and to "enhance one another's ability to bring people to Christ." A group of forty members from the Cathedral Church of Saint James in Uganda committed to pray daily for Trinity parishioners. When delegations from each congregation visited the other, they routinely spoke at revival meetings organized by the host church. By contrast, evangelistic efforts were not central features of the relationships between the Catholic parishes and their partners and the Presbyterian congregations and their partners. These congregations' involvement centered around education, construction, health care, sanitation, or economic empowerment.

Although the congregations differed in how they prioritized and interpreted "otherworldly" and "this worldly" concerns, these differences should not be overstated. For instance, while participants at the evangelical Anglican congregations generally saw evangelism and spiritual enrichment as important goals of their sister church relationships, they also participated in social and economic programs and routinely spoke of "holistic ministry." However, parishioners at the mainline Presbyterian congregations—even at Third Presbyterian, identified by the senior pastor as one of the most progressive in the denomination—often identified "otherworldly" goals in their relationships. Joint prayer, worship, and Bible study were central features of these relationships. While the Presbyterian congregations were loathe to explicitly evangelize, respondents in these congregations often spoke of their participation in the sister church relationship as "bearing witness" to their faith or as part of their own path of Christian discipleship. "The same way that Paul did in the New Testament, I see that when one community of Christians commits to another community of Christians, both of them grow spiritually," said Pastor Henry Hunt. Similarly, respondents from the African American Baptist congregations articulated both "this worldly" and "otherworldly" goals. Construction projects were sponsored to better equip partners to "preach the gospel," while outreach efforts such as shoe drives and training programs were also central to the relationships. While real theological and social differences existed among the congregations, all of the congregations were interested in meeting both the physical and spiritual needs of their own members, members of their sister churches, and the broader community in which both partners were situated.

Perhaps one of the reasons that tensions between "this worldly" and "otherworldly" concerns were rather muted is that, presumably, members of the partnering congregations were already Christians. While many of the Presbyterian respondents and some of the Catholics were leery of trying to "impose" the Christian faith on non-Christians, they were quite comfortable participating in religious activities in conjunction with their coreligionist partners. In many cases, they lent assistance—whether through providing resources or through physically teaching, baptizing, preaching, or praying—to their partner congregations for the purpose of discipleship and catechesis. Likewise, in most cases, Anglican and Baptist congregations focused on equipping and ministering to other Christians rather than entering the thorny territory of cross-cultural evangelism. Whether because they were leery of engaging in evangelism altogether or because they believed that evangelism should be driven by the efforts of local Christians rather than short-term cross-cultural crusades, with the exception of Trinity Anglican the congregations tended to avoid direct proclamation of their faith to non-Christians. Instead, they focused on the spiritual and physical needs of the members of their sister churches and, by extension, the communities in which their partners were situated.

## Projects Versus Relationships

The most important variable that distinguished the sister church relationships from one another was whether the partnership was centered on projects or relationships. While representatives from every congregation gave voice to the value of solidarity in some way, the primacy of building friendship varied among the congregations—as did the degree to which the northern congregations prioritized mutuality. Some congregations focused on the projects they wanted to accomplish in their sister church communities, and they worked to develop respectful relationships with their partners as a means to accomplishing projects more effectively. For other congregations, the interpersonal relationships between members of the two parishes in partnership were seen as ends in themselves.

### Relationships over Projects

One type of sister church relationship gave priority to building mutual relationships over accomplishing projects. Living Faith Anglican Church especially embodied this posture:

From the beginning, we made every effort to avoid a "project mentality" in order to establish the foundational principles of partnership. There are many pitfalls that ignorance, sin, and the devil could open up as brothers and sisters, from radically different contexts, try to walk beside one another. Open, transparent dialogue, and consistent prayer, are critical and can expose much of the potential damage that resource-sharing can cause.[36]

For Living Faith, the relationship with Murambi Parish in Rwanda was first and foremost a matter of Christian friendship and encouragement. For this reason, during the first two years of the partnership, Living Faith concentrated exclusively on building a relationship with their partners. Living Faith began supporting Murambi Parish financially only after the Cross-Continental Partnership Council perceived that a strong foundation of trust and mutuality had been built between the two communities. And even then, the CCPC was careful to fund only modest, targeted projects that the two communities agreed on together after extensive prayer and deliberation.

According to Chris Coulter, assistant pastor at Living Faith, "there is a really strong emphasis in our church, headed by the CCPC, that we can't just go over to Rwanda and throw a bunch of money around, and then say, 'Isn't this great?'" Instead, Coulter continued, "The CCPC emphasize partnership and learning from each other in a reciprocal way. They are very much aware of the power of money and realize that giving a lot of money isn't a good way to approach this type of relationship."

Aaron Thomas, chair of the Cross-Continental Partnership Council added that the committee very carefully tried to avoid falling into the mindset of, "we need you because we want to give, and you need us because you want to receive." While acknowledging that a "huge gap in resources between the two communities" made it difficult to avoid donor/recipient, giver/receiver posturing, Thomas reiterated that both Living Faith and Murambi tried to approach their relationship collaboratively.

Third Presbyterian was another congregation that stood out for its emphasis on building relationships above relief, development, or evangelistic projects. Gloria Feinburg, chair of the partnership committee, explained that because of both practical factors (such as government restrictions and Third's very limited financial resources) and ideological factors (such as the congregation's leeriness of paternalism), the relationship between the two churches centered around "people-to-people connections" rather than money.

I think when money isn't the driving force, you have to get more creative. And from our experience, I would say there are a lot of advantages to the relationship not being about money. I would even say that it is better that way. For Cubans, I don't think what they really want is money. What they really want is to know that they are not alone, that people have not forsaken them, that they are not as isolated as they might feel.

Several other respondents from Third Presbyterian confirmed Feinburg's sentiments.

"Probably as much as anything," said Eleanor Banks about the purpose of the delegation to Cuba in which she participated, "it was just getting to know the parishioners of our sister church, and their Christian feelings, in personal ways . . . allowing us to see a very human side of what they were doing." "The sensory experience of connecting with other people, especially cross-culturally, is very powerful" added Nancy Compton, another member of Third Presbyterian. As these sentiments illustrate, for Third Presbyterian, like Living Faith Anglican, it was the notion of Christian solidarity that most set the tone for the sister church relationship.

### Relationships and Projects in Tension

While the Living Faith and Third Presbyterian communities worried that too much of a focus on projects would compromise the sense of mutuality that they worked so hard to build, most other congregations were less cautious. They valued solidarity but considered it a matter of method more than purpose. These congregations sought to accomplish projects in their sister church community and believed that mutuality and collaboration were effective means of accomplishing projects rather than goals in themselves. As Peter Russell, rector of Christ the King Anglican, explained, "Certainly, solidarity and relationships are very important. But relationships usually don't become very strong if you just go down there and say, 'I'm your friend, and you're my friend.' So, we have various projects as well."

Most congregations did not question *whether* to engage in social or evangelistic projects but rather *how* to engage in them. To one degree or another, they sought to avoid the pitfalls of the sending model of mission and to build egalitarian friendships with their global southern partners. But they also gave money and provided labor or other resources for projects in their sister parish communities such as construction projects, health clinics, educational initiatives, catechesis, evangelistic outreach efforts, microfinance programs, and vocational training. Desiring to carry out projects in the spirit of mutuality and respect, these congregations often emphasized that working cross-culturally among the poor is a matter of social justice rather than charity and that reciprocity is qualitative rather than quantitative. Brian Baker from Trinity Anglican expressed a common sentiment among respondents: "Economically, our relationship with the Cathedral Church of Saint James is one-way. Saint James has a lot of need, and our congregation has been very generous to them. But beyond money, it's equal. We visit each other. We support each other in prayer. We encourage each other."

"Even though the people of Saint James aren't giving money, they are giving in other ways," added fellow Trinity member, Jean Francis. "We try to keep up with *them*! They are incredibly giving people, and they provide tremendous spiritual leadership and support."

Unlike Living Faith Anglican and Third Presbyterian, for most congregations, even those that valued solidarity and reciprocity, supporting the sister parish financially was a key feature of the partnership. John DiGiovanni, social justice minister at Our Lady of Sorrows, explained that Our Lady of Sorrows' primary approach to mission was to give money. Out of a 350,000-dollar annual budget for mission and outreach, Our Lady of Sorrows gave twelve thousand dollars to Reina de la Paz each year. Our Lady of Sorrows is not alone. According to the Center for Applied Research in the Apostate, North-South financial giving is a constitutive part of sister parish relationships. Of US Catholic parishes involved in a sister parish relationship in Latin America, CARA found that 58 percent contributed between one thousand and ten thousand dollars annually to their partners, whereas 10 percent contributed less than one thousand dollars and 32 percent contributed more than ten thousand dollars each year. According to CARA, offering financial and other forms of support—such as providing clothing, food, construction items, educational material, and religious supplies—is the paramount concern of most US parishes involved in sister parish relationships, though many also engage in activities to promote mutuality.[37]

Many respondents from the Washington, DC–area congregations described their priorities in reverse order. Mitch Covington, participant and former mission committee chair at Christ the King Anglican, explained:

> Our relationship with Nueva Jerusalén is not really about money: it's about depth of relationship. They clearly have needs. They recognize that we come from a country that is well-off, and they know that we're a resource for them. They're very willing to ask for financial support, and we're willing to give them what's appropriate. But the relationship is not based on that. In other words, we're just happy to have a connection with them and vise versa and just to deepen the relationship and encourage one another spiritually.

For congregations like Christ the King and others that sought a cooperative relationship yet also chose to contribute money and other resources to
projects in their sister church community, material support was seen as a
complement rather than a barrier to solidarity.

For instance, even though Our Lady of Sorrows members donated a
significant amount of time, labor, expertise, and other resources to countless projects at María Reina de la Paz over the years, Our Lady's sister
parish committee members unequivocally insisted that solidarity, not
charity, drove the relationship. "The purpose of our relationship is building
solidarity, finding commonality, tearing down barriers, sharing stories,
sharing life, and sharing faith," said Susan Travinsky, a long-time participant and former chair of Our Lady of Sorrows' sister parish committee.
"It is not a project-oriented relationship, and it shouldn't be." Travinsky
elaborated:

> We go down and learn from them. They teach us, and we share our reality
> with them and they with us. But it is not a paternalistic, "We're here to do
> something for you." We provide them with a great deal of financial support.
> For instance . . . the preschool would be closed if it wasn't for our financial
> support, so that financial support is vital to them. But they are not interested
> in hearing us say, "This is how we do things. Let us show you how great it
> can be." It's important that it be a relationship that's based on an equal
> footing. It's not an equal financial reality, but in a great many ways they're
> more sophisticated than we are.

Janice Thompson, another committee member, noted that, in different
ways, the two parishes experienced solidarity in the faith in their encounter with each other.

> We've asked the priest at Reina de la Paz, "What is the benefit to you when
> delegations come down?" And he said that for them it is feeling the grace of
> God through us. Everything is difficult for them, so they really appreciate
> the gesture of solidarity on our part. Also, for them the relationship is sus-
> taining, especially financially. But for us, we get to experience solidarity in
> the faith. Solidarity is very strong for them. They are a living example to us
> of community and what loving your neighbor looks like and can do. It is
> quite inspiring to us.

Congregations like Our Lady of Sorrows that imbibed an intentional
approach to mission and regarded mutuality highly, yet also supported and

engaged in projects in their sister church communities, faced a difficult framing task. They sought to distinguish their sister church relationship from the sending model of mission while participating in activities that have long been associated with that model. Several respondents in these congregations were keenly aware that power and money are often connected. Knowing that philanthropic giving could easily jeopardize a sense of reciprocity and equality between the linked congregations, these participants sought to play the role of partners rather than benefactors and commonly differentiated between social justice and charity. "The people of Reina de la Paz are dirt poor," said Kevin Marino, chair of the partnership committee at Our Lady of Sorrows. "But they don't want a paternalistic relationship with us. They don't want to be little brown Americans. They want to decide what to do, with our support. And we recognize and honor that." In conjunction with their partners abroad, leaders like Marino often labored to establish structures of mutual accountability between the two sister parishes and insisted that projects be locally controlled and initiated. By careful selection of vocabulary and attention to structures of power, many congregations maintained that they could give resources to their partners without compromising a sense of solidarity.

*Projects over Relationships*

The tension between solidarity and giving was lost on a few of the congregations.

Their international congregational relationships were driven by programs and oriented around tangible results, and they neither questioned the sending model of mission nor sought to distinguish their efforts from this model. These congregations saw their sister church relationships as avenues for their philanthropy.

Mount Shannon Presbyterian Church was one such congregation. Mount Shannon parishioners did not form personal relationships with anyone at Bensonville Presbyterian beyond Charles and Priscilla Spencer, who had been previous members of Mount Shannon. In fact, the congregation-to-congregation relationship itself was little more than a formality. Mount Shannon concentrated its efforts in the surrounding Carysburg Mission area in Liberia, seeking to aid in various projects there. When Mount Shannon sent a delegation to Liberia, the purpose was strictly reconnaissance for project development. A minority of those who participated in the delegation were members of Mount Shannon; the majority were invited on the delegation because of their professional expertise. Don Lingard, a delegation and committee member, described Mount

Shannon's participation in a sister church relationship as a way to "give back." "To whom much is given, much is expected," he quipped, adding that Mount Shannon's work in Carysburg showed that their congregation is "not just talking, but also walking." Pastor Henry Hunt, who envisioned the relationship as an opportunity for joint discipleship, explained that Lingard's philanthropic approach to the relationship was typical for the Mount Shannon congregation, and indeed the Spencers in Liberia as well. Dissatisfied with how the relationship was framed in his congregation, Hunt considered either discontinuing it or becoming more "autocratic" in its leadership.

Another congregation that emphasized projects over relationships was Victory Baptist Church. Victory Baptist primarily engaged with Ebenezer Baptist by giving money, and respondents referred to Ebenezer with terminology such as "the church we support" rather than "partner" or "sister church." Respondents from Victory Baptist reported that the purpose of their congregation-to-congregation relationship was lending aid to the less fortunate and supporting an under-resourced congregation in its ministry. "We think that we should be our brothers' keeper," explained Lola Evans, Victory's associate minister of evangelism and outreach, expressing sentiments shared by other respondents. Evans added, "If you are blessed, then you need to reach out and bless someone else. Our approach is really to show love, to help people, and to show them the right way."

Building mutual relationships with members of the Ebenezer community was not a priority at Victory. Once Ebenezer's sanctuary had been built, those who served on Victory's mission committee believe they had accomplished their goal and thus shifted their focus to other projects.

Additional Considerations

Besides meeting humans needs and developing relationships cross-culturally with fellow Christians, some congregations had additional goals for their sister church relationships that were not addressed by either the evangelical-to-liberal continuum or the projects-to-relationships continuum. Based on their ethnic composition or theological traditions, some congregations desired to build connections with specific communities with shared affinities to strengthen common bonds. Additionally, while most congregations acknowledged that contributing to the spiritual formation of their own members was a desired outcome of the sister church relationship, some congregations drew special attention to this facet of the relationship.

Because of their very different social location and collective history, African American Christians reckon with a legacy of colonialism and colonial mission in ways distinct from their counterparts of European descent. Seeking to correct the European bias that they believe informs many western Christians' sense of mission, some African American Christians seek to embody an Africentric approach to mission and ministry.[38] "In the broadest sense," explains Ronald Edward Peters, a theoretician of African American spirituality, Africentrism "refers to the practice of examining historical evidence as well as current reality by utilizing pre-colonial black Africa rather than European civilization, expansionism, and colonial activity as the major points of reference."[39] Church Twinning International, a parachurch organization that twins African American congregations in the southern United States with congregations in Africa and the African Caribbean, embraces the Africentric approach to mission. This organization links congregations in order to help African American Christians reconnect to their roots and better appreciate African modes of religiosity.

Despite its important role in the mission and identity of a significant segment of African American Christianity, Africentrism was not a key motif in the partnerships of the profiled African American Baptist congregations. Lawrence Jones, assistant to the pastor at Thirteenth Street Baptist Church, explained that Thirteenth Street's purpose in mission is to "advance the gospel" rather than strengthen cultural ties: "Whether it's from a person of African descent or European descent, the power of the word of Christ is lifting up these communities." Cynthia Adams, chairperson of the board of mission at Victory Baptist, conveyed this sentiment in stronger terms: "If a person is in need, it doesn't make any difference. God doesn't look at who we are, what we are. If we can give in any way, that is how we should give."

Yet, Pastor Clancey Brown of Mount Calvary Baptist, admitted that even though Africentrism is not a formal part of his congregation's vision for mission, he and other members of the congregation gained a better sense of their heritage by strengthening ties to other members of the African diaspora. "This happened to me especially when I went to South Africa," he recalled. "It was a sense of me looking at the mother country and saying, 'I'm part of this.'" Brown also noted that because, as African Americans, members of his congregation knew what it is like to be oppressed, they were careful "not to offend and to come alongside people" rather than trying to control them. He believed that African American

Christians have "raised a flag" to the white gatekeepers of North American evangelicalism with the message: "We don't need you to come in and tell us how to win our own people." Mount Calvary's international congregational relationships provided the congregation with a platform for connecting to coethnics in a culturally sensitive manner.

### Overcoming Cultural and Ethnic Divisions

While it is common for religious communities to reach out to other religious communities on the basis of a shared heritage or ethnicity, some congregations enter into international partnerships at least in part to build connections and heal wounds across cultural and ethnic bounds. Various sociologists of North American religion have pointed out that worshiping communities reinforce ethnicity by providing a common setting in which people of similar backgrounds come together, thereby increasing social interactions among coethnics and providing a space for comfort and belonging.[40] A small percentage of North American Christians are trying to reverse the role of religion in reinforcing ethnic divisions by creating multiethnic congregations. Along the same vein but in a less ambitious way, some of the profiled congregations entered into sister church relationships at least in part to bridge racial, ethnic, and cultural divides. These congregations highlighted the bonds of Christian friendship across economic disparities, geographic borders, and ethnicity with the intent that their parishioners would not only develop a more nuanced global perspective but also begin to understand the various ways that racism and western cultural hegemony have taken their toll on persons of color around the world. Lamont Koerner said that helping American Lutherans make "a change in consciousness" and "develop a global perspective" is the first priority of the Saint Paul Area Synod's Tanzania partnership program. While sister church relationships ideally benefit both parties, in Koerner's mind it is North Americans who are most in need of transformation. Similarly, several of the profiled Washington, DC–area congregations, in addition to various project or relationship-related goals, voiced hope that through their sister church relationships, their own parishioners would see the world and themselves anew.

### Intrachurch Connections

A few congregations sought to strengthen organizational connections or make a political statement through their partnerships. Partners' ecclesiastical affiliation or stance on controversial issues was of little direct consequence to the sister church relationship in most instances. While Presbyterians tended to partner with other Presbyterians and so on, partners were often quite different from each other theologically, politically, and liturgically. Differences in these matters were usually de-emphasized. Even among partners who shared organizational and theological affinities, a common Christian faith and shared humanity were stressed over particular issues.

By contrast, for Trinity Anglican and Living Faith Anglican, a shared theological/political posture was a key feature of the sister church relationship. Trinity Anglican's relationship with the Cathedral Church in Saint James was part of its symbolic and literal process of distancing itself from the Episcopal Church and realigning with African Anglicanism. "The Church of England and the Episcopal Church in the US are drifting around everywhere," said Remy Duke. "The Africans, on the other hand, are the pupils that have become the teachers." For Living Faith, ecclesiastical ties to Africa were part of the founding identity of the congregation, a connection reinforced and expanded by Living Faith's relationship with Murambi Parish. Through sister church relationships, Anglican parishes like Living Faith and Trinity affirmed their identity and organizational alignment.

## Conclusion

Clergy members and other leaders in the participating congregations appropriated and developed collective action frames to help fashion a shared understanding of the purpose of their sister church relationships among their parishioners. While almost all of the congregations highlighted the importance of mutuality to one degree or another, congregations varied in the way framers balanced relational goals vis-á-vis project goals, conceptualized human need, and prioritized other factors such as cross-cultural education and denominational identity. As chapter 7 will explore, however, individuals within a given congregation did not always share the same understanding of the purpose of their sister church relationships. Moreover, frames were not the only factor governing the course of sister church relationships and inspiring participation. Congregations were often drawn into sister church relationships not only because of collective framing but also because of grassroots connections that had already been fostered. Individuals within the congregations were inspired to participate by a vast assortment of psychological, social, and ideological factors, some of them related to congregational frames and some not.

The collective action frames that are employed in efforts to propel sister church relationships on both a macro and a congregational level are multifaceted, evolving, and at times opaque. At the congregational level, participants sorted through myriad and sometimes competing ideas about the purpose of sister church relationships. Mixed with individuals' unique motivations, frames articulated by both intermediaries and congregational leaders set the tone for sister church relationships. Common themes in the collective action frames articulated by spokespersons from denominational agencies and parachurch organizations that facilitate congregation-to-congregation relationships include the value of two-way missional partnership, the goal of solidarity over charity, the departure from the "sending" model of mission, and the intention to minister holistically. At the congregational level, especially among congregations that entered into sister church relationships with an intentional posture, these themes were more or less reiterated, though steered by the particularities of each situation.

From the vantage point of the northern partners, the most important variable that distinguished the profiled relationships from one another was whether the partnership was centered around projects or relationships. Whereas representatives from almost every congregation gave voice to the value of solidarity in some way, the primacy of fostering friendship varied among the congregations. Some congregations placed such a premium on building strong, give-and-take relationships with their partners that they all but avoided project development in their sister church communities. Other congregations tried to balance the two, working on projects but attempting to do so in the context of reciprocal and respectful relationships. A few congregations were decidedly project centered, their sister church relationships perceived as vehicles for philanthropic activity and not as ends in themselves.

A focus on relationships over projects blunted some of the other tensions that often emerge in mission efforts, particularly between liberal and conservative agenda. Those congregations that focused on building mutually enriching relationships with cohorts in their sister churches in Africa or Latin America did not squabble about whether their sights were on this world or the spiritual realm. Rather, they sought to worship, grow in the Christian faith, and meet human needs together with their brothers and sisters abroad. Whether liberal or conservative, congregations intentionally engaged in sister church relationships conceived of meaning relationally. For them, a transformational encounter mattered more than accomplishing something concrete and measurable. Yet, most congregations did not eschew projects all together. These congregations tried to strike a delicate balance between honoring their partners as equals and actors on one hand, and giving resources to curb poverty and economic injustice on the other.

As chapter 7 will explore, individuals within a given congregation did not always share the same perspective. Sometimes congregants subscribed to the same ideological basis for their sister church relationship but differed on how to apply shared principles to concrete situations. Other times the very purpose of the sister church relationship was hotly debated among participants. These scenarios complicated both the collective action of congregations and their framing processes. Moreover, as congregations carried out their sister church relationships, the frames they espoused did not always neatly translate into practice. Many congregations painfully experienced the gap between the ideal and the real, calling into question the viability of the frames themselves.

| Outcomes

*The Effects of Sister Church Relationships on Individuals and Congregations*

"I HAVE TWO LIVES," said Larry Gates, a former parishioner and sister parish committee member at Our Lady of Sorrows, "one before I went to El Salvador, and one since then." Prior to 1991, when Gates first became acquainted with the María Reina de la Paz community in San Salvador as a sister parish delegation member through Our Lady of Sorrows, he "was in the belly of the beast." A long-time lobbyist at a government relations firm, Gates rubbed shoulders with the rich and powerful as a matter of course. When he returned to Washington from his first trip to El Salvador, however, Gates told his secretary that he didn't see himself "doing the Washington thing much longer." He remembered giving the following explanation: "People that have money give us money to lobby for them so they will have more money. I'm done with that. I want to devote my attention to the people who don't have any representation and don't have any place in the system."

Gates' first experience in El Salvador through his parish's sister church relationship sent him down a new path in life. Change wasn't immediate; Gates described his transformation as a gradual process of discerning his calling and reconciling himself to his fears. But two decades later, both the circumstances of Gates's life and the attitudes he embodied were markedly different from those of his previous existence. At the time of the interview, Gates served as the executive director of a homeless shelter and advocacy center in inner-city Washington, DC. He and his family had relocated from the prestigious neighborhood where Our Lady of Sorrows is situated to an impoverished neighborhood, also leaving Our Lady of Sorrows for a historically African American, social-justice oriented urban

Catholic parish. Gates had returned to El Salvador and the Reina de la Paz community fourteen times since his first trip in 1991. Even though he no longer attended Our Lady of Sorrows, he continued to maintain strong relationships with several members of Our Lady's sister parish community in San Salvador, attending their weddings and welcoming them into his home in Washington, DC, for months at a time. Gates also served on the board of a Salvadoran microenterprise organization and planned multiple advocacy events in Washington to raise awareness about the plight of Salvadorans.

Gates explained that his experiences in El Salvador had been a great blessing to him. "I go to El Salvador for the spiritual nourishment, for the living water," he said. Gates maintained that his experiences in El Salvador prompted him to ask questions about himself and his choices in life, to focus on what is important, and to become a better human being and a more dedicated Christian. He reported that the people he met there chastened and inspired him through their stories and their generosity of spirit. Most of all, they redefined for him what it means to be poor. Whether in María Reina de la Paz or his parish in an economically depressed area of Washington, DC, Gates noted that "when you worship with the poor, you soak up the Spirit in a way that is difficult to do among the privileged. . . . The poor suffer from a lot of other poverty," he continued, "but the rich often suffer from poverty of vision."

Gates asserted that he had received much more than he had given in his involvement with the people of María Reina de la Paz. That said, he would not have so drastically altered his life if he didn't believe he could also be a blessing to his friends in El Salvador. Gates aspired to serve as a father figure to the orphaned children of María Reina de la Paz. He listened to the stories of those he met in San Salvador, letting them know they aren't forgotten. He took to heart the advice of Reina de la Paz's long-time pastor: "Pray for us, and tell the truth about what you saw here." Out of relationships of openness and mutual vulnerability, concluded Gates, "we've learned from each other, helped each other, and all benefited greatly."

Larry Gates's story is one of radical personal transformation through his participation in his parish's international relationship. Though much more dramatic for Gates than for most participants, positive personal development attributed to participation in a sister church relationship was a common theme among respondents. Respondents found their faith strengthened, their circle of friends expanded, their assumptions challenged, and their biographies enhanced through their participation in sister church relationships.

Beyond northern participants' stories of personal transformation, the outcomes of the profiled relationships remain opaque. Tangible results of mission efforts are difficult to measure, especially in partnerships oriented around friendship more than projects. Correlation and causation are almost impossible to disentangle, and many outcomes are unintended and unforeseen. Moreover, the study was designed to solicit attitudes of the northern participants, not to solicit attitudes of global southern partners, observe behavior, or trace causation through pretests and posttests. These limitations notwithstanding, the accounts of respondents indicated that the collective action frames that undergirded the profiled sister church relationships were to at least some degree confirmed by experience. Meaningful cross-cultural friendships were formed, and participants' lives were changed—sometimes subtly and sometimes dramatically—through their participation. Gary Marx and Douglas McAdam identify four outcome possibilities for social movements: political or economic change, specific legislation, changes in public opinion and behavior, and the creation of new organizations or institutions.[1] With the exception of legislation, each of these possible outcomes is evident, at least on a small scale, as a result of sister church relationships.

## Stories of Personal Change

As chapter 5 explains, one of the main purposes of sister church relationships, according to the collective action frames espoused at both the micro and macro level, is to educate and reform North American participants. Regardless of how explicitly this goal was promoted in their particular congregation, most respondents spoke of their experiences related to participation in a sister church relationships as personally enriching or even transformative. However, whether or not respondents' participation actually evoked significant, long-term changes in their behaviors and attitudes—as many claimed it did—is a complicated question.

Beyond taking respondents' words at face value, a causal relationship between participation and attitudinal or behavioral change could not be determined by the study. Moreover, as multiple observers of human behavior have noted, attitudes and assumptions are deeply entrenched and often resist change—even, at times, despite evidence to the contrary. People sometimes change their attitudes and corresponding behaviors only to revert over time to their original viewpoints, especially if their environment supports the initial opinions.[2] Additionally, the gap between a people's rhetoric and actual behavior can be pronounced; behavior does not always conform to feelings and beliefs.[3] For this reason, social scientists have made a practice of prioritizing behavior over practice. Drawing on Émile Durkheim, anthropologist David Kertzer remarks, "Socially and politically speaking, we are what we do, not what we think."[4]

Without assuming neat translation of ideas into behavior or linear causation from participation to lifestyle, respondents' accounts of the role of sister church relationships in their lives is still instructive—the narratives scaffolding participants' understanding of themselves and their worlds. Many respondents expressed sentiments commonly voiced by those who return from short-term mission trips to impoverished areas: appreciation for material blessings and a vow to no longer take them for granted, wonder at the happiness of people who have so little, and gratitude for the generosity and hospitality of their hosts. Beyond these somewhat pedestrian responses, however, many participants forged deep and long-lasting bonds with members of their sister parish—bonds that often resulted in return trips, ongoing correspondence, long-term project development, and even social activism. Because of the continuing nature of congregation-to-congregation partnerships, participants were afforded opportunities to sustain and deepen the commitments and relationships that began in the context of sister church relationships. Many reported that their views of Christianity, poverty, and the "other" changed drastically because of their experiences.

## Formation for the Young

Cross-cultural experiences related to sister church relationships were especially formative for young people. Brian Baker, a Trinity Anglican parishioner who joined his congregation's delegation to Uganda the summer before his senior year of high school, described what happened to him on this trip as life changing, and perhaps even a conversion experience. Baker explained that the trip took place shortly before Trinity Anglican formally disaffiliated from the Episcopal Church, in the context of bitter clashes between those who wanted to leave the denomination and those who wanted to stay. "I had been going through a really hard time with all the debates. I knew people really well on both sides, and I was confused about who was right."

This turmoil only intensified for Baker while in Uganda. On one hand, he was repelled by the aggressive evangelistic techniques and dogmatism he perceived among his congregation's Ugandan counterparts as well as his own pastor and fellow delegation members. On the other hand, Baker was impressed by the passion and vibrancy of faith he saw among the Ugandan Christians as well as his cohorts from Trinity.

The cognitive dissonance that plagued Baker eventually subsided as he came to embrace the absolutism of his colleagues. A long-time Boy Scout, Baker had told Ugandan pastor Paul Wamboga of his desire to meet a few Ugandan Scouts. When Baker got to Uganda, he was surprised to learn that a camporee had been prepared for the entire Boy Scout district in recognition of his visit. Honored and humbled by this gesture as well as the hospitality of the Ugandan Scouts, Baker was nervous about the speech he was asked to deliver on the last night of the camporee. But, as days passed, he became increasingly comfortable with what he would say.

> I came out and said that I was honored to be speaking to them. I told them that scouting was a good thing, and that studies are important. And then I did what everyone on our team had been doing; I talked about the faith. I told them that I realized that without Jesus, you can't do anything. And I kind of believed it myself. Even though I knew this message was divisive, I was really starting to believe it myself. He's God; what can I say?

Through Baker's speech, it became clear to him that, to his surprise, he too was embracing the identity of his sister church cohorts.

Baker's experience in Uganda helped steer him on a particular journey of faith, one that he continued to embrace several years later. Although he did not "see things in black and white" as did many of his fellow parishioners at Trinity, he came to identify with the "Anglican" side of the debate among Americans connected to the Church of England. Additionally, he described himself as a more dedicated Christian in the wake of the trip.

> The trip made me think about my faith a lot more. Here in the US, the faith is a lot more watered down. But in Uganda they really knew the Bible and were full of life.
>
> . . . I am a lot more prone to share my faith and stand up for it now than I was before the trip. I still respect other people's faiths, but I see that without Jesus there is nothing. I needed to be woken up, and the trip woke me up. People were talking really boldly, and I wasn't ready for it. But it became a very spiritual time—learning about how to follow God and get to know Jesus. I had grown up in the church my whole life, and there had been a lot of controversy about leaving the Episcopal Church. I think I had misconstrued some of the things the Anglican side was doing, particularly the

missionary aspect. I understand more of it now. You can't understand unless you decide to go where God is pulling you.

Baker did not know it at the time, but after the trip he would face several difficult years, trying times that his newfound faith commitment would propel him through. By remaining in close e-mail contact with friends from Saint James that he had met in Uganda, continuing to attend Trinity Anglican, and fully participating in activities offered in conjunction with Wamboga's frequent visits to Trinity, Baker became more steeped in the religious and cultural milieu of conservative Anglicanism.

Jennifer Mercer, a twenty-eight-year-old former parishioner of Saint Clement Catholic Church who was highly involved in Saint Clement's sister parish relationship as a teenager, also underwent a process of reformation through her sister parish participation. For Mercer, however, the personal development was psychosocial rather than religious. In fact, when interviewed, Mercer was no longer a practicing Catholic—considering herself "spiritual" rather than "religious." Even before she became involved in the sister parish relationship, said Mercer, she was social-justice minded. While she didn't relate to her peers at Saint Clement, she looked up to several adults at the parish involved in social-justice efforts, especially the director for social concerns. Encouraged by these adults to join Saint Clement's annual delegation to Pignon, Haiti, Mercer made the trip during her freshman year of college—a trip which she said enriched her perspective and steered her life choices. Mercer explained that in the wake of the extreme poverty and injustice she witnessed in Haiti, she had a difficult time returning to life back in the United States. "Even though I was pretty well informed about things before I went, when I came back I thought, 'How can I live this lifestyle?', even though my lifestyle wasn't extreme or frivolous. I would see people being totally frivolous; we were taking so many things for granted. It was really difficult to deal with those things."

As an adult, Mercer believed she had matured significantly since her trip to Haiti and was longer as dogmatic or judgmental in her resistance to the consumerist American lifestyle. Yet, she remained committed to living simply, being sensitive to cultural differences, and resisting American heavy-handedness abroad—commitments she traced to her experiences participating in a sister parish relationship as a teen.

Being in Haiti and getting to know Haitians gave me a lot of perspective in the sense that it made me see accurately that being an American in this world affects so much of how people see you. It helped me look at the

American way of life from an outside perspective. As Americans, we think that our way of life is the right way. But you can't just go in and think that, as an American, you have all the answers.

Mercer mentioned that while prior to being involved in St. Clement's relationship in Haiti she had considered a career in international development, she changed her mind after going to Haiti out of a fear of playing into American imperialism. "I decided that maybe it would be better to stay here in the U.S. and work on democracy and equality issues instead of going somewhere else and telling them what to do." For Mercer, being involved in a sister church relationship, and especially visiting her counterparts in Haiti, was instrumental in crafting her identity and actions as a socially conscious American.

Samantha Black was another young adult who believed that her life took a different course because of her involvement in her church's sister parish relationship. Beginning in the fall of 2006, Black began serving on Saint Mariana of Jesus' sister church committee. She ventured to Costa Rica three times out of the relationship, most recently as a young adult delegation leader. She also started a ministry to sponsor children's education in San José. Black explained that because of her involvement in Saint Mariana's sister parish relationship, she felt a great sense of purpose in her life—something her other friends in their mid-twenties struggled to find.

> The first time I was there, I had a really difficult time leaving. I didn't want to go home. I get very frustrated by materialism and American culture: the constant need for more, making money everything. And when I'm in Costa Rica, it's not that life is simpler, but the things that are important are different. Family is important, friendships, relationships, God, spirituality. It's really a peaceful place for me to be.

Black also noted that she found fulfillment in being an advocate for her friends in Costa Rica with her church community in the United States. Black recalled that near the end of her last trip, when she was lamenting to one of her Costa Rican friends that she didn't want to leave, he said to her: "Samantha, I need you to go home. I need you to go home because I know you 'get it,' and I know that you will do what you can to help us. You understand us. You like us. You appreciate us. You can share our stories there."

Because she felt called to do just that, Samantha Black derived both joy and meaning from her participation.

## Spiritual Growth

Because of their life stage, most older adults did not see the kind of drastic changes in their perspective or lifestyles as did young adults like Brian Baker or Jennifer Mercer. But many found themselves deeply influenced by their experiences nonetheless. Many participants considered being involved in a sister church relationship a profoundly spiritual experience. Beyond secular philanthropy or cross-cultural exchange, participants worshiped alongside fellow members of their faith—often being exposed to new and different religious expressions in the process. Many found their faith strengthened and their appreciation for the universal church enhanced. Pastor Henry Hunt at Mount Shannon Presbyterian recalled what for him was an intimate and powerful experience during his trip to Liberia. Called upon to bless a sick child in a remote and impoverished village, Hunt was grateful that for a moment, he could represent the grace and presence of God to this child. Seeing cultural barriers temporarily torn down as those assembled "showed themselves as they were," Hunt maintained that he saw the grace of God in the faces of the Liberians as well.

His voice cracking and his eyes welling with tears, Ricardo Flores from Saint Mariana of Jesus told of his deep admiration for the faith and wisdom he saw in the life of the pastor of Reina de la Paz. He also noted that the sacramental and icon-centered worship style of his sister parish counterparts was a rich personal blessing. Similarly, participants at Kensington Woods were inspired by the vibrant dancing and singing that filled the worship of their Kenyan brothers and sisters, and respondents from New York Avenue were taken aback by the beautiful liturgical art they saw in the sanctuary of Iglesia del Centro in Havana.

## Humanizing the "Other"

The opportunity to build interpersonal cross-cultural friendships with other Christians was also a powerful dimension of sister church partnerships for North American participants. Respondents of all ages reported that the relationships they developed with people in their sister church communities enriched them and challenged them. Instead of viewing poverty, other cultures, or corruption abstractly, they now had faces to associate with victimization, suffering, and otherness. Jean Francis, a participant at Trinity Anglican remarked: "Growing up, I always thought of Africa as way far away and not very humanized in my purview. And when you go, you meet real people—who are just like you except their culture is different and their skin color is different. And that is a neat experience because you pick up new friends."

A similar sentiment was voiced by Gloria Feinburg from Third Presbyterian:

> We have been really enriched and touched through our relationships with Cubans at Del Centro. The relationships have really helped us put names and faces to our understanding of another culture. Now, when a hurricane hits, for example, our concern isn't just abstract. We are thinking, 'How is Elena? How is Oneida?'

Feinburg also noted that people are more likely to respond to suffering if they have a personal connection to those suffering. Shane Ish from Living Faith Anglican added:

> This relationship really does humanize the people on the other side of it, as I hope it has done for them with respect to us. It turns people from projects, who are defined by a handful of attributes that are stereotypically associated with poverty, into people who are really like us in more ways than they are different from us . . . just different situations with the same Lord and fundamentally the same mission.

Not only can face-to-face encounter with people from impoverished regions of the world personalize suffering, said Ish, it can also help North Americans resist defining people by their suffering.

Beyond making difference less strange, sister church relationships also exposed North American participants to compelling character traits, insights, and stories from their counterparts across the ocean. For example, several parishioners at Trinity Anglican remarked that they were inspired by the strong faith they witnessed in their African brothers and sisters. "The church [in Uganda] is in fact the center of people's lives; it is almost totally different from what we have in the U.S.," said Edward Francis, reveling in the strength of Ugandan Christianity. His wife, Jean, added that she was stunned by the generosity, zeal for evangelism, and spiritual maturity she saw among her brothers and sisters at Saint James. Some even noted that their relationships with Ugandans challenged their assumptions on race. Living in a racially segregated area of rural Virginia, said Remy Duke, "we all have our ideas of what people are like, especially the blacks in Africa." Participating in Trinity's sister parish relationship, continued Duke, disavowed him of these stereotypes and exposed him to experiences of people in other parts of the world. As chapter 7 will explore, sister church relationships are far from immune to cultural imperialism. Nor do they erase individuals' prejudices. At least for some respondents, however, participating in a sister church relationship helped them see people who were different from them with new eyes.

## Friendships

Especially for those who were actively involved in sister church partnerships for an extended period of time, the personal friendships they formed with counterparts in their sister church communities were often significant. Susan Travinsky, who had been actively involved in Our Lady of Sorrows' sister parish relationship in El Salvador for ten years, said that her participation is one of the most important pieces of her life. Travinsky had visited her sister parish eight times, including two full summer stays during breaks from her school year as a teacher. Travinsky built deep friendships with both laypeople and clergy from Reina de la Paz and communicated with several of these friends on a weekly basis.

> María Reina de la Paz is my second home. When I decided to sign on for that first delegation ten years ago, I was thinking very much in political and professional terms. That was the sort of growth I thought I would get from it. And when I went, it became such a profound personal and spiritual experience. It has had a tremendous impact on my life.

Aaron Thomas from Living Faith Anglican remarked that forming a relationship with Fabi Gataraiha, pastor of Living Faith's sister parish in Rwanda, had been an extremely rewarding experience in itself. "I personally love Fabi and would do anything for him; we have become great friends." Thomas said that his experience is shared by many Living Faith participants. "Between representatives from Murambi Parish coming here and people from Living Faith going there, strong and legitimate relationships have been formed." Thomas, who worked professionally in international development, said that the rich personal relationships he formed through his participation in Living Faith's sister church partnership has made his volunteer work related to Africa infinitely more fulfilling and enriching than his professional work there.

Many participants remarked that the relationships they formed while visiting their sister parishes were the most meaningful and fulfilling parts of their experience. For some of these people, relationships were not sustained because of communication barriers or simply inertia. While they treasured their memories, memories were all that was left of the relationships. But for other participants, especially those who returned again and again, the relationships only grew stronger.

Extension Projects

In several cases, participants' admiration or concern for the friends they had made across the world inspired them to initiate projects related to their sister church communities that were beyond the pale of their congregations' partnerships. Mitch Covington from Christ the King Anglican reported that from the first year he visited Nicaragua, he was troubled by the absence of men in the sister church community. Because of the lack of economic opportunities in San Fernando, most of the men go elsewhere to find work. "The women are very strong, very determined, very enduring, but it's also very difficult for them. And of course not having a father at home leads to all kinds of problems for the children, and being away is not good for the men either."

Seeing the strain on his friends in the Nueva Jerusalén community, Covington contacted Opportunity International, a Christian microfinance organization working in the region, about the San Fernando community's situation. Largely because of his efforts, Opportunity International eventually instituted a microfinance program specifically among Covington's contacts in San Fernando. The program performed well, so Covington and his family returned to San Fernando the following year to celebrate and reconnect with their friends there—independent from Christ the King's church-sponsored efforts.

For Jack Napoli from Saint Clement Catholic Church, personal initiatives beyond the scope of his parish's partnership climbed to an even greater level. Napoli described himself as "hooked" on the Sacré-Coeur community in Pignon, Haiti. On a midnight truck ride approaching Pignon during his second trip there, Napoli recalled feeling an overwhelming and very personal sense that he was about to be home. "I just felt like I belonged there. It sounds corny, but I felt like I was seeing Jesus in the people I saw. It sounds so corny that I'm almost embarrassed to say it, but that's really what I felt, and I felt it strongly."

Napoli had participated in three delegations through Saint Clement and had also traveled to Haiti three times on his own. His personal trips largely centered around a coffee business that he and a few others from Saint Clement started in order to help their friends in Pignon get a fair price for their beans. In consultation with the Pignon coffee growers, Napoli helped them join a fair-trade Mexican cooperative. He also marketed their coffee in the United States. Napoli explained that his work in Haiti and the relationships he had formed among Haitians had become extremely important to him. "It's my hobby, my pet project, the thing I care the most about besides my immediate family. I probably spend at least twelve hours a week working on this project, and another six or seven thinking about it. This is different. I used to be into sports, but this is different."

## Advocacy Efforts

Direct personal action inspired by sister church involvement could also be seen in the advocacy efforts of some participants. At Living Faith Anglican, one member of the first delegation to Rwanda, Lisa Scott, returned as a filmmaker to shoot a documentary about the Rwandan genocide. Capturing moments of "repentance and forgiveness" among Tutsi and Hutu Christians, Scott aimed to tell the story of her Rwandan brothers and sisters and share "their personal testimony to the immense healing that God is doing in their nation." In addition to sharing the stories of their sister church counterparts for the sake of promoting awareness, respect, and compassion among Americans, some participants felt compelled to advocate for their friends among politicians and other powerbrokers. Particularly at Third Presbyterian and Our Lady of Sorrows, several participants wrote letters to the US government, decrying how US policy in Cuba and El Salvador adversely affected the lives of their friends. Individuals like Susan Travinsky, Larry Gates, and Janice Thompson from Our Lady of Sorrows went further: Travinsky by traveling to El Salvador as an elections observer, Gates by organizing a round table on El Salvador for Washingtonians, and Thompson by making personal efforts to contact a Salvadoran bishop about the particular plight of María Reina de la Paz.

## Behavioral Change

Many respondents maintained that participation in sister church relationships steered their behavior, if in subtle or indirect ways. Several pastors and church leaders reported that their sister church–related experiences steered the course of their ministry in their own congregations. For example, Pastor Ruth Eaton from Kensington Woods said that her Kenyan counterparts inspired her to think differently about her ministry as a pastor. "The power of their Christian faith is demonstrated in very tangible ways.

The whole day is infused with worship and prayer at the Limuru mission. There's a sense in which I feel very complete when I'm over there."

She endeavored to incorporate this worship-infused sense of life into her own spiritual practice and her ministry at Kensington Woods. Similarly, Clancey Brown from Mount Calvary Baptist noted that much of his vision for his work was inspired by visits to international partner congregations. "It has been phenomenal and eye-opening for me to see the word of God come alive in other countries. The passion for God that I have seen there is just out of this world. I wish we could bottle up some of that and bring it back to the States."

While respondents were quick to describe the emotional rewards and altered perspective afforded by their participation in sister parish relationships, it was more difficult for them to identify tangible ways in which their actions or life choices were a direct outcome of their involvement. Of the tangible outcomes, return trips, continued or increased participation in the sister church relationship, and maintenance of cross-cultural friendships were most common. More opaque behavior-related effects identified by respondents included increased willingness to share their faith, an enhanced life of prayer and worship, a greater propensity to befriend immigrants, and less conspicuous consumption of resources.

## A Real Difference?

The vast majority of respondents believed that their involvement in sister church relationships had a positive impact on their lives, making them more conscientious global citizens, more devoted Christians, and better human beings. But these claims should not be trusted uncritically. Attitudinal and behavioral changes are almost impossible to demonstrate or measure. The gap between rhetoric and practice is all too common; what people think and what they do isn't always consistent, and individuals often see their own actions through self-serving biases.

The various studies of international mission trips have not reached a consensus regarding the effects of such trips on participants. As Terence Linhart notes, "Participants continue to report them as significant experiences . . . yet researchers have been unable to clearly describe the nature of that significance."[5] However, if Robert Wuthnow's findings in his comprehensive study of the global outreach of American churches can be trusted, perhaps respondents' claims regarding the impact of sister church relationships on their lives are at least partially valid. Based on a nationally representative survey of more than two thousand church members and qualitative interviews with three hundred individuals involved in transnational ministries, Wuthnow concluded that there is ample evidence to suggest that mission trips encourage deeper and longer-lasting commitments to transcultural ministries among North American participants. Wuthnow discovered that participants in transcultural ministries are more likely than nonparticipants to attend church events related to international issues, to say that their congregation should emphasize international mission, and to give financially to transcultural outreach efforts. Sixty-two percent of respondents to this survey who participated in a mission trip said that it had a major impact on their life, and 92 percent said it made them more hopeful.[6] Although Wuthnow cautions that correlative relationship between these traits and participation in mission trips does not necessarily mean that mission trips cause them, he also cites evidence to lend support to the argument for causation. For instance, transcultural commitment is higher among adults of all ages who went on mission trips as teenagers than those who didn't— even controlling for current levels of congregational involvement as adults. The argument for causation is stronger in this case because longitudinal difference in attitude and behavior is an indication of possible effect.[7]

Wuthnow concludes that "the critical role that personal involvement in international ministries is playing in the global outreach of American Christianity is less in its contribution toward the financing and staffing of these programs and more in its larger influence on hearts and minds." Those who are directly involved in transcultural mission said that their outlook has been altered and reported that they see the world and their own faith differently.[8] To the degree that American participants in short-term mission trips grow in cultural intelligence or mature in faith, this shift in perspective could be more pronounced among participants in sister church relationships than it is among the more general population of participants in international or cross-cultural ministries. Ostensibly, because many participants in sister church relationships sustain their involvement over a greater period of time, the opportunity to develop a transcultural perspective and a globally minded lifestyle is expanded.

Research specifically focused on sister church relationships suggests that the "hearts and minds" of North Americans may indeed be influenced positively by participation. Based on his case study of a relationship between a Liberian congregation and an American congregation—which featured participant observation, surveys, interviews, group discussions, and questionnaires in both congregations—Samuel Reeves concludes that the congregation-to-congregation relationship "led participants to increased cultural awareness and a more culturally cosmopolitan outlook on life, the ministry of the church and the kingdom of God."[9] Reeves maintains that participants recognized the relationship as beneficial in expanding and enriching personal faith and discipleship as well as in cultivating a more global faith perspective.[10] Similarly, in his study of four Lutheran congregations in southeastern Iowa who partnered with Tanzanian congregations, David Cline notes that the Iowa Lutheran participants who traveled to Tanzania expressed a common theme of being overwhelmed by the hospitality of their hosts and being emotionally and spiritually enriched by the "community of saints across cultures."[11] In his study of US Unitarian Universalist congregations partnering in Romania, David Keyes also found that participants became more grounded in their faith tradition and developed a greater awareness of global justice issues.[12] Among the few scholarly studies of sister church relationships, most point to positive outcomes in the lives of northern participants.

Because all of these studies were ethnographic and limited to a few cases or less, however, their findings are not generalizable. Moreover, research on the effects of participation in cross-cultural mission relationships in the lives of North Americans also reveals areas of ambivalence or even negative outcomes. For instance, in her case study of a relationship between a US Catholic parish and a Haitian parish, Tara Hefferan found that whereas members of the US parish voiced more nuanced perceptions of Haitians than the negative stereotypes adopted by most Americans, they still tended to generalize Haitians as lazy and dependent and remained invested in notions of class superiority.[13] In his study of three relationships between US and Ukrainian congregations, C. M. Brown found that American participants either failed to meet learning objectives or learned what they expected to learn; they "did not develop deep understandings informed by Ukrainian cultural perspectives."[14] Each sister church relationship is idiosyncratic, as is each individual's experience. The outcomes of sister church relationships on the lives of northern participants—let alone congregations or southern communities—are at best varied and opaque. Yet, while sister church relationships may not be as capable of changing lives for the better in practice as they are in theory, respondents' stories of personal transformation remain poignant.


## Impact on North American Congregations

In 1995, the Secretariat for Latin America of the National Conference of Catholic Bishops conducted a survey of US parishes that aimed to identify the effects of the relationship between the Catholic Church in the United

States and the Catholic Church in Latin America on the US Church. The Secretariat found that US parish priests reported several changes in their parishes as a result of involvement with Latin America. Of the responding parishes, 32.1 percent acknowledged improvement in commitment to social change and equity, 55.9 percent appreciation of blessings in this country, 58.9 percent awareness of different cultures, 49.6 percent concern for the universal church, and 43.7 percent sensitivity to social justice.[15]

Many of the respondents in this study, especially if they were not pastors or other staff members, were less optimistic than the priests surveyed by the NCCB about the level of transformation in their congregations as a result of participation in sister church relationships. In several congregations, respondents conveyed that impact was limited to a relatively small group of people within the congregation. Those actively involved in the sister church relationship claimed to have changed markedly as a result of their participation, but they saw little difference in their congregation as a whole. Parishioners who were not directly involved in the congregation-to-congregation relationship generally knew little about the partnership and even less about the lives of members of their partner parish. Often, their attitudes and experiences regarding mission, global Christianity, or world needs were marginally affected by their congregation's international partnership. Even so, and especially in congregations in which sister church relationships were well integrated into congregational life, international partnerships helped enrich congregational experience, solidify congregational identity, and create social capital within congregations.

## Congregational Enrichment

Some respondents projected the type of personal enrichment claimed by individuals onto their congregations collectively. Jolene McIntyre from Kensington Woods Presbyterian reported that being in a sister church relationship "gives us a different perspective, of gratitude and appreciation for what we have. We get a chance to meet other Christians who are different from us, to partner with them, to share from our financial advantage and to receive from their spiritual advantage."

For a congregations like Kensington Woods, whose sister church relationship had enjoyed a long and active history, McIntyre's claim that the relationship cultivated a collective sense of transcultural appreciation and generosity may be well founded. Milton Estelle, Kensington Woods's sister church committee chairperson, explained that twenty years into the relationship, a large segment of the congregation had actively participated in the sister church relationship and that the relationship had become a core part of the congregation's identity. Many parishioners had participated in one of Kensington Woods's biennial delegations to Kenya, and even more had participated in initiatives related to the sister parish without going to Kenya. The entire congregation, Estelle added, had been continually reminded of the partnership through prayers, music, and art used in Kensington Woods's liturgy; an annual silent auction; newsletters; and other congregationwide phenomena related to the sister parish. Through all of these things, concluded Estelle, Limuru had permeated Kensington Woods's culture and identity.

For Third Presbyterian, it was through liturgy that the sister church relationship most influenced congregational culture and enriched parishioners' sensibilities. Cuban songs were routinely played and sung at Third Presbyterian, the congregation's choir having learned a whole new repertoire from their music exchange with Iglesia del Centro. Banners from Cuba were prominently displayed at the front of the sanctuary, and clergy vestments were adorned with Cuban-style embroidery. Gloria Feinburg laughed as she gave another example of how Third's relationship with Centro had permeated congregational culture:

> People in our church used to disagree about whether it is appropriate to applaud after a great choir number or moving speech during the worship service. Well, when we were in Cuba, we saw that their congregation waves their bulletins instead of applauding during a worship service. So we brought that back here, and now everyone does it! One of the Cubans was visiting and said, "We do that in our church too!" when he saw us waving our bulletins. We smiled and said, "We learned it from you!"

Feinburg also explained that the impact of Third's sister church relationship extended far beyond those individuals directly involved. For instance, springing from the relationship between Third and Centro, the Presbyterian Women associations of the Washington, DC, and Cuban presbyteries also forged a strong partnership. "Through the personal relationships that have been formed through this congregational partnership, we've seen a domino effect. Our sister church relationship has had some amazing repercussions."

Kensington Woods and Third Presbyterian were among only a few congregations in which congregational life was meaningfully affected by the sister church relationship and in which individuals from across the parish, with varying levels of involvement, claimed to have been significantly refined by the partnership. Still, while nonparticipating members in most congregations may not have seen many individual life changes as a result of their congregation's sister church relationship, congregational identity was influenced by participation in nearly all congregations in the study.

## Congregational Identity

In many of the Washington, DC–area congregations, sister parish relationships were a key component of congregations' collective identity and sense of vitality. They gave congregations something important to rally around and provided parishioners with a shared sense of purpose and meaning. They set participating congregations apart from other congregations, making parishioners feel as if their congregations were unique or special and giving them a reason to see themselves as generous and conscientious. Sister church relationships enabled members of congregations to feel connected to the universal church and enlarged by being part of something greater than themselves.

As many observers of congregational life have noted, congregations thrive when parishioners experience a collective sense of purpose and connectedness and languish when they do not.[16] The 2001 US Congregational Life Survey identified ten key strengths that make congregations successful. Included in this list are providing opportunities for spiritual growth, connecting to the community, providing opportunities for participation, creating a sense of belonging, and equipping parishioners to share their faith.[17] Sister church relationships gave congregations strengthening opportunities in each of these four areas. They enabled parishioners to grow and serve together and, in the process, fashion and bolster congregational identity.

This function of sister church relationships was especially pronounced at Trinity Anglican and Living Faith Anglican. Both congregations partnered with African bodies that shared their position in the Anglican realignment. Through their partnerships, these Anglican congregations solidified their ecclesiastical loyalties and theological commitments. Since Trinity Anglican's partnership with the Cathedral Church of Saint James crystalized as Trinity left the Episcopal Church to affiliate with CANA, it was especially formative for the congregation's new identity within the Anglican Communion. Gini Axelrod, a participant from Trinity, remarked:

> All the vibes that I can sense tell me that the relationship with the Cathedral
> Church of Saint James and Paul Wamboga in Uganda has now eliminated

any possible hesitation for being under African leadership. . . . Had it not been for this relationship, I'm pretty sure that there would have been at least some undercurrents of hesitation if not some concerns expressed.

Axelrod also said that the two congregations' shared commitment to be guardians of orthodoxy, in the midst of secularization and heresy promoted by the liberal wing of Anglicanism, strengthened their relationship as well as both congregations' resolve to continue in the path they had chosen.

> Trinity and Saint James have the same foundation of belief, and we can build on that. We were united in Christ to start with; we didn't have to argue about whether Jesus is the only way and which gospel we were proclaiming. We know where we both stand, and that has only made the relationship stronger. . . . And having that support helped us tremendously in the battles we did have to fight with the Episcopal Church and those from our congregation who chose to stay with that denomination. There's nothing like knowing that there are forty to fifty people halfway around the world who have never seen you, and don't know you, but pray for you every day. The effects of those prayers have been very evident in the last few years, which have been very difficult because of our decision to leave the Episcopal Church.

Fellow Trinity parishioner Remy Duke added that Trinity's African brothers and sisters had been very gracious, strengthening Trinity and assuring the congregation that they were on the right path. "We are prepared to lose our court cases. If we get kicked out of our building, we'll build a church somewhere else. We are more resolved than ever through our relationship with the folks in Uganda."

Since Living Faith Anglican began as an AMiA church plant and thus never had cause to leave the Episcopal Church, the perceived need to choose sides and draw battle lines was not as pronounced at Living Faith as it was at Trinity. However, Living Faith's sister church relationship with Murambi Parish performed a similar function of helping to establish theological and ecclesiastical identity. Living Faith's sister church relationship gave many in the congregation a sense of pride and excitement. Internationally minded, justice-oriented, and theologically conservative, Living Faith parishioners enjoyed not just being tangibly linked to the global church, but also being closely aligned with fellow conservative Anglicans. Being part of a relationship with a parish in Rwanda, said Brian Jones, "gives us a sense that the Christian faith isn't only an American faith, and that we are part of something much larger. That gives us a mission and a drive that is a lot stronger than in so many other churches I've been in."

Chris Coulter, assistant pastor at Living Faith, explained that Living Faith's relationship with Murambi gave parishioners the opportunity to glean from the "spiritual riches" of African Christians in general and African evangelical Anglicans in particular, and in so doing, the relationship invigorated parish morale. Justin Hahn's sentiments were shared by many: "What is being attempted here is very unique—there is something to be said for the way our church is trying to do this."

Although the behavior and attitudes of most congregants beyond those directly involved may not have changed significantly because of their church's relationship, intangible results such as providing a congregation with a greater sense of identity and purpose should not be underemphasized. In the words of James Hopewell,

> A healthy congregation, like a healthy family, is one that understands and tells its stories. Neither families nor parishes can, in any event, escape some kind of narrative exchange, but their vigor in part depends upon the degree to which they know that they know these narratives. Parish self-understanding, like that of a family, depends upon its perception of itself in a particular time and form, with a memory of its past and the capacity for an open yet characteristic future. A vital congregation is one whose self-understanding is not reduced to data and programs but which instead is nurtured by its persistent attention to the stories by which it identifies itself.[18]

The congregations involved in sister church relationships were strengthened by incorporating their experiences into their collective biographies. Sister church relationships allowed congregations to craft their self-understanding around stories of generosity and reconciliation.

## Congregational Bonding

In addition to providing congregations opportunities to enrich parish culture and fashion a shared identity, sister church relationships facilitated a sense of community, or what sociologists call "bonding social capital," within congregations. Rallying around a common cause is a powerful means of establishing a strong group dynamic. Moreover, while outreach and inreach efforts are often pitted against each other in congregations, there is ample evidence to suggest that bonding social capital and bridging social capital—which joins people across social divides—can go hand in hand.[19] Those who work together on a particular project often form strong friendships with one another and vice versa. As the US Congregational Life Survey's findings indicate, reaching outward to others and inward to members are complementary strengths for congregations.

> Congregations with the greatest sense of connectedness to the community are also places where worshippers feel a strong sense of belonging and feel empowered to become leaders. Chances are, these are places where people have figured out an answer to the question, "What is special about us?" They understand what the congregation needs to do in that particular time and place. They understand, in other words, not just that they should do something—but what that "something" is.[20]

Congregations are local by definition. They are composed of a particular group of people in a particular time and place. One of the chief functions of congregations is to give worshipers a sense of belonging within a larger community of fellow adherents. It is often in serving together beyond parish walls that this sense of belonging is created.

Sister church relationships created opportunities for group solidarity in the profiled congregations. Unlike some other parish activities, sister parish participants built relationships with each other not just by spending time together but also by working toward a common goal and engaging in collective ritual behavior. As Émile Durkheim convincingly argued, solidarity is produced by people acting together rather than by thinking together. Because of its symbolic power and emotional evocation, ritual behavior, in Durkheim's mind, is especially conducive to building solidarity.[21] Involvement in sister church relationships provided participants opportunities to work, worship, learn, and encounter difference together—often in vulnerable and highly emotionally charged situations. Taking North Americans away from the familiarity of their everyday lives and throwing them into new and sometimes difficult situations in which they are nearly forced into intimacy with fellow teammates, short-term mission trips often contain a built-in bonding mechanism. Even more so, sister church initiatives can foster such experiences year after year.

Making meaning together by working toward a common goal, sharing powerful experiences, and wrestling with pain and injustice, participants in several congregations established near familial relationships with their fellow teammates. Of course, sometimes these relationships were threatened or destroyed by conflict, and sometimes familiar simulation was short lived. But in many cases, fellow participants became one another's dear and enduring friends. Jack Napoli remarked, "Shortly after we got involved in the sister parish project, my wife and I faced a difficult family crisis. The twinning committee at Saint Clement became a sort of family to us. They were amazingly wonderful. That group supported us and gave us a way to be outside ourselves."

Years later, several of these committee members were still Napoli's close friends.

In-group bonding among participants benefitted not just individuals involved but also congregations. Particularly in larger congregations, sister church relationships enabled participants to find a niche within the congregation and in so doing enhanced a broader sense of belonging. Each of the profiled Catholic parishes had more than twenty-five hundred members. In large parishes like these, a sense of community is often difficult to build since most parishioners are strangers to one another. Those who participate in particular ministries, however, often escape the culture of anonymity and build strong relationships with other parishioners who are also involved. In smaller congregations such as Trinity Anglican and Christ the King Anglican, this sense of in-group solidarity was widespread because a large portion of the congregation directly participated in the sister church relationship. In larger congregations, although the sister parish relationship tended to be less pronounced in parish life if simply because of competition with other programs, the sense of community developed among committee members spread outward to other parishioners through potlucks, fundraisers, slideshows, and debriefing reports in conjunction with the sister parish project. While a few congregations had problems with the sister church partnership being perceived as the pet project of a clique within the congregation, most congregations found parish fellowship enriched because of the sister church relationship. Solidarity was built not just between the northern parish and the southern parish but also within the North American parish.

Other researchers have also found that sister parish relationships increased bonding social capital within congregations. In his study of partnerships between Lutheran congregations in Tanzania and the United States, David Cline concluded that participating in sister church relationships enhanced a sense of community within the American congregations. Members of delegations in particular bonded with one another and brought new energy to their congregations because of their excitement about their visit to the sister parish.[22] Similarly, C. M. Brown found that sister church relationships were vehicles for promoting bonding social capital, in addition to their more overt function of promoting bridging and linking social capital that cross ethnic, cultural, and economic lines.[23]

## Impact on Global Southerners and Global Southern Communities

Although many of the profiled partnerships were designed to increase Americans' cultural intelligence or bolster their congregational life, most were also designed to enhance life in southern communities. Because this study focused on the attitudes and experiences of northern participants, the impact of the congregation-to-congregation relationships on global southerners can only be intimated. Respondents' accounts of the role of sister church relationships in the lives of their partners are biased and incomplete at best. Even so, respondents' testimonies suggest that the profiled relationships did bring about at least some positive outcomes in southern communities.

In many cases, the partnership resulted in tangible differences such as more children enrolled in school or physical improvements to congregational or community assets. Speaking of Saint Clement's fifteen-year relationship with Paroisse Catholique du Sacré-Coeur in Pignon, Haiti, Jack Napoli remarked:

> We have seen a difference in Pignon in the lives of several thousand people. In the old pictures, you see a lot more bald heads and distended bellies among the children, like in Africa. We don't see as much of that any more. At least in the schools, young kids are getting milk. There are 500 kids in the elementary school that Saint Clement supports. That is 1,000 kids in a five-year period, and they have parents and siblings who have also been touched. The secondary school has 350 kids. And they are getting top scores in the district. You say, who are these kids? Why are they doing so well? It is because they have opportunity. In that respect, Saint Clement has every right to be proud, that they made that opportunity available.

Napoli added that Saint Clement's members should resist patting themselves on the back not only because there are still many problems in Pignon but also because changes have come about not just through Saint Clement's benevolence but also through the Haitians' own self-determination and a shared, Spirit-led journey. Still, because of the sister church relationship, Napoli maintained that Pignon is a changed community.

Similarly, Pastor Ruth Eaton from Kensington Woods Presbyterian reminisced that twenty years earlier, the Limuru Mission Area of Kenya consisted of a small dirt-floor multipurpose building, an open-air "classroom" on a piece of carpet under a tree, and a borrowed treadle sewing machine. Thanks in large part to the Kensington Woods partnerships, the

Limuru Mission Area grew to include a vocational center offering training in five trades, a primary school, an orphan-care home, several preschools, and twelve churches. At Our Lady of Sorrows, Susan Travinsky reported that 25 percent of the annual budget of the preschool operated by María Reina de la Paz was covered by Our Lady of Sorrows. "Our financial support is vital to them; they would be closed without it." Even congregations whose financial support was modest or whose relationships were programmatically thin could point to tangible benefits in their sister church communities. Victory Baptist could identify a new sanctuary for Ebenezer Baptist in Jamaica; Living Faith Anglican a tipper lorry for the Murambi community; and Mount Calvary twenty new sewing machines for Jangalia Baptist Church's tailor training program.

But perhaps more important than tangible outcomes or even measurable social change, many North American participants were proud to report that, like themselves, their southern partners were also enriched by the friendships formed between the two communities. Kevin Marino from Our Lady of Sorrows said, "The people of Reina de la Paz are grateful for the money and the support that we give them, but I don't think that is why they are in the relationship. They genuinely like us. It's the friendship, the solidarity, that is most important."

Especially in politically charged settings like El Salvador and Cuba, members of sister church communities, according to their North American counterparts, benefited most by knowing that Christians in other parts of the world stood with them in their struggle. And in situations of dire poverty, while physical support was certainly appreciated, it was overtures of solidarity and compassion that were most treasured.

Respondents with professional experience in international development or mission especially tended to maintain that sister church relationships represent not only a laudable approach to cross-cultural engagement but also an effective means of bringing healing and hope to impoverished communities. Long-time international development professionals such as Ricardo Flores, Felix Mapanje, Kevin Marino, Aaron Thomas, and Janice Thompson all dedicated themselves tirelessly to their church's relationship, believing that faith-based, grassroots partnerships are an important complement, if not a more effective alternative, to government programs. Kensington Woods Presbyterian Pastor Ruth Eaton remarked:

> To me, one of the best commentaries on our relationship is that we had a member from Malawi, Felix Mapanje, who worked here in the U.S. at the World Bank for many years. He went over to Limuru on one of our delegations.

When he came back, he said, "This is better than any of the World Bank projects; this is the way it needs to be done.'" And he has been highly involved in our partnership ever since.

Aaron Thomas, who also worked for the US government in the field of international development, lamented that the programs he helped administer professionally were impersonal and at times ineffective. By contrast, through his participation in Living Faith's sister church relationship, Thomas said, "I feel like I have a chance of making a much greater impact at a much higher level than what I do during the week."

Thomas believed that his passion for long-term, faith-based, grassroots, cross-cultural partnerships as an effective means of combatting poverty and suffering was shared by his Rwandan cohorts. When Rwandan bishop John Rucyahana was asked by North American Anglicans how they could get involved in ministry to Rwandan orphans, recalled Thomas, Rucyahana replied, "First, come and stay with me. First, come and be with me." For Thomas, Rucyahana's words, which he heard echoed by his sister-church cohorts in Gatisbo, served as "really strong affirmation that this isn't just *our* 'enlightened' view of how we are supposed to be approaching this." According to Thomas, people on both sides of the partnership had poured their energy and resources into the relationship, believing in its capacity to bring about positive change in the lives of North Americans and global southerners alike.

Especially since the voices of the southern partners are not represented by this study, respondents' assessment of the role of sister church relationships in the lives of their partners should be compared with scholarship about the effects of American mission efforts abroad based on observations of southern communities and testimonies from Africans and Latin Americans themselves. Although the scholarship assessing the impact of short-term mission trips on North American participants is much more developed than the scholarship gauging the effects of short-term mission trips on southern communities, several scholars have begun exploring this territory. Some of these scholars are global southerners themselves with direct links to communities who host North American visitors in the name of mission.

The wisdom of sending human and physical capital from North America to the global South in the name of mission has become hotly debated territory among such scholars. North American mission efforts sometimes produce unfortunate consequences even when intentions are noble and structures are scrutinized to avoid wasting resources, creating dependency, and fostering paternalism. Costs of sending North Americans and goods are high relative to other alternatives for which the same money might be used. Not only that, but in some cases North American workers may do more harm than good due to their lack of cultural fluency, their potential displacement of local workers, and the short-term nature of their service. And even when money is handled sensitively, North American–funded projects in the global South are often inefficiently carried out and sometimes destabilizing for local economies. Despite their foibles, contemporary North American mission efforts in the global South are deemed worthwhile by some scholars because of the resources they bring to southern communities and the encouragement they offer to southern Christians.

According to David Livermore, however, many scholars and long-term missionaries alike are not convinced that short-term mission trips are helping recipients.[24] For instance, in his study of a North American relief organization's role in helping Hondurans rebuild their homes in the aftermath of Hurricane Mitch in 1998, sociologist Kurt Ver Beek found no lasting impact on the Honduran families and communities whose homes were built by North Americans as compared to those who never saw a short-term mission team. The Hondurans he interviewed stated that, if given the choice, they would rather see the money raised by each team who traveled to Honduras channeled toward building more Honduran homes and employing Hondurans, even as these respondents acknowledged that receiving the money in lieu of the missionaries was not likely a realistic option.[25]

In a 2007 issue of the *Journal of Latin American Theology* dedicated specifically to short-term mission efforts in Latin America, several scholars, most of them Latin Americans themselves, weighed in on the question of how short-term mission trips affect local communities.

Joquín Alegre Villón, pastor at the Christian and Missionary Alliance Church in Calloa, Peru, reported on a mission trip from members of his congregation's sister church in Minnesota, with great enthusiasm. Based largely on more than five thousand "decisions of faith" made in the community during the visit from the partner congregation, Villón considered the short-term visit from the American partner congregation to be wildly successful in bearing fruit in his community.[26]

Other contributors to the issue were not as confident as Villón on the efficacy of short-term mission trips on the ministry of Latin American churches. In his survey of theology students and teachers at the Evangelical University of Paraguay, Martín Hartwig Eitzen found that while two-thirds of respondents stated that short-term missions bring some benefit to the national church they aim to help, 35 percent said that short-term mission efforts produce results that do not last. Eitzen also discovered that most Paraguayan believers are interested in hosting short-term mission efforts not for the money but for the relationships and friendships this type of mission enables.[27] In his analysis of the impact of short-term mission efforts on local churches, Peruvian Rodrigo Maslucán argued that while the local church benefits from the direct work of visiting groups, such help can be damaging to the church if the visitors do not value the national church members or include them in decision making.[28] Maslucán also observed that it is common for Peruvian pastors to note that the money spent on international travel for short-term mission trips could be redirected to local efforts to greater effect.[29] The special issue of the *Journal of Latin American Theology* also included the voices of several North Americans who had served as long-term missionaries in Latin America, many of them critiquing short-term mission trips for bringing about negative or insignificant outcomes in the local communities they intended to serve.

By elevating relationships over programs, focusing on long-term goals and sustainable development over short-term projects, and honoring the agency of southern Christians, proponents of sister church relationships maintain that sister church relationships mitigate some of the potential pitfalls of short-term mission trips and are thus more effective in their impact on local communities. However, the research on the effects of sister church relationships on southern communities is similarly ambiguous to the research on stand-alone short-term mission trips. According to C. M. Brown, one of the most important potential contributions of sister church relationships is in crossing major divides of culture, ethnicity, wealth, and power by creating bridging and linking social capital between communities around the world. However, bridging social capital—which creates networks between people who differ in terms of ethnicity or culture—and linking social capital—which bridges status relating to power and access to resources—are harder to create than bonding social capital.[30] In his case study of three sister church relationships between American and Ukrainian congregations, Brown found that, when aided by bicultural mediation that empowered the Ukrainian congregations, bridging and linking social capital formed between partner congregations. Furthermore, the bridging and linking social capital resulted in both serendipitous and strategically planned benefits for the Ukrainian communities.[31] In his comparison of the three cases in his study, however, Brown notes that social capital creation was not automatic. When bicultural mediation was not effective and systems of decision making were not empowering to the Ukrainian congregations, bridging and linking social capital were not created.

Other research on the effectiveness of sister church relationships in bringing about positive change in southern communities has also yielded a mixed appraisal. Based on his case study of a partnership between a Liberian congregation and a North American congregation, Samuel Reeves argues that northern and southern participants alike discerned the relationship to be mutually beneficial and rewarding for both congregations. Reeves maintained that like northern participants, southern participants also saw their faith enriched and their global perspective enlarged.[32] In his interviews with Tanzanians involved in congregational partnerships with American Lutherans, David Cline found that, like their American counterparts, Tanzanian Lutherans expressed appreciation for their experience of "the community of saints across cultures." Additionally, Cline reports that the Tanzanians he interviewed mentioned the importance of the relationships for bettering the lives of the poor in their communities.[33] While Tara Hefferan also found that parish twinning helps meet some human needs in Haitian communities, she argues that sister parish relationships do not concentrate on systemic issues that create local problems. Rather than subverting differences in wealth, power, and opportunity, says Hefferan, twinning relationships are prone to reinforcing systemic injustice.[34]

As several of the contributors to the special edition of the *Journal of Latin American Theology* noted, the impact of short-term mission trips on local communities depends largely on how the trips are carried out in relation to local communities. Based on participant observation in Peruvian communities, Robert Priest and Tito Paredes concluded that the impact of short-term mission projects depended upon whether Peruvian partners were central to the planning an implementation of collaborative projects, whether projects fit within the long-term strategy and plans of Peruvian Christians, and whether there was energy and commitment to the project on both sides.[35] Short-term mission projects that met these criteria had a stronger positive impact in Peruvian communities than those that did not. Similarly, based on his congregation's experiences of partnership with North American congregations, Dominican pastor Robert Guerrero maintained that partnerships that value relationships and empowerment over tasks and projects can bring about a significant amount of good for both partners, whereas little lasting change happens in either community when short-term volunteers approach their partners from a place of power.

What we have experienced in our Network as we give priority to relationship and community building over task and projects, is that the task becomes a platform for community building. We find people experience deep impact in their personal lifestyle and serious re-evaluation of their ministry approach. Many of our friends from the North that have served us for years have made serious adjustments to their lifestyles and profound impact in their own local Churches back home.[36]

According to Guerrero, when relationships are nurtured and power is used to enable community rather than impose agendas, both host and visiting ministries are transformed in the process.

Believing that sister church relationships are better able to meet these conditions than stand-alone short-term mission efforts, proponents of sister church relationships maintain that sister church relationships can heighten the positive impact of short-term mission efforts. Like stand-alone short-term mission trips, however, the effectiveness of sister church relationships in southern communities is largely dependent upon how they are carried out. As the next chapter will explore, some of the profiled partnerships were more successful than others. In addition to the paralyzing effects of interpersonal conflict, the profiled sister church relationships faced formidable challenges such as the structural imbalance of power, the difficulty of effective cross-cultural communication, and the instability of interpersonal relationships. In some cases, the gap between rhetoric and reality was pronounced, and sustained positive change was elusive. Still, participants believed that something true and beautiful—if imperfect—emerged from their partnerships.

## Conclusion

Despite challenges and setbacks, respondents maintained that sister church relationships brought about a significant amount of good in the lives of North Americans and global southerners alike. It is difficult to determine the extent to which they were right. If one of the chief ends of sister church relationships is in creating bridging social capital—as both C. M. Brown and Robert Priest suggest—then judging the effectiveness of such efforts is especially difficult because friendship defies quantification. Moreover, bridging social capital is a phenomenon that is shared by both communities, with possible reverberations in many directions. The effects of sister church relationships are in some ways intangible, if still significant. To describe their sense of the impact of their congregation's sister church relationship being greater than the sum of its parts, two pastors used the metaphor of marriage as an illustration. Ruth Eaton from Kensington Woods Presbyterian shared:

We are a catalyst for each other, and that to me is a real partnership. Just like a marriage, you often marry your opposite in many ways because that person completes something in you, and you complete something in them. In our sister church relationship, in a sense we come with our material goods to meet their material needs; we come with our spiritual needs and they have their spiritual goods. We're truly inspired in the relationship, and their material circumstances have truly improved since the relationship began. Clean water, education, facilities. It is truly to me a beacon of hope. It's a twenty-year miracle, through the power of the Holy Spirit.

Dave Rice also thought of Living Faith's relationship with Murambi like a marriage:

Both communities have been changed by this relationship. From time to time, Fabi will say, 'I've gotten a new take on this issue from you,' or vise versa. It's like marriage. People think of marriage as this static thing where you take these two perfect porcelain dolls and you put them together on the mantelpiece and look at them. That's just not true. Marriage is this dynamic relationship of two people taking a journey together. I think the same way about our engagement of these two congregations and our marriage together. We're dynamic, and we're constantly changing. It's been very, very good, for both.

Relational therapist and marriage expert Harville Hendrix describes marriage as both "a crucible and a cushion."[37] According to respondents, the same could be said of sister church relationships. Through their experiences related to congregational partnerships, participants found themselves stretched and comforted, convicted and graced.

CHAPTER 7 | Challenges

*The Hurdles for Sister Church Relationships*

IN MARCH OF 2008, Pastor Henry Hunt from Mount Shannon Presbyterian Church led a "scouting delegation" to Carysburg, Liberia, to explore how to develop Mount Shannon's fledgling sister church relationship. Don Lingard, the only other member of Mount Shannon who went on the trip, was chosen to participate because of his position as moderator of Mount Shannon's mission committee. The delegation's other three members were only tangentially connected to the congregation and were recruited to participate because of their professional expertise.

At least for most of the participants, Mount Shannon's delegation to Liberia was not the sort of therapeutic experience that many North Americans have come to expect of cross-cultural mission trips. Strong conflict between Carysburg and Mount Shannon leadership quickly emerged. The legacy of Liberia's colonial history has created a complex and sticky web of power dynamics at Carysburg Mission, a web that Henry Hunt, for one, was not afraid to enter and disturb. Priscilla and Charles Spencer were prominent members of the "Congolese" class as they are called in Liberia, descendants of African American freed slaves who colonized Liberia in the middle of the nineteenth century. As Hunt explained, in Liberia the demarcation between the repatriates, who control the country and almost all of its institutions, and the "country people," who live in dire poverty and enjoy very few rights, is stark.

While in Liberia, Hunt was appalled by the poor treatment of the country people by the Spencers and other Carysburg Mission leaders. He balked at this treatment on several occasions, from refusing to eat until the housekeeper was served to gathering blankets to sleep in the car so the driver could have a bed to circumventing the Spencers' plans for agricultural development by making his own business arrangements with local farmers. "In every situation in which I saw cultural oppressiveness or subhuman treatment, I objected. And that was not OK. And it's still not OK. How much do you go along in order to keep peace, and how much do you speak out for . . . what is a very difficult situation?"

As Hunt saw the situation, it was his obligation to stand up for the dignity of other human beings and children of God, even if that meant angering the Congolese leadership of his congregation's partner church.

Viewing Hunt's behavior as a challenge to her authority and the integrity of the mission, Priscilla Spencer chided Hunt for interfering in a culture he did not understand and undermining her leadership. Spencer and her fellow leaders at Carysburg Mission were not the only ones who had a problem with Hunt's actions. From the perspective of Rose Morrison, an education consultant who joined Mount Shannon's delegation out of humanitarian rather than religious motivation, Henry Hunt's behavior in Liberia was motivated by his "issues with women" and overconfidence in his own religious and cultural perspective.

> The pastor of Mount Shannon and I really didn't see eye-to-eye at all. I tried to acknowledge that I have biases as an American, and to listen to people, to get to know them and to hear their ideas. Liberia is a very complicated country with a complicated history. Pastor Hunt was totally blind to the fact that he was a powerful white man, bringing with him the white man's religion, as a cultural imposition. He kept on challenging the leadership of Carysburg Mission for the way they treated country people. The message he sent was, "I'm not racist, you're racist." He kept challenging the way that things were done, not realizing the fact that his position as a powerful white male from North American might influence his perspective.

For Rose Morrison, Hunt represented not the liberator of the oppressed, but the modern-day northern colonizer.

Meanwhile, Don Lingard and many other members of Mount Shannon who were involved in the Liberian partnership were much more sympathetic to the Spencers and their approach to ministry than was Henry Hunt. Unlike Morrison, who respected the Spencers' literacy and social development efforts but was leery of what she saw as the heavy-handed role of religion at Carysburg, Lingard expressed nothing but admiration for Priscilla and Charles Spencer. A philanthropist without a critical understanding of culture, Lingard, along with many of his fellow parishioners, had no say in the disputes between Hunt and Morrison regarding cultural authority and the proper response to the legacy of colonialism. While Morrison believed that cultural values are relative, that Christianity is a foreign instrument of oppression in Africa, and that North Americans are in no position to offer solutions to African problems, Hunt preached mutual accountability in the name of Christianity, standing up against oppression wherever it may be found, and a relationship-centered approach to ministry. Lingard, on the other hand, saw the Liberian partnership simply as an opportunity for the Mount Shannon congregation to do good by helping the less fortunate. Lingard was proud of the various projects that Mount Shannon initiated related to Carysburg Mission, and he boasted that the Mount Shannon congregation has been "very generous and giving."

The sister church relationship between Mount Shannon Presbyterian Church and Bensonville Presbyterian in the Carysburg Mission of Liberia is a story of colliding worlds. At Mount Shannon, religious philanthropists like Don Lingard, secular humanitarians like Rose Morrison, and abrasive prophets like Henry Hunt combined forces in an effort to reach ill-defined goals in an alien, problem-wrecked, and complicated setting. On the other side of the equation, privileged Congolese Christians struggled to improve their community amid corruption, distrust, and toxic cultural norms, in concert with a North American partner whose support was equivocal and strained. And somewhere in the mix, cross-cultural faith-based friendships struggled to find the value ostensibly assigned to them by both partners.

Given the conflicted nature of Mount Shannon's sister church relationship, Henry Hunt had doubts about the viability of the partnership in the future. Besides questioning the Spencers' leadership and the project-centered approach of his own congregation's mission committee, Hunt questioned the feasibility of travel and communication between the two communities given Liberia's lack of security and infrastructure. On the other hand, Liberian children were being educated and given medical care through the partnership, and Mount Shannon parishioners were growing in faith and cultural intelligence. Because Hunt believed that the good outweighed the bad, he had not encouraged his congregation to discontinue the relationship. Even though he may not have understood why some might look at him, rather than Spencer or Lingard, as the face of colonialism, Hunt recognized that sister church relationships are inevitably messy.

## Challenges Confronting Sister Church Relationships

Mount Shannon Presbyterian's partnership was the most conflicted and troubled of the profiled congregations. While an extreme case, Mount Shannon's story illustrates many of the common challenges that confront

North American congregations involved in international partnerships. Interpersonal conflict made it difficult for the congregation to work well as a team and to establish trust with their partners in Liberia. Although less debilitating, many other challenges presented themselves as barriers to a fruitful sister church relationship. The partnership's reliance on a few individuals and their personal relationships meant that connections between the two congregations at large were difficult to foster. Concerns over safety, distance, and cost made it difficult for members of the two congregations to meet one another and build meaningful friendships. Money and resources spent on sending a scouting delegation from Mount Shannon to Carysburg were not available for other endeavors, and questions about whether these resources were used effectively were difficult to answer.

In addition to these challenges that surface in cross-cultural mission efforts of all types, Mount Shannon also faced several difficulties close to the heart of the sister church model of mission. As Mount Shannon discovered, the ideals of partnership and mutuality, while attractive in theory, are very difficult to embody on the ground—especially in the context of marked material inequality, power differentials, and the difficulty of crossing boundaries of race, class, and culture. Moreover, participants do not always share the same understanding of the ideas that frame sister church relationships or the same strategy for putting ideas into practice. As congregations seek to build relationships with other faith communities across oceans in the name of the partnership model of mission, things do not always turn out as planned. What starts strongly can lose energy and vision over time. Conflict can tear congregational teams apart and compromise their efforts. Economic and cultural barriers can handicap, if not poison, sister church relationships. While most respondents believed that their sister church relationships were still worthy endeavors despite their problems, this conviction was hard won.

## Reliance on Individuals and Personal Relationships

One of the challenges to the vitality of sister church relationships is their reliance on individuals and personal relationships among individuals. Grassroots interpersonal relationships are the lifeblood of the sister parish model. As the previous chapter discussed, interpersonal relationships are a source of strength for sister church relationships; they inspire, intensify, and prolong participation, and they provide meaning and fulfillment for those involved. Still, personal relationships are often unstable and transitory and make for a tenuous base for institutional partnerships. However informal their links to denominational or parachurch networks and however decentralized their leadership systems, sister church relationships are still institutional in nature. They are designed to link congregations, not unaffiliated groups of individuals. For better or for worse, however, in many congregations, sister church relationships effectively link a particular subgroup within one congregation to a subgroup within another congregation. The salient relationships formed are often at an individual level. Parishioners who are not directly involved in the relationships are only marginally invested in their congregation's partnership.

Dependent upon religious institutions and formal networks for survival yet simultaneously eschewing them in favor of personal relationships, sister church partnerships are difficult to sustain organizationally. Whereas globalization facilitates ease of travel and communication, it also enables migration, which is often rapid and recurring and thus destabilizing for personal relationships. North Americans in particular are likely not only to change geographic locations several times in their lives but also to switch congregations or become unaffiliated. When a key actor leaves a congregation or stops participating in the congregation's partnership, the change can often spell a crisis for the congregation's sister church relationship overall.

Several of the profiled congregations faced difficulties in the course of their sister church relationships due to a change in leadership or participation. At Our Lady of Sorrows, Pastor John Mountford's charisma and networks propelled Our Lady's side of the sister parish relationship for nearly a decade. When Mountford and several other key personalities left the parish, the relationship went into decline due to a leadership vacuum, a lack of enthusiasm, and a loss of strong interpersonal relationships between members of the two communities. Of those participants involved more recently, several had left the parish—even while remaining on the sister parish committee. While the personal relationships between these individuals and members of the Reina de la Paz community remained strong, the formal relationship between the two parishes languished. As Our Lady of Sorrows illustrates, the ever-changing composition of congregations can easily destabilize their international partnerships.

The entrance of new personalities into sister church relationships can have similar effects. Several respondents at Saint Mariana of Jesus remarked that Monsignor Peter Krakishaw, who became pastor two years after Saint Mariana's sister parish relationships began, had not been as strong of an advocate for the sister parish relationships as the former pastor. Respondents also voiced concern that Krakishaw was more interested in philanthropy than justice and thus isolated many of the original participants. The other profiled sister church relationships were similarly vulnerable to changes in participation, for good or for ill.

Moreover, particular congregants often wielded significant influence on their sister church relationships. Difficult or domineering personalities stifled participation or generated conflict among participants in several congregations. In programs administered by centralized leadership, the personality of the pastor or other dominant leader often made or broke institutional efforts. In two of the Catholic parishes, participants struggled to satisfy the wishes of a pastor with whom they disagreed, knowing that the pastor's authority was preeminent. In decentralized programs, even though power was ostensibly shared, personality clashes impeded effective organizational functioning. Mount Shannon Presbyterian's case is a fitting illustration. Both centralized and decentralized leadership structures were sensitive to the idiosyncrasies of particular individuals.

Even if individual North American participants in sister church relationships are well liked both in their own congregations and their sister church communities, often they do not possess the same professional expertise and cultural fluency as long-term missionaries or development workers—let alone local leaders. Development efforts in the global South serviced by laypersons from another culture are easily handicapped by ignorance. As Peyton Crowder, a Presbyterian pastor and participant in Mount Shannon's delegation to Liberia, remarked:

> The downside of sister church relationships is that support is based on a personal, emotional relationship rather than the expertise of professionals at the denominational level. Personal relationships are limited, and a potential problem is that you get people from congregations getting involved who don't know what they are doing. There is a place for professionals who have a much better idea of how to assess needs. They provide a guided, directed, planned-out approach to mission that congregations who are doing things at the grassroots level often do not have.

Crowder added that even though he had experience in the field of construction as well as church leadership, it was difficult to assess the needs in Carysburg without the background knowledge that denominational experts might have.

In some ways, the reliance on individuals is the Achilles heel of the sister church model. In other ways, individuals and the bonds they form on a personal level provide the lifeblood of sister church relationships. To see their international partnerships thrive, congregations involved in sister church relationships needed to avoid responsibility for the relationship being too concentrated among one individual or small group while simultaneously encouraging participants to form meaningful, interpersonal, cross-cultural relationships.

## Conflict

In the midst of congregation-to-congregation relationships, conflicts of one sort or another almost inevitably arise. While disagreements and misunderstandings can be a source of growth in relationships if they are addressed and resolved properly, interpersonal conflicts can also tear apart communities and undermine mission efforts. Despite the significant cultural differences between northern and southern partners in sister church relationships, cross-cultural conflict between congregations was much less pronounced in the profiled cases than intracongregational conflict. Moreover, while theological disagreements sometimes surfaced in these sister church relationships, differences in personality and conflicting understandings of collective identity caused the more salient conflicts.

Many of the partners were quite different from each other in theological orientation and practice. As several scholars of global Christianity have observed, southern Christian communities tend to embrace social conservatism, biblical literalism, and an evangelical ethos more than northern ones. Sister church relationships particularly highlight this trend since mainline churches are over-represented among participating congregations in the North. Yet, in the profiled relationships, theological differences did not seem to affect sister church relationships negatively. In their attempts to respect and honor members of their sister church communities, participants often did their best to avoid conflict with their counterparts. Given the barriers of language and distance as well as the short length of time that participants usually spent with their counterparts, intensified theological conflicts simply did not arise.

In most cases, in fact, ideological differences were tolerated and even respected. While respondents with more liberal orientations were often reticent to verbally commend their faith to others, they did not seem to have the same misgivings about their partners' evangelistic efforts or pietistic practices. Delegates from Washington, DC–area congregations with formalized liturgies expressed appreciation for the spirited and spontaneous style of worship of their southern partners. Politically charged differences regarding women in church leadership and homosexuality were generally breached amicably as well. In the latter regard, for instance, Nancy Compton from Third Presbyterian explained that although a formal relationship between the National Capital Presbytery and a Kenyan presbytery had dissolved over differing stances on the issue of homosexuality, projects initiated by the partnership were sustained under the auspices of member congregations of each presbytery. According to Compton, both sides found the compromise workable, and mutual ministry continued. As long as the Washington, DC–area congregations remained quiet about their progressive stance on homosexuality during their interactions with their Kenyan counterparts, said Compton, the issue did not adversely affect their partnership.

In most cases, ideological differences remained benign, but in several cases the tides were turned as northern congregations were found to be more socially conservative than their southern counterparts. Peter Russell, rector of Christ the King Anglican, expressed deep concern about the acceptance of women's ordination by the Anglican Province of Rwanda. According to Russell, the Christ the King congregation felt betrayed by what they perceived to be a compromise of biblical truth on behalf of their Rwandan partners. At Our Lady of Sorrows Catholic Church, several parishioners were uncomfortable with the Marxist commitments they perceived among their counterparts at María Reina de la Paz. Several respondents from Third Presbyterian, who identified their congregation as one of the most liberal in the PC(USA), mentioned that Iglesia del Centro was just as progressive. These findings challenge claims of a global culture war brewing between northern and southern Christians. While theological and political differences did exist between the northern and southern partners, in several cases these differences contradicted stereotypes. And in most cases these differences did not adversely affect the relationship between the two communities in any substantial way.

The heart of the most pronounced conflict among the profiled partnerships was clashing personalities. Priscilla Spencer and Henry Hunt did not battle over politics or theology. Instead, they argued about the best way to run programs, treat people, and exercise authority. Similarly, most of the conflict that occurred within the Washington, DC–area congregations—which was more pronounced that conflict between partnering congregations—centered around personality clashes and differing understandings of identity and mission.

In her study of congregational conflict among Protestant, Catholic, and Jewish congregations in a large midwestern suburb in the early 1990s, Penny Edgell Becker found that congregational conflict was produced not by different polity types and different ideologies but rather by competing understandings of identity.[1] According to Becker, congregations fall into four basic categories based on the "way we do things here." The four identities rest on answers to two questions: whether the congregation fosters debate about issues and whether members expect their internal relationships to be close or remote. In Becker's typology, the "leader" congregation is devoted to public issues but does not expect intimacy in its internal life. Opposite of the leader congregation, the "family" congregation expects intimacy even at the cost of issue-centered engagement. The "community" congregation is both issue centered and close knit, while the "house of worship" congregation is interested in neither intimacy nor activism, but in worship. Becker found that in most cases, as long as congregations could agree on their function as a church, they avoided bitter conflicts, even if members differed markedly from one another in their theological and political leanings. Intractable conflicts, on the other hand, occurred when members lacked consensus on the fundamental identity of their congregation.

Coalescing with Becker's findings, the profiled congregations generally experienced conflict related to their sister church relationships when members disagreed on the purpose of the partnership or when individuals argued about how to carry out projects and relationships. The tension between projects and relationships noted in chapter 5 caused conflict in several cases, especially when participants were not unified in their sense of purpose for their congregation's partnership. At Our Lady of Sorrows, some parishioners believed that one of their responsibilities was to advocate for Salvadorans with the Catholic Church and the US government, whereas other parishioners believed that political advocacy had no place among parish activities. At Saint Mariana of Jesus, some parishioners believed that a focus on financial giving would compromise a sense of mutuality in their relationship with Nuestra Señora. Others maintained that financially supporting the economically disadvantaged parish was the best thing that Saint Mariana could do to help. When participants did not see eye-to-eye regarding the purpose of their sister church relationship, conflict naturally ensued.

In most cases involving discord, intracongregational conflict related to the sister church relationship was as much a function of differences in personality, age, or position of influence as it was anything else. Many participants who came of age before the cultural shifts of the 1960s, for example, approached sister church relationships from a project-centered, philanthropy-based vantage point. Baby boomers and members of Generation X and Y cohorts, on the other hand, tended to be more sensitive to dynamics of power and privilege. On the more banal level, some personalities, regardless of age, were more tolerant of living or travel conditions in the global South than were others. These differences sometimes caused intradelegation tension. Differing leadership styles and contests of power also caused conflicts.

Conflict between partners or within congregations was neither pronounced nor debilitating in most of the relationships. In fact, several respondents from various congregations referenced misunderstandings or differences that were ultimately a source of humor and growth. Yet interpersonal conflict, when protracted, unresolved, or bitter, threatened to undermine the success of sister church relationships.

## Logistical Concerns

Another challenge to the health of sister church relationships is posed by logistical difficulties on both the micro and macro levels. Unlike local or even regional partnerships or projects, the cost of sending visitors across oceans is problematic or even prohibitive in many cases. Even if North American participants can avail themselves of the financial resources required to travel to Asia, Latin America, or Africa, it is usually impossible for their counterparts in their sister church communities to return visits, short of full subsidies from the North American partners. Aside from the question of whether the money to fund cross-continental travel in the name of sister church relationships is well spent, the concept of partnership is compromised when one partner is always the financier.

Beside financial costs, numerous other logistical hurdles present themselves in sister church relationships. Especially in war-torn or politically unstable countries such as Liberia, threats to the safety of North American visitors are significant. While Americans generally find it relatively easy to secure government permission to visit most places in the global South, the reverse is not true, especially in the wake of the events of September 11, 2001. Even where travel is relatively affordable and free from strict government restrictions, on the basis of distance alone it is difficult for delegations from sister church partners to visit one another on a regular basis. Environmental costs of long-distance travel also create a barrier to delegation visits and call into question the sustainability of international short-term mission efforts and sister church relationships in general.

Communication barriers, like travel barriers, can also be significant. While international communication capabilities have improved dramatically since the advent of e-mail and cellular phones, the lack of reliable infrastructure in many communities in the global South can make for intermittent and unreliable communication between sister church communities. Language barriers also pose formidable challenges. Although parishioners often managed to have meaningful encounters with members of their sister congregations amid language barriers, gestures and one-word exchanges only went so far. Some congregations boasted of a surprising number of French or Spanish speakers among their participants, and translators were routinely hired to accompany delegation teams. Moreover, the number of English-speakers in many locations in the global South is ever growing. Still, effective communication across technological, linguistic, and cultural divides remains challenging.

## Opportunity Costs

Congregations, like all human entities, are limited in the amount of time, energy, and resources that are available to them. Congregations that become involved in sister church relationships may forgo other opportunities for growth, mission, or service. Additionally, congregational mission projects often have results that are unplanned and unanticipated by their initiators. As R. Stephen Warner notes, mission is a source of functional diffuseness in congregations.[2] When congregations take on a sister church relationship, they often unwittingly give something up and/or take on unexpected challenges as a result. Of particular concern is the possibility of focusing on international relationships to the neglect of local communities. While several of the congregations engaged in mission efforts in their local communities in addition to their international activity, many congregations found it difficult to sustain multiple time- and energy-intensive ministries. Rather than spread their resources thin, they concentrated on their sister church relationship over local initiatives.

Perhaps their focus on international over local ties was not accidental. Critics of the short-term mission movement have noted that sending teams of volunteers abroad for short periods of time can be an escape mechanism for congregations that are put off by the requirements or discomforts of long-term engagement with their local communities. Engaging with geographic neighbors who impinge upon an individual's or community's sensibilities can be trying and unpleasant. By contrast, congregations can often more easily set their own terms in foreign mission efforts. Short-term mission trips abroad are often more exotic and interesting than engaging in one's own community. They also tend to be less emotionally risky for participants in that sustained interaction is not required, discomfort is usually temporary, and situations of dire need can be easily removed from view by returning home.

## Vulnerability in Frames

As chapter 5 explained, the sister church model of mission is based on the ideals of partnership and mutuality. Framers envision sister church relationships as two-way flows of spiritual and material resources, undertaken in the spirit of solidarity rather than charity or philanthropy. As leaders in the profiled congregations sought to embody the ideal of partnership in their sister church relationships, however, they faced many obstacles. Some participants failed to understand or appreciate the value of mutuality, thus highlighting a gap between rhetoric and reality. Participants differed among themselves regarding how to appropriate this value in practice. And even when congregational teams agreed on the frames they espoused, conditions they encountered as well as their own prejudices often called into question the feasibility of their ideals.

Although leaders in most of the congregations insisted that their sister church relationship was primarily a vehicle of mutuality rather than a funnel for North American philanthropy, often their vision was not internalized by the rest of the congregation. Kevin Marino from Our Lady of Sorrows lamented that despite the committee's many efforts to educate the parish about solidarity, most people "just don't understand." He explained:

> People have a hard time differentiating between charity and solidarity or charity and social justice. Most people just think, "It's great that we are helping these poor people." People here are well educated, and they have good intentions, but they aren't always aware of El Salvador and the issues there. And they don't really understand what we are trying to do.

Similarly, Kimberly Cook, director of social concerns at Saint Clement, said that one of the biggest challenges as facilitator of Saint Clement's sister parish relationship with Sacré-Coeur was helping parishioners understand that "this is not just charity, but a give-and-take situation. Poverty doesn't mean disability." In addition to conveying the reciprocal nature of the relationship, Cook also struggled to frame projects in Pignon as empowerment efforts rather than handouts. She explained that it is tempting for both Haitian brothers and sisters in the Pignon community and St. Clement's parishioners to consider the economic disparities between the two parishes and expect Saint Clement to be Sacré-Coeur's eternal benefactor. Part of Cook's task, as she saw it, was to help her parish carry out their efforts in Pignon in such a way that eventually the support would no longer be needed.

According to long-time committee member Jack Napoli, however, the values of solidarity and social justice were not being internalized in the parish. "When I hear people talk about the sister parish, I often hear about 'how much help we are giving,' and the emphasis is on how much help *we're* giving." Like Cook, Napoli pointed to a culture of dependency in Haiti, "which we only nurture when we encourage people to see us as their benefactors." According to Napoli, Saint Clement's previous director of social concerns emphasized solidarity, relationship building, and empowerment to a much greater degree than Kimberly Cook. From Napoli's perspective, part of the reason the "charity mindset" was so pervasive at Saint Clement is that neither Saint Clement's pastor nor Cook really understood the values they ostensibly espoused. "You know, it's hard," he continued. "I'm not sure I really 'get it' either."

Saint Clement was not the only parish in which leaders' endorsement of the ideal of solidarity was equivocal, at best. Clancey Brown, pastor of Mount Calvary, was committed to long-term relationships with international partners. He spoke of "coming alongside" his congregation's partners rather than "trying to fix their problems," and he stressed that it was pastors Rupini and Luckhoo who set the tone for Mount Calvary's work in their communities. "We are always making sure that we do not overstep our boundaries. We lend ourselves to them." At the same time, there was a paternalistic tenor to Brown's articulation of Mount Calvary's approach to congregation-to-congregation relationships. Brown spoke of "adopting" both Jangalia Baptist and Resurrection Temple, of being named "father" of Resurrection Temple to "provide covering" to Resurrection's female pastor, and of supporting international churches for nothing in return.

Many of the congregations had difficulty disseminating a unified vision for their sister church relationship. Leaders were unsuccessful in getting the rest of the congregation to fully adopt their frames, leaders disagreed among themselves, or they lacked full commitment to a particular vision of partnership. As Gary Marx and Douglas McAdam point out, even when social movement actors share a common ideology, there is often disagreement when it comes to the specific aspects of an ideology or how to apply it to concrete situations.[3] At Saint Mariana of Jesus, for example, at least initially the twinning committee agreed that the purpose of the relationship was solidarity and mutual support. As Mark Downey explained, however, participants soon disagreed among themselves regarding the relationship's priorities. Tension between a focus on projects and a focus on relationships began to erode Saint Mariana's common vision and action on behalf of the sister parish relationship.

Downey, a high school Spanish teacher, was heavily involved in Saint Mariana's twinning relationship in the initial stages and then dropped out when it became clear to him that the relationship was going in a direction that he could not support. Downey explained that the committee's initial goals for the relationship were building strong interpersonal relationships between laypeople in both parishes and serving together side-by-side. When Monsignor Peter Krakishaw became Saint Mariana's new pastor, Krakishaw pulled the project away from lay leadership and began emphasizing money and "works of mercy." Downey started noticing that for many participants, getting involved became "my little thing to do for God. Like Mother Teresa, this is my charity moment where I'm going to be the one in power who is reaching down and giving a handout or doing works of mercy, and not a lot of work in terms of actually building a relationship."

Downey lamented that parishioners at Saint Mariana, encouraged by their pastor, "just wanted to 'do stuff' rather than allowing any kind of real relationship to take place."

Confusion and disagreement regarding the ideal of mutual solidarity as well as difficulty applying this value in concrete situations are not entirely surprising given the vulnerability of partnership as a basis for mission. As missiologist Jonathan Rowe contends, partnership in mission is a benign but not necessarily positive concept. It is defined mostly by what it is against—paternalism—rather than by constructive notions of the purpose of mission.[4] The theory of partnership in mission was developed as a response to the reputation of colonial mission efforts for triumphalism and heavy-handedness on the part of northerners. Its attractiveness, says Rowe, is at least partially based on it being considered unobjectionable—a shaky foundation for a vision for mission.[5]

Additionally, the ideal of partnership is somewhat at odds with a basic notion of mission as an act of sending.[6] When individuals embark on a missionary endeavor, they do so because they believe they have something to give to others. Whether they seek to proclaim a message, teach a skill, meet a need, or fix a problem, missionaries believe that change is needed in the target community and that they can be instruments of change.[7] Of course, giving and receiving are not necessarily mutually exclusive, as framers of sister church relationships are quick to point out. Still, a focus on mutuality and relationship building can obscure what, for many North American participants, is at the heart of their motivation. They want to see suffering diminished and needs met in the global South. A focus on relationships takes pressure off of congregations to be accountable for the resources they expend and to see measurable accomplishments as a result of their mission efforts. This makes many North American participants uncomfortable. Whatever good comes out of cross-cultural, faith-based friendships, in the minds of many participants, is simply not enough.

## Structural Imbalances of Power and Resources

The frame of mutual partnership as a basis for sister church relationships is called into question not only by attitudes of North American participants but also by the glaring reality of global inequality. As Samuel Escobar observes:

> Globalization has facilitated communication to the point that material and technological means are now available to create and develop transnational and transcontinental partnerships for the recruitment, training, and sending of missionaries. On the other hand, the growth of economic and social disparities adds difficulties to the development of effective global partnerships.[8]

When there is a vast disparity in access to power and resources between the two partners of an international sister church relationship—as is almost always the case—the call to mutual giving and receiving is complicated and compromised.

Several respondents remarked that while they wanted to honor the dignity of their partners and acknowledge that both communities were rich in some ways and poor in others, it was difficult to avoid a patronage scenario because of the dire material circumstances of their partners and the powerful influence of wealth. Mike Vallez, founder of Global Faith Partners, phrased the dilemma this way: "It's not about the money, yet it's always about the money." When financial contributions from the northern partner to the southern partner become a significant part of a sister church relationship, it is easy for both sides to begin to see the relationship as one of benefactor and beneficiary. For this reason, as was discussed in chapter 5, some of the congregations in my study were hesitant to give money to their sister congregations. Yet, even leaders in these congregations acknowledged that refusing to give out of one's abundance, albeit for good reasons, can easily be construed as simply a lack of generosity.

Given the dire poverty in most partner communities, it is unsurprising that some North American participants viewed their relationship as primarily philanthropic, despite the frame of mutuality endorsed by their congregations. Chet Greenstreet from Christ the King Anglican, for example, believed that his congregation's relationship with Nueva Jerusalén could not possibly be anything but donor-to-recipient.

> Other than appreciation and love toward us, they have nothing physical that they can give back. A family who basically lives in a one room block building and has no income, other than just to show their appreciation for what you're doing for them, there isn't anything else really that they can give you.

Many respondents saw immense value in the nonmaterial resources of their sister church communities and considered themselves blessed to a greater degree than they had been a blessing. But a few participants, like Greenstreet, placed a higher priority on material giving. When considering tangible resources, mutuality seems little more than an illusion in sister church relationships.

Even if they had good intentions of treating their international partners as friends and equals, many North American participants were blind to their own position of power in the relationship bestowed on them because of their material advantage. In the interest of making sure their money was used effectively, most of the Washington, DC–area congregations asked their partner congregations to give an accounting of how donations were spent. To simply give money indiscriminately, some respondents argued, would be irresponsible. Yet, no such accountability was asked of them in return. While protocols were created in many of the sister church relationships to ensure that southern partners maintained most of the control over their budget and program priorities, northern partners were not required to be financially accountable to their southern partners in any way.

On the other side of the equation, southern communities may feel a sense of indebtedness to their northern partners, which also compromises equal footing in the relationships. Out of a fear that children will go hungry or schools will close if they express concerns about their congregation-to-congregation relationships or make decisions that are unpopular with their sister churches, leaders in southern communities may feel that their hands are tied or their mouths gagged. Or, perhaps like Father Jean-Claude Germain from Pignon, Haiti, who visited Saint Clement every year to thank the parish for their generosity, leaders in southern communities may feel pressure to ingratiate themselves with their northern partners. Several respondents strongly believed that their counterparts in their sister church communities were not motivated by financial concerns and did not feel pressure to protect their financial interests. Other respondents spoke of a "culture of dependency" among members of their sister parish communities. The mindset was hard to escape when reinforced by both partners. Since only northern participants were interviewed, the degree to which the southern partners experienced a sense of mutuality in the relationships is unknown. However, given the powerful influence of money and the inescapable reality of vast material inequality on a global scale, it is likely that southern partners did not always experience the sister church relationships as liberating or dignifying.

As Jonathan Bonk contends in his treatise on mission and money based largely on his experience as a western missionary in Africa, the disparity in access to resources between northerners and southerners is more complex than wealth alone. Western affluence, says Bonk, is at least partially due to factors that cannot be re-created by the poor today.[9]

> We are now haunted by distressing indications that for most of our fellow human beings, there neither *is* nor *can be* any possible road to our way of life, with its visions of ever increasing levels of comfort and consumption. . . . the stark and brutal truth is that the natural resources of our planet are sufficient to support "developed" life for only a tiny fraction of its human population.[10]

Because western affluence is predicated on centuries of slavery, genocide, military conquest, and economic and political imperialism, no amount of "development" can replicate the conditions of this wealth among the poor in other parts of the world today. Moreover, Bonk argues that possession of wealth virtually ensures northern missionaries' insulation since it is a social reality that people almost always fraternize with economic peers. Bonk's arguments relate to sister church relationships and short-term mission efforts as well. The legacy of colonialism cannot be erased by efforts to form relationships across cultures, no matter how well intentioned.

### Barriers in Crossing Boundaries of Race, Class, and Culture

According to many critics, western humanitarian and religious mission efforts in the global South have historically functioned as thinly veiled attempts to expand empires and impose white cultural values on nonwhite populations. Frantz Fanon famously added to this line of reasoning by arguing that nonwhite subjects internalized this message of inferiority and as a result tried to appropriate and imitate the cultural code of the colonizer.[11] Recent generations of missiologists and development professionals have tried to reverse this trend by promoting structures of development and mission that engender respect for local cultures and empower local communities. Part of the rationale of the sister church model of mission is that long-term, reciprocal, mutually accountable relationships are a solution for overcoming the colonizing tendency by building trust and goodwill between partners.

Unfortunately, however, northern participants in sister church relationships are prone to perpetuate the very systems of cultural imperialism that they seek to overcome. In her case study of a relationship between a Catholic parish in the United States and a parish in Haiti, Tara Hefferan concluded that inasmuch as the American Catholics sought to save Haitians from poverty through the twinning relationship, their participation was an exercise of power. According to Hefferan, sister church relationships are a form of "alternative development" that fall prey to many of the same pitfalls of conventional secular development efforts. Although they can be contrasted to secular development efforts in their refusal to divide economic and spiritual realms, sister church initiatives share with secular development efforts a notion of progress based on a "generalized experience of middle-class Western modernity."[12] By focusing on "development," northern participants in sister church relationships imply that a group or nation is somehow deficient and requires outside intervention in order to "fix" it.[13] Predicated on the need to correct the seeming deficiencies of Haitians, the twinning relationship Hefferan studied was envisioned as a vehicle for equipping individuals with proper tools to build their own self-sufficiency rather than a way to change the structural forces that keep Haitians marginalized and impoverished.[14]

Unlike Hefferan's subjects, many respondents from the twelve Washington-area congregations did not view their sister church participation primarily through the lens of development. Whether or not development was part of their frame, however, respondents were often ignorant of entrenched patterns of cultural imperialism and unwittingly reinforced such patterns. Sometimes participants preached a gospel of respect and deference but then acted in ways to indicate that the structures and norms governing their sister church communities were inferior to North American systems and values. Other times, participants so idolized their sister church counterparts for their joy amid suffering as to minimize the ugliness of poverty or foster caricatures of the people they encountered. Many respondents took middle-class

American values for granted as universal and attributed local problems to cultural deficiencies rather than systemic injustices.

Ironically, a posture of paternalism was especially pronounced in the African American congregations. Contemporary African American Christian communities generally enjoy a culture of respect and compassion for the marginalized and oppressed. However, their institutions tend to be younger, less affluent, and more locally focused than those of their predominantly white counterparts. African Americans involved in mission efforts at the congregational level are often not privy to the same historical reflection, technical assistance from intermediaries, framing resources, and structural networks as members of predominantly white congregations. For the profiled African American congregations, reciprocity with their international partners was generally not a strong priority.

Still, no matter their demographic composition, most of the congregations sought to escape patterns of northern control and southern dependency Many, in fact, were so sensitive to this tendency that they overcompensated by idolizing their sister church communities and in so doing erected racial and cultural barriers of a different nature. Not wanting their sister church relationships to become "projects," several participants played the role of religious and cultural tourists when they visited their sister church communities. In these scenarios, it was easy for North American participants to objectify members of their sister church communities by reducing them to cultural artifacts or particular idealized traits.

In their attempts to make sense of alterity, northern participants sometimes fell prey to oversimplification or idolization of members of their sister church communities. Instead of seeing their counterparts as complex human beings, they relied on trite assumptions about what "they" are like. Tara Hefferan observed that sister parish committee members of the US parish she studied tended to invest more heavily in notions of difference than sameness with their Haitian counterparts. Haitians were at once models to emulate and repudiate: they were admired for their dignity, fortitude, focus on family, and joyfulness but ridiculed for their unworldliness, perceived laziness, and dependence on outsiders.[15] Similarly, respondents from the twelve Washington, DC–area congregations also tended to create one-dimensional portraits of their counterparts in an effort to discern authenticity in an alien culture. A prominent part of this discourse was the presumption that the poor are happy. Not wanting to see themselves as complicit in oppression or to be compelled to change their lifestyles, some North American participants risked minimizing the suffering of the poor and marginalized in their eagerness to read their partners as content in their circumstances.

Another way that participants patronized their counterparts was by suggesting that global southerners expressed particular opinions or traits principally because they had been co-opted by westerners. While it is true that political battles within western Christianity have often been recapitulated in Africa, Latin America, and Asia, some participants were quick to strip their sister church communities of responsibility, especially on matters in which they disagreed with them. At Third Presbyterian, Associate Pastor Stacy James Forester claimed that Presbyterians in Africa took a conservative stance on homosexuality because they had been conditioned by conservative American missionaries. Conversely, Rector Peter Russell from Christ the King Anglican suggested that leaders within the Anglican Church of Rwanda endorsed women's ordination because they had been indoctrinated by American liberals. Instead of seeing their sister church counterparts as agents, some North American participants preferred to view them as easily swayed or victimized.

By and large, respondents viewed themselves as crusaders against racism and ethnocentrism. Some even attributed what they perceived to be an increased level of cultural sensitivity to their participation in a sister parish relationship. However, racialized frames run deep, especially in American culture, and Americans' self-perceptions of their egalitarianism are often belied by their behavior. Hefferan describes several examples of Americans exhibiting disrespect and paternalism toward their partners with seeming oblivion.[16] Even without observing respondents' interactions with their partners, entrenched prejudices could be depicted among respondents. For instance, when Earl Henderson from Trinity Anglican explained how the Christians he met from Uganda challenged his stereotypes about "backwards Africans" with their intelligence, sophistication, and knowledge about Christianity, he noted that "I'm not talking about the locals on the street, but the Christian leaders." Similarly, Remy Duke, also from Trinity Anglican, remarked that when Africans are "educated and have a calling, they are just as sharp and intelligent as anyone you have encountered." Duke's and Henderson's caveats about which Africans they esteemed call into question the extent of their egalitarianism. As multiple students of race relations have observed, people often retain negative views of other groups despite evidence to the contrary. If they meet individuals who contradict their racial stereotypes, they simply see those individuals as exceptions to the rule.

Even if participants were loathe to acknowledge racism or paternalism in their own interactions with their partners, several recognized the ugliness of cultural imperialism inasmuch as they perceived it in the cross-cultural encounters of other North Americans. Respondents from each of the realigned Anglican congregations contrasted their open embrace of global southerners with what they perceived to be racism and arrogance on behalf of their Episcopalian counterparts. Rector Peter Russell from Christ the King Anglican remarked:

> I think how the Episcopal Church has responded to the Anglican realignment is a direct result of the "noble savage" concept. And what you've seen is that the noble savages have much to teach us, sort of like the American Indian. But when the noble savages rose up and said, "maybe we're not so savage," the Episcopal Church said, and I use my words advisedly, "Who the hell do you think you are? You are noble *savages*, and we are welcome to recognize the nobility of your savagery, but you are still savages." So what you see is this thin veneer of tolerance, love, acceptance, that hides a kind of arrogance or perhaps even tyranny.

Gini Axelrod expressed similar sentiments about former members of Trinity Anglican who decided to stay with the Episcopal Church when Trinity ceded from the denomination.

> Everyone supports the relationship now. But before we left the Episcopal Church there were complaints coming from people who ended up leaving Trinity to stay Episcopalian. They didn't want to be associated with Africa or to give our money there.

According to Axelrod and fellow parishioners like Edward and Jean Francis, it is the liberal Episcopalians, not the conservatives, who are intolerant and culturally insensitive.

Hailey Beckett from Living Faith Anglican, though much more sympathetic to the liberal wing of American Christianity than Russell or Axelrod, observed that though mainline liberals, as proponents of the social gospel, fight against being imperialistic, "they actually end up being more imperialistic because they come and say, 'Well, we are going to fix you,' but never take the time to look inward." Beckett continued:

> I just wonder how much self reflection . . . is going on among them and if anything is being transformed in them. They are so focused on transforming the outside and helping *other* people.

Evangelicals were not the only ones to identify imperialistic or culturally insensitive attitudes elsewhere. Contrasting Our Lady of Sorrows's approach to mission in El Salvador with that of evangelical groups who are also active there, Kevin Marino remarked that not only were the evangelicals that he had encountered in Latin America antagonistic to Catholicism, but they also endorsed the economic and political status quo and tried to "make brown people white." In Marino's eyes, evangelicals are like adolescents with an immature approach to mission. "I just want to say to them, 'Do you think you are going to create a better world for [Salvadorans] by trying to conform them into your own image?'"

The case of Mount Shannon Presbyterian is another illustration of the tendency among respondents to recognize racism or imperialism in someone else. According to Rose Morrison, Pastor Henry Hunt was a powerful white American male with an authoritarian personality—quick to act unilaterally in a culturally alien context and undermine local authority. Hunt, on the other hand, saw himself as an advocate for the oppressed who was willing to stand up to the Congolese colonizers. And as far as he was concerned, Rose Morrison, who "was supposed to be enlightened and culturally sensitive," failed to live up to her reputation by spending large amounts of time away from the group, alone with adult males. And in Hunt's mind, Priscilla Spencer, though her skin was black, was a true colonizer.

Mission efforts across boundaries of race, class, and culture have historically been fraught with misunderstanding, contests of power, and suspicion. Despite their desire to do things differently, participants could not obliterate the baggage of historical precedence, cultural privilege, and racialized norms. Parishioners from the Washington, DC–area congregations generally sought reconciliation across boundaries of race, class, and culture. Yet, their efforts were sometimes compromised by unquestioned assumptions, unacknowledged privilege, and unfair expectations regarding alterity. Moreover, participants' very desire to do good in their sister church communities was often linked to notions of progress or development that presumed the superiority of the industrialized West.

## Conclusion

The litany of challenges confronting sister church relationships gave congregations pause and forced them to evaluate whether their sister church relationship was indeed helping them fulfill their call to Christian mission. The obstacles of troublesome personalities, transient relationships, logistical nightmares, framing weaknesses, material inequality, and cultural barriers—to name a few—were problems with no easy solutions.

In her exploration of the friendship ideal in mission, in which cross-cultural relationships are seen as both a means of mission and an end in themselves, Dana Robert raises important questions about the feasibility of the model in today's milieu:

> [I]n an age characterized by short-term mission service, what is the deeper meaning of friendship? Is true friendship of equals possible across widening economic divides, or is it a self-deluding rationalization that makes the wealthy feel good about their charitable activities? . . . Does anyone have time to make friends today, or is cross-cultural service a kind of global networking that looks good on a résumé? Is friendship now defined by Facebook rather than walking in someone else's shoes?[17]

As this chapter illustrates, the critique of sister church relationships embedded in these questions deserves to be taken very seriously. Any celebration of the congregation-to-congregation model of mission that does not acknowledge the pitfalls and—often unintended—negative consequences of such relationships is unearned.

Many of the vexations of sister church relationships plague cross-cultural mission efforts of all stripes. The historical legacy of colonialism in particular saddles virtually all contemporary encounters between northerners and southerners with heavy baggage. However, cultural isolation, an alternative to cross-cultural mission, poses its own set of problems. And compared to other forms of mission, many respondents maintained that sister church relationships are better poised to facilitate fruitful exchange. Despite the difficulties, respondents overwhelmingly agreed that sister church relationships, when well designed and executed, are worthwhile. Because they believed the blessings of sister church relationships to far outweigh the curses, participants strove to scale the mountain of obstacles that stood in their way to generative and reciprocal congregation-to-congregation relationships. While their efforts were imperfect, many did claim to steal a glimpse of the other side of the precipice.

CHAPTER 8 | Opportunities

*The Sources of Strength for Sister Church Relationships*

MEMBERS OF LIVING FAITH Anglican Church maintained that their partnership with an African parish created significant opportunities to rewrite the scripts for faith-based, cross-cultural encounters. Living Faith's rector, Dave Rice, recounted that during Living Faith's first delegation to Murambi, the team quickly realized that despite their intentions, they were falling into tired and unhealthy patterns of North-South Christian engagement on African soil. He recalled visiting a Christian school in Gatsibo with the rest of his team:

> After [our presentation] the principal took over and gave an altar call for children to come forward and make a decision for Christ. About ten or fifteen kids came forward. Afterwards, one of the teachers took several of us outside. As we were talking, the teacher mentioned that those were the same ten or fifteen kids who had made a decision for Christ the last time the white *muzungus* had come to town.

Troubled by this revelation, the leaders of Living Faith's delegation called a team meeting. After a lengthy discussion about the patterns of Christian mission that have long existed in East Africa and the scripts of colonialism that Living Faith delegation members were unwittingly executing during their visit, Rice and other team members expressed their concerns to Archdeacon Gataraiha.

> That night, we had a worship service with Marambi Parish, and they paraded all of us up to the front of the church and sat us in chairs up on the

pulpit, honoring us as special visitors. At a certain point in the service, we all left those chairs and sat in the midst of the congregation and demonstrated to them that we were, first of all, equals and secondly, profoundly uncomfortable with being honored guests like that. We were pretty uncertain about how this would be received. But they went wild; they loved it. They responded very well, and we sensed that they were just as uncomfortable with the scripts as we were.

Rice asserted that, in the context of the sister church relationship, Living Faith participants continually re-evaluated their expectations. Rice believed that as Living Faith members collectively considered whether or not their actions and goals were healthy, and as they formed deeper relationships with their Rwandan counterparts, the congregation did an increasingly better job in engaging in mission in Rwanda.

Just as the sister church relationship gave members of Living Faith opportunities to express their concerns to their Rwandan counterparts, so too the relationship afforded Rwandan Christians opportunities to be honest with Living Faith about their own disappointments and discomforts. Speaking about the importance of honest dialogue in the relationship, Hailey Beckett, a parishioner from Living Faith, recounted:

> I remember a conversation a group of us from Living Faith had with some Rwandans through our sister church relationship. They asked if we had heard about the genocide in East Africa when it was happening. Those of us from Living Faith talked about how O.J. Simpson's trial was at the same time. I remember watching that case, but I had no idea that people were dying in Rwanda. "No," I told them, "if anything Rwanda was probably on the fifth page of the newspaper in a little world news column."
>
> And they just looked at us like, "I can't believe this. I can't believe that is all we were to you."
>
> We said, "We're so sorry. We didn't know. It's not that we don't care about you."
>
> On that level, they think that people heard about it and just didn't care and said, "Well, just die, you Africans."
>
> We had to explain to them over and over, "We do care about you, and we had no idea, and we are so sorry."

Beckett, who was a teenager during the East African genocide, desperately desired to be reconciled to African Christians beyond the gap between the oppressors and the oppressed, the haves and the have-nots. She maintained that Living Faith's sister church relationship with Murambi Parish was a step in the right direction, believing that the partnership afforded both sides opportunities to bring cross-cultural pain and misunderstanding to light and to chart a new course together.

Shane Ish, a member of Living Faith's sister parish committee and a government employee specializing in relief and development, explained that cultivating this sort of honest, mutually respectful, and mutually beneficial relationship with Murambi Parish was not always easy. Ish noted that Murambi's request for a tipper lorry was an instance that especially tested the resolve of the two communities to carry out their sister church relationship in this way. Even though the relationship was centered around Christian friendship, said Ish, "we do see that they have real needs and that we have real capabilities and resources." With this in mind, two years after the relationships began, Living Faiths' sister parish committee asked the corresponding committee at Murambi Parish to identify prominent needs that Living Faith could help meet. After a considerable amount of exchange, the Murambi committee reported that acquiring a tipper lorry was Murambi's first priority as a microfinance initiative. Considering the expense of a tipper lorry along with advice from professional colleagues cautioning against such a purchase, Ish especially was leery of honoring this request and said as much to Living Faith's partners in Rwanda. Next, Ish recalled,

> They came back to us, and really emphasized, "You all asked, and we took it very seriously, and this is our answer. We're here, and we see the need, and we see the opportunity." They walked us through some of their considerations and reiterated that this was where the partnership should go. It put us in a tough spot because we had some qualms about it. But on the other hand, we asked, and in the spirit of partnership, we really had to take that seriously.

Eventually, Living Faith wired the funds to purchase the tipper lorry to their partners.

Aaron Thomas, chair of Living Faith's committee added that the tipper lorry situation was especially challenging because before the relationship even began, Rwandan Bishop Kolini had said to Living Faith's leadership, "Go be involved in partnership. Keep me informed. I'm not going to tell you what to do, just don't buy them a car."

Of course, said Thomas, a car—which eventually evolved into a tipper lorry—was the exact thing that Murambi Parish requested! Thomas supplemented Ish's account of the situation by explaining that after months of deliberation, scores of exchanges between the two communities, several misunderstandings, and some hurt feelings, the two communities came to an agreement that was ultimately a cause for celebration and a symbol of growth. Even Bishop Kolini eventually lent his support to the plan to buy the tipper lorry.

As these vignettes illustrate, sister church relationships such as the one between Living Faith and Murambi help open up opportunities for trust and goodwill to develop between Christian communities in different parts of the world. Even though the accounts of the exchange between the two communities are one-sided and thus incomplete, they profile some of the strengths of the sister church model of mission from a North American vantage point. Both the particularities of today's religious, cultural, political, and economic climate as well as unique features of the sister church model of mission render such partnerships promising vehicles for facilitating fruitful cross-cultural encounters and engaging North American Christians in mission.

## The Context of Sister Church Relationships: Structural Considerations

Prominent features of both the international milieu of religious globalization and the ecology of contemporary American religiosity create opportunities for locally-rooted, faith-based, ocean-crossing endeavors such as sister church relationships to succeed. In addition to providing a compelling response to the "southernization" of Christianity in the postcolonial era, sister church relationships are well poised to take advantage of the sense of interconnectedness and the compression of time and space brought on by globalization. Moreover, North American congregations that participate in international congregation-to-congregation relationships navigate an organizational field and a spiritual climate that encourages such participation.

### Capitalizing on Globalization

As the first chapter highlighted, sister church relationships are an artifact of a postcolonial, transnational milieu—improbable in another historical situation. Though iterations of what is now labeled the partnership model of mission have been around since the dawn of Christianity, the contemporary setting of globalization has made cross-cultural missional partnerships feasible as never before. The growing consciousness of the world as a single place and the compression of time and space, both of which are hallmarks of contemporary globalization, are crucial factors in the life of international sister church relationships. In fact, a sense of human interdependence and the capacity to breach barriers of distance through modern technology make sister church relationships possible.

Across the globe, borders separating nations, people groups, and cultures from one another have become increasingly permeable as the processes of globalization have accelerated over the last generation. In addition to borderlessness, contemporary globalization signals an expanding sense of interconnectedness. It implies interdependence not just among local communities but among people across the planet, entailing a complex dialectic between the local and the global.[1] As Jehu Hanciles recognizes,

> The processes of globalization are collapsing distance and juxtaposing cultures in an unprecedented fashion and, especially for Western societies, posing profound questions related to cultural identity and managing religious plurality. Contemporary migration has helped to create new societies in which the cultural "other" is not a geographically distant curiosity or a random stranger one might perchance encounter on the street but a distinct, sizable presence within and impinging on the same social space.[2]

As Hanciles sees it, while nonwesterners have long experienced upheaval in their cultural and religious identities because of western influence, the favor is now being increasingly returned. Through their encounters with nonwesterners due especially to South-North migration but also to travel to the Southern Hemisphere, westerners are confronted by alterity face-to-face.

Religion is especially influenced by the border-collapsing dynamic of globalization. The process of migration, a hallmark of globalization, often both intensifies and renegotiates religious commitment for migrants. Hanciles observes that the religious impacts of migration go beyond the lives of migrants themselves; every migrant is a potential missionary, with a new community of possible converts.[3] Moreover, because of globalization, social networks are restructured and/or expanded for many of the world's citizens whether through migration, short-term travel, or technology. Since religious norms, meaning, and expression are so intimately connected to social context, the restructuring of social networks entails the transformation of religion.

While an increased sense of borderlessness has heightened religious conflict in some cases, it has also facilitated cross-cultural and transnational religious connections. Globalization not only causes people to encounter members of other religious traditions, it also causes them to encounter coreligionists from other countries and cultures—fellow pilgrims whose journey of faith is at once shared and alien. In addition, it enables coreligionists from disparate cultures who desire to form connections with each other to do so in fluid and accessible ways. Increased migration, foreign exchange and study abroad programs, short-term mission trips, and "reverse mission efforts" have enabled greater contact between majority-world and minority-world groups and individuals and rendered the face of the "other" within reach. As Mark Juergensmeyer notes, one possible outcome of the interplay between religion and globalization is the globalization of religion itself. Globalization has enabled religious groups to expand their influence around the world and to foster greater bonds among adherents.[4]

Even if American Christians of European ancestry never leave their own country, they are much more likely than ever before to encounter people whose skin color, country of birth, and cultural identification is different from their own. More than twenty-five million global southerners have immigrated to the United States since legislation changed dramatically under the Immigration and Nationality Act in 1965.[5] Most of the new immigrants are Christians, and native-born American Christians are slowly forging connections with Christian immigrants from around the world. As Mark Chaves and his colleagues discovered in the National Congregations Survey, American congregations are increasingly located in census tracts with significant immigrant populations, and congregations themselves are diversifying to reflect these changes.[6]

As chapter 4 explained, immigrants from the Global South played a crucial role in the profiled sister church relationships, linking coreligionists separated by geographic and cultural boundaries. Nonwhite immigrants, students, and other sojourners from the Global South featured prominently in the partnerships, serving as catalysts or intermediaries. Immigrants and other transnational figures bridged oceans and cultures by personally connecting global southerners and North Americans, both logistically and symbolically. Turning the "other" into "one of us," they facilitated and enhanced the partnership by transferring ownership and creating a sense of shared identity.

Globalization heightens coreligionists' opportunities for cross-cultural, faith-based friendship and collaboration. As Hanciles writes, "The encounter between different groups of people . . . inevitably expands the horizons of knowledge on both sides and fosters interconnectedness—causing the world to shrink."[7] Following the initial encounter with people from other cultures—individuals, congregations, and other entities are also in a better position to sustain cross-cultural relationships because of globalization. The technological revolution of the Information Age affords an ease of cross-continental travel and communication never before possible. The National Congregations Survey found that even in the last decade, the increasing use of computer technology was marked among American congregations.[8] The digital divide between the northern and southern hemispheres is still pronounced, and congregations in the global South do not enjoy near the same level of technologically based connectedness as their counterparts in the North. Yet, Internet, e-mail and cellular phone technology are increasingly available to institutions and their leaders in the global South.

Respondents were quick to acknowledge the facilitating role of modern technology in their sister church relationships. While they often found it difficult to communicate with parishioners in their partner congregations, many respondents, especially those in leadership positions, routinely exchanged e-mails and telephone calls with leaders in their partner congregations. The majority of respondents, in fact, relied so heavily on the availability of airplane travel, cellular phone communication, e-mail, and the Internet to sustain their sister church relationships that they believed that any recognizable form of their congregation's relationship would not have been possible fifty or even twenty-five years ago. Shane Ish from Living Faith Anglican articulated the sentiments of many respondents:

> Today's communication and transportation capabilities have made [sister parish relationships] so much more possible. That's one of the things that makes this an exciting time to be alive, really—the possibility of real relationship with people on the far side of the world where you actually see one another and can communicate, even with the flaws, with some success. A generation or two ago you would have been stuck with letters that took a month or two to arrive.

Technological developments combined with changing economic realities, political structures, and migratory patterns around the world have dramatically altered patterns of North-South religious engagement. Globalization creates new opportunities for the partnership approach to mission in general and sister church relationships in particular. Nancy Eiesland and R. Stephen Warner write that the movement back and forth among communities of faith around the world creates transnational circuits of relationships—relationships that, in turn, result in new songs, altered rituals, and new perspectives on global politics, economics, and culture. Whether in exurban Atlanta or rural Nigeria, increasingly congregations recognize their shared conversations, common practices, and structures of cooperation and exchange and find their place within a transnational religious ecology in which their local practices, values, and habits are shaped by far-flung relations.[9]

Combined with the maturation of the church in the global South and the widespread currency of the new paradigm in missiology, the forces of globalization have facilitated missional relationships between Christians at the grassroots level from the North and the South.

## The Restructuring of American Religion: New Opportunities for Practice-Oriented Spirituality and Congregation-Based Ministry

In addition to changes in cross-cultural and religious exchange on a global scale, the restructuring of religion on American soil has also created new opportunities for phenomena such as sister church initiatives. In an era in which denominational salience is waning and religious institutions are weakening and restructuring, sister parish relationships illustrate how North American Christianity has adapted to these changes by focusing on grassroots initiatives and harnessing practice-oriented spirituality.

Social scientists have charted the shifts in American religiosity over the latter half of the twentieth century and into the twenty-first—from the religious and cultural hegemony of mainline Protestantism to religious pluralism, from a spirituality of "dwelling" to a spirituality of "seeking," from prescribed and institutionalized religious identity to voluntarism and reflexivity, and from centralization and bureaucratization within religious institutions to fragmentation and localization.[10] Addressing the relationship between postmodern cultural forces and Christian religious institutions in particular in the United States, William Dinges draws attention to four trends: the loss of institutional salience, the cultural uncoupling of spirituality from religion, the loss of institutional control of religious symbols, and the rise of transdenominationalism—which together signal a seismic shift in American religiosity.[11] The institutional crisis that has befallen American Christianity has been particularly destabilizing for mission agencies. Since the 1990s, especially, mission agencies have been forced to reduce their programming and scope and have shifted from administering broad-scale programs to supporting grassroots efforts.[12]

### Practice-Oriented Spirituality

The institutional restructuring of religion combined with the renegotiating of spirituality among Americans over the last half-century, while spelling death for various forms of religiosity, have also created new opportunities in religious life. One of these opportunities is a newfound interest in practice-oriented spirituality. In his widely influential study of American religion since World War II, sociologist Robert Wuthnow frames the story of postwar religion as a shift from a spirituality of "dwelling" to a spirituality of "seeking." Wuthnow suggests that a spirituality of "practice"—in which people engage intentionally in activities that deepen their relations to the sacred—has been gaining strength in recent years against the dominant backdrop of seeker-oriented spirituality.[13] While dwelling-oriented spirituality has become unsustainable because of "complex social realities [that] leave many Americans with a sense of spiritual homelessness," and seeking-oriented spirituality has left many unfulfilled because it "results in a transient spiritual existence characterized more often by dabbling than depth," practice-oriented spirituality offers a recipe for religious vitality in the contemporary milieu.[14] Like seeker-oriented spirituality, practice-oriented spirituality respects the individualist temper of America culture. But it also satiates contemporaries' need for belonging by emphasizing strong connections to a community. In practice-oriented spirituality, sacred space is revered, though negotiable, and discipline is valued alongside freedom of exploration.[15] The giving of self in service, often envisioned as an outgrowth of devotional life, is a central component of practice-oriented spirituality.[16]

Particularly among American Christians, Craig Dykstra and Dorothy Bass have drawn significant attention to the critical role of practice for vital religiosity. Borrowing from Alasdair MacIntyre, Dykstra and Bass define practices as "those shared activities that address fundamental needs of humanity and the rest of creation that, woven together, form a way of life."[17] Dykstra and Bass invite Christian communities to see themselves as constituted by practices of faithfulness. Their project has achieved wide resonance among theologians and practitioners alike.

Sister church relationships capitalize on the participatory, communal, and service-minded nature of the practice-oriented spirituality to which Dykstra, Bass, and Wuthnow point. They link the contemplative life of prayer with social action as participants from partnering congregations pray for each other and work together to meet human needs.

Respondents who represented sister church programs at the denominational or parachurch level commonly referred to their programs' designs to enable parishioners to participate in mission firsthand. Alisa Schmitz from Food for the Hungry reported that Food for the Hungry's partnership program was begun in an effort to offer "opportunities for engagement," beyond giving money, to people in the pew.[18] Dan Shoemaker from Reciprocal Ministries International attributed the formation of RMI's partnership program to its leaders' recognition that people "wanted to get their hands dirty" in mission.[19] Patrick Friday from the United Methodist Church's General Board of Global Ministries spoke of his work as an effort to "catch the wave" begun by grassroots initiatives, helping to guide and organize "the movement of the spirit" among ordinary people.[20] At the congregational level as well, multiple respondents indicated that participating in a sister church relationship was a response to their desire to "do something" in the name of their faith.

Sister church relationships enable ordinary parishioners to become involved in mission in a tangible way. While many of the Washington, DC–area congregations relied on individuals with professional expertise to help steer the course of their participation in a sister church relationship, these individuals were usually members of the congregation who worked alongside other members with no such expertise. The experience and skills of "experts" were generally helpful resources for congregations involved in congregation-to-congregation relationships. But it was the congregations that were also able to employ the passions, time, labor, and relational gifts of a broad swath of the congregation whose sister church initiatives thrived the most. Congregations in which participation was limited to a committee of mostly experts had difficulty generating enthusiasm and creating a congregationwide sense of ownership for their sister church relationships. By contrast, congregations that provided an opportunity for a variety of parishioners to express their faith through service and spiritual practices in the context of community saw their sister church program thrive—and their parishioners enriched in the process.

### Local Communities

A second opportunity for sister church relationships created by the restructuring of American religion is the renaissance of local communities as a focal point of religious life. Despite the weakening of religious institutions over the last half-century, local congregations—whether traditional or experimental—clearly remain the central way in which American religion is socially organized.[21] Congregations play a central role in nurturing religious commitment and channeling voluntary religious activity in contemporary society.[22] The waning salience and changing roles of denominations and other umbrella religious institutions has shifted influence to local communities in the practice of religiosity.[23] While acknowledging the declining importance of denominations in American religious life, architects of the Baylor Religion Survey suggest that rather than religion itself being on the wane, "Americans may simply be more likely to connect with religion at the local level."[24]

Facing less competition from broad-scale mission programs and better able to meet participants' desire for hands-on, relationally driven, locally initiated ministry, grassroots mission efforts have been given new buoyancy by the decline of denominational and parachurch institutions. In her discussion of American congregations and their patterns of partnership, based on findings from the Organizing Religious Work project, Nancy Ammerman draws attention to the importance of informal coalitions such as clergy associations, loose networks of local congregations, and ad-hoc grassroots partnerships alongside congregations' affiliations with formal nonprofit organizations and denominational agencies.[25] When congregations do link with broad-scale intermediaries and service providers, they do so in the interest of extending the reach of their congregations and forming strategic alliances to mobilize needed resources. Congregational actors tend to see themselves as partners rather than subsidiaries in these relationships.[26]

Mission efforts seem to be more appealing to prospective participants when such efforts arise out of local communities rather than "from above." The Center for Applied Research in the Apostolate, for example, found that when relationships of solidarity between Catholic parishes in the United States and parishes in Latin America were initiated by either a lay minister or parish council, nearly two-thirds sent at least five parishioners to visit the sister parish. By contrast, where relationships were initiated by a bishop or religious community, only a quarter sent five or more parishioners to visit.[27] In addition to this research, Ammerman found that giving was more generous in congregations that had personal and direct connections to specific projects.[28]

Because sister church relationships are rooted in the institutional life of local congregations, they sidestep some of the structural hurdles plaguing not only expansive bureaucracies but also nonaffiliated mission initiatives. As discussed in chapter 7, one of the challenges to the health of sister church relationships is their dependence on individuals and personal relationships among individuals. However, compared to ad-hoc mission trips or independent missionaries who cobble together support from a variety of sources, the structure of sister church relationships is more stable.

The relational base of sister church relationships is generally shared throughout congregations. While personal connections are crucial for generating and sustaining participation in sister church partnership, these connections generally transcend any one individual or any one relationship. The sister church phenomenon as it is embedded in North American Christianity strikes a workable balance between routine and charisma; it caters to individuals while also providing institutional controls.

In addition to drawing attention to the vulnerability of sister church relationships because of their reliance on individuals and interpersonal relationships, chapter 7 also highlighted potential opportunity costs of sister church relationships, most notably the neglect of the local community. While congregations are decidedly local institutions in many ways, the evolution of American spirituality from dwelling to seeking, among other factors, has resulted in increasing geographic dispersion among congregations' members. Contemporary North Americans not only commute to work, they also commute to church. Nancy Ammerman, in concert with various other scholars of congregational life, points out that most North American congregations, whatever their tradition, are now "niche congregations" that cater to a particular set of needs, style of worship, demographic group, or cultural posture rather than functioning as parishes defined by geographic boundaries.[29]

The geographic diffusion of congregational membership combined with the shift in self-understanding of congregations from parish to niche has left many congregations with no particular sense of belonging or responsibility in their physical neighborhoods. While it is important for congregations to create a sense of community and build a shared sense of purpose among their members, members' collective sense of "neighborhood" could just as well be international as local for many North American congregations. Nancy Eiesland and R. Stephen Warner write that congregations' environments are increasingly wide in scope and open-ended in character. Congregations are linked to networks and events across geography and temporal space, bound to the "global village" through conversations, practices, and structures.[30]

Sister church relationships capitalize on the interpenetrating and reflexive relationship between the global and the local brought on by globalization as well as the restructuring of North American religion. Congregation-to-congregation relationships are quintessentially local as two geographically bound communities partner with each other for the sake of ministry that takes place on a local scale in one of the two communities. But they also transcend the boundaries of local communities, countries, and even continents, forging international connections that are rooted in congregations and grassroots relationships.

### The Convergence of Practice-Oriented Spirituality and the Local Congregation

The ascent of practice-oriented spirituality and a renewed sense of the importance of local religious communities are ever coalescing, especially through phenomena such as sister church relationships. Wuthnow notes that the collective dimension of religion, particularly as expressed in local faith communities, is a prominent feature of practice-oriented spirituality. According to some proponents of practice-oriented spirituality, the vitality of the congregation is the measure of true religious commitment.[31] In *Practicing Congregations*, Diana Butler Bass charts the reinvigoration of congregations that have shifted focus away from propositional doctrines and toward the practices and narratives of the Christian faith. In the last generation, says Bass, the story of mainline Protestant decline has been rewritten through the emergence of these practicing congregations.[32]

Extending Brooks Holifield's periodization scheme of congregational history, Bass contends that practicing congregations signal a new wave of religious identity in the United States.[33] As Bass explains, participatory congregations, which began in the 1950s and which serve as Holifield's last classification, still dominate the landscape. They tend to be democratic, experimental, therapeutic, and market-savvy, and they focus on techniques and programs. Recently, however, practicing congregations have emerged alongside these participatory congregations. Thriving in a postmodern setting of fragmentation and pluralism, practicing congregations construct faith as a way of life in community as they prioritize worship, spiritual formation, justice, and social action. Practicing congregations seek to overcome the moral fragmentation of the contemporary world by making faith-filled meaning together. Whereas voluntarism is a mark of contemporary religious participation in general, practicing congregations specifically celebrate intentionality as parishioners embrace a sense of their own spiritual and ethical responsibility.[34]

Although not all of the congregations that participate in sister church relationships could be considered practicing congregations, the two trends are related. Whereas rituals are at the center of religious meaning, social service and mission activity often go hand-in-hand with rituals by linking moral virtue to sacred presence. The profiled sister church relationships straddled the line between social service and specifically religious activities.

Because of their dual focus on social service and spiritual solidarity, they enabled participants to express and transmit religious meaning while seeking to meet others' needs. And because of their rootedness in local faith communities, these sister church relationships were particularly equipped to function in a decentralized organizational milieu.

## Flexibility

Because congregations that participate in sister church relationships tend to focus on community engagement and faith formation over propositions and programs, they often do not fit neatly into the bipolar schema of American Christianity that divides individuals and institutions into the camps of "liberal" and "conservative." As discussed in chapter 4, sister church relationships can be found among congregations across the spectrum of American Christianity. But they especially cater to congregations that emphasize a holistic gospel and that focus on orthopraxy over orthodoxy—congregations whose identity is not bound by the demarcations of the culture wars or theological posturing.

Accommodating both liberals and conservatives and everyone in between, sister church relationships are flexible enough to suit various purposes. Through congregational partnerships, progressive Christians can get involved in mission without feeling pressure to proselytize. After all, they are interacting with people who are already Christians, and charitable giving can seem more dignified when cloaked in the structures and rubric of partnership. The sister parish model is also attractive to traditionalist North American Christians. It affords those tied to ecclesiastical leadership in the global South—such as realigned Anglicans—a more significant point of contact with their spiritual overlords and brothers and sisters in the "parent" church. For others, it facilitates exposure to Christians famed for a high level of spiritual capital and/or "unreached peoples" via southern congregations. Whatever their theological and political orientation, participants are attracted to the relational and cross-cultural dimensions of sister church relationships.

The flexibility of sister church relationships also extends to ethnicity and other demographic characteristics. Predominantly European-American congregations can partner with global southern congregations in mission, while congregations made up of immigrants from the global South, through international sister church relationships, can maintain relationships with their compatriots back home, offering support to those they left behind and using the relationship as a springboard for their own local ministry. Regardless of how long their families have lived in North America, other people of color in North America employ congregational partnerships as a vehicle for connecting to an ethnic heritage, a beloved history, or a group of people with whom affinities are shared.

## Transcending Bipolar North American Christianity

Sister church partnerships themselves can help bridge and transcend ideological divides among North American Christians. More than simply appealing to Christians across the theological and political spectrum because of its flexibility, the sister church model of mission also spans differences between "this worldly" and "otherworldly" postures, otherwise known as "liberal" verses "evangelical." Sister church relationships solicit participation in both direct outreach (often considered the domain of conservatives) and efforts to evoke societal change (considered the domain of liberals), therein attempting to foster holistic mission and ministry. In many sister church initiatives, social justice is valued alongside Christian unity and spiritual growth. Because of their focus on organic relationships and personal and communal transformation over programs and doctrines, congregation-to-congregation partnerships can help participants move beyond a fixation on being "right." As Lamont Koerner from the Saint Paul Area Synod of the ELCA maintained, sister church relationships are promising venues for helping liberals and conservatives alike move beyond bickering and power-brokering because of their focus on serving and learning in the context of meaningful encounters with God and others.

According to Hailey Beckett from Living Faith Anglican, the relational basis of sister church partnerships also helps North American Christians from both ends of the spectrum look inward at their own foibles rather than focusing on other people's missteps. Beckett maintained that through honest dialogue with their Rwandan counterparts, Living Faith parishioners were continually confronted by their own areas of weakness and beckoned to change. Living Faith's sister church initiative challenged the liberal-conservative paradigm. Disdainful of triumphalism and imperialism yet sympathetic to the worldview of their global southern counterparts, Living Faith participants rejected both absolutism and relativism. Seeing both the soul and the body as arenas of the gospel, their approach to mission called into question the divide between this-worldly and otherworldly spirituality.

## Mitigating the Weaknesses of Other Models of Mission

As chapter 5 explained, proponents of international sister church relationships often elevate the partnership model of mission above other models as a more effective approach to mission. They are particularly critical of the sending model of mission, which was prominent during the colonial era and remains operative in the contemporary scene under multiple guises. Some North American champions of the sister church model view career missionary sponsorship, stand-alone short-term mission trips, and broad-scale western relief and development efforts as inherently flawed approaches to mission in the global South because of their connection to the sending model. Other sister church proponents conceive of these efforts as complementary to the sister church model, assuming the initiatives are responsible. Whatever their level of support for other models of mission, however, advocates maintain that sister church relationships represent a particularly effective approach to mission in the postcolonial milieu in their capacity to build trust between partners and foster sustained engagement.

Of alternative models of mission, stand-alone short-term mission trips receive the most targeted criticism from proponents of the sister church model. Justin Hahn's comparison of his experiences on short-term mission trips with his participation in Living Faith's sister church relationship illustrate this critique. Hahn, a twenty-five-year-old Korean American, had participated in several short-term mission trips with other organizations before he started attending Living Faith.

> Contrasted with short-term mission trips, I think our relationship we have in Gatsibo is much more effective because not only can we do things for them, but there is something much deeper than an act. There is a relationship there that resists the tendency to view other parties in terms of just their functionality and what they can offer you. My experience in past mission trips was that we would show up somewhere and people would look at us only through the lens of, "Oh, they are here to give us more money," or "they are here to give us a new building."
> But with the sister church relationship, I think we have overcome that as two parishes. We have built a relationship built on trust. I think they know that we love them and we trust them and we want what is best for them, and vice versa. And if that entails monetary transactions, so be it. But if it involves something deeper than monetary transactions, such as praying for one another or sharing the concerns or the struggles of the church, I think

that is something that the sister church model offers that the traditional "send a group of twenty high school kids to a foreign country" model may not present.

Sister church relationships are more closely related to the short-term mission movement than this binary portrayal suggests, and proponents' claims that sister church relationships are more effective in responding to needs in southern communities have not been demonstrated.

Still, Hahn's account draws attention to some of the structural advantages of sister church relationships over stand-alone mission trips.

Short-term mission trips have become extremely popular among North American Christians, experiencing a dramatic increase in popularity during the 1980s and 1990s that has continued to the present day.[35] Proponents argue that short-term mission trips enrich the lives of North American participants and expand the work of Christianity in other countries by the labor, expertise, energy, and Christian witness they supply.[36] As the STM movement has expanded, sponsoring agencies have increasingly sought to develop uniform standards, and a growing body of literature has encouraged reflection on best practices in short-term mission.[37]

Despite these gains, critics contend that North-South short-term mission trips function largely outside of structures of accountability, easily fall prey to promoting religious tourism over serious engagement, drain badly needed resources from career missionaries and local organizations as well as sending congregations, and fail to deliver promised long-term benefits either to communities in the global South or to North American participants. David Livermore writes that "Some scholars are concerned that not only do these trips fail to bring about lasting life change for the participants, worse yet, they actually perpetuate the very things they are intended to counter." North American participants return home assuming that developing countries are "backward" and that the poor are happy in their poverty, and well-rehearsed stereotypes and power relationships are reinforced.[38]

Sister church relationships have much in common with short-term mission trips and are thus implicated by many of the same critiques. Indeed, many congregation-to-congregation relationships grow out of short-term trips, and it is largely through short-term mission trips that such partnerships are nourished and sustained. Congregation-to-congregation relationships are similar to STM in their reliance on lay volunteers and intermittent cross-cultural engagement.

Like short-term mission efforts, sister church relationships can be accused of poor stewardship of resources, promoting religious tourism over significant engagement, and sending ill-equipped North American volunteers to accomplish ill-defined goals in global southern communities.

However, sister church relationships also have structural advantages over stand-alone short-term mission efforts. While North American sister church participants are not immune to attitudes of cultural superiority or insensitivity, they generally have access to extensive cross-cultural training prior to traveling to the global South as well as ongoing contact with global southerners after they return home. This ongoing contact prolongs North American participants' opportunity to re-evaluate destructive stereotypes and assumptions and also enhances the possibility of trust developing between partners.

In response to evidence that most short-term mission trips as they are currently practiced do not bring about lasting change in the lives of participants, Kurt Ver Beek suggests that a greater sense of accountability and encouragement would improve the effectiveness of STM.[39] North Americans who participate in short-term mission trips are much less vulnerable to life changes as a result of their experiences than is commonly thought among proponents of short-term mission trips, says Ver Beek. Rather than being easily changed, volunteers "more closely resemble young saplings, which can be bent and even held in one place for a week or more, but once let loose quickly go back to their original position."[40] Like saplings, short-term volunteers need to be confronted with the types of issues they encounter while on mission trips for much longer periods of time in order for change to become permanent. Ver Beek contends that lasting change would be much more likely if, first of all, short-term mission groups would establish long-term partnerships with organizations, missionaries, and churches that are involved in outstanding work among those they serve. Second, sustained change would be more likely if participants would set specific, demanding, and public goals and then be regularly held accountable and encouraged to put them into practice by their community.[41]

While some short-term mission efforts are also embedded in long-term commitments to partner organizations in the global South, this sense of accountability is part of the very structure of sister church relationships. North Americans who embark on delegations to their sister church abroad, assuming they remain members of the participating congregation, are regularly reminded of their experiences and commitments made while overseas as their congregation continues to nurture its sister church relationship. Moreover, participants are often afforded ample opportunity to continue their involvement with their sister church community, whether through return visits, committee work, advocacy, fundraising, or other projects. Ostensibly, accountability and encouragement are also provided to North American participants by members of the sister church community, assuming cross-cultural relationships are maintained. And on the other side of the equation, there is also more promise for long-term change to be seen among communities abroad within the structure of sister church relationships than stand-alone short-term mission trips.

The sister church model of mission also enjoys certain advantages over other models of mission involving North American participation abroad, such as career and organizational mission efforts and direct monetary donations. Unlike many short-term mission efforts, long-term engagement and accountable relationships are structural priorities for both sister church relationships and full-time mission and relief efforts, whether on behalf of career missionaries or organizations. But while the more traditional models of mission restrict North American participation mainly to professionals, sister church relationships allow scores of ordinary laypeople to engage in cross-cultural mission efforts in a tangible way. In contrast to fundraising campaigns in which North American congregations and organizations give money directly to global southern entities with limited personal contact, sister church relationships place financial gifts within the context of relationships at the grassroots level. Although interpersonal relationships are arguably an inefficient channel for the flow of physical resources, they offer more promise than bureaucratic programs for participant transformation. Placing financial contributions within the context of cross-cultural relationships at the grassroots level can help blunt the misuse and excessive influence of money in mission efforts.


## Creating Social Capital

Researchers such as C. M. Brown, Robert Wuthnow, Robert Priest, and Kersten Bayt Priest have argued that, when done well, missional partnerships between northern and southern communities create social capital as they help people build bridges across divides. Particularly important in this equation is linking social capital, featuring vertical connections across marked differentials of wealth, status, and power. Individuals and communities that are socially subordinate and economically poor need not only social ties but also vertical ties to those with access to power and resources.[42] Partnering with Christians from North America and Europe can afford this opportunity to southern Christians. Writing about short-term mission trips to Peru, Robert Priest says that the linking social capital created through partnerships with northern Christians has given Peruvians greater access to both physical resources and social influence in their communities.[43]

Participation in social networks and accompanying patterns of trust, interpersonal commitment, and reciprocity are central to individual well-being and community strength—both for rich and poor alike. The capacity of sister church relationships to create social capital is important for northerners as well as southerners. In her study of North American women who participated in short-term mission trips, Kersten Bayt Priest found that serving as "resource brokers" to southern communities through their involvement in STM was good for participants. "Involvement in STM nurtures the soul, pries away 'suburban blinders' and allows women to care in contexts which obviously need resources," writes Priest. According to Priest, missional partnerships between northerners and southerners have helped propel the "globalization of empathy" along with new patterns of "resource brokering" across international borders.[44]

The exchange of resources can undermine a sense of mutuality between partners, and empathy does not always translate into a change in lifestyle. Still, the capacity of sister church relationships to create social capital in both northern and southern communities is a source of strength for the model. Respondents recognized the bonding, bridging, and linking social capital created by their sister church relationships as valuable assets that enriched their lives and helped them develop increased cultural intelligence. Evidence of antipathy, fear, or mistrust was difficult to find in respondents' accounts of their interactions with their sister church counterparts. Instead, respondents celebrated the global nature of Christianity, admired the faith of their counterparts in the global South, and envisioned their partners as brothers and sisters.

Respondents tended to be relatively well informed about the shape of global Christianity. Most respondents rejected the notion of Christianity as a western religion and instead identified Christianity as a universal faith, rooted in the Middle East and now truly global. Most respondents were well aware that Christianity is numerically stronger in the global South than it is in the global North. While many lamented what they saw as the decline of Christianity in their own context, they celebrated the vibrancy of the faith they witnessed among members of their sister church communities. Many also believed that though the Christian gospel has certain universal elements, no one culture has a privileged interpretation of Christianity, and the faith is contextualized uniquely in each cultural setting.

More than just appreciating global southern Christianity, many respondents believed that the witness of their brothers and sisters in the global South is both a model for North American Christians and a gift to American culture. According to Chris Coulter, assistant pastor at Living Faith, multicultural evangelism on American soil can be particularly effective.

When an African comes in and says, "I've been through suffering and I've been through pain, and let me tell you about Christ," [Americans] listen to him. And [Africans] have a cultural authority, for some reason. When [Africans] come and talk about their life, it is just really compelling and it is received as an authentic expression of spirituality. I think people are more jaded and are more cynical to the white approaches to this question. They like to see an African, or an Asian, a Latin American get up and say, "I believe in Jesus and here is why. I've come out of a totally different culture and I don't care about any of these issues you are talking about. Here is what Jesus has done for my people." I think people love that. I wish we had a lot more of it.

Coulter asserted that the African Christians he has met not only are effective evangelists in North America but also offer compelling stories and insights to North American churchgoers.

We've had some of these African leaders come in and preach and teach in our congregations, in some pretty direct and unmediated, unfiltered ways. And, you know, that is an experience for western people in Washington, D.C.—to have an African come in . . . and to really let him free to speak his mind and his heart. I think that has been interesting for people. Rather than being repelled by it, people have said, 'Boy, there are different ways of looking at the world. Isn't this interesting and challenging?"

There was one night in particular where one of our African friends was speaking and the power went out. He was speaking up there for fifty-five minutes. It was long, and it was hot in there, and the lights were out. But for a lot of people—you know, you could just see people—you would expect modern Americans to say, "Okay, this is awkward." But most people were pretty hooked in.

It was not just evangelicals who believed that global southern Christians offer North Americans a compelling faith witness. Respondents from the Catholic, Presbyterian, and African American Baptist congregations also reported that they found the faith of their sister church counterparts to be encouraging and exemplary. The mutual exchange between Christians from different hemispheres, especially when these exchanges featured North American deference to southerners, was also a source of celebration. According to Hailey Beckett from Living Faith,

> Anyone I've ever told about that relationship, Christian or not, is always intrigued. I think their initial reaction is always, "Huh, that is really cool." Especially non-Christians, I think, have this idea that Christians are cultural imperialists going out to conquer the world and make everyone disciples by word or by sword. Explaining that we are a church planted by Africa is a quick way to shut them up, almost.

Rather than recoiling from global southern Christianity as strange, distasteful, or threatening, respondents celebrated and embraced the faith of their counterparts.

Respondents did not see eye-to-eye with their southern counterparts on all scores. Nor did they always display postures of sensitivity and respect. Still, many developed genuine relationships with their counterparts that not only linked southern communities with needed resources but also afforded both parties the benefits of friendship. The ethos of cross-cultural, faith-based connectivity fuels the sister church movement, and the sister church movement in turn fuels this ethos.


## Conclusion

The sobering effect of chapter 7's litany of challenges confronting sister church relationships is offset by the fact that many of the factors that erect obstacles for sister church relationships also create opportunities for them to succeed. While the precariousness of personal relationships and the idiosyncrasies of individuals can destabilize sister church relationships, the grassroots, relational nature of sister church relationships is also a source of strength for the model. Individuals serve as advocates within a congregation, inspiring others to become involved through their stories. Their hard work moves projects forward, and the relationships they form across oceans are both the seeds and the fruit of sister church relationships. While the difficulties of travel and communication across oceans are significant, the processes of globalization in the contemporary milieu have enabled inhabitants of different continents to forge connections never before possible in the same way. While the restructuring of North American religion has compromised many of the pillar institutions and protocols of North American mission efforts, it has also created new opportunities for grassroots, faith-based initiatives. While the frames of mutuality and solidarity that propel sister church relationships are vulnerable on several scores, they inspire countless participants to give of themselves and to discover their common humanity in fruitful ways. While disparities in privilege and power call into question the possibility of reciprocity, they also force participants to be creative, reflective, and self-transcending in order to make sister church relationships work. While barriers of race and culture can be sources of pain and oppression, relationships can become all the more meaningful when understanding is reached across such divides. And while interpersonal conflict can compromise sister church relationships, it can also make them stronger.

Living Faith's relationship with Murambi Parish serves as a particularly compelling illustration of how the circumstances of modern life and the humor of cultural trends can be harnessed to propel strong sister church relationships. Living Faith and Murambi parish were able to capitalize on the compression of time and space on a global scale brought on by modern technology. Even though Washington, DC, and Gatsibo, Rwanda are thousands of miles away both literally and figuratively speaking, parishioners from the two communities were able to visit one another on a regular basis and communicate by e-mail and cellular phone almost daily. Even the fact that the two communities came into contact with each other at all was largely a function of the increased mobility and South-North migration of recent decades. As a young congregation with a unique institutional structure and a significant amount of local autonomy, Living Faith could accommodate the demand for practice-oriented spirituality and grassroots-based ministry that have emerged in the context of the restructuring of American religion. Priding themselves on navigating a third way between what they considered the hollow spirituality of liberal Christianity and the dogmatism and insularity of fundamentalism, Living Faith parishioners were attracted to the promise of holistic ministry and barrier-crossing connections afforded by sister church relationships. Drawn to participate in Christian mission in the world, members of Living Faith were at once leery of western imperialism and eager to establish meaningful and reciprocal relationships with people from other parts of the planet.

For the members of Living Faith Anglican as well as countless other North American Christians, the sister church model of mission, despite its inherent pitfalls, represents an attractive vehicle of cross-cultural Christian engagement. The structure of sister church relationships combined with attitudes of respect and humility, which the model celebrates, provide a promising platform for mission in the contemporary world.

# Conclusion

*The Confluence of Civilizations*

JUSTIN HAHN WAS A twenty-five-year-old Korean American who worked on Capitol Hill as a congressional aid. After graduating from college and moving to Washington, DC, Hahn began attending Living Faith Anglican, where he became actively involved in the congregation's sister church relationship. Hahn maintained that Living Faith's relationship with Murambi Parish in Rwanda was simply an attempt for both parties to implement the call to Christian mission.

> The primary focus of our relationship is that this is really what the church, the catholic church, in terms of the universal church, should look like. We're all part of the body of Christ. There is certain diversity of context and diversity of how churches are structured and run, but at the end of the day we are all followers of Jesus and we are all part of the Christian church. Living Faith's sister church relationship is about what we feel should always be done. We wouldn't say we are blazing a revolutionary trail and that we should be put on a pedestal. Our sister church relationship is something that is a natural, logical connection of taking the gospel and the mission of the church to heart.

According to Hahn, participating in the mission of the church means reaching out across borders of geography, race, economics, and creed to share the love of Christ to those both inside and outside of the church.

> Our church is active in ministering to people's needs in all sorts of ways because of the love of Christ, and I would argue that that is the point of being Christians. It is what Christians should always be doing. Our sister

church relationship is a logical extension of that. You start with your family, then your city, and work your way out. At the end of the day, you are working across geopolitical and international lines.

While Hahn was not bashful in his support for various American mission and outreach efforts in other parts of the world, he was also quick to acknowledge that the border-crossing dynamic of mission in today's climate is and should be multidirectional. Hahn became especially convinced of the multidirectional nature of mission after he traveled to Rwanda as part of Living Faith's sister church delegation. Referencing the words of a Rwandan bishop whom he met during his travels, Hahn remarked that missionaries are being sent not only from North to South and South to North but also from everywhere to everywhere.

According to Hahn, the burgeoning of African Christianity and the global revolution in Christian mission are exciting and refreshing. Seeing sister church relationships and other examples of the partnership approach to mission as Christians from around the world "going where Jesus is leading us as a church," Hahn was thrilled to participate in what he strongly believed is the work of God in the world.

## Reframing Global Christianity in the Context of Globalization

Justin Hahn's respect for global southern Christians, desire to form meaningful and mutual relationships across borders, sense of excitement about the changing shape of global Christianity, and advocacy for multidirectional international mission efforts were sentiments that were shared by nearly all respondents among the twelve profiled Washington, DC–area congregations. Respondents were attracted to global southern Christians and to their faith. Appearing to be unthreatened by shifts in influence and numerical strength from northern to southern Christianity, respondents celebrated the global reach of the Christian faith, the diversity of the church, and the opportunity for northern Christians to learn from coreligionists representing other regions, perspectives, and backgrounds.

The twelve relationships featured in this study, and arguably sister church relationships at large, serve as counterexamples to the patterns of global religious engagement identified by leading theorists of contemporary globalization. Instead of confirming one camp of scholars' expectations of cross-cultural misunderstanding and hostility, or another camp of scholars' assumptions of global homogenization under the banner of western imperialism, international sister church relationships present patterns of cross-cultural religious engagement that are generally interpenetrating, reflexive, and amicable.

The predominant theory of contemporary globalization holds that the processes of globalization in today's world perpetuate structures of western—and principally American—hegemony. In various ways, proponents of this global-culture argument contend that the world is becoming more homogenous as economic dominance and technological supremacy drive the spread of western modernization in ways that erode local cultures and indigenous identities.[1] From Peter Berger's "four faces of globalization" and Francis Fukuyama's "end of history" to Benjamin Barber's "Jihad versus McWorld" and various iterations of secularization theory, advocates of the universal-culture thesis suggest that cross-cultural engagement in the contemporary setting generally serves to instill western values in the rest of the world's citizens. Religious forces, in this schema, are seen as secondary to economic and political processes.

Critics of this cultural-homogenization approach to globalization, however, draw attention to resistance to westernization among various groups of people living outside North America and Europe. In his *Clash of Civilizations*, for example, Samuel Huntington postulates a fragmented global cultural landscape marked by contending "civilizations." According to Huntington, "the world is becoming more modern and less Western,"[2] while the forces of integration and globalization are generating "counter forces of cultural assertion and civilizational consciousness."[3] Huntington maintains that the response of nonwestern societies to western ones ranges from rejection, amalgamation, absorption, and substitution. The post–Cold War world is multipolar and multicivilizational rather than homogenous. Moreover, in Huntington's eyes, religion is not a spent force in an increasingly secular global society but rather a major constituent of civilization and an impetus of cultural parochialism and ferment in today's world.[4]

Building upon Huntington's thesis, Jehu Hanciles argues that "far from being a one-directional, single, unified phenomenon, the processes of globalization are multidirectional, inherently paradoxical, and incorporate movement and countermovement."[5] According to Hanciles, religion is an especially potent force in the complex web of globalization. The spread of socioeconomic modernization has not bankrupted religious life, as proponents of the universal-culture thesis maintain, but rather revitalized it. In addition to the increased religious vitality of local communities in the global South, Hanciles notes a growing religious gap between the West and the non-West that significantly troubles the single global-culture perspective. As he sees it, South-North migration and religious expansion are powerful aspects of contemporary globalization that signal diversification and conflict rather than homogenization.

> If the entrenched religiosity and unbridled spiritual outlook of poorer (mainly non-Western) societies constitutes a key component in arguably the most fundamental cultural divide of the new global order, then the admixture of migration and religious expansion represents one of the most important aspect of globalization.[6]

Such movements, sometimes referred to as "globalization from below," says Hanciles, have received all too little attention in studies of globalization, their impact minimized by the dominant perspective that holds that western cultural modes and values set the standard for the rest of the world.

Like Hanciles, many of the prominent scholars of contemporary global Christianity emphasize the differences between the church in the North and the church in the South. As chapter 1 explained, scholars such as Philip Jenkins, Lamin Sanneh, Andrew Walls, and Samuel Escobar draw attention to the shifting center of gravity in the landscape of global Christianity. In addition to maintaining that Christianity has become numerically stronger in the South than the North over the course of the twentieth century, these scholars contend that Christianity's spiritual heartland has also shifted to the global South. Primarily through the efforts of indigenous and often Pentecostal churches, Christianity has become especially vibrant and authentic in the global South. In contrast to the liberalism, stagnancy, and defensive posture of many northern Christians, southern Christians are powerfully on the move—even sending missionaries to the North to challenge its decadence and secularism. While they restrict their scope to the religious features of globalization, many scholars of global Christianity essentially endorse the "clash of civilizations" hypothesis.

Among both theorists of contemporary globalization and students of global Christianity, insufficient attention has been paid to the multidirectional connections forged between Christians representing various geographic, cultural, and ideological poles. Sister church relationships are examples of cross-cultural encounters in the contemporary world that serve as vehicles primarily of collaboration and friendship rather than homogenization or conflict. Certainly sister church relationships are imperfect carriers of these values. The potential for engendering conflict and misunderstanding between partners, as well as for promoting patterns of northern imperialism and southern disempowerment, are real possibilities in the course of sister church relationships. Yet, the overall trajectory of sister church relationships is cross-cultural, faith-based collaboration and kinship at the grassroots level. Though significant and broad-reaching, the sister church movement and other embodiments of the partnership approach to mission are nearly ignored by proponents of both the universal-culture and the "clash of civilizations" hypotheses. Neither paradigm gives due currency to examples of cross-cultural collaboration of a religious nature.

As Robert Wuthnow contends in *Boundless Faith*, the prevailing tendency to portray northern and southern Christians using an us/them dichotomy misses the central logic of the globalization thesis: that different parts of the world are becoming more closely connected.[7] Instead of a bipolar map of global Christianity in which the North and South are seen as competing centers, a truer picture of global Christianity is pluriform and multicentric. Rather than ascertaining the strength of Christianity primarily on the basis of demography, it should be recognized that the global influence of Christian institutions and movements originating in the North remains strong. While southern forms of Christianity are gaining leverage around the world, northern forms of Christianity also significantly influence the practice of the faith all over the globe. Moreover, such influences are often celebrated rather than resisted in local communities. Northern Christians enjoy singing African choruses and displaying Latin American liturgical art, while southern Christians eagerly use North American Sunday school curriculum. Christianity develops singularly in each particular context rather than following a uniform trajectory. So also, religious adherents around the world influence one another jointly and uniquely in each context of encounter.

In the past, European and North American influence in Africa, Asia, and Latin America has often been overstated. As a correction, many contemporary scholars of global Christianity have highlighted the autonomy and internal vitality of indigenous churches in the formerly colonized world, attributing the growth of Christianity in the global South almost exclusively to indigenous efforts and maintaining that the character of the Christian faith in the global South is almost entirely homegrown.[8] However, this line of argument tends to minimize the impact of northern Christians in the global South, especially in a positive sense.

It is hard to deny that the forty thousand Americans serving as career missionaries abroad affect individuals and communities in the areas in which they work in some way. Similarly, the 3.7 billion dollars invested annually by US churches on overseas ministries, as well as efforts of the one to two million American church members who participate in international short-term mission efforts each year, are not without consequence.[9] Through their en-counters with global southerners, North Americans and Europeans are also changed—even if in subtle or unmeasurable ways. Focusing on difference can too easily eclipse instances of northern and southern Christians interact-ing collaboratively and constructively.

As Wuthnow contends, "globalization begs for a new paradigm that emphasizes not only the autonomous vitality of the churches in the global South but also the cultural and organizational mechanisms through which Christianity in its scattered global locations has become more intricately connected."[10] Using the analogy of the body, Wuthnow advocates for a reformulation of the narrative of global Christianity that recognizes each organ's dependence on others and the importance of various parts working together.[11] Seen in this light, the story of global Christianity is less about "shifting centers of gravity" than it is about "mutual edification and interaction."[12]

Wuthnow's treatment of the global outreach of American churches in *Boundless Faith* is an attempt to frame American overseas mission efforts according to this new narrative. Similarly, this study of sister church re-lationships attempts to rethink how global citizens, and particularly coreli-gionists around the world, have become interdependent. While acknowledging the serious disparities in power as well as the threat these disparities pose for the prospect of mutuality and interdependence, this study demonstrates that interactions between Westerners and non-Westerners need not be under-stood as uniformly imperialistic. Nor should western Christianity be con-ceived as an impotent or irrelevant force in global affairs amid the dominance of nonwestern iterations of the faith. Patterns of cross-cultural engagement among Christians reveal a complex dialectic in an era of globalization. Co-religionists around the world are interconnected, and their outreach efforts are interpenetrating. The encounters among Christians hailing from various parts of the world carry not only the potential for conflict but also the possi-bility for solidarity.

## Contributions and Findings

Wuthnow's study is broad-reaching and comprehensive, but it does little to address the qualitative character of grassroots cross-cultural connections of a religious nature. Nor does it examine the attitudes of North American Christians toward their counterparts in the global South or the effects of American outreach efforts in any detail. By contrast, this study shows not just what Americans do abroad, but how they do it. This book considers international religious connections from an American vantage point as does *Boundless Faith*, but it more thoroughly elucidates the multidirectional nature of contemporary Christian mission. This study presents a specific yet multilayered case study of new patterns of religious engagement in the contemporary setting, focusing on both the sending and receiving missional capacity of particular communities. Through sister church relationships, American Christians are both the subjects and objects of global missionary outreach.

In addition to recasting global patterns of religious engagement, this study also illuminates the international sister congregation phenomenon itself. As one of the few historical and comparative studies of sister church relationships to date, this book chronicles the history and development of the sister parish model of mission as well as shedding light on the ways in which the model is embodied in particular contexts.

As chapter 2 recounts, sister church relationships began in the early 1980s among Catholics and mainline Protestants as a reaction against colonial patterns of mission and an outgrowth of grassroots cross-cultural encounters among Christians. Since then, on the North American scene, sister church relationships have become increasingly popular among Christians from virtually all traditions. While denominational agencies and parachurch ministries often perform facilitating roles in sister church relationships, the model is decidedly local. It is fueled by grassroots efforts and functions as a bottom-up rather than a top-down phenomenon.

Because of the local character of the sister church phenomenon, the rest of the book focuses on how the model is embodied among specific congregations. Based on interviews from respondents in the profiled congregations, similarities and differences in the ways sister church relationships were envisioned and carried out are highlighted. Of the twelve congregations in the study, most were significantly larger than the national average and operated large congregational budgets. Vibrant community life and a shared passion for mission also marked most of the congregations. Beyond these commonalities, however, the congregations varied greatly. Some gravitated toward the liberal end of the theological spectrum while others could be classified as conservative and evangelical. Some of the congregations operated under a hierarchical polity, while the polity of others was connectional or congregational.

Surprisingly, however, these differences did not affect the character of the congregations' sister church relationships as much as one might suppose. Beyond the congregational level, polity factored little in sister church relationships since denominational oversight was almost always highly limited. Even at the congregational level, sister church relationships were generally decentralized and controlled largely by lay leadership in committee. Thus, whether a congregation was Catholic, Presbyterian, Anglican, or Baptist did not influence the structure of its sister church relationship to a significant degree in most cases. In the Catholic and African American Baptist congregations, the high level of authority given to the pastors over parish matters generally entailed less autonomy for sister parish committees than in the Protestant congregations. Some respondents among the Catholic parishes resented this authority as meddling without sufficient information or investment on behalf of the pastor. Among the African American Baptist congregations, by contrast, pastoral control was so fixed that parishioners were not nearly as involved or invested in their congregation's relationships. In the mainline Presbyterian and evangelical Anglican congregations, lay leaders were generally given more control of their congregation's sister church program. However, more than polity, the personality of the pastor as well as the leadership structures of the congregation in relation to its sister church relationship set the tone for the governance of each congregational partnership program.

Theological orientation, like polity, was not as salient of a factor in the nature of the profiled sister church relationships as one might imagine. Across traditions, congregations employed frames for their sister church relationships based on mutual solidarity and joint edification over charity. Whether a congregation was "this worldly" or "otherworldly" in its approach to mission affected how a congregation prioritized goals and carried out ministry in the context of its sister church relationship, but the more important distinction was whether a congregation focused more on projects or relationships. The more intentional and vibrant sister church partnerships tended to center on friendship-building and solidarity, whereas other sister church relationships functioned mostly as vehicles for philanthropic or evangelistic transactions and thus recapitulated more program-oriented models of mission. Among the profiled African American Baptist churches, sister church relationships tended to center on financial uplift for impoverished congregations in the Caribbean or Africa. The evangelical Anglican congregations, meanwhile, capitalized on a sense of spiritual kinship with their counterparts as well as opportunities for evangelism. Carrying out Catholic social teaching and celebrating the universality of the Church were foci of parish partnerships among Catholic parishes, and Presbyterian congregations concerned themselves with humanitarian efforts. In these ways, the profiled sister church relationships reflected the traditions and ideological postures of the congregations involved. However, the majority of the congregations sought most of all to minister holistically in the context of mutual relationships with their sister church counterparts. The manner in which congregations sought to embody these goals and the degree to which they succeeded set congregations apart from each other more than the traditions they represented.

Individual participants, like congregations, varied in their experience, motivation, influence, and goals related to sister church relationships. They were both old and young, male and female, conservative and liberal, blue collar and white collar. Immigrants from the global South and other transnational figures played crucial roles in most of the sister church relationships. They often served as both catalysts and intermediaries, bridging cultures by turning the "other" into "one of us." Participants and especially leaders who were native to the United States, like immigrant participants, tended to be well endowed in cross-cultural exposure as well as social and material capital. With discretionary time, money, and energy available for their sister church relationships, many sought to apply their professional expertise—often in the "helping professions" or international development—to another context while being personally enriched in the process.

Based on respondent testimony, it appears that the overwhelming majority of participants did find their experiences related to their sister church involvement to be edifying or even transformative on a personal level. Cross-cultural experiences within the context of sister church relationships were especially formative for young adults. But many adults who were middle aged or advanced in years also described their experiences as challenging or moving. Participants commonly reported that their Christian faith had been strengthened or that their hearts had been opened in a new way to people who were different from them. Some participants were inspired to instigate development projects, advocate for marginalized communities, or alter their patterns of consumption. Many returned over and over to their sister church communities and established meaningful and enduring cross-cultural friendships.

On a collective level, sister church relationships often enhanced parish life by providing congregations with a shared understanding of identity or purpose. While their direct influence was typically limited to a subset within each congregation, sister church programs created opportunities for parishioners to build a sense of community and belonging within their churches. This book focused on the attitudes and experiences of North American participants. Hence, the impact of sister church relationships on communities in the global South can only be hypothesized. American

Christians should not be perceived as trustworthy spokespersons for Christians in the global South. Although respondents were not able to accurately judge the impact of their sister church relationships on their partner communities, most of them believed that the overall impact was positive. Because the sister church model elevates relationships over programs, focuses on long-term goals and sustainable development over quick fixes, and promotes ongoing partnerships over one-time projects, proponents believed that sister church relationships more effectively bring hope and healing to communities in the global South than do many other forms of mission. Respondents from the profiled congregations, while quick to acknowledge the ways in which they had benefited from their congregations' sister church relationships, also concluded that their counterparts profited materially and spiritually.

Despite these convictions, a substantial collection of obstacles threatened the ability of sister church relationships to thrive and called into question their effectiveness. The model's reliance on individuals and interpersonal relationships, while in many ways a source of strength, often rendered the sister church partnerships as fragile as the individuals involved. The logistical demands of sustaining travel and communication across oceans, cultures, and political boundaries also proved debilitating at times. Whatever resources a congregation dedicated to its sister church relationship, those resources were not available for other endeavors—an opportunity cost that sometimes caused concern or tension. While disagreements between sister church partners were rare, intracongregational conflict and personality clashes plagued several of the Washington, DC–area congregations. Moreover, many of the congregations struggled to translate the frames in which their sister church relationships were staged into practice. Participants disagree among themselves regarding how to embody the ideals of solidarity and reciprocity in concrete situations, but also the glaring structural imbalances in access to power and resources on a global scale called into question the feasibility of achieving mutuality between partners. Given the reality of economic inequalities, racial biases, and cultural misunderstandings that have long plagued cross-continental encounters, it was easy for partnering congregations to fall into patterns of soft imperialism and dependency.

Though some aspects of the cultural dimension of religion in today's world pose barriers for sister church relationships, prominent features of both the international milieu of religious globalization and the ecology of contemporary American religiosity create opportunities for locally rooted, faith-based, ocean-crossing endeavors such as sister church relationships to succeed.

Sister church relationships take advantage of the sense of interconnectedness and the compression of time and space brought about by globalization. Moreover, North American congregations that participate in international congregation-to-congregation relationships navigate an organizational field and a spiritual climate that encourages such participation. The waning importance of denominationalism, the loss of institutional salience, and the renegotiating of spirituality among Americans over the last half century, while spelling decline for various forms of religiosity, have also created new opportunities in religious life. Sister church relationships capitalize on the growing interest in practice-oriented spirituality among American Christians by allowing ordinary parishioners to become involved in mission in a tangible way. Sister church relationships also tap into the renaissance of local communities as focal points of American religious life. American congregations with international partnerships often illustrate the marriage of practice-oriented spirituality and congregational vitality. As "practicing congregations," they are on the vanguard of a trend whereby religious communities make meaning together by combining service, friendship, and sacred presence.

Other strengths of the sister church model of mission include its plasticity, its ability to transcend ideological divides, and its greater capacity to build trust between partners, foster sustained engagement, and create social capital than many other models. Accommodating both liberal and conservative Christians and everyone in between, sister church relationships are flexible enough to suit various purposes. More than simply appealing to North American Christians across the theological and political spectrum, the sister church model of mission also spans differences between "this worldly" and "otherworldly" postures by promoting social justice, Christian unity, spiritual growth, and evangelism in a holistic way. The relational basis of sister church relationships encourages participants to venture outside the territories of doctrines and programs and into the realm of "I and Thou."[13] By placing short-term mission trips in the context of long-term relationships, the sister church model fosters accountability while still allowing ordinary parishioners to become involved in mission— therein eschewing some of the common pitfalls of other models of mission.

## Implications, Unanswered Questions, and Final Remarks

Conceptualizing mission not as expansion from a fixed geographic center but rather as flows of people, resources, and messages "from everywhere to everywhere," the sister church model of mission reflects a new map of global Christianity. No longer do Europe and other places inhabited by people of European descent function as the heartland of Christianity. Nor is the global South the next Christendom. The sister church phenomenon points to a picture of global Christianity that is multipolar and interactive. In this sketch, Christianity operates cross-culturally, not primarily as a tool of homogenization nor a weapon of conflict but rather as a vehicle of encounter and exchange.

The sister church relationships profiled in this study evidence collaboration between northern and southern Christians alongside other motifs of hostility, domination, or avoidance. This research suggests that, while not immune to the potential to promote soft imperialism on the part of northerners or compromise human dignity on the part of southerners, sister church relationships embody an approach to mission oriented around partnership. The profiled northern Christians, while imperfect in many ways and bound to entrenched systems of global inequality, generally sought to embody reciprocity and solidarity in their sister church relationships. Respondents from Washington, DC–area congregations involved in sister church relationships celebrated the global nature of Christianity, admired the faith of their southern counterparts, and embraced these counterparts as friends. They prioritized relationships over programs and sought to promote mutual accountability and reciprocal benefit between partners in the structures they employed and the norms they embraced.

As a qualitative and case-oriented study, however, this book is limited in its ability to gauge the extent to which sister church relationships succeed in bringing anticipated changes to northern and southern communities. Quantitative studies on the outcomes of sister church relationships would surely prove illuminating on this score. Comparisons of the effects of sister church relationships on participants to the effects of short-term mission trips on participants would be especially beneficial. Such studies could help ascertain whether the sister church model of mission is more effective than other models of mission in promoting trust and accountability and sustaining individual and communal transformation, as proponents of sister church relationships claim. Additional studies of sister church relationships from the vantage point of global southerners would also be illuminating. Ethnographic studies are inherently steered by the biases of respondents. Without speaking in one voice, global southern participants in international sister church relationships articulate alternative perspectives and lend different biases from the ones profiled in this study.

Further exploration of the decentralized, multidirectional, and interpenetrating nature of contemporary religious engagement on a global scale is also needed. The sister church phenomenon is but one outgrowth of significant twentieth-century developments such as the maturation of southern Christianity, the technological revolution, mass South-North migration, the ecumenical movement, and a new paradigm in Christian missiology. While a number of scholars have highlighted the shifts in global Christianity in the twentieth century and other scholars have drawn attention to the outreach efforts of particular groups, more attention should be paid to the cross-cultural linkages that are becoming ever more pronounced among Christians around the world. Christianity is not alone on this score. The networking capacity of other religions, too, has evolved in the contemporary era, while inter-religious encounter is also heightened by globalization. Additional scholarship is needed to elucidate the new dynamics of religious expansion and engagement in a globalizing world.

As this study of the sister parish movement illustrates, religious traditions are ever reinventing themselves to accommodate contemporary trends and circumstances. On one hand, the sister church phenomenon is an artifact of the contemporary global milieu—improbable in another historical situation. On the other hand, the sister church movement highlights not just the responsive dimension of religion vis-á-vis culture but also the prophetic dimension. Sister church relationships push against the currents of today's vast global inequalities, potent ideological battles, striking cultural divides, and tendencies toward religious privatization on one hand and religious totalism on the other.

Intentionally blurring the lines between "sending" and "receiving" communities, the sister parish model of mission is designed to recognize the truly global nature of contemporary Christianity. Proponents attempt to eschew patterns of paternalism or isolationism and strive to foster mutuality and partnership between American Christians and their counterparts in the global South. Recognizing that in themselves, short-term mission trips can be a poor use of resources, proponents seek to build lasting and purposeful ties between communities. In some cases and in some ways, sister church relationships are just another iteration of western imperialism, little more than veiled attempts to tame or co-opt Christianity in the global South. But in many cases and in many ways, sister parish relationships embody a missionary approach that Central Africans might refer to as *bega kwa bega* or *maboko na maboko*, mission "shoulder to shoulder" or "hand in hand."[14]

Sister church relationships represent both philosophical shifts in the understanding of Christian mission and changing structures of global religious engagement. As sister church relationships illustrate, emerging trajectories of religious globalization are marked not only by cross-cultural conflict but also by cross-cultural connection. In this sense, Stephen Aron's use of the term *confluence* to refer to the coming together of two or more streams of people is a better metaphor than Huntington's "clash of civilizations" motif. Describing the "American confluence" of the Missouri, Ohio, and Mississippi Rivers, Aron writes that the "coming together of rivers and peoples involved both collisions and collusions," resulting in "new worlds for all."[15] Similarly, the cross-culture encounter between Christians through international congregation-to-congregation relationships also involves both clash and cooperation, leaving all parties changed.

In many ways, Justin Hahn's story is a prototype of cross-cultural connection among contemporary Christians. A member of an ethnic minority in his own country, Hahn crossed borders merely by attending Living Faith Anglican Church. But attending a predominantly white congregation rooted in an English tradition was only the beginning of Hahn's journey across borders. His congregation not only belonged to the Anglican Province of Rwanda but also forged close ties with Rwandan Christians who shared this identity. By participating in his congregation's sister church relationship, Hahn acknowledged that he not only recognized but also celebrated the border-crossing dimension of Christianity. "Missionaries are being sent not only from Africa to America and America to Africa, but from everywhere to everywhere," said Hahn. "And that is the way it ought to be."

| NAME (PSEUDONYM) | ROLE IN SISTER CHURCH PROGRAM | AGE RANGE | OCCUPATION | SEX | ETHNICITY/ RACE |
|---|---|---|---|---|---|
| **Christt the King Anglican Church** | | | | | |
| Mitch Covington | participant | 45–49 | financial advisor | male | white |
| Chet Greenstreet | participant | 70–74 | electrical engineer | male | white |
| Corey Kimsey | leader | 30–34 | business professional | male | white |
| Edward Mulkowski | nonparticipating parishioner | 55–59 | corporate executive | male | white |
| Peter Russell | nonparticipating clergy member | 50–54 | rector and canon | male | white |
| Layla Shepard | participant | 45–49 | housekeeper | female | white |
| **Kensington Woods Presbyterian Church** | | | | | |
| Ruth Eaton | leader/clergy member | 55–59 | senior pastor | female | white |
| Milton Estelle | leader | 65–69 | retired forester | male | white |
| Felix Mapanje | leader | 60–64 | retired international development professional | male | African immigrant |
| Jolene McIntyre | participant | 60–64 | speech pathologist | female | white |
| Jason Rushmore | participant | 30–34 | federal civil servant | male | white |
| Brad Steen | nonparticipating parishioner | 65–69 | retired geologist | male | white |

(*continued*)

| NAME (PSEUDONYM) | ROLE IN SISTER CHURCH PROGRAM | AGE RANGE | OCCUPATION | SEX | ETHNICITY/ RACE |
|---|---|---|---|---|---|
| **Living Faith Anglican Church** | | | | | |
| Hailey Beckett | participant | 30–34 | Journalist | female | white |
| Chris Coulter | nonparticipating clergy member | 30–34 | associate pastor | male | white |
| Pierce Gatewood | nonparticipating parishioner | 35–39 | art gallery associate | male | white |
| Justin Hahn | participant | 25–29 | congressional staff person | male | Asian American |
| Shane Ish | participant | 40–44 | international development professional | male | white |
| Brian Jones | participant | 25–29 | advertising professional | male | white |
| Dave Rice | leader/clergy member | 35–39 | pastor | male | white |
| Aaron Thomas | leader | 30–34 | international development professional | male | white |
| **Mount Calvary Baptist Church** | | | | | |
| Clancey Brown | leader/clergy member | 55–59 | senior pastor | male | African American |
| Jocelyn Parker | participant/staff member | 45–49 | church administrator | female | African American |
| Olivia West | participant | 50–54 | management analyst | female | African American |
| **Mount Shannon Presbyterian Church** | | | | | |
| Jim Cassidy | nonparticipating parishioner | 45–49 | mechanic | male | white |
| Peyton Crowder | participant (nonmember) | 55–59 | pastor of another congregation | male | white |
| Henry Hunt | leader/clergy member | 55–59 | senior pastor | male | white |
| Karen Klingdon | nonparticipating parishioner | 40–44 | administrative assistant | female | white |
| Don Lingard | leader | 65–69 | retired sales manager | male | white |
| Rose Morrison | participant (nonmember) | 35–39 | educational researcher | female | white |

| NAME (PSEUDONYM) | ROLE IN SISTER CHURCH PROGRAM | AGE RANGE | OCCUPATION | SEX | ETHNICITY/ RACE |
| --- | --- | --- | --- | --- | --- |
| **Our Lady of Sorrows Catholic Church** | | | | | |
| John DiGiovanni | nonparticipating staff member | 65–69 | social justice minister | male | white |
| Larry Gates | former participant | 55–59 | director of nonprofit organization | male | white |
| Jasper Horner | nonparticipating parishioner | 65–69 | retired federal civil servant | male | white |
| Kevin Marino | leader | 40–44 | international development professional | male | white |
| Silas McConnell | nonparticipating parishioner | 70–74 | director of nonprofit organization | male | white |
| Janice Thompson | participant | 65–69 | retired international development professional | female | white |
| Susan Travinsky | former leader | 40–44 | teacher | female | white |
| **Saint Clement Catholic Church** | | | | | |
| Bernadette Bellemy | participant/former leader | 65–69 | retired social worker | female | Haitian immigrant |
| Kimberly Cook | leader/staff member | 45–49 | director of social concerns | female | African American |
| Jennifer Mercer | former participant | 25–29 | data analyst | female | white |
| Arnold Monroe | nonparticipating clergy member | 70–74 | pastor | male | white |
| Jack Napoli | leader | 55–59 | federal civil servant | male | white |
| Walter Rosedale | nonparticipating parishioner | 65–69 | retired professor | male | white |
| Deborah Sorens | non-participating parishioner | 75–79 | retired teacher | female | white |
| **Saint Mariana of Jesus Catholic Church** | | | | | |
| Alejandro Alvarez | non-participating staff member | 55–59 | custodian | male | Hispanic immigrant |
| Faith Berkholder | participant | 18–24 | college student | female | white |
| Julie Berkholder | participant | 40–44 | homemaker | female | white |

*(continued)*

| NAME (PSEUDONYM) | ROLE IN SISTER CHURCH PROGRAM | AGE RANGE | OCCUPATION | SEX | ETHNICITY/ RACE |
|---|---|---|---|---|---|
| Samantha Black | leader | 25–29 | federal civil servant | female | white |
| Mark Downey | former participant | 50–54 | teacher | male | white |
| Ricardo Flores | leader | 40–44 | international development professional | male | Hispanic |
| Peter Krakishaw | non-participating clergy member | 65–69 | pastor | male | white |
| Diego Rodríguez | participant/clergy member | 40–44 | deacon | male | Hispanic immigrant |

### Third Presbyterian Church

| | | | | | |
|---|---|---|---|---|---|
| Benjamin Banks | participant | 70–74 | retired military officer | male | white |
| Eleanor Banks | participant | 70–74 | retired teacher | female | white |
| Gertrude Chalmers | participant | 65–69 | social worker | female | white |
| Nancy Compton | non-participating parishioner | 60–65 | retired attorney | female | white |
| Gloria Feinburg | leader | 60–65 | retired congressional staffer | female | white |
| Stacy James Forester | participant/clergy member | 35–39 | associate pastor | female | white |
| Robert Hamilton | participant/clergy member | 55–59 | senior pastor | male | white |

### Thirteenth Street Baptist Church

| | | | | | |
|---|---|---|---|---|---|
| Bessie Graham | non-participating parishioner | 60–65 | retired | female | African American |
| Lawrence Jones | participant/staff member | 50–54 | assistant to the pastor | male | African American |
| Lionel Morris | leader/clergy member | 40–44 | pastor | male | African American |

### Trinity Anglican Church

| | | | | | |
|---|---|---|---|---|---|
| Gini Axelrod | participant/staff member | 65–69 | church musician | female | white |
| Brian Baker | participant | 18–24 | college student | male | white |
| Remy Duke | non-participating parishioner | 75–79 | retired military officer | male | white |
| Edward Francis | participant | 65–69 | retired military officer | male | white |

| NAME (PSEUDONYM) | ROLE IN SISTER CHURCH PROGRAM | AGE RANGE | OCCUPATION | SEX | ETHNICITY/ RACE |
|---|---|---|---|---|---|
| Jean Francis | participant | 60–64 | management consultant | female | white |
| Earl Henderson | non-participating parishioner | 70–74 | retired military officer | male | white |
| Craig Mora | leader/clergy | 60–64 | rector | male | white |
| **Victory Baptist Church** | | | | | |
| Cynthia Adams | participant | 60–64 | retired administrative assistant | female | African American |
| Milton Barclay | leader/clergy member | 60–64 | pastor | male | Jamaican immigrant |
| Lola Evans | non-participating staff member | 70–74 | associate minister | female | African American |
| Anita Wallace | participant | 60–64 | cosmetologist | female | African American |

# NOTES

## Introduction

1. The social distribution and theological underpinnings for each of these terms are somewhat distinct, as the book will explore in greater detail. *Companion congregation* and *twinning* are terms linked to Lutheran and Catholic communities, respectively. For descriptive purposes, the other terms are employed interchangeably throughout the book because of their widespread use even though "sister church" language could be considered problematic because of its gendered connotations, its association with the relationship between Roman Catholicism and Eastern Orthodoxy, and its conflation of *church* with the local congregation. While Catholics and Anglicans, among other groups, tend to use the word *parish* rather than *congregation* to describe local units of the church, this book employs *congregation* in the broad sociological sense as a description for local religious communities rather than as a particular type of polity.

2. Lamont Koerner (associate coordinator of the companion relationship between Saint Paul Area Synod and the Iringa Diocese of Tanzania), telephone interview by author, 24 March 2008.

3. See Robert Wuthnow and Stephen Offutt, "Transnational Religious Connections," *Sociology of Religion* 69, no. 2 (2008): 214. While scholars of global Christianity have recognized several ways in which cross-pollination has occurred within the worldwide church, they tend to emphasize the autonomy of the church outside the West over the influence of outsiders. Moreover, literature on the history and practice of Christian mission, while abundant, has tended to focus either on the sending or receiving capacity of particular Christian communities or individuals.

4. Omar M. McRoberts, *Streets of Glory: Church and Community in a Black Urban Neighborhood* (Chicago: University of Chicago Press, 2003), 153.

5. Brenda Brasher, *Godly Women: Fundamentalism and Female Power* (New Brunswick, NJ: Rutgers University Press, 1998), 6.

6. See chapter 4 for a working definition of *congregation* employed in this study.

7. See Nancy Tatom Ammerman, *Pillars of Faith: American Congregations and Their Partners* (Berkeley: University of California Press, 2005), 4. Although these categories are helpful, they are also problematic. The bounds of the "Black Church," for

instance, are notoriously difficult to delineate, and predominantly African American congregations in predominantly white denominations are hard to classify. Moreover, immigrant Christian communities such as African Initiated Churches (AICs) that do not fit neatly into either Protestantism or Catholicism are excluded from this schema. Eastern Orthodox Christians, though a small percentage of American churchgoers, are also excluded. Despite these limitations, I structured my field research according to these four general traditions in the interest of covering a broad and representative—though not comprehensive—swath of American Christianity. In addition to the issue of inclusion, terminology is also a problem in that *mainline* is no longer an accurate description, if it ever was, of American Protestants whose denominations affiliate with the World Council of Churches. Following the lead of Ammerman and a host of other scholars, I use *mainline* as a shorthand for liberal or conciliar Protestants rather than in a technical sense.

8. See chapter 4 for further discussion.

9. See Gerardo Marti, *A Mosaic of Believers: Diversity and Innovation in a Multiethnic Church* (Bloomington: Indiana University Press, 2005), 204–205.

10. See Scott Thumma, "Methods for Congregational Studying," in *Studying Congregations: A New Handbook*, ed. Nancy Ammerman et al. (Nashville: Abingdon Press, 1998), 205–208.

11. See Clem Adelman, David Jenkins, and Stephen Kemmis, "Rethinking Case Study: Notes from the Second Cambridge Conference," in *Case Study: An Overview. Case Study Methods 1* (Victoria, Australia: Deakin University, 1983), 3. See also Gretchen B. Rossman and Sharon F. Rallis, *Learning in the Field: An Introduction to Qualitative Research*, 2d ed. (Thousand Oaks, CA: Sage Publications, 2003), 104–106.

12. See Matthew Miles and Michael Huberman, *Qualitative Data Analysis: An Expanded Sourcebook*, 2d ed. (Thousand Oaks, CA: Sage Publications, 1994).

13. See John and Lyn Lofland, *Analyzing Social Settings*, 3d ed. (Belmont, CA: Wadsworth, 1995), 127–145.

14. See James Hopewell, *Congregation: Stories and Structures* (Philadelphia: Fortress Press, 1987).

15. Thumma, "Methods for Congregational Studying," 235.

16. See Pew Global Attitudes Project, "What the World Thinks in 2002: How Global Publics View: Their Lives, Their Countries, The World, America" (Washington, DC: Pew Research Center, December 4, 2002), http://pewglobal.org/reports/display.php?ReportID=165 (accessed 10 April 2013).

17. See Gurminder K. Bhambra, "Historical Sociology, Modernity, and Postcolonial Critique," *The American Historical Review* 111, no. 3 (June 2011): 653–662.

18. See, for example, Talal Asad, ed., *Anthropology and the Colonial Encounter* (Reading, UK: Ithaca Press, 1973); Tony Ballantyne and Antoinette Burton, eds., *Bodies in Contact: Rethinking Colonial Encounters in World History* (Durham, NC: Duke University Press, 2005); Sandra E. Greene, *Sacred Sites and the Colonial Encounter: A History of Meaning and Memory in Ghana* (Bloomington: Indiana University Press, 2002).

19. See Edward Said, *Orientalism* (New York: Vintage Books, 1978).

20. James H. Mittelman, *The Globalization Syndrome: Transformation and Resistance* (Princeton: Princeton University Press, 2000).

21. See Samuel Huntington, *The Clash of Civilizations and the Remaking of World Order* (New York: Simon and Schuster, 1996).

22. Koerner, telephone interview.

23. Ibid.


*Chapter 1*

1. David B. Barrett, ed., *World Christian Encyclopedia*, Vol. 1, 2nd ed. (Oxford: Oxford University Press, 2001), 12; Lamin Sanneh, "The Changing Face of Christianity: The Cultural Impetus of a World Religion," in *The Changing Face of Christianity: Africa, the West, and the World*, ed. Lamin Sanneh and Joel Carpenter (New York: Oxford University Press, 2005), 4. Sanneh points out that this modest growth is only because patterns of immigrant religiosity have mitigated against the general pattern of decline of Christianity in Europe in North America.

2. David B. Barrett, Todd M. Johnson, and Peter F. Crossing, "Missionometrics 2007: Creating Your Own Analysis of Global Data," *International Bulletin of Missionary Research* 31, no. 1 (January 2007): 32.

3. Andrew F. Walls, *The Cross-Cultural Process in Christian History: Studies in the Transmission and Appropriation of Faith* (Maryknoll, NY: Orbis Books, 2002), 64; Barrett, Johnson, and Crossing, "Missionometrics 2007," 32.

4. Philip Jenkins, *The Next Christendom: The Coming of Global Christianity* (Oxford: Oxford University Press, 2002), 2.

5. Lamin Sanneh, *Whose Religion Is Christianity? The Gospel Beyond the West* (Grand Rapids, MI: W. B. Eerdmans Publishing Co., 2003), 3.

6. Walls, *Cross-Cultural Process in Christian History*, 65.

7. Ibid., 47.

8. Ibid., 34.

9. Jenkins, *Next Christendom*, 12.

10. I follow Philip Jenkins's lead in using the term *global South* to refer to Africa, Latin America, and Asia, even though Asia is not technically in the Southern Hemisphere. Although not without problems, *global South* is a less pejorative term than *Third World* or *developing world*.

11. Kenneth Scott Latourette coined the phrase "the great century" with reference to the nineteenth-century western missionary endeavor in his *History of the Expansion of Christianity*, 7 vols. (Grand Rapids, MI: Zondervan Publishing House, 1970).

12. Dana Robert, "Shifting Southward: Global Christianity Since 1945," *International Bulletin of Missionary Research* 24, no. 2 (April 2000): 50–58.

13. Allan Anderson, "The Gospel and Culture in Pentecostal Mission in the Third World," *Missionalia* 27, no. 2 (February 1999): 220–230; cited in Stephen B. Bevans and Roger P. Schroeder, *Constants in Context: A Theology of Mission for Today* (Maryknoll, NY: Orbis Books, 2004), 386.

14. Sanneh, *Whose Religion Is Christianity?*.

15. David Martin, "Evangelical Expansion in Global Society," in *Christianity Reborn: The Global Expansion of Evangelicalism in the Twentieth Century*, ed. Donald M. Lewis (Grand Rapids, MI: W. B. Eerdmans Publishing Co., 2004): 273–294.

16. Jenkins, *Next Christendom*, 8.

17. Philip Jenkins, *The New Faces of Christianity: Reading the Bible in the Global South* (New York: Oxford University Press, 2006).

18. Christopher J. H. Wright, "An Upside-Down World: Distinguishing Between Home and Mission Field No Longer Makes Sense." *Christianity Today* 51, no. 1 (January 2007): 43.

19. "About the Anglican Church in North America," The Anglican Church in North America, accessed 10 April 2013, http://anglicanchurch.net/?/main/page/about-acna. See also Andrew Higgins, "Divided Flock: Episcopal Church Dissidents Seek Authority Overseas," *Wall Street Journal* (20 September 2007), sec. A1.

20. Claudia Währisch-Oblau first used the concept of "reverse mission" in 2000 in her categorization of immigrant churches within the Rhein-Ruhr region of Germany. In her work, the term "reverse missionary" refers to congregations planted in Germany by overseas "mother churches" in Africa, Latin America, or Asia. While reverse missionary congregations put much effort into evangelizing immigrants of the same national/ethnic origin, many also seek to evangelize native populations and re-evangelize native "spiritless" churches. Claudia Währisch-Oblau, "From Reverse Mission to Common Mission . . . We Hope," *International Review of Mission* 89, no. 354 (2000): 467–483.

21. Christopher Wright reports that 50 percent of all Protestant missionaries in the world come from non-western countries, and the proportion is increasing annually. "An Upside-Down World," 43.

22. Nancy Tatom Ammerman, *Pillars of Faith: American Congregations and Their Partners* (Berkeley: University of California Press, 2005), 200.

23. Walls, *Cross-Cultural Process in Christian History*, 45.

24. "The Latest Korean Mission Status (2008)," Korea Research Institute for Missions, accessed 10 April 2013, http://krim.org/2010/english.html. See also Steve S. C. Moon, "The Recent Korean Missionary Movement: A Record of Growth, and More Growth Needed," *International Bulletin of Missionary Research* 27, no. 1 (2003): 11–16.

25. Barrett, Johnson, and Crossing, "Missionometrics 2007," 31.

26. Claudia Währisch-Oblau, "'We Shall Be Fruitful in This Land': Pentecostal and Charismatic New Mission Churches in Europe," in *Fruitful in This Land: Pluralism, Dialogue and Healing in Migrant Pentecostalism*, ed. André Droogers et al. (Zoetermeer, NL: Boekencentrum, 2006), 33.

27. Ibid., 26.

28. See Rebecca Y. Kim, "Acts of Sacrifice," *Faith and Leadership*, 21 June 2011, accessed 10 April 2013, http://www.faithandleadership.com/content/rebecca-y-kim-acts-sacrifice. The extent to which foreign missionaries in western countries influence native-born populations is contested. For instance, Jehu Hanciles argues that African immigrant pastors in the United States almost universally claim that they are missionaries, while Robert Wuthnow notes that most African or Latin Americans serving churches in the United States are serving their own ethnic communities. See Jehu Hanciles, *Beyond Christendom: Globalization, African Migration, and the Transformation of the West* (Maryknoll, NY: Orbis Books, 2008), 364–373; Robert Wuthnow, *Boundless Faith: The Global Outreach of American Churches* (Berkeley: University of California Press, 2009), 56.

29. Sanneh, "Changing Face of Christianity," 3.

30. See Walls, *Cross-Cultural Process in Christian History*, 49–71. See also Brian Stanley, *The World Missionary Conference, Edinburgh, 1910* (Grand Rapids, MI: W. B. Eerdmans Publishing Co., 2009).

31. Sanneh, "Current Transformation of Christianity," in *Changing Face of Christianity*, 220.

32. Philip Jenkins, "The Next Christianity," *The Atlantic Monthly* 290, no. 3 (October 2002): 55.

33. See Wuthnow, *Boundless Faith*. See also Robert Schreiter, "Short Term, Long Term, on Whose Terms?," *Mission Update*, Periodic Paper #3 (Fall 2006): 1–8.

34. Wilbert R. Shenk, *Changing Frontiers of Mission* (Maryknoll, NY: Orbis Books, 1999), 143.

35. See Edward Said, *Orientalism* (New York: Vintage Books, 1978).

36. See, for example, Dana Robert, "Cross-Cultural Friendship in the Creation of Twentieth-Century World Christianity," *International Bulletin of Missionary Research* 35, no. 2 (April 2011): 100–107.

37. See Sanneh, *Whose Religion Is Christianity?*. See also Robert, "Shifting Southward."

38. Andrew F. Walls, *The Missionary Movement in Christian History: Studies in the Transmission of the Faith* (Maryknoll, NY: Orbis Books, 1996); Joel Carpenter, interview by author, Grand Rapids, MI, 14 July 2008.

39. Shenk, *Changing Frontiers of Mission*, 153.

40. Stephen Neill, *A History of Christian Missions* (London: Penguin Books, 1986), 215.

41. Ibid., 286.

42. Kenneth Scott Latourette, *The Great Century in the Americas, Australasia, and Africa* (New York: Harper, 1953), 469.

43. Shenk, *Changing Frontiers of Mission*, 149.

44. Jenkins, *Next Christianity*, 42.

45. Mary M. McGlone, *Sharing Faith Across the Hemisphere* (Maryknoll, NY: Orbis Books, 1997), 114.

46. Shenk, *Changing Frontiers of Mission*, 160–163. See also Angelyn Dries, *The Missionary Movement in American Catholic History* (Maryknoll, NY: Orbis Books, 1998), 215–246.

47. David Bosch, *Transforming Mission: Paradigm Shifts in Theology of Mission* (Maryknoll, NY: Orbis Books, 1991).

48. Unlike Protestantism, Catholic ecclesiology has long crossed geographic borders. The Second Vatican Council and other twentieth-century developments, however, helped the Catholic Church re-evaluate international relationships and structures.

49. McGlone, *Sharing Faith Across the Hemisphere*, 109. See *Guadium et Spes*, §§1, 4; *Ad Gentes*, §11; *Lumen Gentium*, §13; in Austin Flannery, ed., *Vatican Council II: Constitutions, Decrees, Declarations* (Newtown, Australia: E. J. Dwyer, 1992).

50. McGlone, *Sharing Faith Across the Hemisphere*, 111.

51. Robert Schreiter, "Globalization and Reconciliation," in *Mission in the Third Millennium*, ed. Robert Schreiter (Maryknoll, NY: Orbis Books, 2001), 137.

52. Ibid.

53. Ibid., 138.

54. McGlone, *Sharing Faith Across the Hemisphere*, 147.

55. *Redemptoris Missio*, §85, in *Origins*, Catholic News Service Documentary Service, 31 January 1991.

56. United States Conference of Catholic Bishops, *To the Ends of the Earth: A Pastoral Statement on World Mission* (New York: The Society for the Propagation of the Faith, 1987), ¶¶15–16.

57. United States Conference of Catholic Bishops, *Called to Global Solidarity: International Challenges for U.S. Parishes* (Washington, DC: United States Council of Catholic Bishops, 1997), ¶¶1, 4–5.

58. Bevans and Schroeder, *Constants in Context*, 394.

59. Ibid., 285.

60. Timothy Yates, *Christian Mission in the Twentieth Century* (New York: Cambridge University Press, 1994), 221.

61. "Evangelization, Proselytism, and Common Witness: The Report from the Fourth Phase of the International Dialogue (1990–1997) between the Roman Catholic Church and Some Classical Pentecostal Churches and Leaders," in *Pneuma* 21, no. 1 (Spring 1999): 16, ¶129.

62. Yates, *Christian Mission in the Twentieth Century*, 246. See also the Second Lausanne Conference's "Manilla Manifesto," in *New Directions in Mission and Evangelization I: Basic Statements 1974–1991*, ed. James A. Scherer and Stephen B. Bevans (Maryknoll, NY: Orbis Books, 1992), 293.

63. Van Engen attributes the paradigm shift in missiology to the inclusion of the cognate studies of anthropology, linguistics, communication theory, and spiritual power in the field. Charles Kraft was a key interlocutor in this new dialogue, calling cross-cultural missionaries to deal with the expanding cultural diversity of the church and the world. Charles E. Van Engen, preface to *Paradigm Shifts in Christian Witness: Insights from Anthropology, Communication, and Spiritual Power: Essays in Honor of Charles H. Kraft*, ed. Charles E. Van Engen, Darrell Whiteman, and J. Dudley Woodberry (Maryknoll, NY: Orbis Books, 2008), xvii.

64. Bosch, *Transforming Mission*, 368.

65. Ibid.

66. *The Witness of a Revolutionary Church: Whitby, Ontario, Canada, 4–24 July 1947* (London: International Missionary Council, 1947), 19–20; quoted in Colin Marsh, "Partnership in Mission: To Send or To Share?" *International Review of Missionary Research* 92, no. 366 (2003), 370.

67. Marsh, "Partnership in Mission," 371.

68. Bosch, *Transforming Mission*, 389–393.

69. The 1963 conference sponsored by the WCC's Commission on World Mission and Evangelism, for example, emphasized the church's universal call to "mission in six continents" instead of sending and receiving. See Yates, *Christian Mission in the Twentieth Century*, 165.

70. Marsh, "Partnership in Mission," 372.

71. James A. Scherer, *Gospel, Church, and Kingdom: Comparative Studies in World Mission Theology* (Minneapolis: Augsburg Press, 1987), 167.

72. In J. D. Douglas, ed., *Let the Earth Hear His Voice. International Congress on World Evangelization in Lausanne* (Minneapolis: World Wide Publications, 1975), 6.

73. Bruce K. Camp, "Major Paradigm Shifts in World Evangelization," *International Journal of Frontier Missions* 11, no. 3 (1994): 135.

74. Quoted in Paul E. Pierson, "Lessons in Mission from the Twentieth Century: Conciliar Missions" in *Between Past and Future: Evangelical Missiology Entering the Twenty-first Century*, ed. Jon Bonk (Pasadena, CA: William Carey Library, 2003), 73.

75. Bevans and Schroeder, *Constants in Context*, 355. The Center for Parish Development and the Ekklesia Project also speak of a "missional church."

76. Scherer, *Gospel, Church, and Kingdom*, 191.

77. Douglas, *Let the Earth Hear His Voice*, 5, §6.

78. Lesslie Newbigin, *The Gospel in a Pluralist Society* (Grand Rapids, MI: W. B. Eerdmans Publishing Co., 1989), 222–233.

79. Pierson, "Lessons in Mission from the Twentieth Century," 73.

80. Bruce K. Camp, "A Survey of the Local Church's Involvement in Global/Local Outreach," in Bonk, *Between Past and Future*, 234.

81. See Pope Paul VI, *Evangelii Nuntiandi*, §21, Papal Encyclicals Online, accessed 10 April 2013, http://www.papalencyclicals.net/Paul06/p6evan.htm.

82. Bevans and Schroeder, *Constants in Context*, 363. See also Robert Rivers, *From Maintenance to Mission: Evangelization and the Revitalization of the Parish* (Mahwah, NJ: Paulist Press, 2005), 186.

83. Simon Chan, "Mother Church: Toward a Pentecostal Ecclesiology," *Pneuma* 22, no. 2 (Fall 2000): 189.

84. In 1972, Shoki Coe, Director of the Fund for Theological Education, introduced the term *contextualization* to missiological vocabulary where it has gained traction ever since. Before this, discussions of similar values took place among both conciliar and evangelical Protestants under the rubric of *indigenization*. For instance, evangelical anthropologists had been differentiating gospel and culture for several decades in the journal, *Practical Theology*.

85. Lesslie Newbigin wrote extensively on this topic, concluding that rather than being the world's evangelist, the West needs to be re-evangelized. Newbigin called for a "missionary encounter" with Enlightenment culture, which, he maintained, is antithetical to Christianity on many scores. See Lesslie Newbigin, *The Other Side of 1984: Questions for the Churches* (Geneva: World Council of Churches, 1983).

86. In Douglas, *Let the Earth Hear His Voice*, 285–300; quoted in Yates, *Christian Mission in the Twentieth Century*, 205.

87. René Padilla, *Mission Between the Times: Essays on the Kingdom* (Grand Rapids, MI: W. B. Eerdmans Publishing Co., 1985), 108.

88. See, for example, David Hesselgrave, *Communicating Christ Cross-Culturally: An Introduction to Missionary Communication* (Grand Rapids, MI: Zondervan Publishing Co., 1978), 85.

89. Yates, *Christian Mission in the Twentieth Century*, 203.

90. This emphasis was not new. For instance, in the nineteenth century many Catholics promoted social justice in conjunction with the teachings of Pope Leo XIII, and Protestants saw the Social Gospel movement come to preeminence. The social dimensions of the gospel gained renewed attention, however, with the ascent of liberation theology and increased receptivity to the voices of global southerners as colonial empires crumbled.

91. In Douglas, *Let the Earth Hear His Voice*, 129–133, 116–120.

92. Bevans and Schroeder, *Constants in Context*, 337.

93. Ibid., 262. For instance, the theme of the Lausanne Committee's 1989 conference in Manila was for the "whole church to take the whole gospel to the whole world."

94. Samuel Escobar, *Changing Tides: Latin America and World Mission Today* (Maryknoll, N.Y.: Orbis Books, 2002). See also Andrew F. Walls, "The American Dimension in the History of the Missionary Movement," in *Earthen Vessels: American Evangelicals and Foreign Missions, 1880–1980*, ed. Joel Carpenter and Wilbert Shenk (Grand Rapids, MI: W. B. Eerdmans Publishing Co., 1990), 1–25.

95. Michael Pocock, Gailyn Van Rheenen, and Douglas McConnell, eds., introduction to *The Changing Face of World Mission: Engaging Contemporary Issues and Trends* (Grand Rapids, MI: Baker Books, 2005).

96. Todd M. Johnson, "'It Can Be Done': The Impact of Modernity and Postmodernity on the Global Mission Plans of Churches and Agencies," in Bonk, *Between Past and Future*, 37–49.

97. Escobar, *Changing Tides*, 11.

98. A. T. Kearney/Foreign Policy Magazine, "Globalization Index (2006)," accessed 10 April 2013, http://atkearney.com/. The United States recently ranked third overall in globalization on the basis of several indicators spanning trade, business, politics, and information technology.

99. Robert Wuthnow and Stephen Offutt, "Transnational Religious Connections," *Sociology of Religion* 69, no. 2 (2008): 214.

100. Ibid., 218.

101. Carpenter, interview by the author.

102. Doug McAdam, John D. McCarthy, and Mayer N. Zald, introduction to *Comparative Perspectives on Social Movements: Political Opportunities, Mobilizing Structures, and Cultural Framings* (New York: Cambridge University Press, 1996), 6. See also David A. Snow and Robert D. Benford, "Ideology, Frame Resonance, and Participation Mobilization," in Bert Klandermans, Hanspeter Kriesi, and Sidney Tarrow, eds., *From Structure to Action: Social Movement Participation Across Cultures* (Greenwich, CT: JAI Press, 1988), 197–217. Social movement theory provides a helpful lens for viewing the contemporary practice of mission in general and the sister church movement in particular. While the literature on social movements is diverse, three factors to explain the emergence of social movements are salient in the various strands of social movement theory: political opportunities, mobilizing structures/forms of organization, and framing processes. See also Chapter 5 for a more thorough discussion of social movement theory, particularly with regard to framing processes.

103. Pierson, "Lessons in Mission from the Twentieth Century," 74.

104. See Camp, "A Survey of the Local Church's Involvement in Global/Local Outreach," 221.

105. Bevans and Schroeder, *Constants in Context*, 262.

106. Korea Research Institute on Missions, "The Latest Korean Mission Status (2008)."

107. Johnson, "It Can Be Done," 42.

108. See Robert Schreiter, "Short Term, Long Term, on Whose Terms?" *Mission Update*, Periodic Paper #3 (Fall 2006).

109. Barrett, Johnson, and Crossing, "Missionometrics 2007," 28.

110. Ibid., 25. See also Dotsey Welliver and Minnette Northcutt, eds., *Mission Handbook: U.S. and Canadian Protestant Ministries Overseas, 2004–2006* (Wheaton, IL: Billy Graham Center, 2004) and Wuthnow, *Boundless Faith*.

111. Andrew Walls writes that "Americans represent Western characteristics exemplified to the fullest extent." This comes through in the way Americans conduct missions, especially in the primacy they place on numerical success, technique, efficiency, volunteerism, inventiveness, and entrepreneurialism. Walls also argues that, often unwittingly, Americans tend to be evangelists for American culture just as much as for Christianity. Walls, "The American Dimension in the History of the Missionary Movement," in Bonk, *Between Past and Future*, 3–8.

112. Many denominations and mission agencies span both the United States and Canada. While my study essentially pertains to residents of the United States, many of its general conclusions apply to Canadians as well. At times I reference US residents and North Americans interchangeably. My desire is neither to exclude Canadians or Mexicans from North American Christianity nor to imply that religious distinctions between these groups are insignificant, but rather to communicate fluidly. Additionally, while it is problematic to use the term *American* to apply to residents of the United States to the exclusion of other inhabitants of the Americas, I also apply this conceit upon occasion to avoid awkward and cumbersome language.

113. Welliver and Northcutt, eds., *Mission Handbook*, 12.

114. Dana Robert, "Cross-Cultural Friendship in the Creation of Twentieth-Century World Christianity," *International Bulletin of Missionary Research* 35, no. 2 (April 2011): 105.

115. Ibid., 106.

116. For other examples, see Kai Michael Funkschmidt, "New Models of Mission Relationship and Partnership," *International Review of Mission* 91, no. 363 (2002): 558–576; Jacqueline L. Salmon, "Churches Retool Mission Trips: Work Abroad Criticized for High Cost and Lack of Value," *The Washington Post* (5 July 2008), sec. B1. The following initiatives are also among those seeking to embody the partnership ideal: Amahoro Africa (http://www.amahoro-africa.org), Encuentro 2000 (http://www.usccb.org/hispanicaffairs/encuentro.shtml), Glocal (http://www.glocal.net), Partners International (http://www.partnersintl.org) (accessed 10 April 2013).

117. See Richard Lubawa, *Shoulder to Shoulder: Bega Kwa Bega: A Lutheran Partnership Between Minnesota and Tanzania* (Minneapolis: Lutheran University Press, 2007).

## Chapter 2

1. Mike Vallez, introduction to *The New Mission Book: Mission Possible*, e-book only (Minneapolis: by the author, 2005). Accessed 21 April 2008, www.globalfaithpartners.com/ebook.html (site discontinued).

2. Vallez, telephone interview by author; 9 March 2008.

3. Vallez, *New Mission Book*, chapter 7.

4. Vallez, telephone interview.

5. Vallez, *New Mission Book*, chapter 11.

6. Ibid.

7. Dan Shoemaker, telephone interview by author, 16 September 2008.

8. "Background," on Global Faith Partners, accessed 8 March 2008, http://www. globalfaithpartners.com/vision.html (site discontinued).

9. Because of the diffuse nature of the sister church phenomenon, its scope is nearly impossible to measure. Neither the definition nor the terminology of "sister church" relationships is universal or even widespread. The organizational dynamics of the sister church phenomenon also lack solidity. While many partnerships are started and/or overseen by denominational or parachurch mission agencies, perhaps as many originate among congregations themselves and function independently. Often, partnerships are informal and evolving rather than contractual. With the exception of Catholics, American denominational bodies have not mapped the sister church phenomenon among their constitutive congregations with any precision. For Catholics, the last survey that gathered information on sister parish relationships was conducted in 2001 through the National Parish Inventory. With these limitations in mind—based on correspondence with representatives of national mission agencies, data published by research institutes such as the Center for Applied Research in the Apostolate and the U.S. Catholic Mission Association, and informal congregational mapping of the Washington, DC, metropolitan area—I estimate that 5 to 10 percent of Christian congregations in the United States are involved in long-term international congregation-to-congregation relationships.

10. Mary L. Gautier and Paul Perl, "Partnerships of Solidarity with the Church in Latin American and the Caribbean," Special Report of the Center for Applied Research in the Apostolate (Washington, DC: Georgetown University, Fall 2003), 1.

11. See Tara Hefferan, *Twinning and Faith Development: Catholic Parish Partnering in the U.S. and Haiti* (Bloomfield, CT: Kumarian Press, 2007), 19–20. As a backdrop to the growth of international partnerships between parishes, Hefferan notes increasing levels of volunteerism and service in the United States, a shifting of social service delivery from government to nongovernmental organizations, and growing lay involvement in mission, especially among Catholics.

12. Dennis P. O'Connor, *Bridges of Faith: Building a Relationship with a Sister Parish* (Cincinnati: St. Anthony Messenger Press, 2007), 58–60.

13. Ibid., 61–63.

14. Catherine Nerney, telephone interview by author, 18 April 2008.

15. Mary Campbell, telephone interview by author, 4 April 2008.

16. Ibid.

17. Roger Peterson, "Innovation in Short-term Mission," in *Innovation in Mission*, ed. Jim Reapsome and Jon Hurst (Waynesboro, GA: Authentic, 2006), 51–66. See also Robert Wuthnow and Stephen Offutt, "Transnational Religious Connections," *Sociology of Religion* 69, no. 2 (2008). The number of short-term international missionaries from the United States and from around the globe continues to grow. Current estimates range from one to four million annually.

18. "A Brief History," on Reciprocal Ministries International, accessed 10 April 2013, http://www.rminet.org/aboutrmi/history.htm.

19. Shoemaker, phone interview.

20. O'Connor, *Bridges of Faith*, 42.

21. Nancy Bernhardt-Hsu, "Partnering Relationships for Mission (An Inquiry & Overview of Diocesan and Parish Twinning)," United States Catholic Mission Association (Washington, DC: Spring 2003), 6. See also Gautier and Perl, "Partnerships of Solidarity," 5–7.

22. Gautier and Perl, "Partnerships of Solidarity," 6.

23. O'Connor, *Bridges of Faith*, 41–42.

24. Mary M. McGlone, *Sharing Faith Across the Hemisphere* (Maryknoll, NY: Orbis Books, 1997), 213.

25. Gautier and Perl, "Partnerships of Solidarity," 2–3.

26. Bernhardt-Hsu, "Partnering Relationships for Mission," 4.

27. Gautier and Perl, "Partnerships of Solidarity".

28. O'Connor, *Bridges of Faith*, 33.

29. Hefferan, *Twinning and Faith Development*, back cover.

30. Gautier and Perl, "Partnerships of Solidarity," 7.

31. Ibid.

32. Robert Pelton (director of Latin American/North American Church Concerns, Kellogg Institute for International Studies, University of Notre Dame), telephone interview by author, 10 May 2008; Nerney, telephone interview.

33. "Primary Ministry Work Activity," 2005 Mission Survey/Statistics, on United States Catholic Mission Association, accessed 20 May 2013, http://67.59.160.66/Work%20Activity.htm.

34. Gautier and Perl, "Partnerships of Solidarity," 4.

35. Bernhardt-Hsu, "Partnering Relationships for Mission," 7.

36. Richard Lubawa, *Shoulder to Shoulder: Bega Kwa Bega: A Lutheran Partnership Between Minnesota and Tanzania* (Minneapolis: Lutheran University Press, 2007).

37. Ibid., 10.

38. Ibid., 38.

39. Ibid., 5.

40. "Global Mission in the Twenty-first Century: A Vision of Evangelical Faithfulness in God's Mission," Evangelical Lutheran Church in America, Division for Global Mission (Chicago: 1999), 38.

41. Campbell, telephone interview.

42. "Mission Strategy for Latin America," Evangelical Lutheran Church of America, Division for Global Mission (Chicago: 1995), 9.

43. Campbell, telephone interview.

44. Lubawa, *Shoulder to Shoulder*, 9.

45. Campbell, telephone interview.

46. Ibid.

47. Charles Jones, telephone interview by author, 14 April 2008.

48. Ibid.

49. "How International Ministries Approaches our Work," on American Baptist Church, USA, International Ministries, accessed 20 May 2013, http://www.international-ministries.org/read/3819.

50. Jones, telephone interview.

51. "Manual for Congregational Partnerships," The Alliance of Baptists/Fraternity of Baptist Churches of Cuba (Washington, DC: June 2005), 1.

52. Stan Hastey, telephone interview by author, 30 April 2008.

53. "Manual for Congregational Partnerships," 3.

54. Connectional polity holds that the church is defined not by formal structures, doctrine, or systems of authority but by connections between people. For a discussion of

how United Methodist connectional polity informs Methodist international mission efforts, see Bruce W. Robbins, *A World Parish? Hopes and Challenges of the United Methodist Church in a Global Setting* (Nashville: Abingdon Press, 2004).

55. Patrick Friday, telephone interview by author, 1 May 2008.

56. "In Mission Together," on United Methodist Church, General Board of Global Ministries, accessed 10 April 2013, http://gbgm.umc.org/connections/partnerships/inmissiontogether/.

57. Friday, telephone interview.

58. "Presbyterians Do Mission in Partnership," General Assembly of the Presbyterian Church (USA) (Louisville: 2003).

59. Doug Welch, telephone interview by author, 1 April 2008.

60. See Samuel Escobar, *Changing Tides: Latin America and World Mission Today* (Maryknoll, NY: Orbis Books, 2002).

61. Christopher Bader et al., "American Piety in the Twenty-first Century: New Insights to the Depth and Complexity of Religion in the US; Selected Findings from the Baylor Religion Survey, September 2006," (Waco: Baylor Institute for Studies of Religion, 2006), 8.

62. Robert Priest, Douglas Wilson, and Adelle Johnson, "U.S. Megachurches and New Patterns of Global Missions," *International Bulletin of Missionary Research* 34, no. 2 (April 2010): 101.

63. "About Us," on Covenant Merge Ministries, accessed 10 April 2013, http://covmerge.org/about/.

64. Dale Lusk, telephone interview by author, 5 December 2008.

65. "Decade of Change in the Philippines," on Converge Worldwide, accessed 5 December 2008, http://www.scene3.org/content/view/1604/74/ (www.scene3.org is now www.convergeworldwide.org).

66. "Our Values," on Converge Worldwide, accessed 5 December 2008, http://www.scene3.org/content/view/1014/69/ (www.scene3.org is now www.convergeworldwide.org).

67. "Our Genesis," on The Anglican Church in North America, accessed 10 April 2013, http://anglicanchurch.net/media/genesisJuly2010.pdf. The 2003 ordination of Bishop Gene Robinson, who is openly gay, prompted several dioceses and hundreds of traditionalist parishes to leave the Episcopal Church over the last decade. Initially, many linked with provinces representing other parts of the worldwide Anglican Communion, most in the global South. More recently, approximately one hundred thousand realigned American Anglicans formed their own rival Anglican Church in North America.

68. "The Companion Diocese Network Consultant: A Ministry and a Job Description," Office of Anglican and Global Relations, The Episcopal Church of the United States of America (New York: The Episcopal Church Center, n.d.).

69. James Teets (manager of partnership service, Office of Anglican and Global Relations, The Episcopal Church of the United States of America), e-mail correspondence with author, 30 April 2008.

70. "The Companion Diocese Network Consultant."

71. The Anglican Church in North America is still seeking recognition as a province in the Anglican Communion. During the transition period, ACNA bishops retain membership in the House of Bishops of the province in which they were members prior to the formation of the ACNA. It is unclear whether this will change if the ACNA gains

recognition as a province of the Anglican Communion. See "Our Genesis," http://angli-canchurch.net/media/genesisJuly2010.pdf. See also Suzane Sataline, "Episcopalians Form Rival Church," *The Wall Street Journal*, December 3, 2008) accessed 10 April 2013, http://online.wsj.com/article/SB122834564219177337.html.

72. "Relationships," on Anglican Global Mission Partners, accessed 10 April 2013, http://www.anglican-missions.org/.

73. "Calling," on Sharing of Ministries Abroad International, accessed 10 April 2013, http://www.somausa.org/calling.

74. Initially, Rwanda's Anglican Mission was named "Anglican Mission in America" (AMiA). In 2007, "Anglican Mission in the Americas" (AMiAs) was created by the Archbishop of Rwanda as an umbrella organization for AMiA, and its sisters, the Anglican Coalition of Canada and the Anglican Coalition in America, to accommodate diverse practices on women's ordination within Rwanda's Anglican Mission. See The Anglican Mission in the Americas, "Questions and Answers," on The Anglican Mission in the Americas, accessed 8 December 2008, http://www.theamia.org/experience/pqanda (page no longer on website).

75. "General Understandings for Sister-to-Sister Church Partnerships: Province of Rwanda and the Anglican Mission in the Americas," The Anglican Mission in the Americas, working document (August 2008).

76. Tim Smith, telephone interview by author, 11 September 2008.

77. Ibid.

78. "General Understandings."

79. See C. Eric Lincoln and Lawrence H. Mamiya, *The Black Church in the African-American Experience* (Durham, NC: Duke University Press, 1990), 1. I follow Lincoln and Mamiya's lead in using "Black Church" as sociological and theological shorthand for the pluralism of black Christian churches in the United States. Whereas black congregations in predominantly white denominations as well as black individuals in predominantly white congregations usually are not included in the definition of "Black Church," the following denominations, which represent more than 80 percent of all black Christians in the United States, fall under its scope: African Methodist Episcopal (AME), African Methodist Episcopal Zion (AME Zion), Christian Methodist Episcopal (CME), National Baptist Convention, USA, Incorporated (NBC), National Baptist Convention of America, Unincorporated (NBCA), Progressive National Baptist Convention (PNBC), and Church of God in Christ (COGIC).

80. Angelique Walker-Smith, "A Global Vision of Unity, Mission, and Evangelism: Ecumenism," National Baptist Convention, 2007 Annual Session, 3–5.

81. See Ronald Edward Peters and Marsha Snulligan Haney, eds., *Africentric Approaches to Christian Ministry: Strengthening Urban Congregations in African American Communities* (Lanham, MD: University Press of America, 2007).

82. Nancy Tatom Ammerman, *Pillars of Faith: American Congregations and Their Partners* (Berkeley: University of California Press, 2005), 198.

83. See Evelyn Brooks Higginbotham, *Righteous Discontent: The Women's Movement in the Black Baptist Church, 1890–1920* (Cambridge, MA: Harvard University Press, 1993).

84. David Emmanuel Goatley, telephone interview by author, 9 June 2008. See also James Melvin Washington, *Frustrated Fellowship: The Black Baptist Quest for Social Power* (Macon, GA: Mercer University Press, 1986).

85. Goatley, telephone interview.

86. Robert Wuthnow, *The Restructuring of American Religion: Society and Faith Since World War II* (Princeton, NJ: Princeton University Press, 1988).

87. Ibid., 101.

88. Gautier and Perl, "Partnerships of Solidarity," 18.

89. When first incorporated, the organization's name was Haiti Parish Twinning Program, which later became Adopt-a-Parish Program. PTPA switched to its current name after it began facilitating partnerships outside of Haiti in the late 1990s.

90. McGlone, *Sharing Faith Across the Hemisphere*, 203.

91. "History," on Parish Twinning Program of the Americas, accessed 10 April 2013, http://www.parishprogram.org/history.

92. McGlone, *Sharing Faith Across the Hemisphere*, 213.

93. "Sister Relationships," on Parish Twinning Program of the Americas, accessed 10 April 2013, http://www.parishprogram.org/sister-relationships.

94. McGlone, *Sharing Faith Across the Hemisphere*, 214.

95. Richard Fenske, *En La Buena Lucha: In the Good Struggle: The Sister Parish Movement* (Shippensburg, PA: Ragged Edge Press, 1996), 9–11.

96. "Our Story," on Sister Parish, Incorporated, accessed 10 April 2013, http://sisterparish.org/our-work/our-story/; see also Fenske, *En La Buena Lucha*, 14.

97. "Definition of the Sister Church Program," on Reciprocal Ministries International, accessed 10 April 2013 http://www.rminet.org/aboutrmi/.

98. "Ministry Philosophy," on Food for the Hungry, accessed 10 April 2013, http://fh.org/about/vision.

99. Alisa Schmitz, telephone interview by author, 14 October 2008.

100. "More Information About Community 2 Community," on Food for the Hungry, accessed 14 October 2008, http://www.fh.org/c2c/find-out-more-information-about-c2c (page no longer on website).

101. "Vision Statement," on SHARE Foundation, accessed 9 December 2008, http://www.share-elsalvador.org/about/vision.htm (page no longer on website).

102. O'Connor, *Bridges of Faith*, 16.

103. "Church Twinning International . . . An Ecumenical Ministry," Church Twinning International, brochure.

104. "Silver Anniversary," Church Twinning International, brochure, 26 September 2006.

105. Sidney Holston, interview by author, 27 September 2007.

106. Jones, telephone interview.

107. Priest, Wilson, and Johnson, "U.S. Megachurches and New Patterns of Global Missions," 101.

108. See Wade Clark Roof, *Spiritual Marketplace: Baby Boomers and the Remaking of American Religion* (Princeton, NJ: Princeton University Press, 2001); Dean R. Hoge, Benton Johnson, and Donald A. Luidens, *Vanishing Boundaries: The Religion of Mainline Protestant Baby Boomers* (Louisville: Westminster John Knox Press, 1994).

109. See R. Stephen Warner, "Work in Progress Toward a New Paradigm for the Sociological Study of Religion in the United States," *American Journal of Sociology* 98, no. 5 (1993): 1044–1093. Addressing the plight of mission societies in particular, Wilbert R. Shenk notes that as early as the 1960s, mainline mission agencies began to decline,

burdened by the laws of bureaucracy and an inability to adjust to a changing environment. By the 1990s, evangelical agencies appeared to be facing the same forces. See Shenk, *Changing Frontiers in Mission* (Maryknoll, NY: Orbis Books, 1999), 179–180.

110. Ibid., 181.

111. Rates of religious membership, giving, and participation have decreased while rates of "switching" and disaffiliating have increased. See Barry A. Kosmin and Ariela Keysar, *Religion in a Free Market: Religious Americans Who, What, Why, Where* (Ithaca, NY: Paramount Market Publishing, 2006); Darren E. Sherkat, "Tracking the Restructuring of American Religion: Religious Affiliation and Patterns of Religious Mobility, 1973–1998," *Social Forces* 79 (2001):1459–1493; Wade Clark Roof and William McKinney, *American Mainline Religion* (New Brunswick, NJ: Rutgers University Press, 1987).

112. See Nancy Tatom Ammerman, *Congregation & Community* (New Brunswick, NJ: Rutgers University Press, 1997); Ammerman, *Pillars of Faith*; Mark Chaves, *Congregations in America* (Cambridge, MA: Harvard University Press, 2004).

*Chapter 3*

1. See Nancy Ammerman, "Culture and Identity in the Congregation," in *Studying Congregations: A New Handbook*, ed. Nancy Ammerman et al. (Nashville: Abingdon Press, 1998), 78–104.

2. "Mission Statement," Saint Clement Catholic Church, undated online document.

3. "Sister Parish Project," Saint Clement Catholic Church, undated online document.

4. "Kensington Woods Presbyterian Church Limuru Mission Work Camp 2005," DVD, narrated by Ruth Eaton, senior pastor.

5. "What Is Crossroads?" on Operation Crossroad Africa, accessed 12 April 2013, http://operationcrossroadsafrica.org/index2013.php?div[content]=1202; see also Nina Mjagkijj, "Operation Crossroads Africa," in *Organizing Black America: An Encyclopedia of African American Associations* (Oxford: Taylor and Francis Group, 2001), 542–543.

6. "Partners in God's Global Village: Limuru Narok Presbyterian Church, Limuru, Kenya," Kensington Woods Presbyterian Church, undated online document.

7. Ibid.

8. "Kensington Woods Presbyterian Church Limuru," DVD.

9. Ibid.

10. "Partners in God's Global Village."

11. According to Robert Hamilton, senior pastor of Third Presbyterian Church, the majority of the adults at Third were either elderly or in their twenties and thirties, reflecting the recent migration of young professionals to the urban core and the suburbanization of baby boomers a generation ago.

12. "Understanding of Partnership between Iglesia del Centro Presbiteriana-Reformada de la Habana and Third Presbyterian Church," Third Presbyterian Church, May 2005.

13. "Sister Church Relationship: Five-year Joint Resolution," Third Presbyterian Church and Iglesia del Centro Presbiteriana-Reformada, 14 December 1999.

14. Remy Duke, Trinity's delegate to the Anglican District of Virginia and former senior warden, paraphrased the message Trinity received from their Ugandan partners as the following: "All we are doing is bringing the love of Christ and support as you chart

the right path. You don't owe us anything. We are not asking anything from you. We are poor, and we are used to it."

15. "Living Faith Anglican Church 2005 Rwanda Mission Report" (October 2005), 17.

16. "Practicing Partnership: The Theory and Practice of Building Sister Church Relationships between the AMiA and the Anglican Church in Rwanda," Cross-Continental Partnership Council, Living Faith Anglican Church, draft, fall 2007.

17. "Practicing Partnership."

18. Ironically, the Rwandan Anglican Church's definition of orthodoxy proved not to be conservative enough for Christ the King's sensibilities on biblical authority. In 2007 the Rwandan Church created an umbrella organization for AMiA (Anglican Mission in America), called AMiAs (Anglican Mission in the Americas), which allowed for the ordination of women to the presbyterate, therein disgruntling many at Christ the King.

19. "Mission/Vision Statements," Thirteenth Street Baptist Church, undated online document.

20. "Building Networks, Broadening Visions: Enhancing African American Pastoral Ministry," on Lott Carey Foreign Mission Convention, accessed 10 January 2009, http://www.lottcarey.org/PEP.html (page no longer on website).

21. "Our Culture, Our History: Pastor Morris' Missionary Trip to South Africa," *Thirteenth Street Baptist Herald*, newsletter, summer 2008.

*Chapter 4*

1. "Practicing Partnership: The Theory and Practice of Building Sister Church Relationships between the AMiA and the Anglican Church in Rwanda," Cross-Continental Partnership Council, Living Faith Anglican Church, draft, fall 2007.

2. Ibid., 431.

3. Mary L. Gautier and Paul Perl, "Partnerships of Solidarity with the Church in Latin American and the Caribbean," Special Report of the Center for Applied Research in the Apostolate (Washington, DC: Georgetown University, Fall 2003), 4. Of the parishes in my study, Saint Clement had five thousand members, Our Lady of Sorrows had seven thousand members, and Saint Mariana had thirteen hundred families. Catholic parishes tend to be much larger than Protestant congregations. The National Congregations Study reported that 18 percent of Roman Catholic parishes had more than twenty-five hundred people associated with the parish, while less than 1 percent of other congregations were that large. Mark Chaves, *Congregations in America* (Cambridge, MA: Harvard University Press, 2004), 29–36.

4. Nancy Tatom Ammerman, *Pillars of Faith: American Congregations and Their Partners* (Berkeley: University of California Press, 2005), 202.

5. Gautier and Perl, "Partnerships with Solidarity," 4.

6. Mark Chaves and Shawna Anderson, "Continuity and Change in American Congregations: Introducing the Second Wave of the National Congregations Study," *Sociology of Religion* 69, no. 4 (2008): 432.

7. Social scientists define multiethnic congregations as those in which at least 20 percent of the congregation are members of ethnic groups other than the dominant ethnic group in the congregation. See Gerardo Marti, *A Mosaic of Believers: Diversity and Innovation in a Multiethnic Church* (Bloomington: Indiana University Press, 2005).

8. Gautier and Perl, "Partnerships with Solidarity," 4.

9. Indeed, both of the multiethnic parishes in my study were Catholic.

10. Ammerman, *Pillars of Faith*, 198.

11. R. Stephen Warner, *A Church of Our Own: Disestablishment and Diversity in American Religion* (New Brunswick, NJ: Rutgers University Press, 2005), 257.

12. See Peggy Levitt, *God Needs No Passport: Immigrants and the Changing American Religious Landscape* (New York: New Press, 2007).

13. Immigrant congregations often lie "off the grid" of traditional American religious organization and can be very difficult to study. Fortunately, a growing body of literature on immigrant religiosity is emerging to fill what was, until recently, a wide gap in coverage. In addition to Levitt, see Dean Hoge and Michael Foley, *Religion and the New Immigrants: How Faith Communities Form Our Newest Citizens* (New York: Oxford University Press, 2007); Lowell Livezey, ed., *Public Religion and Urban Transformation: Faith in the City* (New York: New York University Press, 2000); Cecilia Menjivar, "Religious Institutions and Transnationalism: A Case Study of Catholic and Evangelical Salvadoran Immigrants," *International Journal of Politics, Culture, and Society* 12, no. 4 (1999): 589–612; Fenggang Yang and Helen Rose Ebaugh, "Religion and Ethnicity Among New Immigrants: The Impact of Majority/Minority Status in Home and Host Countries," *Journal for the Scientific Study of Religion* 40, no. 3 (2001): 367–378.

14. See the 2010 US Census, available online at http://www.census.gov.

15. For a discussion of the various models of church polity, see Nancy Tatom Ammerman, *Congregations and Community* (New Brunswick, NJ: Rutgers University Press, 1997), 51–54; Nancy T. Ammerman, "Denominations: Who and What Are We Studying?" in *Reimagining Denominationalism: Interpretive Essays*, ed. Robert Bruce Mullin and Russell E. Richey (New York: Oxford University Press, 1994); Mark Chaves, "Denominations as Dual Structures: An Organizational Analysis," *Sociology of Religion* 54 (1993):147–169.

16. Robert Priest, Douglas Wilson, and Adelle Johnson, "U.S. Megachurches and New Patterns of Global Missions," *International Bulletin of Missionary Research* 34, no. 2 (April 2010): 97–104.

17. The emerging/emergent movement is an important example. While Christians who identify with this movement resist organizing into centralized institutions and some even resist organizing into congregations, their vast and powerful social networks have generated vibrant international partnerships and consultations.

18. Paul J. DiMaggio and Walter W. Powell, "The Iron Cage Revisited: Institutional Isomorphism and Collective Rationality in Organizational Fields," *American Sociological Review* 48 (April 1983): 147–160.

19. R. Stephen Warner, "Work in Progress Toward a New Paradigm for the Sociological Study of Religion in the United States," *American Journal of Sociology* 98, no. 5 (1993): 36.

20. Ibid.

21. The trend toward de facto congregationalism should not be overgeneralized, however. For instance, parishes belonging to hierarchical religious institutions such as the Roman Catholic Church continue to be governed differently from most Protestant congregations.

22. See Marti, *Mosaic of Believers*. Marti argues that successful multiethnic churches help members reconstruct identity around a shared purpose rather than an ethnic difference.

23. Ammerman, *Pillars of Faith*, 202.

24. Carl S. Dudley and Sally A. Johnson, *Energizing the Congregation: Images That Shape Your Church's Ministry* (Louisville: Westminster John Knox Press, 1993).

25. For five of the six (nonclergy) parishioners interviewed from Living Faith, the congregation's connection to Rwanda was a compelling factor in their decision to join the church.

26. See Mark Noll, *American Evangelical Christianity: An Introduction* (Hoboken, NJ: Wiley-Blackwell, 2001).

27. David A. Roozen, William McKinney, and Jackson W. Carroll, *Varieties of Religious Presence: Mission in Public Life* (Cleveland: Pilgrim Press, 1984).

28. See Martin E. Marty, *Righteous Empire: The Protestant Experience in America* (New York: Dial Press, 1970); Robert Wuthnow, "Old Fissures and New Fractures in American Religious Life," in *Religion and American Culture*, ed. David G. Hackett (New York: Routledge, 1995); James Davison Hunter, *Culture Wars: The Struggle to Define America* (New York: Basic Books, 1992).

29. Chaves, *Congregations in America*, 28.

30. See Nancey Murphy, *Beyond Liberalism and Fundamentalism: How Modern and Postmodern Philosophy Set the Theological Agenda* (Harrisburg, PA: Trinity Press International, 1996).

31. David Sikkink, "'I Just Say I'm a Christian': Symbolic Boundaries and Identity Formation Among Church-going Protestants," in *Re-forming the Center: American Protestantism, 1900-Present*, ed. Douglas Jacobsen and William Vance Trollinger (Grand Rapids, MI: W. B. Eerdmans Publishing Co., 1998), 55; see also George Barna, *Index of Leading Spiritual Indicators* (Dallas: Word Publishing Company, 1996), 9.

32. CARA's report mirrors these findings, suggesting that parish participation in twinning relationships is stronger when leadership is decentralized; Gautier and Perl, "Partnerships with Solidarity," 7. More broadly, some research has shown that decentralized administration is more self-regulating and resilient than centralized organization. See Ori Brafman and Rod Beckstrom, *The Starfish and the Spider: The Unstoppable Power of Leaderless Organizations* (London: Portfolio, 2006).

33. See Bernand M. Bass and Bruce J. Avolio, *Training Full Range Leadership* (Redwood, CA: Mind Garden, 1999).

34. Brafman and Beckstrom, *Starfish and the Spider*.

35. See Roger Daniels, *Coming to America: A History of Immigration and Ethnicity in American Life* (New York: Harper Collins, 2002).

36. Chaves and Anderson, "Continuity and Change," 424.

37. See Peggy Levitt, *The Transnational Villagers* (Berkeley: University of California Press, 2001).

38. Because the Washington, DC, metropolitan region is home to a large concentration of immigrants, highly educated professionals, and people employed in the field of international relations, the following portraits are at least to some degree peculiar to the specific cases in this study.

39. By contrast, recent immigrants with limited English skills, a population that was prevalent at Saint Mariana of Jesus, did not get involved in their parish's twinning relationship, despite recruiting attempts by the twinning committee. Saint Mariana of Jesus was a shared parish with masses conducted in various languages. Hence, it attracted many recent immigrants. At all the other parishes, most worshipers were well assimilated.

40. See the appendix for further information.

41. To compare these findings to more wide-reaching studies on the relationship between demographics and volunteering, see Jone L. Pearce, *Volunteers: The Organizational Behavior of Unpaid Workers* (New York: Routledge, 1993), 68–69. Pearce notes that several studies have found that volunteering peaks in individuals from age forty to sixty, while the median age of participants in my study was higher.

42. Gary T. Marx and Douglas McAdam, *Collective Behavior and Social Movements: Process and Structures* (Englewood Cliffs, NJ: Prentice Hall, 1994), 33.

43. Pearce, *Volunteers*, 61–85.

44. Marx and McAdam, *Collective Behavior and Social Movements*, 86.

45. William A. Gamson, "The Social Psychology of Collective Action," in *Frontiers in Social Movement Theory*, ed. Aldon Morris and Carol Mueller (New Haven, CT: Yale University Press, 1992), 56.

46. Pearce, *Volunteers*, 69.

47. Ibid., 66.

48. Mary M. McGlone, *Sharing Faith Across the Hemisphere* (Maryknoll, NY: Orbis Books, 1997), 221.

49. Ibid., 253.

50. Robert Putnam, *Bowling Alone: The Collapse and Revival of American Community* (New York: Simon and Schuster, 2000).

*Chapter 5*

1. Doug McAdam, John D. McCarthy, and Mayer N. Zald, introduction to *Comparative Perspectives on Social Movements: Political Opportunities, Mobilizing Structures, and Cultural Framings* (New York: Cambridge University Press, 1996), 2. See also Gary T. Marx and Douglas McAdam, *Collective Behavior and Social Movements: Process and Structures* (Englewood Cliffs, NJ: Prentice Hall, 1994).

2. Stuart Hall, "The Rediscovery of 'Ideology:' Return on the Repressed in Media Studies," in *Culture, Society and the Media*, ed. Michael Gurevitch et al. (London: Methuen, 1982), 56–90.

3. Robert D. Benford and David A. Snow, "Framing Processes and Social Movements: An Overview and Assessment," *Annual Review of Sociology* 26 (2000): 613.

4. Ibid., 614.

5. Mayer N. Zald, "Culture, Ideology, and Strategic Framing," in McAdam, McCarthy, and Zald, *Comparative Perspectives on Social Movements*, 262.

6. Benford and Snow, "Framing Processes and Social Movements," 615.

7. Ibid., 623.

8. McAdam, McCarthy, and Zald, *Comparative Perspectives on Social Movements*, 6.

9. Nancy Bernhardt-Hsu, "Partnering Relationships for Mission (An Inquiry & Overview of Diocesan and Parish Twinning)," United States Catholic Mission Association (Washington, DC: Spring 2003), 5.

10. United States Conference of Catholic Bishops, *Called to Global Solidarity*, ¶¶21, 26.

11. See Janet Carsten, ed., *Cultures of Relatedness: New Approaches to the Study of Kinship* (Cambridge: Cambridge University Press, 2000). Fictive kinship has a long history in Christianity and other missionizing faiths. Familial metaphors to describe the Christian community are replete in the New Testament—a fact that is embraced by proponents of sister church relationships.

12. "Sister Relationships," on Parish Twinning Program of the Americas, accessed 10 April 2013, http://www.parishprogram.org/sister-relationships.

13. "International Sister Church Relationships: Advice from International Ministries," American Baptist Church, USA, 5.

14. Lamont Koerner (associate coordinator of the companion relationship between Saint Paul Area Synod and the Iringa Diocese of Tanzania), telephone interview by author, 24 March 2008.

15. "Mission Statement," on Sister Parish, Incorporated, accessed 8 September 2008, http://www.sisterpari sh.org/missionstatement.html (page no longer on website).

16. Richard Fenske, *En La Buena Lucha: In the Good Struggle: The Sister Parish Movement* (Shippensburg, PA: Ragged Edge Press, 1996), 14.

17. Ibid., 17.

18. "General Guidelines for International Partnerships Between PC(USA) Congregations, Presbyteries, and Synods and International Church Governing Bodies and Institutions," Presbyterian Church, USA, Worldwide Ministries Division (Louisville: 2004), 1.

19. Doug Welch, telephone interview by author, 1 April 2008.

20. Patrick Friday, telephone interview by author, 1 May 2008.

21. Welch, telephone interview.

22. Charles Jones, telephone interview by author, 14 April 2008.

23. Friday, telephone interview.

24. Companion Synod Task Force File, no. 3, Evangelical Lutheran Church of America, quoted in Richard Lubawa, *Shoulder to Shoulder: Bega Kwa Bega: A Lutheran Partnership Between Minnesota and Tanzania* (Minneapolis: Lutheran University Press, 2007), 8.

25. "Mission Strategy for Latin America," Evangelical Lutheran Church of America, Division for Global Mission (1995).

26. David Cline, "Cross-Cultural Companionship: Initial Barriers and Impacts of a Companion Congregation Relationship," (D.Min. diss., Luther Seminary, St. Paul, MN: 2006), 10.

27. "Developing a Sister Church Relationship," American Baptist Church, USA, International Ministries (2008).

28. "Manual for Congregational Partnerships," The Alliance of Baptists/Fraternity of Baptist Churches of Cuba (Washington, DC: June 2005), 3.

29. Stan Hastey, telephone interview by author, 30 April 2008.

30. "Mission Statement," on Sister Cities International, accessed 24 April 2009, http://www.sister-cities.org/about/mission.cfm (page no longer on website).

31. "Sistering Partnerships with SHARE: Information and Recommended Steps for Discerning Groups," SHARE Foundation (May 2006), 2.

32. Mike Vallez, *The New Mission Book: Mission Possible* e-book only (Minneapolis: by the author, 2005), chapter 4, accessed 21 April 2008, www.globalfaithpartners.com/ebook.html (site discontinued).

33. See Paweł Załęski, "Ideal Types in Max Weber's Sociology of Religion: Some Theoretical Inspirations for a Study of the Religious Field," *Polish Sociological Review* 3, no. 171 (2010): 319–325.

34. See David A. Roozen, William McKinney, and Jackson W. Carroll, *Varieties of Religious Presence: Mission in Public Life* (Cleveland: Pilgrim Press, 1984).

35. R. Stephen Warner, *New Wine in Old Wineskins: Evangelicals and Liberals in a Small-Town Church* (Berkeley: University of California Press, 1988), 56. See also Talcott Parsons, *The Social System* (New York: Free Press, 1951).

36. "Practicing Partnership: The Theory and Practice of Building Sister Church Relationships between the AMiA and the Anglican Church in Rwanda," Cross-Continental Partnership Council, Living Faith Anglican Church, draft, fall 2007.

37. Mary L. Gautier and Paul Perl, "Partnerships of Solidarity with the Church in Latin American and the Caribbean," Special Report of the Center for Applied Research in the Apostolate (Washington, DC: Georgetown University, Fall 2003), 4.

38. Ronald Edward Peters, introduction to *Africentric Approaches to Christian Ministry: Strengthening Urban Congregations in African American Communities*, ed. Ronald E. Peters and Marsha Snulligan Haney (Lanham, MD: University Press of America, 2006), xvi.

39. Ronald Edward Peters, "Africentrism as a Challenge to Contemporary Christian Ministry" in Peters and Haney, *Africentric Approaches to Christian Ministry*, 37.

40. Dean Hoge and Michael Foley, *Religion and the New Immigrants: How Faith Communities Form Our Newest Citizens* (New York: Oxford University Press, 2007), 183; Fenggang Yang, *Chinese Christians in America: Conversion, Assimilation, and Adhesive Identities* (University Park: Penn State University Press, 1999), 33.

*Chapter 6*

1. Gary T. Marx and Douglas McAdam, *Collective Behavior and Social Movements: Process and Structures* (Englewood Cliffs, NJ: Prentice Hall, 1994), 112.

2. See *Gale Encyclopedia of Psychology*, 2nd ed. (Farmington Hills, MI: Gale Group, 2001), s.v. "Attitudes and Attitude Change." For this reason, says Cur Verbeek, short-term mission trips have a bad track record in effecting long-term change in participants.

3. The discrepancy between attitudes and behavior has been borne out by countless studies. See Marx and McAdam, *Collective Behavior and Social Movements*, 109.

4. David Kertzer, *Rituals, Politics and Power* (New Haven, CT: Yale University Press, 1988), 68.

5. Terence D. Linhart, "Planting Seeds: The Curricular Hope of Short-Term Mission Experiences in Youth Ministry," *Christian Education Journal* 3, no. 2 (2005): 257.

6. Robert Wuthnow, *Boundless Faith: The Global Outreach of American Churches* (Berkeley: University of California Press, 2009), 181.

7. Ibid., 182.

8. Ibid., 183. Wuthnow's findings should be compared to the conclusions of other scholars studying the impact of American short-term mission efforts on participants. David Livermore observes that a growing number of studies are questioning the efficacy of short-term mission trips in bringing about long-term personal transformation ("CQ and Short-Term Missions: The Phenomenon of the 15-Year-Old Missionary," *Handbook of Cultural Intelligence: Theory, Measurement, and Applications*, ed. Soon Ang and Linn Van Dyne [New York: M.E. Sharpe, 2008], 271–288. For instance, in their survey of the research on short-term mission efforts, Robert Priest, Terry Dischinger, Steve Rasmussen, and C. M. Brown cite that the explosive growth in the number of short-term mission trips has not been accompanied by similarly explosive growth in the number of career

missionaries, that it is not clear whether participation in service trips causes participants to give more money to alleviate poverty once life returns to normal, that participants' ethnocentrism does not decrease over the long term, and that participating in service trips does not seem to reduce participants' tendencies toward materialism. See Robert J. Priest et al., "Researching the Short-Term Mission Movement," *Missiology: An International Review* 34, no. 4 (October 2006): 431–450. See also Terence D. Linhart, "The Curricular Nature of Youth Group Short-Term Cross-Cultural Service Projects" (PhD diss., Purdue University, Purdue, IN: 2004).

9. Samuel Broomfield Reeves, Jr., *Congregation-to-Congregation Relationship: A Case Study of a Partnership Between A Liberian Church and a North American Church* (Lanham, MD: University Press of America, 2004), 76.

10. Ibid., xii.

11. David Cline, "Cross-cultural Companionship: Initial Barriers and Impacts of a Companion Congregation Relationship," (DMin diss., Luther Seminary, St. Paul, MN: 2006), 74–77.

12. David Keyes, *Most Like an Arch: Building Global Church Partnerships* (Chico, CA: Center for Free Religion, 1999), 132.

13. Tara Hefferan, *Twinning and Faith Development: Catholic Parish Partnering in the U.S. and Haiti* (Bloomfield, CT: Kumarian Press, 2007), 111–120.

14. C. M. Brown, "Friendship Is Forever: Congregation-to-Congregation Relationships," in *Effective Engagement in Short-Term Missions: Doing It Right!*, ed. Robert Priest (Pasadena, CA: William Carey Library, 2008), 230.

15. Cited in Mary M. McGlone, *Sharing Faith Across the Hemisphere* (Maryknoll, NY: Orbis Books, 1997), 254.

16. For example, in *A Mosaic of Believers*, Gerardo Marti argues that a shared sense of purpose, one that transcends ethnic identity, is the key feature of thriving multiethnic churches.

17. Cynthia Woolever and Deborah Bruce, *Beyond the Ordinary: 10 Strengths of U.S. Congregations* (Louisville: Westminster John Knox Press, 2004).

18. James Hopewell, *Congregation: Stories and Structures* (Philadelphia: Fortress Press, 1987), 193.

19. See Robert Putnam, *Bowling Alone: The Collapse and Revival of American Community* (New York: Simon and Schuster, 2000), 367–401.

20. "What Makes Us Special: The Magic Balance," US Congregational Life Survey (2001), on US Congregations, accessed 11 June, 2009, http://www.uscongregations.org/10strengths-whatmakesusspecial.htm.

21. Émile Durkheim, *Elementary Forms of Religious Life* (New York: Free Press, 1995).

22. Cline, "Cross-cultural Companionship," 91.

23. Brown, "Friendship Is Forever," 212–215, 221.

24. Livermore, "CQ and Short-Term Missions," 274–275.

25. Kurt Alan Ver Beek, "The Impact of Short-Term Missions: A Case Study of House Construction in Honduras After Hurricane Mitch," *Missiology: An International Review* 34, no. 4 (2006): 477–496.

26. Joaquín Alegre Villón, "Short-Term Missions: Experiences and Perspectives from Calloa, Peru," *Journal of Latin American Theology* 2, no. 2 (2007): 133–135.

27. Martín Hartwig Eitzen, "Short-Term Missions: A Latin American Perspective," *Journal of Latin American Theology* 2, no. 2 (2007): 45.

28. Rodrigo Maslucán, "Short-Term Missions: Analysis and Proposals," *Journal of Latin American Theology* 2, no. 2 (2007): 143.

29. Ibid., 145.

30. Robert D. Putnam, Lewis M. Feldstein, and Don Cohen, *Better Together: Restoring the American Community* (New York: Simon and Schuster, 2003), 3.

31. Brown, "Friendship Is Forever," 231.

32. Reeves, *Congregation-to-Congregation Relationship*, xii.

33. Cline, "Cross-cultural Companionship," 98–99.

34. Hefferan, *Twinning and Faith Development*, 205–206.

35. Robert Priest, "Introduction: Short-Term Missions and the Latin American Church," *Journal of Latin American Theology* 2, no. 2 (2007): 13.

36. Robert Guerrero, "Short term Missions within Relational and Empowering Partnerships," Trinity Evangelical Divinity School Missiology Conference (Deerfield, IL: April 2008).

37. Harville Hendrix, *Getting the Love You Want: A Guide for Couples* (New York: Henry Holt and Company, 2001).

*Chapter 7*

1. Penny Edgell Becker, *Congregations in Conflict: Cultural Models of Local Religious Life* (Cambridge University Press, 1999). Amid all of the media attention on political conflicts within American congregations, Mark Chaves and Shawna Anderson note that, according to the results of the 2006–2007 National Congregations Study, only 2 percent of American congregations reported a conflict over the issue of homosexuality in the last two years ("Continuity and Change in American Congregations: Introducing the Second Wave of the National Congregations Study," *Sociology of Religion* 69, no. 4 (2008): 420).

2. R. Stephen Warner, "The Place of the Congregation in the Contemporary American Religious Configuration," in *A Church of Our Own: Disestablishment and Diversity in American Religion* (New Brunswick, NJ: Rutgers University Press, 2005), 155. See also Carl S. Dudley, "From Typical Church to Social Ministry: A Study of the Elements Which Mobilize Congregations," *Review of Religious Research* 32 (March 1991): 196–212.

3. Gary T. Marx and Douglas McAdam, *Collective Behavior and Social Movements: Process and Structures* (Englewood Cliffs, NJ: Prentice Hall, 1994), 34.

4. Jonathan Rowe, "Dancing with Elephants: Accountability in Cross-Cultural Christian Partnerships," *Missiology* 37, no. 2 (April 2009): 149.

5. Ibid.

6. *Merriam-Webster Online Dictionary*, s.v. "mission," accessed 19, April 2013, http://www.merriam-webster.com/dictionary/mission.

7. I owe this insight to Rebecca Y. Kim, associate professor of sociology at Pepperdine University.

8. Samuel Escobar, *The New Global Mission: The Gospel from Everywhere to Everyone* (Downers Grover, IL: InterVarsity Press, 2003), 165.

9. See Jonathan Bonk, *Missions and Money: Affluence as a Missionary Problem*, rev. and exp. ed. (New York: Orbis Books, 2007).

10. Jonathan Bonk, *"Missions and Money . . .* Revisited," McLure Lectures, Pittsburgh Theological Seminary, 27 September 2010, accessed 10 April 2012, http://www.pts.edu/Jonathan_Bonk_Addresses_Christian_Faith_During_McClure_Lectures.

11. See Frantz Fanon, *The Wretched of the Earth*, trans. Constance Farrington (New York: Grove Press, 1963); Fanon, *Black Skin, White Masks*, trans. Charles Lam Markmann (New York: Grove Press, 1968).

12. Tara Hefferan, *Twinning and Faith Development: Catholic Parish Partnering in the U.S. and Haiti* (Bloomfield, CT: Kumarian Press, 2007), 4.

13. Ibid., 43.

14. Ibid., 156.

15. Ibid., 119.

16. Hefferan, "Encountering Development 'Alternatives': Grassroots Church Partnering in the U.S. and Haiti," in *Bridging the Gaps: Faith-Based Organizations, Neoliberalism, and Development*, ed. Tara Hefferan, Julie Adkins, and Laurie Occhipinti (Lanham, MD: Lexington Books, 2009), 69–82.

17. Dana Robert, "Cross-Cultural Friendship in the Creation of Twentieth-Century World Christianity," *International Bulletin of Missionary Research* 35, no. 2 (April 2011): 106.

*Chapter 8*

1. See James H. Mittelman, *The Globalization Syndrome: Transformation and Resistance* (Princeton: Princeton University Press, 2000).

2. Jehu Hanciles, *Beyond Christendom: Globalization, African Migration, and the Transformation of the West* (Maryknoll, NY: Orbis Books, 2008), 377.

3. Ibid., 296.

4. Mark Juergensmeyer, introduction to *Religion in Global Civil Society*. (Oxford: Oxford University Press, 2005).

5. See Roger Daniels, *Coming to America: A History of Immigration and Ethnicity in American Life* (New York: Harper Collins, 2002). While a number of projects have been undertaken to study the interplay between religion and the new immigration, these studies tend to focus on how immigrants maintain religious ties to their homelands or how religion affects immigrants' integration into American life. See Linda Basch, Nina Glick-Schiller, and Christina Szanton Blanc, *Nations Unbound: Transnational Projects, Postcolonial Predicaments, and Deterritorialized Nation-States* (Langhorne, PA: Gordon and Breach, 1994); Dean Hoge and Michael Foley, *Religion and the New Immigrants: How Faith Communities Form Our Newest Citizens* (New York: Oxford University Press, 2007); Peggy Levitt, *God Needs No Passport: Immigrants and the Changing American Religious Landscape* (New York: New Press, 2007); R. Stephen Warner, ed., *Gatherings in Diaspora: Religious Communities and the New Immigration* (Philadelphia: Temple University Press, 1998); Fenggang Yang and Helen Rose Ebaugh, "Transformations in New Immigrant Religions and Their Global Implications," *American Sociological Review* 66, no. 2 (April 2001): 269–288. Unfortunately, the religious connections immigrants and other transnational figures forge between their old homes and their new ones have not been sufficiently addressed by scholars.

6. Mark Chaves, *Congregations in America* (Cambridge, MA: Harvard University Press, 2004), 245.

7. Hanciles, *Beyond Christendom*, 4.

8. Mark Chaves and Shawna Anderson, "Continuity and Change in American Congregations: Introducing the Second Wave of the National Congregations Study," *Sociology of Religion* 69, no. 4 (2008): 422.

9. Nancy L. Eiesland and R. Stephen Warner, "Ecology: Seeing the Congregation in Context," in *Studying Congregations: A New Handbook*, ed. Nancy Ammerman et al. (Nashville: Abingdon Press, 1998), 41.

10. See Robert Wuthnow, *After Heaven: Spirituality in America Since the 1950s* (Berkeley: University of California Press, 1996); Dean R. Hoge, Benton Johnson, and Donald A. Luidens, *Vanishing Boundaries: The Religion of Mainline Protestant Baby Boomers* (Louisville: Westminster John Knox Press, 1994); Barry A. Kosmin and Ariela Keysar, *Religion in a Free Market: Religious Americans Who, What, Why, Where* (Ithaca, NY: Paramount Market Publishing, 2006); Wade Clark Roof and William McKinney, *American Mainline Religion* (New Brunswick, NJ: Rutgers University Press, 1987); R. Stephen Warner, "Work in Progress Toward a New Paradigm for the Sociological Study of Religion in the United States," *American Journal of Sociology* 98, no. 5 (1993). An important caveat to the story of denominational decline, voiced by Nancy Ammerman is that the "elaborate breakdown and reconstitution" of denominationalism has occurred principally among white Protestant denominations rather than Catholics, black Protestants, or other groups (*Pillars of Faith: American Congregations and Their Partners* (Berkeley: University of California Press, 2005), 252).

11. William Dinges, "Postmodernism and Religious Institutions," *The Way: A Review of Christian Spirituality* 36, no. 3 (July 1996): 215–224.

12. Ibid., 181.

13. Wuthnow, *After Heaven*, 170.

14. Ibid., 168.

15. Ibid., 17.

16. Ibid., 192.

17. Dorothy C. Bass, ed., *Practicing Our Faith: A Way of Life for a Searching People*, 2d ed. (San Francisco: Jossey-Bass, 2007), xxv.

18. Alisa Schmitz, telephone interview by author, 14 October 2008.

19. Dan Shoemaker, telephone interview by author, 16 September 2008.

20. Patrick Friday, telephone interview by author, 1 May 2008.

21. Congregations can be defined as "the relatively small-scale, local collectivities and organizations in and through which people engage in religious activities." Mark Chaves et al., "The National Congregations Study: Background, Methods, and Selected Results," *Journal for the Scientific Study of Religion* 38 (December 1999): 458. Chaves reports that there are more than three hundred thousand religious congregations in the United States, and that more than 60 percent of American adults attend services at a religious congregation at least once a year while one quarter attend weekly. See Chaves, *Congregations in America*, 3. The 2006 Baylor Religion Survey found that almost half of Americans attend church once a month. Christopher Bader et al., "American Piety in the Twenty-first Century: New Insights to the Depth and Complexity of Religion in the US; Selected Findings from the Baylor Religion Survey, September 2006" (Waco: Baylor Institute for Studies of Religion, 2006), 4–10.

22. See Wuthnow, *After Heaven*, 30. See also R. Stephen Warner, *A Church of Our Own: Disestablishment and Diversity in American Religion* (New Brunswick, NJ: Rutgers University Press, 2005), 145.

23. While church attendance and affiliation have declined in recent decades, this trend is often overstated. Moreover, new patterns of collective religious activity at the local level have emerged outside of traditional structures. See Diana Butler Bass, *Christianity After Religion: The End of Church and the Birth of a New Spiritual Awakening* (New York: HarperOne, 2012).

24. "American Piety," 7.

25. Ammerman, *Pillars of Faith*, 177–179.

26. Ibid., 158–205.

27. Mary L. Gautier and Paul Perl, "Partnerships of Solidarity with the Church in Latin American and the Caribbean," Special Report of the Center for Applied Research in the Apostolate (Washington, DC: Georgetown University, Fall 2003), 7.

28. Ammerman, *Pillars of Faith*, 204.

29. Nancy Tatom Ammerman and Arthur Emery Farnsley, *Congregation and Community* (New Brunswick, NJ: Rutgers University Press, 1997), 130. Wade Clark Roof, revising H. Richard Niebuhr's thesis in *The Social Sources of Denominationalism*, speaks of contemporary congregations being organized around "lifestyle enclaves." See Roof, *Spiritual Marketplace: Baby Boomers and the Remaking of American Religion* (Princeton, NJ: Princeton University Press, 2001).

30. Eiesland and Warner, "Ecology," 41.

31. Wuthnow, *After Heaven*, 168–170.

32. Diana Butler Bass, *The Practicing Congregation: Imagining a New Old Church* (Herndon, VA: The Alban Institute, 2004), 4.

33. See E. Brooks Holifield, "Toward a History of American Congregations," in *American Congregations: New Perspectives in the Study of Congregations*, ed. James P. Wind and James W. Lewis (Chicago: University of Chicago Press, 1994), 23–53.

34. Bass, *Practicing Congregation*, 14, 152.

35. For a comprehensive appraisal of the short-term mission model, see Kurt Ver Beek, "International Service Learning: A Call to Caution," in *Commitment and Connection: Service-Learning and Christian Higher Education*, ed. Gail Gunst Heffner and Claudia Beversluis (Lantham, MD: University of America, 2002), 55–69.

36. See Roger Peterson, Gordon Aeschliman, and R. Wayne Sneed, *Maximum Impact Short-term Mission: The God-Commanded, Repetitive Deployment of Swift, Temporary, Non-Professional Missionaries* (Minneapolis: STEM Press, 2003).

37. For instance, more than seventy evangelical organizations have adopted the US Standards of Excellence in Short-Term Mission. See "Overview: The Seven U.S. Standards of Excellence in Short-Term Mission," on US Standards of Excellence in Short-term Mission, accessed 20 May 2013, http://www.soe.org/explore/the-7-standards/. For discussion on best practices in STM, see Don Richter, *Mission Trips that Matter: Embodied Faith for the Sake of the World* (Nashville: Upper Room Books, 2008) and Robert Priest, ed., *Effective Engagement in Short-Term Missions: Doing It Right!* (William Carey Library, 2008).

38. David Livermore, "CQ and Short-Term Missions: The Phenomenon of the 15-Year-Old Missionary," in *Handbook of Cultural Intelligence: Theory, Measurement, and Applications*, ed. Soon Ang and Linn Van Dyne (New York: M.E. Sharpe, 2008), 273. For an analysis of common attitudes among North American participants that derail short-term mission efforts, see also Glenn Schwartz, "How Short-Term Missions Can Go Wrong," *International Journal of Frontier Missions* 20, no. 4 (Winter 2003): 27–34.

39. Kurt Alan Ver Beek, "Lessons from the Sapling: Review of Quantitative Research on Short-Term Missions," in Priest, *Effective Engagement in Short-Term Missions*, 469–496.

40. Ibid., 491.

41. Ibid., 494–495.

42. See Robert Wuthnow, "Religious Involvement and Status-Bridging Social Capital," *Journal for the Social Scientific Study of Religion* 41, no. 4 (2002): 669–684; Michael Woolcock and Deepa Narayan, "Social Capital: Implications for Development Theory, Research, and Policy," *World Bank Research Observer* 15, no. 2 (2000): 225–249.

43. Robert Priest, "Peruvian Churches Acquire 'Linking Social Capital' Through STM Partnerships," *Journal of Latin American Theology* 2, no. 2 (2007): 175–189.

44. Kersten Bayt Priest, "Women as Resource Brokers: STM Trips, Social and Organizational Ties, and Mutual Resource Benefits," in Priest, *Effective Engagement in Short-Term Missions*, 274–275.

*Conclusion*

The conclusion's title references two seminal works exploring cross-cultural encounters. In *American Confluence: The Missouri Frontier from Borderland to Border State* (Bloomington: Indiana University Press, 2009), historian Stephen Aron introduced the concept of "confluence," generally reserved for the meeting of two bodies of water, as a metaphor to describe the coming together of two or more streams of people. In *The Clash of Civilizations and the Remaking of World Order*, political scientist Samuel Huntington articulated the theory that people's cultural and religious identities serve as the primary source of conflict in the post–Cold War world.

1. Jehu Hanciles, *Beyond Christendom: Globalization, African Migration, and the Transformation of the West* (Maryknoll, NY: Orbis Books, 2008), 48.

2. Huntington, *The Clash of Civilizations and the Remaking of the World Order* (New York: Simon and Schuster, 1996), 78.

3. Ibid., 36.

4. Ibid., 68–78; 96–97.

5. Hanciles, *Beyond Christendom*, 2.

6. Ibid., 47.

7. Robert Wuthnow, *Boundless Faith: The Global Outreach of American Churches* (Berkeley: University of California Press, 2009), 51.

8. Ibid., 53.

9. Ibid., 38.

10. Ibid., 58.

11. Ibid., 61.

12. Ibid.

13. See Martin Buber, *I and Thou*, trans. Ronald Gregor Smith (New York: Scribner's, 1958).

14. See Richard Lubawa, *Shoulder to Shoulder: Bega Kwa Bega: A Lutheran Partnership Between Minnesota and Tanzania* (Minneapolis: Lutheran University Press, 2007).

15. Stephen Aron, *American Confluence: The Missouri Frontier from Borderland to Border State* (Bloomington: Indiana University Press, 2009), xviii.

# BIBLIOGRAPHY

Adelman, Clem, David Jenkins, and Stephen Kemmis. "Rethinking Case Study: Notes from the Second Cambridge Conference." In *Case Study: An Overview. Case Study Methods 1.* Victoria, AU: Deakin University Press, 1983.

Ahlberg, Dean C. "Our Identity: The Story That Gathers Us In, Sends Us Out." DMin diss., Hartford Theological Seminary, 2005.

Alberoni, Francesco. *Movement and Institution.* New York: Columbia University Press, 1984.

Ammerman, Nancy Tatom. *Bible Believers: Fundamentalists in the Modern World.* New Brunswick, NJ: Rutgers University Press, 1987.

———. *Pillars of Faith: American Congregations and Their Partners.* Berkeley: University of California Press, 2005.

Ammerman, Nancy, Jackson Carroll, Carl Dudley, and William McKinney, eds. *Studying Congregations: A New Handbook.* Nashville: Abingdon Press, 1998.

Ammerman, Nancy Tatom, and Arthur Emery Farnsley. *Congregation and Community.* New Brunswick, NJ: Rutgers University Press, 1997.

Anderson, Allan. "The Gospel and Culture in Pentecostal Mission in the Third World." *Missionalia* 27, no. 2 (February, 1999): 220–230.

Aron, Stephen. *American Confluence: The Missouri Frontier from Borderland to Border State.* Bloomington: Indiana University Press, 2009.

Asad, Talal, ed. *Anthropology and the Colonial Encounter.* Reading, UK: Ithaca Press, 1973.

A. T. Kearney/Foreign Policy Magazine. "Globalization Index (2006)." Accessed 15 August 2008. http://atkearney.com/.

Babbie, Earl R. *The Practice of Social Research,* 10th ed. Belmont, CA: Wadsworth Publishing, 2003.

Bader, Christopher, Kevin Dougherty, Paul Froese, Byron Johnson, F. Carson Mencken, Jerry Z. Park, and Rodney Stark. *American Piety in the Twenty-first Century: New Insights to the Depth and Complexity of Religion in the US: Selected Findings from The Baylor Religion Survey.* Waco, Texas: Baylor Institute for Studies of Religion, September 2006.

Ballantyne, Tony, and Antoinette Burton, eds. *Bodies in Contact: Rethinking Colonial Encounters in World History*. Durham, NC: Duke University Press, 2005.

Barber, Benjamin R. *Jihad vs. McWorld: How the Planet Is Both Falling Apart and Coming Together and What This Means for Democracy*. New York: Crown, 1995.

Barna, George. *Index of Leading Spiritual Indicators*. Dallas: Word Publishing Company, 1996.

Barrett, David B., ed. *World Christian Encyclopedia*, 2nd Ed., Vol. 1. Oxford: Oxford University Press, 2001.

Barrett, David B., Todd M. Johnson, and Peter F. Crossing. "Missionometrics 2007: Creating Your Own Analysis of Global Data." *International Bulletin of Missionary Research* 31, no. 1 (January 2007): 25–32.

Basch, Linda, Nina Glick-Schiller, and Christina Szanton Blanc. *Nations Unbound: Transnational Projects, Postcolonial Predicaments, and Deterritorialized Nation-States*. Langhorne, PA: Gordon and Breach, 1994.

Bass, Bernard M., and Bruce J. Avolio. *Training Full Range Leadership*. Redwood, CA: Mind Garden, 1999.

Bass, Diana Butler. *Christianity After Religion: The End of Church and the Birth of a New Spiritual Awakening*. New York: HarperOne, 2012.

———. *Christianity for the Rest of Us: How the Neighborhood Church is Revitalizing the Faith*. San Francisco: Harper San Francisco, 2006.

———. *The Practicing Congregation: Imagining a New Old Church*. Herndon, VA: The Alban Institute, 2004.

Bass, Dorothy C., ed. *Practicing Our Faith: A Way of Life for a Searching People*, 2d ed. San Francisco: Jossey-Bass, 2007.

Becker, Penny Edgell. *Congregations in Conflict: Cultural Models of Local Religious Life*. Cambridge, UK: Cambridge University Press, 1999.

Benford, Robert D., and David A. Snow. "Framing Processes and Social Movements: An Overview and Assessment." *Annual Review of Sociology* 26 (2000): 611–639.

Berger, Peter L. "Four Faces of Global Culture." *National Interest* 49 (Fall 1997): 23–29.

Bernhardt-Hsu, Nancy. "Partnering Relationships for Mission (An Inquiry & Overview of Diocesan and Parish Twinning)." United States Catholic Mission Association. Washington, DC: Spring 2003.

Bevans, Stephen B., and Roger P. Schroeder. *Constants in Context: A Theology of Mission for Today*. Maryknoll, NY: Orbis Books, 2004.

Bhabha, Homi. *The Location of Culture*. New York: Routledge, 1994.

Bhambra, Gurminder K. "Historical Sociology, Modernity, and Postcolonial Critique," *The American Historical Review* 111, no. 3 (June 2011): 653–662.

Bonk, Jonathan. *Missions and Money: Affluence as a Missionary Problem*, rev. and exp. ed. New York: Orbis Books, 2007.

———. *"Missions and Money . . . Revisited."* McLure Lectures, Pittsburgh Theological Seminary, September 27, 2010. Accessed 10 April 2012. http://www.pts.edu/Jonathan_Bonk_Addresses_Christian_Faith_During_McClure_Lectures.

Bosch, David. *Transforming Mission: Paradigm Shifts in Theology of Mission*. New York: Orbis Books, 1991.

Brafman, Ori, and Rod Beckstrom. *The Starfish and the Spider: The Unstoppable Power of Leaderless Organizations*. London: Portfolio, 2006.

Brasher, Brenda. *Godly Women: Fundamentalism and Female Power*. New Brunswick, NJ: Rutgers University Press, 1998.

Brown, C. M. "Friendship Is Forever: Congregation-to-Congregation Relationships." In *Effective Engagement in Short-Term Missions: Doing it Right!*, ed. Robert Priest, 203–231. Pasadena, CA: William Carey Library, 2008.

Camp, Bruce K. "Major Paradigm Shifts in World Evangelization." *International Journal of Frontier Missions* 11, no. 3 (1994): 133–138.

Carpenter, Joel, and Wilbert Shenk, eds. *Earthen Vessels: American Evangelicals and Foreign Missions, 1880–1980*. Grand Rapids, MI: W. B. Eerdmans Publishing Co., 1990.

Carsten, Janet, ed. *Cultures of Relatedness: New Approaches to the Study of Kinship*. Cambridge: Cambridge University Press, 2000.

Chan, Simon. "Mother Church: Toward a Pentecostal Ecclesiology." *Pneuma* 22, no. 2 (Fall 2000): 177–208.

Chaturvedi, Vinayak, ed. *Mapping Subaltern Studies and the Postcolonial*. London: Verso, 2000.

Chaves, Mark. *Congregations in America*. Cambridge, MA: Harvard University Press, 2004.

———. "Denominations as Dual Structures: An Organizational Analysis." *Sociology of Religion* 54 (1993): 147–169.

———. "Religious Congregations and Welfare Reform: Who Will Take Advantage of 'Charitable Choice'?" *American Sociological Review* 64 (December 1999): 836–846.

Chaves, Mark, and Shawna Anderson. "Continuity and Change in American Congregations: Introducing the Second Wave of the National Congregations Study." *Sociology of Religion* 69, no. 4 (2008): 415–440.

Chaves, Mark, Mary Ellen Konieczny, Kraig Beyerlein, and Emily Barnan. "The National Congregations Study: Background, Methods, and Selected Results." *Journal for the Scientific Study of Religion* 38 (December 1999): 458–476.

Cline, David. "Cross-cultural Companionship: Initial Barriers and Impacts of a Companion Congregation Relationship." DMin diss., Luther Seminary, 2006.

Daniels, Roger. *Coming to America: A History of Immigration and Ethnicity in American Life*. New York: Harper Collins, 2002.

DiMaggio, Paul J., and Walter W. Powell. "The Iron Cage Revisited: Institutional Isomorphism and Collective Rationality in Organizational Fields." *American Sociological Review* 48 (April 1983): 147–160.

Dinges, William. "Postmodernism and Religious Institutions." *The Way: A Review of Christian Spirituality* 36, no. 3 (July 1996): 215–224.

Douglas, J. D., ed. *Let the Earth Hear His Voice. International Congress on World Evangelization in Lausanne*. Minneapolis: World Wide Publications, 1975.

Dries, Angelyn. *The Missionary Movement in American Catholic History*. Maryknoll, NY: Orbis Books, 1998.

Dudley, Carl S. "From Typical Church to Social Ministry: A Study of the Elements Which Mobilize Congregations." *Review of Religious Research* 32 (March 1991): 196–212.

Dudley, Carl S., and Sally A. Johnson. *Energizing the Congregation: Images That Shape Your Church's Ministry*. Louisville: Westminster John Knox Press, 1993.

Durkheim, Émile. *Elementary Forms of Religious Life*. Translated by Karen Fields. New York: Free Press, 1995.

Eitzen, Martín Hartwig. "Short-Term Missions: A Latin American Perspective." *Journal of Latin American Theology* 2, no. 2 (2007): 33–47.

Escobar, Samuel. *Changing Tides: Latin America and World Mission Today*. Maryknoll, NY: Orbis, 2002.

———. *The New Global Mission: The Gospel from Everywhere to Everyone*. Downers Grover, IL: InterVarsity Press, 2003.

"Evangelization, Proselytism, and Common Witness: The Report from the Fourth Phase of the International Dialogue (1990–1997) between the Roman Catholic Church and Some Classical Pentecostal Churches and Leaders." *Pneuma* 21, no. 1(Spring 1999): 11–51.

Fanon, Frantz. *Black Skin, White Masks*. Translated by Charles Lam Markmann. New York: Grove Press, 1968.

———. *The Wretched of the Earth*. Translated by Constance Farrington. New York: Grove Press, 1963.

Fenske, Richard. *En La Buena Lucha: In the Good Struggle: The Sister Parish Movement*. New York: Ragged Edge Press, 1996.

Fetterman, David. *Ethnography: Step by Step*, 2nd Ed. Thousand Oaks, CA: Sage Press, 1998.

Flannery, Austin, ed. *Vatican Council II: Constitutions, Decrees, Declarations*. Newtown, AU: E.J. Dwyer, 1992.

Fretz, Glenn. "Toward Interdependent Ministry Partnerships: Fueling Ministry Without Fostering Dependency." *Evangelical Missions Quarterly* 38, no. 2 (2002): 212–218.

Fukuyama, Francis. *The End of History and the Last Man*. New York: Free Press, 1992.

Funkschmidt, Kai Michael. "New Models of Mission Relationship and Partnership." *International Review of Mission* 91, no. 363 (2002): 558–576.

Gamson, William A. "The Social Psychology of Collective Action." In *Frontiers in Social Movement Theory*, edited by Aldon Morris and Carol Mueller, 53–76. New Haven, CT: Yale University Press, 1992.

Gautier, Mary L. and Paul Perl. "Partnerships of Solidarity with the Church in Latin American and the Caribbean." Special Report of the Center for Applied Research in the Apostolate. Washington, DC: Georgetown University, Fall 2003.

Geertz, Clifford. *The Interpretation of Cultures*. New York: Basic Books, 1973.

Greene, Sandra E. *Sacred Sites and the Colonial Encounter: A History of Meaning and Memory in Ghana*. Bloomington: Indiana University Press, 2002.

Guder, Darrell, ed. *Missional Church: A Vision for the Sending of the Church in North America*. Grand Rapids, MI: W. B. Eerdmans Publishing Co., 1998.

Guerrero, Robert. "Short term Missions Within Relational and Empowering Partnerships." Trinity Evangelical Divinity School Missiology Conference. Deerfield, IL: April 2008.

Guidry, John A., Michael D. Kennedy, and Mayer N. Zald, eds. *Globalizations and Social Movements: Culture, Power, and the Transnational Public Sphere*. Ann Arbor: University of Michigan Press, 2000.

Hanciles, Jehu. *Beyond Christendom: Globalization, African Migration, and the Transformation of the West*. Maryknoll, NY: Orbis Books, 2008.

Haney, Marsha Smulligan. *Evangelism Among African American Presbyterians: Making Plain the Sacred Journey*. Lanham, MD: University Press of America, 2007.

Hall, Stuart. "The Rediscovery of 'Ideology:' Return on the Repressed in Media Studies." In *Culture, Society and the Media*, edited by Michael Gurevitch, Tony Bunnett, James Curran, and Janet Wollacott, 56–90. London: Methuen, 1982.

Hefferan, Tara. "Encountering Development 'Alternatives': Grassroots Church Partnering in the U.S. and Haiti." In *Bridging the Gaps: Faith-Based Organizations, Neoliberalism, and Development*, edited by Tara Hefferan, Julie Adkins, and Laurie Occhipinti, 69–82. Lanham, MD: Lexington Books, 2009.

———. *Twinning Faith and Development: Catholic Parish Partnering in the U.S. and Haiti.* Bloomfield, CT: Kumarian Press, 2007.

Hesselgrave, David. *Communicating Christ Cross-Culturally: An Introduction to Missionary Communication.* Grand Rapids, MI: Zondervan Pub. Co., 1978.

Higginbotham, Evelyn Brooks. *Righteous Discontent: The Women's Movement in the Black Baptist Church, 1890–1920.* Cambridge, MA: Harvard University Press, 1993.

Higgins, Andrew. "Divided Flock: Episcopal Church Dissidents Seek Authority Overseas." *Wall Street Journal*, 20 September 2007, sec. A1.

Hoge, Dean, and Michael Foley. *Religion and the New Immigrants: How Faith Communities Form Our Newest Citizens.* New York: Oxford University Press, 2007.

Hoge, Dean R., Benton Johnson, and Donald A. Luidens. *Vanishing Boundaries: The Religion of Mainline Protestant Baby Boomers.* Louisville: Westminster John Knox Press, 1994.

Holifield, E. Brooks. "Toward a History of American Congregations." In *American Congregations: New Perspectives in the Study of Congregations*, edited by James P. Wind and James W. Lewis, 23–53. Chicago: University of Chicago Press, 1994.

Hopewell, James. *Congregation: Stories and Structures.* Philadelphia: Fortress Press, 1987.

Hunter, James Davison. *Culture Wars: The Struggle to Define America.* New York: Basic Books, 1992.

Huntington, Samuel P. *The Clash of Civilizations and the Remaking of World Order.* New York: Simon and Schuster, 1996.

Hutchinson, Mark, and Ogbu Kalu, eds. *A Global Faith: Essays on Evangelicalism and Globalization.* Sidney, AU: CSAC, 1998.

Jenkins, Philip. *The New Faces of Christianity: Reading the Bible in the Global South.* New York: Oxford University Press, 2006.

———. *The Next Christendom: The Coming of Global Christianity.* New York: Oxford University Press, 2002.

———. "The Next Christianity." *The Atlantic Monthly* 290, no. 3 (October 2002): 54–66.

Johnson, Todd M. "'It Can Be Done': The Impact of Modernity and Postmodernity on the Global Mission Plans of Churches and Agencies." In *Between Past and Future: Evangelical Missiology Entering the Twenty-first Century*, edited by Jon Bonk, 37–49. William Carey Library: Pasadena, CA, 2003.

Juergensmeyer, Mark, ed. *Religion in Global Civil Society.* Oxford: Oxford University Press, 2005.

Kertzer, David. *Rituals, Politics and Power.* New Haven, CT: Yale University Press, 1988.

Keyes, David. *Most Like an Arch: Building Global Church Partnerships.* Chico, CA: Center for Free Religion, 1999.

Kim, Rebecca Y. "Acts of Sacrifice." *Faith and Leadership*, June 21, 2011. Accessed 2 August 2011. http://www.faithandleadership.com/content/rebecca-y-kim-acts-sacrifice.

Korea Research Institute for Missions. "The Latest Korean Mission Status" (2008). Accessed 20 August 2008. http://krim.org/2010/english.html.

Kosmin, Barry A., and Ariela Keysar. *Religion in a Free Market: Religious Americans Who, What, Why, Where*. Ithaca, NY: Paramount Market Publishing, Inc., 2006.

Lakeland, Paul. *Postmodernity: Christian Identity in a Fragmented Age*. Minneapolis: Fortress Press, 1997.

Latourette, Kenneth Scott. *The Great Century in the Americas, Australasia, and Africa*. New York: Harper, 1953.

———. *History of the Expansion of Christianity*, 7 Vols. Grand Rapids: Zondervan Publishing House, 1970.

Levitt, Peggy. *God Knows No Passport: Immigrants and the Changing American Religious Landscape*. New York: New Press, 2007.

———. *The Transnational Villagers*. Berkeley: University of California Press, 2001.

Lincoln, C. Eric, and Lawrence H. Mamiya. *The Black Church in the African-American Experience*. Durham: Duke University Press, 1990.

Linhart, Terence D. "The Curricular Nature of Youth Group Short-Term Cross-Cultural Service Projects." PhD diss., Purdue University, 2004.

———. "Planting Seeds: The Curricular Hope of Short-Term Mission Experiences in Youth Ministry," *Christian Education Journal* 3, no. 2 (2005): 256–272.

Livermore, David. "CQ and Short-Term Missions: The Phenomenon of the 15-Year-Old Missionary." In *Handbook of Cultural Intelligence: Theory, Measurement, and Applications*, ed. Soon Ang and Linn Van Dyne, 271–288. New York: M.E. Sharpe, 2008.

Livezey, Lowell, ed. *Public Religion and Urban Transformation: Faith in the City*. New York: New York University Press, 2000.

Lofland, John, and Lyn Lofland. *Analyzing Social Settings*, 3rd Ed. Belmont, CA: Wadsworth, 1995.

Lubawa, Richard. *Shoulder to Shoulder: Bega Kwa Bega: A Lutheran Partnership Between Minnesota and Tanzania*. Minneapolis: Lutheran University Press, 2007.

Marsh, Colin. "Partnership in Mission: To Send or To Share?" *International Review of Missionary Research* 92, no. 366 (2003): 370–381.

Marti, Gerardo. *A Mosaic of Believers: Diversity and Innovation in a Multiethnic Church*. Bloomington: Indiana University Press, 2005.

Martin, David. "Evangelical Expansion in Global Society." In *Christianity Reborn: The Global Expansion of Evangelicalism in the Twentieth Century*, ed. Donald M. Lewis, 273–294. Grand Rapids, MI: W. B. Eerdmans Publishing Co., 2004.

Marty, Martin. *Righteous Empire: The Protestant Experience in America*. New York: Dial Press, 1970.

Marx, Gary T., and Douglas McAdam. *Collective Behavior and Social Movements: Process and Structures*. Englewood Cliffs, NJ: Prentice Hall, 1994.

Maslucán, Rodrigo. "Short-Term Missions: Analysis and Proposals." *Journal of Latin American Theology* 2, no. 2 (2007): 139–158.

McAdam, Doug, John D. McCarthy, and Mayer N. Zald, eds. *Comparative Perspectives on Social Movements: Political Opportunities, Mobilizing Structures, and Cultural Framings*. New York: Cambridge University Press, 1996.

McCutcheon, Russell T., ed. *The Insider/Outsider Problem in the Study of Religion: A Reader*. New York: Cassell, 1999.

McGlone, Mary M. *Sharing Faith Across the Hemisphere*. Maryknoll, NY: Orbis Books, 1997.

McRoberts, Omar M. *Streets of Glory: Church and Community in a Black Urban Neighborhood*. Chicago: University of Chicago, 2003.

Menjivar, Cecilia. "Religious Institutions and Transnationalism: A Case Study of Catholic And Evangelical Salvadoran Immigrants." *International Journal of Politics, Culture, and Society* 12, no. 4 (1999): 589–612.

Miller, Donald. *Reinventing American Protestantism: Christianity in the New Millennium*. Berkeley: University of California Press, 1997.

Mittelman, James H. *The Globalization Syndrome: Transformation and Resistance*. Princeton: Princeton University Press, 2000.

Mjagkijj, Nina. "Operation Crossroads Africa." In *Organizing Black America: An Encyclopedia of African American Associations*, 542–543. Oxford: Taylor and Francis Group, 2001.

Moon, Steve S. C. "The Recent Korean Missionary Movement: A Record of Growth, and More Growth Needed." *International Bulletin of Missionary Research* 27, no. 1 (2003): 11–16.

Moreau, A. Scott, Harold A. Netland, Charles Edward van Engen, and David Burnett, eds. *Evangelical Dictionary of World Missions*. Grand Rapids, MI: Baker Books, 2000.

Mullin, R. Bruce, and Russell E. Richey, eds. *Re-Imagining Denominationalism: Interpretive Essays*. New York: Oxford University Press, 1994.

Murphy, Nancey. *Beyond Liberalism and Fundamentalism: How Modern and Postmodern Philosophy Set the Theological Agenda*. Harrisburg, PA: Trinity Press International, 1996.

Neill, Stephen. *A History of Christian Missions*. London: Penguin Books, 1986.

Newbigin, Lesslie. *The Gospel in a Pluralist Society*. Grand Rapids, MI: W. B. Eerdmans Publishing Co., 1989.

———. *The Other Side of 1984: Questions for the Churches*. Geneva: World Council of Churches, 1983.

Niebuhr, H. Richard. *The Social Sources of Denominationalism*. New York: H. Holt and Company, 1929.

Noll, Mark. *American Evangelical Christianity: An Introduction*. Hoboken, NJ: Wiley-Blackwell, 2001.

O'Connor, Dennis P. *Bridges of Faith: Building a Relationship with a Sister Parish*. Cincinnati: St. Anthony Messenger Press, 2007.

Ott, Craig. *Globalizing Theology: Belief and Practice in an Era of World Christianity*. Grand Rapids, MI: Baker Academic, 2006.

Padilla, René. *Mission Between the Times: Essays on the Kingdom*. Grand Rapids, MI: W. B. Eerdmans Publishing Co., 1985.

Parsons, Talcott. *The Social System*. New York: Free Press, 1951.

Pearce, Jone L. *Volunteers: The Organizational Behavior of Unpaid Workers*. New York: Routledge, 1993.

Peters, Ronald Edward and Marsha Snulligan Haney, eds. *Africentric Approaches to Christian Ministry: Strengthening Urban Congregations in African American Communities*. Lanham, MD: University Press of America, 2007.

Peterson, Roger. "Innovation in Short-term Mission." In *Innovation in Mission*, ed. Jim Reapsome and Jon Hurst, 51–66. Waynesboro, GA: Authentic, 2006.

Peterson, Roger, Gordon Aeschliman, and R. Wayne Sneed. *Maximum Impact Short-term Mission: The God-Commanded, Repetitive Deployment of Swift, Temporary, Non-Professional Missionaries*. Minneapolis: STEM Press, 2003.

Pew Global Attitudes Project. "What the World Thinks in 2002: How Global Publics View: Their Lives, Their Countries, The World, America." Washington, DC: Pew Research Center, December 4, 2002. Accessed 1 October 2009. http://pewglobal.org/reports/display.php?ReportID=165.

Pierson, Paul E. "Lessons in Mission from the Twentieth Century: Conciliar Missions." In *Between Past and Future: Evangelical Missiology Entering the Twenty-first Century*, ed. Jon Bonk, 65–84. Pasadena, CA: William Carey Library, 2003.

Pocock, Michael, Gailyn Van Rheenen, and Douglas McConnell. *The Changing Face of World Missions: Engaging Contemporary Issues and Trends*. Grand Rapids, MI: Baker Academic, 2005.

Pope Paul VI. *Evangelii Nuntiandi*. Papal Encyclicals Online, 8 December 1975. Accessed 21 September 2008. http://www.papalencyclicals.net/Paul06/p6evan.htm.

Priest, Kersten Bayt. "Women as Resource Brokers: STM Trips, Social and Organizational Ties, and Mutual Resource Benefits." In *Effective Engagement in Short-Term Missions: Doing it Right!*, ed. Robert Priest, 256–275. Pasadena, CA: William Carey Library, 2008.

Priest, Robert. "Introduction: Short-Term Missions and the Latin American Church." *Journal of Latin American Theology* 2, no. 2 (2007): 7–20.

———. "Peruvian Churches Acquire 'Linking Social Capital' Through STM Partnerships." *Journal of Latin American Theology* 2, no. 2 (2007): 175–189.

Priest, Robert J., Terry Dischinger, Steve Rasmussen, and C. M. Brown. "Researching the Short-Term Mission Movement." *Missiology: An International Review* 34, no. 4 (October 2006): 431–450.

Priest, Robert J., Douglas Wilson, and Adelle Johnson. "U.S. Megachurches and New Patterns of Global Mission." *International Bulletin of Missionary Research* 34, no. 2 (April 2010): 97–104.

Putnam, Robert. *Bowling Alone: The Collapse and Revival of American Community*. New York: Simon and Schuster, 2000.

Putnam, Robert D., Lewis M. Feldstein, and Don Cohen. *Better Together: Restoring the American Community*. New York: Simon and Schuster, 2003.

Reeves, Samuel Broomfield Jr. *Congregation-to-Congregation Relationship: A Case Study of a Partnership Between A Liberian Church and a North American Church*. Lanham, MD: University Press of America, 2004.

Richter, Don. *Mission Trips that Matter: Embodied Faith for the Sake of the World*. Nashville: Upper Room Books, 2008.

Rivers, Robert. *From Maintenance to Mission: Evangelization and the Revitalization of the Parish*. Mahwah, NJ: Paulist Press, 2005.

Robbins, Bruce W. *A World Parish? Hopes and Challenges of the United Methodist Church in a Global Setting*. Nashville: Abingdon Press, 2004.

Robert, Dana. "Cross-Cultural Friendship in the Creation of Twentieth-Century World Christianity." *International Bulletin of Missionary Research* 35, no. 2 (April 2011): 100–107.

———. "Shifting Southward: Global Christianity Since 1945." *International Bulletin of Missionary Research* 24, no. 2 (April 2000): 50–58.

Roberts, Bob, Jr. *Glocalization: How Followers of Jesus Engage a Flat World.* Grand Rapids, MI: Zondervan Publishing House, 2007.

Roof, Wade Clark. *Spiritual Marketplace: Baby Boomers and the Remaking of American Religion.* Princeton: Princeton University Press, 2001.

Roof, Wade Clark, and William McKinney. *American Mainline Religion.* New Brunswick, NJ: Rutgers University Press, 1987.

Roozen, David A., William McKinney, and Jackson W. Carroll. *Varieties of Religious Presence: Mission in Public Life.* Cleveland: Pilgrim Press, 1984.

Rossman, Gretchen B., and Sharon F. Rallis. *Learning in the Field: An Introduction to Qualitative Research*, 2nd Ed. Thousand Oaks, CA: Sage Publications, 2003.

Rowe, Jonathan. "Dancing with Elephants: Accountability in Cross-Cultural Christian Partnerships." *Missiology* 37, no. 2 (April 2009): 149–163.

Rubin, Herbert, and Riene Rubin. *Qualitative Interviewing: The Art of Hearing Data.* Thousand Oaks, CA: Sage Publications, 1995.

Said, Edward. *Orientalism.* New York: Vintage Books, 1978.

Salmon, Jacqueline L. "Churches Retool Mission Trips: Work Abroad Criticized for High Cost and Lack of Value." *The Washington Post*, July 5, 2008, sec. B1.

Sanneh, Lamin. *Encountering the West: Christianity and the Global Cultural Process: The African Dimension.* Maryknoll, NY: Orbis Books, 1993.

———. *Whose Religion Is Christianity? The Gospel Beyond the West.* Grand Rapids, MI: W. B. Eerdmans Publishing Co., 2003.

Sanneh, Lamin, and Joel Carpenter eds. *The Changing Face of Christianity: Africa, the West, and the World.* New York: Oxford University Press, 2005.

Sataline, Suzane. "Episcopalians Form Rival Church." *The Wall Street Journal*, December 3, 2008. Accessed 9 December 2008. http://online.wsj.com/article/SB12283456 219177337.html.

Scherer, James A. *Gospel, Church, and Kingdom: Comparative Studies in World Mission Theology.* Minneapolis: Augsburg Press, 1987.

Scherer, James A., and Stephen B. Bevans, eds. *New Directions in Mission and Evangelization I: Basic Statements 1974–1991.* Maryknoll, NY: Orbis Books, 1992.

Schreiter, Robert J., ed. *Mission in the Third Millennium.* Maryknoll, NY: Orbis Books, 2001.

Schreiter, Robert. "Short Term, Long Term, on Whose Terms?." Mission Update, Periodic Paper #3 (Fall 2006): 1–8.

Schwartz, Glenn. "How Short-Term Missions Can Go Wrong." *International Journal of Frontier Missions* 20, no. 4 (Winter 2003): 27–34.

Shenk, Wilbert R. *Changing Frontiers of Mission.* Maryknoll, NY: Orbis Books, 1999.

Sherkat, Darren E. "Tracking the Restructuring of American Religion: Religious Affiliation and Patterns of Religious Mobility, 1973–1998." *Social Forces* 79 (2001): 1459–1493.

Sikkink, David. "'I Just Say I'm a Christian': Symbolic Boundaries and Identity Formation Among Church-going Protestants." In *Re-forming the Center: American Protestantism, 1900-Present*, ed. Douglas Jacobsen and William Vance Trollinger, 49–71. Grand Rapids, MI: W. B. Eerdmans Publishing Co., 1998.

Smith, Christian. *Evangelicalism: Embattled and Thriving*. Chicago, IL: University of Chicago Press, 1998.

Smith, R. Drew, ed. *Freedom's Distant Shores: American Protestants and Post-colonial Alliances with Africa*. Waco, TX: Baylor University Press, 2006.

Snow, David A., and Robert D. Benford. "Ideology, Frame Resonance, and Participation Mobilization." In *From Structures to Action: Social Movement Participation Across Cultures*, Bert Klandermans, Hanspeter Kriesi, and Sidney Tarrow, eds., 197–217. Greenwich, CT: JAI Press, 1988.

Stanley, Brian. *The World Missionary Conference, Edinburgh, 1910*. Grand Rapids, MI: W. B. Eerdmans Publishing Co., 2009.

Sundkler, Bengt, and Christopher Steed. *A History of the Church in Africa*. Cambridge, UK: Cambridge University Press, 2000.

Swedish, Margaret, and Marie Dennis. *Like Grains of Wheat: A Spirituality of Solidarity*. Maryknoll, NY: Orbis Books, 2004.

United States Catholic Mission Association. "Primary Ministry Work Activity." *Mission Survey/Statistics*, 2005. Accessed 23 February 2009. http://www.uscatholicmission. org/go/missionersurveystatistics.

United States Conference of Catholic Bishops. "Called to Global Solidarity: International Challenges for U.S. Parishes." Washington, DC: United States Council of Catholic Bishops, 1997.

United States Conference of Catholic Bishops. "To the Ends of the Earth: A Pastoral Statement on World Mission." New York: The Society for the Propagation of the Faith, 1987.

U.S. Congregational Life Survey. "What Makes Us Special: The Magic Balance." 2001. Accessed 11 June 2009. http://www.uscongregations.org/10strengths-whatmakesus-special.htm).

Van Engen, Charles E., Darrell Whiteman, and J. Dudley Woodberry. *Paradigm Shifts in Christian Witness: Insights from Anthropology, Communication, and Spiritual Power: Essays in Honor of Charles H. Kraft*. Maryknoll, NY: Orbis Books, 2008.

Ver Beek, Kurt Alan. "The Impact of Short-Term Missions: A Case Study of House Construction in Honduras After Hurricane Mitch." *Missiology: An International Review* 34, no. 4 (2006): 477–496.

———. "International Service Learning: A Call to Caution." In *Commitment and Connection: Service-Learning and Christian Higher Education*, ed. Gail Gunst Heffner and Claudia Beversluis, 55–69. Lanham, MD: University of America, 2002.

———. "Lessons from the Sapling: Review of Quantitative Research on Short-Term Missions." In *Effective Engagement in Short-Term Missions: Doing it Right!*, ed. Robert Priest, 469–496. Pasadena, CA: William Carey Library, 2008.

Villón, Joaquín Alegre. "Short-Term Missions: Experiences and Perspectives from Calloa, Peru." *Journal of Latin American Theology* 2, no. 2 (2007): 119–138.

Währisch-Oblau, Claudia. "'We Shall be Fruitful in This Land': Pentecostal and Charismatic New Mission Churches in Europe." In *Fruitful in This Land: Pluralism, Dialogue and Healing in Migrant Pentecostalism*, ed. André Droogers, Cornelis van der Laan, and Wout van Laar, 32–46. Zoetermeer, NL: Boekencentrum, 2006.

Walls, Andrew F. *The Cross-Cultural Process in Christian History: Studies in the Transmission and Appropriation of Faith*. Maryknoll, NY: Orbis Books, 2002.

————. *The Missionary Movement in Christian History: Studies in the Transmission of the Faith*. Maryknoll, NY: Orbis Books, 1996.

Warner, R. Stephen. *A Church of Our Own: Disestablishment and Diversity in American Religion*. New Brunswick, NJ: Rutgers University Press, 2005.

————. *New Wine in Old Wineskins: Evangelicals and Liberals in a Small-Town Church*. Berkeley: University of California Press, 1988.

————. "Work in Progress Toward a New Paradigm for the Sociological Study of Religion in the United States." *American Journal of Sociology* 98, no. 5 (1993): 1044–1093.

————, ed. *Gatherings in Diaspora: Religious Communities and the New Immigration*. Philadelphia: Temple University Press, 1998.

Washington, James Melvin. *Frustrated Fellowship: The Black Baptist Quest for Social Power*. Macon, GA: Mercer University Press, 1986.

Welliver, Dotsey, and Minnette Northcutt, eds. *Mission Handbook: U.S. and Canadian Protestant Ministries Overseas, 2004–2006*. Wheaton, IL: Billy Graham Center, 2006.

Wheeler, Barbara. "You Who Were Far Off: Religious Divisions and the Role of Religious Research." *Review of Religious Research* 37, no. 4 (June 1996): 289–301.

Whiteman, Darrell L. "Creative Partnerships in Mission." *Missiology* 29, no. 1 (2001): 3–61.

Woolcock, Michael, and Deepa Narayan. "Social Capital: Implications for Development Theory, Research, and Policy." *World Bank Research Observer* 15, no. 2 (2000): 225–249.

Woolever, Cynthia, and Deborah Bruce. *Beyond the Ordinary: 10 Strengths of U.S. Congregations*. Louisville: Westminster John Knox Press, 2004.

Wright, Christopher J. H. *Mission of God: Unlocking the Bible's Grand Narrative*. Downers Grove, IL: InterVarsity Press, 2006.

————. "An Upside-Down World: Distinguishing Between Home and Mission Field No Longer Makes Sense." *Christianity Today* 51, no. 1 (January 2007): 42–46.

Wuthnow, Robert. *After Heaven: Spirituality in America Since the 1950s*. Berkeley: University of California Press, 1998.

————. *Boundless Faith: The Global Outreach of American Churches*. Berkeley: University of California Press, 2009.

————. *The Restructuring of American Religion: Society and Faith Since World War II*. Princeton, NJ: Princeton University Press, 1988.

————. "Old Fissures and New Fractures in American Religious Life." In *Religion and American Culture*, ed. David G. Hackett, 359–374. New York: Routledge, 1995.

————. "Religious Involvement and Status-Bridging Social Capital." *Journal for the Social Scientific Study of Religion* 41, no. 4 (2002): 669–684.

Wuthnow, Robert, and Stephen Offutt. "Transnational Religious Connections." *Sociology of Religion* 69, no. 2 (2008): 209–232.

Yang, Fenggang. *Chinese Christians in America: Conversion, Assimilation, and Adhesive Identities*. University Park: Penn State University Press, 1999.

Yang, Fenggang, and Helen Rose Ebaugh, "Religion and Ethnicity Among New Immigrants: The Impact of Majority/Minority Status in Home and Host Countries." *Journal for the Scientific Study of Religion* 40, no. 3 (2001): 367–378.

———. "Transformations in New Immigrant Religions and Their Global Implications." *American Sociological Review* 66, no. 2 (April 2001): 269–288.

Yates, Timothy. *Christian Mission in the Twentieth Century*. New York: Cambridge University Press, 1994.

Young, Robert. *Postcolonialism: An Historical Introduction*. Oxford, UK: Blackwell, 2001.

Załęski, Paweł. "Ideal Types in Max Weber's Sociology of Religion: Some Theoretical Inspirations for a Study of the Religious Field." *Polish Sociological Review* 3, no. 171 (2010): 319–325.

# INDEX